An Encyclopedia of
American Women at War

An Encyclopedia of
American Women at War

From the Home Front to the Battlefields

Volume I:
A–L

Lisa Tendrich Frank, Editor

 ABC-CLIO

Santa Barbara, California • Denver, Colorado • Oxford, England

Library of Congress Cataloging-in-Publication Data

An encyclopedia of American women at war : from the home front to the battlefields / Lisa Tendrich Frank, editor.

p. cm.

Includes bibliographical references and index.

ISBN 978–1–59884–443–6 (hbk. : alk. paper) — ISBN 978–1–59884–444–3 (ebook) 1. United States—Armed Forces—Women—Biography—Encyclopedias. 2. Women and war—United States—Encyclopedias. 3. Women and the military—United States—Encyclopedias.
I. Frank, Lisa Tendrich.

UB418.W65E53   2013
355.0092′520973—dc23   2012018244

ISBN: 978–1–59884–443–6
EISBN: 978–1–59884–444–3

17 16 15 14 13   1 2 3 4 5

This book is also available on the World Wide Web as an eBook.
Visit www.abc-clio.com for details.

ABC-CLIO, LLC
130 Cremona Drive, P.O. Box 1911
Santa Barbara, California 93116-1911

This book is printed on acid-free paper ∞

Manufactured in the United States of America

For Shayna

Contents

List of Entries

Introduction

Anxiety over the prospect of women serving in the military has been a recurring theme in the history of the United States. In the contemporary United States, as they did in the past, politicians and others occasionally decry the gender-specific meanings of the implications for society if women were to fight, get captured, or die in battle. The details and specters have changed over time, but opponents of gender equality in the military have consistently raised concerns about the disintegration of unit cohesion with the addition of women. These critics have also pointed to potential problems related to housing, privacy, and, of course, sexual relations. Furthermore, they have declared that women's physical strength and emotional resolve are inferior to men's and therefore make women unfit for duty. However, the history of women who have served in the U.S. military has shown many of these concerns to be baseless. For the past two centuries, women have demanded and claimed an expanded place in the military even as detractors have warned the public of its disastrous potential. Women, whether for patriotic or pragmatic reasons, have increasingly moved from the homefront to the warfront, and they now participate in all aspects of military life short of serving in combat units. Even this distinction has become remarkably blurry as modern warfare has all but eliminated the concept of clearly delineated combat zones and safe supply lines. The use of drones and intercontinental missiles, the waging of urban warfare, and the use of the military as a peacekeeping force have all brought women into combat even as they remain excluded from combat units. In other instances, the military has "attached" rather than "assigned" women to units heading to the front lines—a distinction that adheres to policy but nevertheless results in many women being intentionally deployed in combat situations. As a result, female soldiers and sailors have served and died for the United States for many years.

The path toward official gender integration in the U.S. military has been a slow and uneven one. For hundreds of years, most women who participated in the military did so in unofficial ways. Prohibited by law and restrained by social mores from fighting in military units, women in the 18th and 19th centuries frequently supported the military through roles traditionally and nontraditionally reserved for women. During the colonial wars, American Revolution, War of 1812, and American Civil War, for example, women were allowed to travel with the troops as camp followers who did laundry, cooked, and cleaned for the soldiers. The military fed and housed these camp followers, but they were not recognized as part of the military. In any case, these women played vital roles in keeping the troops ready for battle.

Other American women volunteered by caring for the sick or spying on the enemy. In a few instances, women successfully managed to get paid for their efforts after the fact, but they almost always did so without any earlier financial arrangement and without actually getting hired for the position. Instead, women tended to offer the skills and knowledge that they possessed and found willing partners in military leaders who could not afford to ignore these crucial needs. For example, during the American Revolution and Civil War, many women served as unofficial spies. These women obtained information when they served as domestic laborers to the enemy. Military officers sometimes willingly revealed secrets in the presence of women because they did not see them as a threat. Men assumed that women, even enemy women, were not paying attention to the conversations, could not understand the information, and were not dangerous. In this manner, domestic laborers or sociable hostesses often became de facto spies. In other instances, women happened to be in the right place with the right information. Many Americans, for example, are familiar with the efforts of former slave Harriet Tubman to help other slaves escape to freedom. Fewer, however, are familiar with her role in passing to Union General David Hunter information about Confederate war plans that she gathered from former slaves. Tubman also led an armed excursion of Union troops in the Combahee River Raid in South Carolina. Tubman's actions parallel those of countless women in the early United States, women who served their nation without either sanction or public acknowledgement.

Prior to the 20th century, some American women were determined to engage in combat in the same manner as was expected of the men of their communities. These women dressed up as and took identities as men, or, in the case of wars fought on American soil, they picked up weapons and defended their homes and communities. In 1782, for example, Deborah Samson donned a disguise and enlisted in the Continental Army under the alias Timothy Thayer. After her sex was discovered and she was dismissed from the unit, the determined Samson reenlisted in the army under the name Robert Shurtliff. Although wounded twice, her true identity was not discovered until she fell ill with fever. Samson was honorably discharged and received a pension for her service. Other women took similar actions in the Civil War.

In other instances, enemy soldiers made women unwilling participants in the wars, as women were taken captive or faced occupation by invading Native American, British, Confederate, Union, or other armies. Such was the case for Susannah Willard Johnson and hundreds of other women in early America who were captured by Indians for either ransom or adoption. In Johnson's case, the Abenakis attacked her home during the French and Indian War and took her captive for three years before she was finally ransomed home. Other American women in this raid and others fought back and died in their homes or were captured and never ransomed home.

The nature of women's military history shifted dramatically in the 20th century, partially as a response to the extensive manpower needs of the two world wars and the sustained challenge to women's position in the social order that they created. During the 20th century, as women in civilian life demanded that economic, labor, and educational barriers be taken down, some women looked to the military to become a leader in gender equality.

In many ways, the military has acted as a tremendous agent of change in regards to women's equality and racial equality, and it has provided tremendous opportunities for women of every background. By some measures, the military has even been ahead of efforts by women to achieve equality in aspects of civilian life. For example, in the 1940s, when women were traditionally expected to care for their families, the women who joined the war effort as members of the Women Accepted for Volunteer Emergency Service (WAVES), Women's Army Corps (WAC), Women Air Force Service Pilots (WASP), Women Marines, and other military branches or auxiliaries played vital military roles that helped lead to American successes on the battlefields. Female spies gathered invaluable information and broke codes that saved American lives. Female nurses in mobile Army surgical hospital (MASH) units faced the dangers of being near the front lines.

Women's military efforts in the 20th century did not go unnoticed. Many servicewomen rose in the ranks and distinguished themselves, including Annie G. Fox, who earned a Purple Heart for her heroism at Pearl Harbor; Cordelia Elizabeth "Betty" Cook, who earned a Bronze Star in 1944; and Mary Roberts Wilson, who earned a Silver Star for her actions at the 1944 Battle of Anzio. Since then, women have earned medals in all of the branches of the military, and they have graduated and taught at each of the military academies. In 1970, the military promoted the first women to general: Anna Mae Hays of the Army Nurse Corps (ANC) and Elizabeth Hoisington of the WAC. In November 2008, Army lieutenant general Ann E. Dunwoody became the first female four-star general, and in February 2012, President Barack Obama nominated Janet Wolfenbarger to become the Air Force's first female four-star general. These achievements are not isolated incidents. In terms of percentages, at the end of the 20th century a greater percentage of military officers than of elected officials, in either the federal or state governments, were women.

Women in the military have also been able to overcome racial barriers. For example, after serving for years in the ANC, Margaret E. Bailey became the first black nurse to become lieutenant colonel, in 1964, and the first African American to hold the rank of full colonel, in 1970. Both achievements occurred as the racial idea of separate and unequal remained a norm throughout much of civilian life. Bailey also spent much of her time encouraging women of color to join the ANC. In addition, the first African American to be appointed chief of the ANC, Hazel Winifred Johnson-Brown, was also the first African American promoted to brigadier general (1979). African Americans and other women of color continue to advance through the ranks of the military.

As the U.S. military has erased many of the barriers to the full integration of women, thousands of women have excelled in ways that conflict with earlier fears about their full incorporation into the ranks. Women, who were once believed to be incapable of nursing wounded soldiers because they would faint at the sight of blood, became essential contributors to the medical needs of soldiers in the American Civil War and the wars that came after it. Women, who were once believed to be ill equipped for the mental agility needed for cryptology, became essential codebreakers in World War I and World War II. Even women's participation in the space program had initially been denied on account of their gender. When 13 women who had qualified for NASA's Mercury program petitioned to participate in the program, President Lyndon B. Johnson had an easy, four-word answer: "Let's stop this now." Since then, women have piloted and otherwise participated in the space shuttle program without incident. Their participation on naval submarines had also been opposed on account of the close quarters and lack of privacy inherent to the vessels. This issue, too, has been resolved, and female submariners have served with distinction without the feared signs of declining unit cohesion. Whether as nurses, soldiers, pilots, spies, or scientists, thousands of women have honorably served their country and have otherwise allayed many of the anxieties that resulted from the belief that women are unsuited for the rigors of military life.

Despite these accomplishments by women, the U.S. military has also been a place of resistance to gender equality. In these instances, the military is more a mirror of social norms and less a leader of social reform. Perhaps most troubling, sexual assault and harassment have continually plagued the military, even after military leadership acknowledged it as a problem. For example, in 1991, at the 35th Annual Tailhook convention in Las Vegas, Nevada, 83 female and 7 male military personnel reported being sexually harassed or assaulted. Naval command responded by blaming the accusers and otherwise burying the claims of the victims. A later Pentagon report on the incident implicated 117 officers in indecent acts or failed acts of leadership, reiterating the Pentagon's 1988 "zero tolerance" policy on sexual harassment. It is difficult to know what, if anything, has changed. Sexual assault and harassment continue in the military, as they do in civilian life. Furthermore, despite many efforts, the military has yet to address adequately the systemic problems. A formal 2004 investigation into harassment and sexual assault against female soldiers in Iraq, for example, revealed that approximately 30 percent of female soldiers had been raped, 71 percent sexually assaulted, and 90 percent sexually harassed. The same report indicated that most of the victims never stepped forward, a reflection of a community that values settling matters locally and punishing those who report abuse.

In other ways, military women continue to face informal barriers. For many years, women necessarily ended their careers in the military when they either married or had children. It was not until 1976 in *Crawford v. Cushman* that the Second Circuit Court ruled it was unconstitutional for the military to automatically discharge pregnant servicewomen. Only a few years earlier, the Supreme Court ruled in *Frontiero v. Richardson* (1973) that servicewomen did not have to prove that their civilian spouses were dependent on them to receive medical benefits and on-base family housing that was available to civilian wives of servicemen. Some scholars believe that women face a continued double standard regarding family as they may be overlooked for promotion and desired assignments.

This encyclopedia examines the various ways that women have participated in military life. Whether formally a part of the military or standing apart from it, the women in this volume have combined to create a dynamic and often contradictory record of female experiences. This volume includes topics that, when overlapped upon each other, form a mosaic that is the female experience with the U.S. military. Entries cover specific professions, organizations, court cases, military policies, wars, branches of the military, American ethnic and racial groups, and individuals. Some of the entries cover topics widely known by the educated public; others tell the history of aspects of women's history that are primarily known only by scholarly specialists. Some of the entries explore barrier breakers; others examine the barriers. Some entries explore those who waged war; others look at those who opposed them.

As with many other reference works, the topics covered are still alive and changing before us. The history of women in the military and the larger quest for equal opportunity is ongoing, and the future is unknown. Although many of the barriers have been broken and women are widely acknowledged as integral members of the armed forces, resistance remains, and some barriers simply await women who are willing and able to achieve those distinctions. Indeed, many of the women in this volume are still alive and serving our nation. Countless others serve, and their achievements have yet to unfold before us. As much as possible, this encyclopedia brings this story up the present.

A

ABZUG, BELLA
(1920–1998)

Attorney Bella Abzug served as U.S. congresswoman (1971–1977) and as a leader in the civil rights, antiwar, women's rights, and environmental movements.

She was born Bella Savitsky to poor Russian immigrant parents in the Bronx, New York, on July 24, 1920. Her admirers have jokingly claimed that she was born yelling. Certainly her indomitable spirit manifested itself at an early age, when she began to challenge the status quo in her synagogue and school. When her father died when she was 13 years old, she defied Jewish tradition— and her rabbi—by insisting that she say *kaddish*, or special prayers for the departed, even though tradition prohibited women from doing so. She asserted that because her father did not have a son, she was the one who should offer the prayers.

Savitsky graduated from Hunter College (New York) in 1942, and, after defiantly applying to Harvard Law School, which at the time did not admit women, she received a scholarship to Columbia University, from which she earned a law degree in 1945. A brilliant student, she married Martin Abzug that same year and passed the New York bar exam in 1947. Her lengthy legal career centered on labor law and civil rights and liberties, and she handled a number of civil rights cases in the South during the 1950s and 1960s. Her law career was remarkable, not least of all because very few women became attorneys in the 1940s and 1950s.

Although she did not attain elective office until 1970, Abzug was very much in the vanguard of American politics and political causes in the 1950s and 1960s. Indeed, she was one of the few lawyers willing to stand up against the excesses of McCarthyism and the House Un-American Activities Committee in the early 1950s. During the next decade, she cofounded and led Women Strike for Peace, an organization dedicated to ending nuclear testing, curbing the nuclear arms race, and bringing to a close American involvement in the Vietnam War. In the meantime, Abzug continued to work for the civil rights agenda and women's rights. She also became a prominent voice in the anti–Vietnam War movement. Disgusted with the Lyndon Johnson administration's war policies, she actively campaigned for Democratic senator Eugene McCarthy for president in 1968. By this time, she was already noted for her seemingly endless array of colorful and sometimes overwrought hats, which became her trademark.

In 1970, Abzug ran for a U.S. congressional seat as a Democrat and won. She was the first Jewish woman to serve in the House of Representatives. She served three full terms, during which she lambasted the Richard Nixon administration for its continuation of the Vietnam War, excoriated Republican economic policy, and introduced or cosponsored numerous landmark legislative initiatives. Her outspoken brashness reportedly earned her a high spot on Nixon's infamous "enemies list" in the early 1970s. Before long, her congressional colleagues were referring to her as "Battling Bella" and "Hurricane Bella." Indeed, on her first day in Congress, she introduced a resolution calling for the immediate withdrawal of American troops from Vietnam.

In 1974, Abzug introduced the first gay rights bill in Congress. She also actively advocated a feminist agenda, which included ardent backing of the Equal Rights Amendment. When the Watergate scandal became public in 1973, Abzug was the first in Congress to call for Nixon's impeachment.

In 1976, Abzug lost a Democratic primary to become a U.S. senator for New York state by the narrowest of margins to Daniel Patrick Moynihan. She left Congress in January 1977. She ran unsuccessfully for mayor of New York that same year but continued her advocacy of civil rights, women's rights, and increased economic opportunity. Two other attempts to regain a seat in the U.S. House, once in 1978 and again in 1986, ended in failure. In the late 1970s, she headed the Jimmy Carter administration's National Advisory Committee on Women until she was asked to step down in 1979 after she criticized Carter's economic policies.

Later that same year, Abzug founded Women USA, a nonprofit women's advocacy group that counted among its leadership many of the illuminati of the women's movement, including Gloria Steinem. In the meantime, she continued to practice law, gave many speeches and talks, took a key role in the International Women's Conferences sponsored by the United Nations, and published numerous articles, books, and opinion pieces. In 1990, Abzug established the Women's Environment and Development Organization (WEDO), an international association that wedded environmental activism and women's rights. In her later years, her health declined precipitously due to a bout with breast cancer and then heart failure. Abzug died in New York on March 31, 1998, one of the great liberal voices of the post–World War II era.

Paul G. Pierpaoli Jr.

See also: Cold War (ca. 1947–1991); Vietnam War (1965–1973); Women Strike for Peace (WSP).

References and Further Reading

Abzug, Bella. *Bella!: Ms. Abzug Goes to Washington*. New York: Saturday Review Press, 1972.

Faber, Doris. *Bella Abzug*. New York: William Morrow, 1976.

Levine, Suzanne Braun, and Mary Thom. *Bella Abzug*. New York: Farrar, Straus and Giroux, 2007.

ADDAMS, JANE (1860–1935)

The cofounder of Hull House in Chicago, president of the Women's International League for Peace and Freedom, and corecipient of the 1931 Nobel Peace Prize, Jane Addams was one of the most notable female reformers in early-20th-century America.

Reformer Jane Addams won the Nobel Peace Prize in 1931 for her work for social justice. She was the founder of Hull House, an urban social settlement for the poor in Chicago, Illinois. (Library of Congress)

Addams was born on September 6, 1860, in Cedarville, Illinois, and graduated from Rockford College in 1881. She achieved notoriety, along with Ellen Gates Starr, when she cofounded Hull House in Chicago in 1889 to assist in teaching the immigrant population about adjustment to and improvement in American society. Their settlement house symbolized the growing popularity of progressive reform in the urban United States at the dawn of the 20th century.

Having joined the American Anti-Imperialist League during the Spanish-American War of 1898, Addams was strongly committed to world peace and antimilitarism. A member of the League's Chicago branch, Addams warned schoolteachers about the way patriotism elevated the virtues of militarism through songs and flag salutes rather than the more noble civic responsibility of community service. In 1907, she expounded upon her peace views in a popular book, *Newer Ideals of Peace*. In this work, Addams rejected "idealistic" pacifism and argued that only a "dynamic" version, based upon the constant growth of human needs and relationships, was necessary to secure civilization's harmonious survival.

The outbreak of World War I directly challenged her progressive ideals. In 1914, Addams chaired the Chicago Emergency Peace Federation and along with other female antiwar advocates formulated a plan for neutral mediation. In 1915, she helped found the Women's Peace Party and served as its elected chairperson. From April to June 1915, Addams presided at the International Congress of Women held at The Hague, Netherlands, and was subsequently elected president of the International Committee of Women for Permanent Peace. During this period, Addams traveled throughout Europe with other notable female antiwar opponents, proposing mediation plans at the capitals of the belligerent nations. Witnessing firsthand the war's destructiveness, Addams surmised that military conflict not only challenged men's moral sensibilities but also women's strongest desires for survival. In February 1917, shortly before the United States entered the conflict, Addams helped organize the Emergency Peace Committee in an effort to arouse public opinion in support of peace.

After the declaration of war, Addams's pacifism was directed at protecting the civil liberties of Americans opposed to military participation and calling attention to the basic needs of people faced with starvation in Europe. She worked closely with Roger Baldwin and the National Civil Liberties Bureau (later the American Civil Liberties Union), spoke out against the passage of the Espionage Act (1917), studied carefully the treatment of conscientious objectors, and lobbied legislators for provisions in the conscription law protecting the rights of nonreligious objectors. During the war, Addams also lectured for the U.S. Food Administration on the preservation and conservation of food and its increased distribution to war victims.

In January 1919, at the height of the post–World War I Red Scare, a U.S. Senate judiciary committee listed in the record 62 eminent citizens considered dangerous radicals. Addams, as a result of her role as one of the nation's leading females in the areas of social reform, women's suffrage, and peace, was on this list.

After the war, the International Committee of Women for a Permanent Peace reconvened in Zurich and Vienna and established the Women's International League for Peace and Freedom. The Women's Peace Party became the U.S. section, and Addams was elected the League's first president. She held that office until 1927, after which she served as honorary president until her death in 1935. During the postwar years, Addams continued to oppose military preparedness and criticized the creation of the Reserve Officers Training Corps (ROTC) program for colleges and schools, supported disarmament treaties, and continued to call for the mediation of international disputes. In 1922, the publication of her book *Peace and Bread in Time of War* highlighted women's historic role in nurturing, protecting, and conserving human life. *Peace and Bread* sought to make the connection between institutional violence, militarism, and the social and economic exploitation of women. A reformer to the core, Addams persisted in calling for full equality for all citizens and a warless world. In 1931, for her efforts, she was awarded the Nobel Peace Prize, along with Columbia University president Nicholas Murray Butler. She died in Chicago on May 21, 1935.

Charles F. Howlett

See also: Reserve Officer Training Corps (ROTC); Spanish-American War (1898); World War I (1914–1918).

References and Further Reading

Addams, Jane. *Newer Ideals of Peace*. New York: Macmillan Co., 1907.

Addams, Jane. *Peace and Bread in Time of War*. New York: Macmillan Co., 1922.

Addams, Jane, E. G. Balch, and A. Hamilton. *Women at The Hague: The International Congress of Women and Its Results*. 1915. Urbana: University of Illinois Press, 2003.

Alonso, Harriet. *Peace as a Women's Issue: A History of the U.S. Movement for World Peace and Women's Rights*. Syracuse, NY: Syracuse University Press, 1993.

Davis, Allen F. *American Heroine: The Life and Legend of Jane Addams*. New York: Oxford University Press, 1973.

Ferrell, John. *Beloved Lady: A History of Jane Addams' Ideas on Reform and Peace*. Baltimore, MD: The Johns Hopkins University Press, 1967.

Howlett, Charles, and Ian Harris. *Books, Not Bombs: Teaching Peace since the Dawn of the Republic*. Charlotte, NC: Information Age Publishing, 2010.

Knight, Louise W. *Jane Addams and the Struggle for Democracy*. Chicago: University of Chicago Press, 2005.

Levine, Daniel. *Jane Addams and the Liberal Tradition*. Madison: Wisconsin History Society, 1971.

AFGHANISTAN

The Islamic Republic of Afghanistan is located in south-central Asia bordering Turkmenistan, Uzbekistan, and Tajikistan in the north; China in the northeast; Pakistan in the southeast; and Iran in the west. Its capital city is Kabul. Due to its geostrategic location connecting India and East Asia to the Middle East and Europe, throughout history Afghanistan has been invaded by foreign armies, including those of Alexander the Great, Genghis Khan, the British, the Soviets, and most recently the United States. Its hardy terrain and climate and the successful guerilla tactics of local tribes have frustrated all major military operations by outsiders and earned Afghanistan the title "Graveyard of Empires." The history of modern Afghanistan began in 1747, when Ahmed Shaha Durrani unified the rival ethnically diverse tribes under his leadership and established the Afghan state. In the 19th century, Afghanistan became a buffer state between British India and an expanding Russian Empire. British forces invaded the Afghan lands unsuccessfully three times between 1838 and 1919, when the country finally declared independence from the British. In 1979, the Soviet army entered Afghanistan to support the existing Marxist government, which resulted in a decade-long, embarrassing operation for Moscow and, ultimately, withdrawal in 1989. The Afghan Civil War (1992–1996) following the Soviet retreat ended when the Taliban, a hardline Islamist group, gained control of the Afghan government. U.S. military involvement in Afghanistan began in October 2001 as a response to the September 11 terrorist attacks on U.S. soil, in which 3,000 American citizens were killed in four coordinated attacks.

In his September 20, 2001, address to the U.S. Congress, President George W. Bush identified the Al Qaeda terrorist organization, then based in Afghanistan, as the perpetrator of the attacks. In the same speech, Bush demanded from the Taliban the immediate delivery of the Al Qaeda leadership to the U.S.

authorities and full U.S. access to the terrorist camps and training grounds in Afghanistan. Bush also announced that this was the beginning of a lengthy global War on Terror and that the nations that did not support the U.S. cause would be considered to have sided with the terrorists. Upon the Taliban's refusal to agree to the United States' terms, coordinated U.S. and NATO military operations in Afghanistan, titled Operation Enduring Freedom (OEF), began on October 7, 2001.

The main objectives of OEF were to dismantle Al Qaeda, to remove the Taliban from power, and to establish a pro-Western democratic regime in Afghanistan. In addition to the NATO troops, the U.S. government also recruited the Northern Alliance (the Taliban's political rivals) and various other local anti-Taliban forces in its fight against the Taliban and Al Qaeda. By 2011 around 68 countries had participated in the operations of the international coalition forces in Afghanistan in various capacities. The initial attacks of the coalition troops under U.S. leadership were very successful. Within the first five weeks of OEF, the Taliban regime was dismantled and the critically important cities of Mazar-i-Sharif, Kabul, Kanduz, and Kandahar were taken. In the second week of December 2001, the U.S. forces laid siege to and quickly took control of what was believed to be the Al Qaeda headquarters in the Tora Bora region of Afghanistan. Although several hundred Taliban and Al Qaeda members were killed in this operation, Osama bin Laden and other high-ranking members of Al Qaeda were not captured and were believed to have escaped to Pakistan.

Despite the failure to apprehend bin Laden, the operational capacity of Al Qaeda was seriously crippled. On December 20, the UN Security Council established the International Security Assistance Force (ISAF) to secure Kabul and its surrounding areas. An interim government was established under the leadership of Hamid Karzai, who became the head of the first democratically elected government of Afghanistan in 2004. However, in 2003 the radical segments of the Taliban, who had regrouped in Pakistan, organized resistance against the invasion forces and the Karzai government. After 2006, the violence in Afghanistan escalated to an extreme as the Taliban-led insurgency began to perpetrate terrorist attacks against not only the coalition troops and the Karzai government but also the civilian population. In the face of intensifying violence in December 2009, President Barack Obama ordered a dramatic increase in the U.S. military presence in Afghanistan, with the deployment of an additional 30,000 soldiers to the country. By December 2011, an estimated 101,000 U.S. troops were deployed in Afghanistan.

A major development in the Afghan War and the U.S. global War on Terror was the killing of bin Laden by U.S. special operations units in Pakistan on May 2, 2011. Upon this development, in June 2011, Obama declared that the U.S. troops would fully withdraw from Afghanistan by the end of the year 2014. As of January 2012, 168 service members had been killed in OEF. The Afghan War from 2001 to 2011 cost the United States an estimated $468 billion. The Afghan War stands as the United States' second longest overseas military involvement, after the Vietnam War.

The global War on Terror also marked a turning point for servicewomen in the U.S. military. Since 2001, the number of female military personnel deployed in Iraq and Afghanistan has reached unprecedented levels. By October 2009, an estimated 11 percent of all troops deployed in Operation Iraqi Freedom and OEF were female. By November 2011, 30 women had died in OEF. Although American women may serve as combat pilots and on naval vessels according to the current military regulations, they are still banned from serving in ground combat units. However, since the beginning of the Afghan War, female servicemembers have increasingly been used for missions "outside the wire," or outside the military base, for intelligence work and at search stations.

In 2009, the Navy initiated the Female Engagement Teams (FET) project to establish contact with the Afghan women, who are traditionally banned from contact with foreign men. The teams are composed of four or five female members who accompany male infantry units on patrols. The female marines are encouraged to wear headscarves when visiting Afghan homes and socializing with Afghan women. Upon the reported success of the FET, in 2011 the Army formed Cultural Support Teams (CSTs), elite female units, to work with the special forces troops during the raids. Both the Navy and the Army teams receive training in Afghan culture, and they aim to establish positive relations with Afghan women while also collecting strategic intelligence.

The FET and the CSTs present a dramatic shift in the gender roles in the U.S. military as, despite the de jure ban on combat assignments for women, female soldiers are now taking active part in infantry operations in the war zones. Although some women soldiers welcome this development as an opportunity for career enhancement, the war claims a high toll on the family life of the female servicemembers. With the longer tours of duty overseas, reaching up to 12 months in the Army and 7 months in the Navy, female soldiers face intensifying challenges in balancing family life and work. Among the main issues reported by women are insufficient maternity deferments (4 months in the Army, 6 months in the Navy), high divorce rates (almost three times higher for female servicemembers than for male soldiers), inadequate health care, sexual harassment and assault, high rates of post-traumatic stress disorder (PTSD), and higher unemployment rates. The U.S. Department of Veteran Affairs and various nongovernmental organizations (NGOs), such as Iraq and Afghanistan Veterans of America (IAVA), address these issues and aim to contribute to their solutions.

Suphan Kirmizialtin

See also: Cold War (ca. 1947–1991); Iraq War (2003–2011); War on Terror (2001–).

References and Further Reading

Barfield, Thomas J. *Afghanistan: A Cultural and Political History.* Princeton Studies in Muslim Politics. Princeton, NJ: Princeton University Press, 2010.

Bumiller, Elisabeth. "Letting Women Reach Women in Afghan War." *New York Times*, March 6, 2010.

Cave, Damien. "Women at Arms: A Combat Role, and Anguish, Too." *New York Times*, November 1, 2009.

Harrison, Todd. "Analysis of the Fy 2011 Defense Budget." Washington, D.C.: Center for Strategic and Budgetary Assessments, 2011.

Jones, Seth G. *In the Graveyard of Empires: America's War in Afghanistan.* New York: W. W. Norton & Co, 2009.

Larner, Brad, and Adrian Blow. "A Model of Meaning-Making Coping and Growth in Combat Veterans." *Review of General Psychology* 15, no. 3 (2011): 187–97.

Mulhall, Erin. "Women Warriors: Supporting She 'Who Has Born the Battle.' " In *IAVA Issue Reports.* Washington, D.C.: Iraq and Afghanistan Veterans of America, 2009.

Obama, Barack. "Address to the Nation on the Way Forward in Afghanistan and Pakistan." West Point, NY, December 1, 2009.

"President Bush's Speech on Terrorism." *New York Times*, September 6, 2006.

Ryan, Maria. " 'War in Countries We Are Not at War With': The 'War on Terror' on the Periphery from Bush to Obama." *International Politics* 48, nos. 2–3 (2011): 364–89.

Tanner, Stephen. *Afghanistan: A Military History from Alexander the Great to the War against the Taliban.* New York: Da Capo Press, 2009.

AFRICAN AMERICAN WOMEN

In all U.S. military conflicts, African American women have played active roles. When laws prevented them from enlisting in the armed forces because of their gender and race, they found alternative means to aid their country. Over time, the military gradually began to officially make use of their abilities. Even when permitted to join the armed forces, they frequently experienced discrimination because of their race and gender. Although extremely limited in the beginning, black women eventually secured a respectable and significant presence within the U.S. military.

During the American Revolution, most of the black women in the American colonies were slaves. As a result, black women could aid the cause by taking over the duties at home so that white women might then go to the battlefront to aid their husbands. Additionally, some black women served as nurses, laundresses, and spies during the Revolutionary War. Others may have

During the Civil War, escaped slave Susie Baker King Taylor joined her husband's regiment, the 33rd U.S. Colored Troops, as a laundress. She also served as a teacher, cook, and nurse for the regiment. (Library of Congress)

disguised themselves as men to fight alongside the soldiers.

Although their official participation in the War of 1812 was limited, black women did their best to aid the cause. To help ease the stress on the homefront, they often tended to farms, helped make bandages for wounded soldiers, and nursed soldiers.

The Civil War saw an increase in African American women's involvement. In the North, many black women became camp followers of black regiments. They stayed close to enlisted husbands, fathers, or brothers as they cooked, laundered, and served as nurses. In addition, the Union paid some black women to grow cotton on plantations for the U.S. government to sell. Other African American women served as Union spies. Still others served as nurses in battlefield hospitals or on hospital ships.

Several African American women distinguished themselves during the Civil War. For example, Susie King Taylor, a slave freed during the war, served as a cook and nurse to Union troops. She also worked as an employee of the Union Army for over four years but never received any pay. She also taught other freed slaves how to read. Another former slave, Harriet Tubman, served as not only a Union spy and scout but also as an unpaid soldier, cook, and volunteer nurse. Tubman was the first woman to lead an armed excursion in the war as she guided Union troops in the Combahee River Raid in South Carolina. Although she received some money for her scouting efforts, she put most of it toward paying other spies for information.

African American women in the Confederacy also participated in the Civil War, although often in hidden and subversive ways. In particular, they supported male family members who ran away to the Union Army, and they subtly disturbed plantation work.

After the Civil War, Cathay Williams disguised herself as a man and enlisted in the U.S. Regular Army in St. Louis, Missouri. She used the alias William Cathey. Her height helped her remain disguised for several months. She was discharged after several hospital stays and had to return to life as a woman. Other women similarly served unnoticed in the Army.

African American women's wartime contributions became more public after the end of slavery. Black women served as nurses during the Spanish-American War, fulfilling a vital role. When yellow fever and typhoid epidemics broke out among the troops, 32 black women were recruited as nurses and shipped to Santiago, Cuba, to care for the soldiers. Although they were assumed to be immune to the diseases because of their dark skin, two African American nurses contracted typhoid fever and died while tending to sick soldiers.

During World War I, African American women took on many roles to aid their nation. They once again worked as nurses, this time with the help of the National Association of Colored Graduate Nurses (founded in 1908), which helped blacks fight stereotypes and racial discrimination. To help the U.S. war effort, black women were urged to enroll in the Red Cross. They worked in hospitals, made bandages for the wounded, and relieved men of their jobs so that they could serve as soldiers. Eventually, 18 black Red Cross nurses were offered Army Nurse Corps (ANC) assignments. Their duty was to care for

German prisoners of war and for black soldiers. In addition, four black women served as volunteers for the Young Men's Christian Association (YMCA), which provided support for soldiers overseas. Overall, public pressure to enlist black women greatly increased during World War I.

During World War II, 56 African American women were admitted into the ANC. In addition to serving as nurses, black women enrolled in the Women's Army Auxiliary Corps (WAAC). The 10 percent of WAAC women who were black served in segregated units working as postal clerks, stenographers, switchboard operators, truck drivers, and typists. When, in 1943, the WAAC was replaced with the Women's Army Corps (WAC), these women continued their work for their nation. After Congress passed a bill barring racial bias in 1943, 2,000 black women enrolled in the Cadet Nurse Corps. In 1948, Harry S. Truman signed the Women's Armed Services Integration Act, which authorized women to enter the Regular Army and created a permanent place for women in the armed forces. African American women still faced segregation, but at least one hurdle had been made easier.

In 1945, the all-black 6888th Central Postal Directory Battalion was sent to England to sort a serious backlog of mail. Led by Maj. Charity Adams Earley, America's first black female officer, the 6888th worked nonstop to filter piles of mail that reached the ceiling; they completed their mission three months before the deadline.

It was not until the Vietnam War that the United States had a fully integrated military. Increasing numbers of African American women volunteered for duty and excelled. Army nurse Diane M. Lindsay was the first black nurse to receive the Soldier's Medal of Heroism for convincing a bewildered soldier to hand over a grenade at the 95th Evacuation Hospital. Olivia Theriot, a flight nurse for the 902nd Aeromed Evacuation Squad, repeatedly flew in and out of Saigon to move wounded soldiers. Following the war, Hazel W. Johnson became the first black woman general officer when she was promoted to chief of the ANC in 1979.

It is estimated that of the 35,000 women that served in the Gulf War in 1991, 40 percent of them were African American. They effectively served as officers, noncommissioned officers, and enlisted soldiers. For example, Lt. Phoebe Jeter headed an all-male platoon and was the first woman to shoot down a Scud missile. Although still forbidden to fight in combat, women were involved in combat support duties. They served as pilots, directed artillery, operated prisoner-of-war camps, and repaired ships.

In 1994 the Army opened up 90 percent of its jobs to women. Women were finally permitted to fill roles that had a substantial risk of capture. Shoshana Johnson became the United States' first black female prisoner of war when she was captured in Iraq in 2003. Today women of all races and backgrounds train alongside their male peers in the military. The wars in Iraq and Afghanistan showed a reduction in the number of enlisted women as compared to those who served in the Gulf War. Even so, increasing numbers of women have been killed in combat or suffer from combat-related wounds.

Siobhan Elise Ausberry

See also: Afghanistan; Air Force Nurse Corps (AFNC); American Red Cross; American Revolution (1775–1783); Army Nurse Corps (ANC); Bailey, Margaret E. (1915–); Baker, Josephine (1906–1975); Bethune, Mary McLeod (1875–1955); Brown, Monica Lin (1988–); Cadet Nurse Corps; Cadoria, Sherian Grace (1940–); Camp Followers; Civil War (1861–1865); Cold War (ca. 1947–1991); Curtis, Namahyoke Sockum (1861–1935); Earley, Charity Adams (1918–2002); Espionage; Fields, Evelyn Juanita (1949–); Gold Star Mothers' Pilgrimages (1930s); Gulf War (1991); Harris, Marcelite Jordan (1943–); Howard, Michelle (1960–); Hunton, Addie Waites (1866–1943); Iraq War (2003–2011); Jackson, Gilda A. (1950–); Johnson, Shoshana Nyree (1973–); Johnson-Brown, Hazel Winifred (1927–2011); Keys (Evans), Sarah Louise (1929–); Korean War (1950–1953); Leftenant Colon, Nancy (1921–); Mammy Kate (n.d.–n.d.); Navy Nurse Corps; Nursing; Rodgers, Marie Louise (1926–); Roundtree, Dovey Mae Johnson (1914–); Spanish-American War (1898); Tubman, Harriet [Araminta Ross] (ca. 1820–1913); United States Coast Guard Women's Reserve (SPAR); Vietnam War (1965–1973); War of 1812 (1812–1815); War on Terror (2001–); Williams, Cathay [William Cathey] (ca. 1844–n.d.); Women Accepted for Volunteer Emergency Service (WAVES); Women Air Force Service Pilots (WASP); Women in Military Service for America Memorial; Women in the Air Force (WAF); Women Marines; Women Strike for Peace (WSP); Women's Armed Services Integration Act of 1948 (Public Law 80-625); Women's Army Auxiliary Corps (WAAC); Women's Army Corps (WAC); World War I (1914–1918); World War II (1941–1945); Young Men's Christian Association (YMCA); Young Women's Christian Association (YWCA).

References and Further Reading

Hunt, C. S. M. Harold. *Transforming the Ranks: Black Female Sergeants Major.* Hanover, MD: Hunt Enterprises, 2008.

Latty, Yvonne. *We Were There: Voices of African American Veterans from WWII to the War in Iraq.* New York: Amistad, 2004.

Moore, Brenda L. *To Serve My Country, to Serve My Race: The Story of the Only African American WACS Stationed Overseas During WWII.* New York: New York University Press, 1996.

Shockley, Megan Taylor. *"We, Too, Are Americans": African American Women in Detroit and Richmond, 1940–1954.* Chicago: University of Illinois Press, 2004.

Tucker, Phillip Thomas. *Cathy Williams: From Slave to Female Buffalo Soldier.* Mechanicsburg, PA: Stackpole Books, 2002.

AIR FORCE NURSE CORPS (AFNC)

The first flight nurses graduated from the United States Army's School of Air Evacuation in 1943, four years before the creation of the Air Force. Rotating between air evacuation squadrons and hospital assignments, experienced flight nurses were ready to transfer into the Nurse Corps of the Air Force Medical Service (AFNC) when it was established on July 1, 1949. Its primary mission is to provide nursing duties for active-duty military personnel in wartime and peacetime situations.

The earliest recruitment guidelines stipulated that only women who were registered nurses, aged 21 to 45, with no dependents under age 18 could be considered. African American Army nurses were among the 1,199 nurses who voluntarily transferred into the AFNC, so this component of military service has always been integrated. The first two direct commissions into the Air Force Nurse Service Reserve occurred on August 24, 1949. Capt. Verena Zeller served as the first chief nurse from 1949 to 1956, reporting to the Air Force surgeon general. Lt. Col. Margaret McKenzie developed the Corps' first career program, defining the scope of nurse specialties. The AFNC had less than a year to get organized before the outbreak of the Korean War in June 1950.

Ground transportation challenges in Korea led to a transformation in the logistics of dealing with the wounded. Aeromedical evacuation of casualties to treatment facilities away from the front lines resulted in higher survival rates. The Air Force evacuated over 333,000 patients during the Korean War, with flight nurses responsible for in-flight medical decisions. AFNC Capt. Vera M. Brown died on September 26, 1950, in a plane crash and was posthumously awarded the Distinguished Flying Cross.

In June 1954, AFNC nurses participated in Operation Wounded Warrior, evacuating wounded French soldiers out of Vietnam. Later, over 770 Air Force women served in the Vietnam War, participating in the Medical Civil Assistance Program with villagers when not on evacuation flights or working at casualty staging facilities or base hospitals. On April 1, 1973, AFNC nurses participated in Operation Homecoming, flying to Hanoi to return 367 released American prisoners of war to the United States. On April 4, 1975, AFNC Capt. Mary Klinker died in an Operation Babylift plane crash while evacuating orphans from Vietnam. Flight nurse Regina Aune became the first woman to receive the Cheney Award for her rescue efforts after surviving the crash. Klinker is listed on the Vietnam Veterans Memorial. In addition, to honor her service the McDonnell Douglas Corporation sponsors the Mary T. Klinker Flight Nurse of the Year Award.

In the 1970s, anticipating a physician shortage with the transition to an all-volunteer military, the Air Force began developing master's degree training for clinical nurse positions. Expanded responsibilities for nurses enabled more efficient use of physicians. The growing emphasis on clinical and deployment readiness also influenced the Corps' training efforts. In 1971, the Air Force opened its Reserve Officer Training Program to women and ended the Nurse Corps' ban on commissioning women with dependents. A 1970s legal challenge by Air Force nurse Susan Struck led to a Supreme Court ruling allowing pregnant military women to remain on active duty.

In the 1960s, the Air Force developed a Bioastronautic Operational Support Group, including nurses, to support manned space flights and aerospace medical research. In the 1970s, NASA and the AFNC conducted research to prepare for women's participation in space shuttle flights. A Nursing Internship Program was launched in 1977 to better prepare new Air Force nurses for patient care. From 1982 to 2002, a bachelor of science degree in nursing was mandatory for being commissioned as an AFNC officer.

In 1972, Col. E. Ann Hoefly became the first chief nurse promoted to the rank of brigadier general. In 1988, Col. Gloria Hernandez became the first active-duty nurse assigned as commander of an aeromedical evacuation unit. In 1990, Col. Judith Hunt was the first Air Force nurse to become commander of a medical treatment facility, Pope Air Force Base. About 4,000 AFNC nurses served in the Gulf War, with the first wartime deployment of air transportable clinics. In 1992, Col. Gloria Lamoureux became the first nurse to serve as a hospital commander. In 1995, Brig. Gen. Linda Stierle became the first nurse appointed director for medical readiness doctrine and planning for the Air Force.

In 2011, Maj. Gen. Kimberly Siniscalchi, assistant surgeon general, nursing services, reported that the 18,000 members of the total nursing force—comprised of the Air Force, the Air National Guard, the Air Force Reserve, and the Aerospace Medical Service—were responsible for nursing care of patients in all Air Force facilities and would continue to participate in military operations other than war. Focusing on education and research, the Nurse Corps' priorities are patient-centered care, development of professional competencies, excellent health care, and leadership for global operations. Aeromedical evacuation continues to be a core competency, with technological advances driving the need for ongoing nursing research. The Nurse Corps' mission statement reflects its proud tradition: "We lead, we partner, we care, every time, everywhere."

Betty J. Glass

See also: Afghanistan; African American Women; Cold War (ca. 1947–1991); Gulf War (1991); Hoefly, E. Ann (1919–2003); Iraq War (2003–2011); Korean War (1950–1953); Mobile Army Surgical Hospital (MASH); Nursing; Reserve Officer Training Corps (ROTC); Vietnam War (1965–1973); World War II (1941–1945).

References and Further Reading

Lindberg, Kerrie G. "The History of the Air Force Nurse Corps from 1984 to 1998, a Research Paper." Maxwell Air Force Base, AL: Air War College, 1999.

Rank, Melissa A. "What Influenced the Development of the Air Force Nurse Corps from 1969 through 1983." Maxwell Air Force Base, AL: Air War College, 1999.

Smith, Donald George, Jr. "A Study of the Persian Gulf War as a Catalyst for Change in the Air Force Nurse Corps' Clinical and Deployment Readiness." Ph.D. dissertation, New York University, 2003.

Smolenski, Mary C., Donald G. Smith Jr., and James Nanney. "A Fit, Fighting Force: The Air Force Nursing Services Chronology." Washington, D.C.: Office of the Air Force Surgeon General, 2005.

Vairo, Sharon A. "History of the United States Air Force Nurse Corps, 1949–1954." Doctor of Nursing Science dissertation, University of San Diego, Philip Y. Hahn School of Nursing, 1998.

ALBRIGHT, MADELEINE KORBEL [MARIE JANA KORBELOVÁ] (1937–)

Madeleine Korbel Albright has served as Democratic Party foreign policy adviser, U.S. ambassador to the United Nations (1993–1997), and secretary of state (1997–2001).

Albright was born Marie Jana Korbelová (the family later shortened the name) in Prague, Czechoslovakia, on May 15, 1937. Her father, Josef Korbel, was a diplomat, and he and his wife had converted to Catholicism from

Madeleine Albright served as secretary of state from 1997 until 2001. Prior to that she was the U.S. ambassador to the United Nations. (Department of State)

Judaism. In 1939, when the Germans took over Czechoslovakia, the Korbel family fled to Britain. Following the defeat of Germany, the family returned to Prague, where Josef Korbel was appointed Czechoslovakian ambassador to Yugoslavia and Albania. A few months after the February 1948 communist coup in Czechoslovakia, the family again sought asylum, this time in the United States. In 1949 they settled in Denver, Colorado, where Korbel became a professor at the University of Colorado and developed an acclaimed program in international relations. He would become an adviser to two U.S. secretaries of state and his own daughter.

An excellent student, she graduated from Wellesley College in Massachusetts in 1959 and married Joseph Albright, a journalist from a distinguished family. Later they divorced. While rearing three

daughters, Albright earned a PhD in government and public law from Columbia University, where she worked with Professor Zbigniew Brzezinski, later named the national security adviser to President Jimmy Carter.

Following extensive volunteer work for the Democratic Party, in 1976 Albright became chief legislative assistant to Maine senator Edmund Muskie. In 1982 she became a professor of international affairs and director of the Women in Foreign Service Program at Georgetown University's School of Foreign Service. Albright was active in the presidential campaigns of Walter Mondale (1984) and Michael Dukakis (1988), serving as chief foreign policy adviser to both candidates. Meanwhile, she built her reputation as an authority on foreign policy and women's issues while forming close personal ties with fellow Wellesley alumna Hillary Rodham Clinton. Upon his 1993 election to the presidency, William Jefferson Clinton appointed Albright U.S. ambassador to the United Nations, a post she took up in February 1994. Her extensive knowledge of foreign languages and Balkan ethnic politics served her well at the United Nations.

In January 1997, Clinton chose Albright to be secretary of state, the highest government post held up to that time by an American woman. Her charm, sense of humor, and sharp wit garnered wide press attention. The exhilaration of Albright's first days in office was clouded by a journalist's revelation that three of her grandparents had perished in Nazi concentration camps and that Albright's immediate family had purposefully obscured their Jewish background. Albright, who had been baptized Roman Catholic at the age of five and had joined the Episcopal Church upon her marriage, knew nothing of her Jewish ancestry.

Early in Albright's term, questions were raised about the effectiveness of a woman, especially one with a Jewish heritage, negotiating with Middle Eastern heads of state, but Albright soon established effective ties with Saudi Arabian officials and forged a strong friendship with King Hussein of Jordan. Still, the Israeli-Palestinian conflict proved intractable. The Clinton administration had made numerous efforts to bring both parties to the negotiating table, beginning with the 1993 Oslo Accords. In January 1998, Israeli prime minister Benjamin Netanyahu and Palestine Liberation Organization (PLO) chairman Yasir Arafat traveled to Washington for talks but showed little willingness to compromise on the status of Jerusalem, a release of prisoners, or Jewish settlements.

Albright and the administration persisted, however, sponsoring talks again in October 1998 at Wye River in Maryland. Albright was able to bring in King Hussein of Jordan and his wife, Queen Noor, as intermediaries. These talks ultimately resulted in the Wye River Memorandum, which pledged more cooperation in security for the Israelis and additional land rights for the Palestinians.

Any expectations that Albright and Clinton may have had for settling disputes in the Middle East were dashed in September 2000 when Israeli hardline politician Ariel Sharon made a provocative visit to Temple Mount/Haram al-Sharif (al-Aqsa Mosque), the Muslim holy site in Jerusalem. The visit not only dashed hopes of Palestinian-Israeli peace but also sparked a new wave of violence known as the al-Aqsa Intifada. Albright's experience alerted her to the importance of understanding religious passions in framing global policy. After she left office in 2001, her writings and speeches stressed the importance of educating policy makers in the tenets of major world religions.

Albright also played a central role in the Balkans, which had descended into chaos and spasms of genocidal violence. She was influential in shaping policy during the Kosovo conflict (1996–1999), which resulted ultimately in NATO's bombing campaign against Serbian-Yugoslavian targets from March through June 1999. The campaign forced Serbian strongman Slobodan Milosevic to the negotiating table. Albright also helped bring to an end the Bosnian War, culminating in the December 1995 Dayton Agreement.

By the end of her four-year term, Albright's critics charged that she dealt with problems on a case-by-case basis and lacked a coherent foreign policy doctrine. Many in the Republican Party also believed that the Clinton administration, basking in prosperous times and relative world peace, had neglected the growing problems of terrorism and collapsing economies in a world no longer held in check by the communist-capitalist rivalry.

However, Albright could cite solid achievements. Her strong personality had generated wide public interest in foreign affairs while her presence in high office had advanced women worldwide. As a refugee from European oppression, she had been an unquestioned American patriot and a strong proponent of worldwide democracy and human rights. She had pointedly warned of American smugness at the beginning of the new millennium, had identified a new world order, and had faced down aggression in the Balkans while maintaining cordial relations with Russia. And despite disappointments, she had kept Israeli-Palestinian peace negotiations from collapsing completely during the difficult tenures of Benjamin Netanyahu and Yasser Arafat.

Allene S. Phy-Olsen

See also: World War II (1941–1945).

References and Further Reading

Albright, Madeleine. *Madam Secretary: A Memoir.* New York: Miramax, 2003.

Albright, Madeleine. *Memo to the President Elect: How We Can Restore America's Reputation and Leadership.* New York: HarperCollins, 2008.

Albright, Madeleine. *The Mighty and the Almighty: Reflections on America, God, and World Affairs.* New York: HarperCollins, 2003.

Blackman, Ann. *Seasons of Her Life: A Biography of Madeleine Korbel Albright.* New York: Scribners, 1998.

Dobbs, Michael. *Madeleine Albright: A Twentieth-Century Odyssey.* New York: Henry Holt, 1999.

Lippman, Thomas W. *Madeleine Albright and the New American Diplomacy.* Boulder, CO: Westview Press, 2000.

ALLEN (BILLINGS), ELIZA [GEORGE MEAD] (1826–N.D.)

Disguised as a man, Eliza Allen served during the Mexican War (1846–1848). She later published her autobiography, *The Female Volunteer; Or the Life and Wonderful Adventures of Miss Eliza Allen, A Young Lady of Eastport, Maine* (1851).

Eliza Allen, later Eliza Allen Billings, remains shrouded in mystery. The only substantial source on her life comes from her own pen; several historians have raised doubts that Allen existed outside the realm of fiction, arguing that her autobiography bears hallmark plot devices of popular 19th-century literature. No definite account proving or disproving her existence has yet been authored.

Allen gives her birth date as January 27, 1826. She was the firstborn to George H. Allen and Sarah Allen, a family of means in the town of Eastport, Maine. From her writing it can be surmised that prior to the outbreak of the Mexican War the Billings family relocated from Canada to her hometown. The Billings were respectable but poor. The eldest son, William, found employment working for Allen's father.

Romance blossomed between Allen and Billings despite established social lines. When Allen's parents discovered their relationship, they forbade her from having any further contact with Billings. In response he wrote Allen a farewell note and enlisted in the Army, thinking a military career would grant him a better chance in the future of securing Allen's hand in marriage.

Influenced by accounts of Revolutionary War heroine Deborah Sampson and of the War of 1812 service of Lucy Brewer, Allen reportedly decided to follow her love by masquerading as a man to enlist. Taking advantage of her parents' absence during an extended trip, she boarded a ship under the alias George Mead.

She successfully enlisted in Portland, Maine, and boarded a transport for the theater of war. Her unit participated in the Battle of Monterey, September 21 through 24, 1846, in which she claims to have personally fought. When her first period of enlistment expired and she had not yet been reunited with Billings, she decided to reenlist.

During her second term she saw action again at the Battle of Cerro Gordo, April 18, 1847. According to her account she was wounded by a sword cut during this engagement. While being treated in the field hospital, Allen discovered her beloved, Billings, also under the care of the surgeons for a battlefield injury. Allen did not reveal herself to Billings but shadowed him as much as possible as George Mead. During this period, through deceptions and candid conversations, "Mead" was able to divine the true nature of Billings's devotion to their love. The two recovered from their wounds, and both planned to muster out as the war had come to a close.

Allen's hopes for a reunion faced a setback after Billings and several of his companions were swindled out of their pay. Rather than return back to Maine empty-handed, Billings and his friends decided to gamble again, this time on the California Gold Rush, which erupted in 1848 with the discovery of gold near Sutter's Sawmill near Coloma, California. They struck out to find their fortune onboard the *Omo*. The ship collided with reefs, leaving it a floating wreck.

Aware of their plan, Allen had followed Billings and his company on another ship. During a passage through the Straits of Magellan, her vessel picked up the survivors of the *Omo*, one of which, miraculously, was Billings. Allen helped nurse him back to health and gave him another chance at prospecting by utilizing her resources.

In September 1849, Billings and Allen arrived in Boston, bolstered by some success in prospecting. When it seemed that Billings would once again foolishly lose his money, Allen revealed herself. Together at last, Allen wrote a plea to her parents to accept her choice of husband. The elder Allens were overjoyed at the return of the daughter they thought they had lost and made amends by granting her request.

In 1851, Allen Billings published an account of her time as Mead. She asserted that she had published the account to convince parents to be careful in their treatment of their daughters and, in particular, to allow them choice in their marriages.

Michael D. Coker

See also: American Revolution (1775–1783); Brewer, Lucy [Louisa Baker, George Baker, Lucy West, Eliza Bowen] (ca. 1793–n.d.); Samson [Sampson] (Gannett), Deborah [Robert Shurtliff] (1760–1827); War of 1812 (1812–1815).

References and Further Reading

Billings, Eliza. *The Female Volunteer; Or the Life and Wonderful Adventures of Miss Eliza Allen, A Young Lady of Eastport, Maine*. Cincinnati, OH: H.M Rulison, 1851.

Johannsen, Robert Walter. *To the Halls of Montezumas: The Mexican War in American Imagination*. New York: Oxford University Press, 1998.

ALL-VOLUNTEER FORCE (AVF)

When the government allowed the military draft to expire in 1973, the United

States military resorted to an all-volunteer force (AVF). Such a switch of manpower required an adjustment to retention and recruitment policies and encouraged the full integration of women and minorities into the armed forces.

In 1968, Richard Nixon's presidential campaign included the promise to end the draft. This proposal had positive results for the candidate. It had the potential to appease constituents who were growing increasingly critical of the war in Vietnam and to temper the student antiwar and antidraft movements. Once elected, Nixon assembled the Gates Commission in 1969, headed by former secretary of defense Thomas Gates. The 15-person committee was comprised of free-market economists like Milton Freedman, W. Allen Wallis, and Alan Greenspan. They researched the subject of an AVF from an economic framework to consider if demand could be created within a new marketplace for recruitment. The draft regulated the relationship between serviceperson supply and serviceperson demand. In deregulating the supply mechanisms required for thriving armed forces, the commission argued that a free-market approach to recruitment could succeed provided there was demand. The key to this success was creating that demand. Economic instability and job scarcity fostered the demand for individual enlistment incentives including pay, benefits, lodging, job training, and travel. Recruitment advertising campaigns in print, poster, and, for the first time ever, on television aimed to transform mass target audiences of young people into supply.

In February 1970, the commission released a unanimous recommendation in its report in favor of ending the draft. As a result, Congress did not extend the draft law. On July 1, 1973, the draft expired and the recruitment structure within the U.S. armed force branches shifted to reflect an "all-volunteer concept." Research economist and military manpower recruitment and retention expert Bernard Rostker wrote that women, perhaps more so than any other group, were responsible for the success of the AVF. Women in service and women supportive of their enlisted partners, spouses, and family members were integral to the AVF's success and long-term viability. Despite the reality of women's influence, the Gates Commission never considered expanding the number of women in uniform in its proposal to Nixon. Within the Department of Defense, it became clear that servicewomen were less costly to enlist than servicemen. In consideration of this disparity, coupled with servicemen shortages in branches and the passage by Congress of the Equal Rights Amendment (ERA) to the Constitution in 1972, a designated task force was set up to increase the number of women in each branch.

The shift to an AVF included higher salaries and attractive benefits, but those details had to be advertised widely in order to retain enlisted servicepeople and to recruit enough new ones. The advertising and recruitment budget allocations were increased accordingly, and a flurry of ad campaigns followed. While draft-era ads evoked abstract ideas about heroism, patriotism, and civic duty, AVF ads emphasized individual benefits and targeted underrepresented and underprivileged groups. The AVF could not advertise broadly to an audience loosely presumed to be male and overwhelmingly white. In conjunction with the use of new forms of media like television and eventually digital websites and video games, AVF marketing tactics tightened in focus to narrowcast specialized messages to increasingly important audiences of women, African Americans, and Hispanics. Although the practice of recruiting specific genders, ethnicities, and races predated the AVF and was prolific near the end of the Vietnam War, the new ads aimed toward minority groups positioned army service as a means of equalizing access to upward mobility. The economic downturns of the 1970s facilitated further demand creation in this regard.

The recruiting tactics aimed at women and minorities evolved pre- and post-AVF. The pre-AVF placements for women were in the Women's Army Corps (WAC). The eventual assimilation of the WAC in 1978 required integrating women into the general army branch and accommodating the changing social norms of gender. Although it was common for pre-AVF WAC ads to address young women as "girls," post-AVF ads aimed at women appropriated the equal-pay-for-equal-work rhetoric of second-wave feminism, arguing that the gender of a soldier was irrelevant and that Army life meant equality and respect for all. Similarly, the AVF ads targeted to African American audiences visually demonstrated a utopian meritocracy in which racism posed no obstacles. Ads claimed that the only color the Army saw was green. Spanish-language ads featured Hispanic protagonists to reach targets more effectively. In ads aimed at minorities, the theme was that rank ascension facilitated class

ascension. Ads aimed specifically at women touted perks like travel, experience, and community in addition to fair pay. In all cases, neoliberal rhetoric, central to selling the end of the draft to politicians, became central in creating supply within targeted audiences. The social climate was not always hospitable to the expansion of women's service roles in the all-volunteer era.

Some scholars have argued that the ERA failed in part because of public anxieties over a gender-equitable AVF. Conservative political activist Phyllis Schlafly condemned the women's movement and the ERA. ERA criticisms waged by Schlafly and others bolstered fears about the potential requirement for women to register into the Selective Service System. Additionally, the debates over removing women's combat exclusion statutes further incited a growing conservative backlash against the women's movement that led to the defeat of the ERA. Despite these problems, women continued to enlist to serve their country in the AVF.

The ongoing recruitment and retention of women soldiers and women supportive of soldiers transformed the AVF into a more family-friendly institution. Morale and quality of life improved with the development of Army family programs ensuring comfortable housing, comprehensive health care, and stable salaries for men and women. As the number of married enlisted soldiers multiplied, it became increasingly necessary to expand programs like the army branch's Quality of Life Program and Family Assistance Center. As the all-volunteer concept continued to succeed, the AVF adapted to be more inclusive and attentive to the needs of women soldiers and women supportive of soldiers.

Jessica L. Ghilani

See also: African American Women; Hispanic American Women; Vietnam War (1965–1973); Women's Army Corps (WAC).

References and Further Reading

Anderson, Martin. "Meeting with the President's Commission on an All-Volunteer Armed Force: Memorandum for the President's File." Washington, D.C., February 21, 1970.

Bailey, Beth. *America's Army: Making the All-Volunteer Force*. Cambridge, MA: Harvard University Press, 2009.

Meckling, William H. "Comment on 'Women and Minorities in the All-Volunteer Force.' " In *The All-Volunteer Force after a Decade: Retrospect and Prospect*, edited by Rodger Little and G. Thomas Sicilia William Bowman. New York: Pergamon-Brassey's, 1986.

Rostker, Bernard D. *I Want You!: The Evolution of the All-Volunteer Force*. Santa Monica, CA: RAND, 2006.

AMERICAN RED CROSS

The American Red Cross is a humanitarian relief organization that was founded in Washington, D.C., on May 21, 1881, by Civil War nurse Clara Barton. The Red Cross is primarily a volunteer organization that provides community services that provide help for the needy; offer support and comfort for military members and their families; coordinate the collection, processing, and distribution of lifesaving blood and blood products; provide educational programs that promote health and safety; and run international relief and development programs. Throughout its history, the American Red Cross has played a vital role in supporting the U.S. armed forces at home and on the battlefield during war.

The creation of the American Red Cross resulted from Clara Barton's Civil War work for Union soldiers. During the war she collected supplies for Union troops, read to and wrote letters for Union soldiers, and served as a battlefield nurse. After the war, she continued her work, helping families to find missing soldiers and to locate the graves of soldiers killed in battle and in prison camps. After serving as a nurse in Europe through the International Red Cross, she decided to bring the Red Cross to the United States. In 1881 she founded the American Red Cross and became its first president, serving as such until 1904.

The Spanish-American War of 1898 was the first event that required that the American Red Cross provide war relief services to the armed forces. During the conflict, the American Red Cross sought to provide assistance to troops fighting the Spanish in Cuba and the Philippines. By the war's end, Barton had recruited over 700 nurses for these efforts. Her recruitment efforts were especially impressive considering that the Army's surgeon general was reluctant to allow women to nurse the wounded. In Cuba, the American Red Cross provided nursing care, medical supplies, food, and other necessities.

During the Spanish-American War, nurse Jane Delano joined the ranks of the American Red Cross. Delano simultaneously served as superintendent of

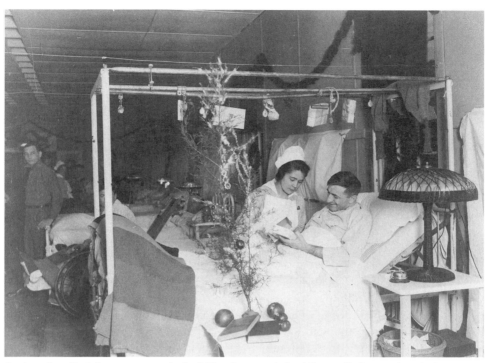

An American Red Cross nurse at the bedside of a wounded soldier at Christmas time during World War I. (Library of Congress)

the Army Nurse Corps (ANC) and chairman of the National Committee on Red Cross Nursing Service. Prior shortages convinced Delano of the importance of having a sufficient supply of nurses. Through her guidance and instruction, the American Red Cross Nursing Service became the primary nursing reserve for the Army, Navy, and Public Health Service. After resigning from the Army Nurse Corps, Delano traveled the country in search of recruits for the American Red Cross. Her efforts proved successful. When the country entered World War I in 1917, the American Red Cross had 8,000 trained nurses ready for duty. The American Red Cross Nursing Program continued to thrive and produced 20,000 registered nurses by 1918.

World War I and its demands on the American Red Cross helped the fledgling organization grow. After the United States declared war on April 6, 1917, demands flooded the still-small American Red Cross. Recognizing that patriotism was high, President Woodrow Wilson asked his fellow Americans to contribute their time and energy to the Red Cross relief effort. Millions responded by offering their voluntary support. Almost overnight, the American Red Cross became a major humanitarian organization.

One of the American Red Cross's most prominent services during World War I was its Camp Services. This service provided soldiers with essential supplies such as clothing, comfort items, and welfare services. Red Cross workers showed movies and served refreshments to soldiers as a means of recreation. In addition, the Red Cross ran canteen services at railroad stations and ship ports, offering food, snacks, and leisure articles to the soldiers. By the end of the war, the American Red Cross had set up 830 canteens in France and the United States.

The American Red Cross also served in many other important capacities during World War I. Its Production Corps produced garments, surgical dressings, and an abundance of other medical supplies. Furthermore, its Nursing Service continued to expand during World War I, providing registered nurses for the Army and Navy.

On the homefront the American Red Cross provided aid to family members of military personnel through financial assistance, communication with soldiers, and information about government-funded programs. In all, the Home Services branch provided aid to 500,000 families during World War I. The American Red Cross Motor Service consisted primarily of women who volunteered their time and cars to provide soldiers with transportation to canteens, military hospitals, and camps. Many of the women took classes in auto mechanics to be prepared in case of a breakdown.

The Red Cross Hospital Service worked to readjust veterans to civilian life through a staff of licensed medical and psychiatric social workers. Female volunteers at Walter Reed Hospital in Washington, D.C., acted as hostesses and provided recreational activities to veterans. As a result of their gray dresses and veils, the female volunteers became known as the Gray Ladies. Demands for their services quickly spread to military and civilian hospitals across the country.

The American Red Cross began preparations for World War II before the United States entered the conflict on December 7, 1941. By then, the organization was already operating a blood donor service in order to provide lifesaving plasma for the armed forces. Dr. Charles Drew oversaw the project that processed the blood donations into liquid plasma. By the end of the war, 13.4 million pints of blood from over 6 million donors had been collected and used to help the men on the battlefield.

Many services offered during World War II were continuations of programs started during World War I. Once again Camp Services provided meals, counseling, financial assistance, comfort items, and communication between soldiers and family. Canteen Services provided snacks in ship ports, railroad stations, and even child care centers and schools. The Gray Ladies continued to provide assistance to soldiers and veterans by writing letters, reading, and running errands for patients. The Motor Corps and the Production Corps also remained popular. The Nursing Service continued to expand. Over half of the 212,000 enrolled nurses were certified to the military and made up a total of 90 percent of all enlisted military nurses during World War II.

During World War II, the American Red Cross again provided a variety of services. Club services were available for troops overseas and on the homefront. The clubs served as hotels and as a place where troops could obtain a hot meal. Many also provided barbershops and laundry facilities. For example, the Rainbow Corner club in London operated around the clock and was capable of serving 60,000 meals in a 24-hour period. Many clubs gained nicknames such as Donut Dugouts and Fleet Clubs. In 1942 the American Red Cross began using large trucks and buses that the organization converted into clubmobiles that served coffee and donuts and distributed newspapers, chewing gum, and other items. Some provided music for troops through the use of phonographs while others used projectors to show movies ("cinemobiles").

Some of the American Red Cross's wartime work was tied directly to the survival of the troops. For example, the organization's First Aid and Water Safety program taught men how to save lives and swim under battle conditions. Trainees underwent drills that instructed them how to navigate through water covered with burning fuel. Soldiers were also trained to swim while weighted down with heavy packs. In addition, the Prisoner of War Relief program was largely credited for keeping many prisoners of war alive. The packages that the organization shipped to prison camps contained nonperishable foods such as raisins, corned beef, sugar, biscuits, dried milk, canned tuna, cigarettes, and hygiene products.

Other programs helped better the lives of soldiers and veterans. For example, the Victory Book Campaigns collected millions of books, magazines, and newspapers from Americans to provide reading material to soldiers. The War Brides program prepared foreign women and their children for transport to the United States to be with their new American soldier husbands. Many Red Cross workers accompanied the brides on ships bound for the United States. In addition, once the women reached their destination, many received assistance for several years after the war.

The American Red Cross again came to the aid of American soldiers during the Korean War. The organization's service at military installations served armed forces personnel in combat zones and military installations at home and abroad. As it had in earlier wars, the Red Cross provided key services such as emergency communication with family, financial assistance, verification for emergency leave, counseling, and the distribution of comfort items. It also provided support to American hospitals in Korea and to Mobile Army Surgical Hospital (MASH) units. Red Cross volunteers also placed calls home to notify families when soldiers were wounded, provided moral support to the wounded, assisted with personal problems, offered social work support, and distributed mailing supplies. The Home Service within the United States provided assistance to families of armed service members. It provided family members with counseling, emergency links to their soldier, assistance in filling out applications for government benefits, financial assistance, and referrals to other community resources. Upon the conclusion of the war, the American Red Cross opened 10 Supplemental Recreational Activities Overseas units. These units were run by college-educated women and provided light refreshments and entertainment to servicemen. This program lasted for 20 years.

During the Vietnam War, American Red Cross workers worked in South Vietnam, where they provided assistance to the armed forces. Conditions for Red Cross workers in Vietnam proved to be particularly dangerous. Five Red Cross workers died in Vietnam, and countless others were injured. The American Red Cross set up field stations to provide deployed soldiers with services that included counseling, aid with communications with family, assistance with personal and family problems, and help in emergency situations. Vietnam veterans were also provided access to such services. Additionally, drug-abuse treatment programs were offered to drug-addicted servicemen. The programs were designed to combat the dramatic increase of marijuana, heroin, and opium use by soldiers during the Vietnam War. Supplemental Recreational Activities programs that were popular at the end of the Korean War continued during the Vietnam era. Young women provided interactive programs and games for military personnel that included fun activities like quizzes, games, and musical performances.

The American Red Cross also remained active on the homefront during the Vietnam War. As soldiers headed to Vietnam, the American Red Cross saw servicemembers off to war, visited families of deployed soldiers, organized clubs for military spouses, and sponsored family nights. It offered families counseling, assistance with communication, and help applying for benefits. The Shop Early program provided Christmas gifts to servicemembers away at war. Local chapters ran Operation Helpmate, a program that organized the collection of books and magazines to send to soldiers in Vietnam. Once veterans had returned home, the organization assisted veterans with applications for compensation, pensions, and other government benefits.

Throughout other U.S. wars, the Red Cross has continued to support the troops and their families. Although not exclusively a war-relief organization, the American Red Cross has generously assisted members of the U.S. armed forces, their family members, and allies in times of great distress. The organization has established a model nursing program, helped troops and family members stay in touch, fed millions, and provided counseling and financial services and countless other means of assistance. Often placing themselves in the path of danger, American Red Cross volunteers have provided troops with not just tangible aid but a sense of hope in times of need.

Siobhan Elise Ausberry

See also: Army Nurse Corps (ANC); Barton, Clara Harlowe (1821–1912); Civil War (1861–1865); Delano, Jane Arminda (1862–1919); Gray Lady Corps; Korean War (1950–1953); Mobile Army Surgical Hospital (MASH); Nursing; Prisoners of War; Red Cross Volunteer Nurse's Aide Corps; Spanish-American War (1898); Vietnam War (1965–1973); World War I (1914–1918); World War II (1941–1945).

References and Further Reading

Burton, David H. *Clara Barton: In the Service of Humanity*. Westport, CT: Praeger, 1995.

Davison, Henry P. *The American Red Cross in the Great War*. Ithaca, NY: Cornell University Library, 2009. First published 1919.

Foster, Rhea Dulles. *The American Red Cross: A History*. New York: Harper and Brothers, 1950.

Kernodle, Portia B. *The Red Cross Nurse in Action 1882–1948*. New York: Harper and Brothers, 1949.

Kotcher, Joann P. *Donut Dolly: An American Red Cross Girl's War in Vietnam*. Denton: University of North Texas Press, 2011.

AMERICAN REVOLUTION (1775–1783)

The American Revolution was a violent conflict between England and the original 13 American colonies that raged on American soil from 1776 to 1783. Colonists, tired from oppression, turned to armed rebellion to gain their independence from England. After many years of battle and much bloodshed, the colonists emerged victorious and formed the United States of America. Colonial women played many vital roles during the American Revolution. The dedication and support of revolutionary women contributed significantly to the outcome of the war.

The years leading up to the war had been difficult ones causing much agitation for both sides. Prior to the American Revolution, the Seven Years' War had recently come to a close. More commonly referred to as the French and Indian War, this war in North America was an effort by Britain to protect the colonists from Indian raids. Because of common interests, many Indians of North America formed alliances with the French. The British eventually conquered their French and Indian enemies but not without accumulating an enormous debt. In addition, the British determined that the occupation of British regulars in the colonies was imperative to suppress future uprisings among French, Spanish, or Indian rivals.

British officials searched for a solution to relieve their nation's massive war debt. They decided that because their efforts had been to protect the colonists, it was only logical to expect monetary assistance from those colonists. As a result, Britain proceeded to pass a new series of tax laws on the colonies. In 1764, the Sugar Act was passed, followed by the Stamp Act in 1765, which required that a duty be placed on all legal documents, newspapers, playing cards,

and dice. The Quartering Act of 1765 required colonists to house British soldiers. Still not satisfied, Britain passed the Townshend Revenue Act of 1767, which taxed essential goods such as tea, paper, paint, glass, and lead.

Colonists were enraged by the new taxes and united to boycott British goods. In 1770, friction among British regulars and Boston citizens resulted in violence and the death of five men. This event became known as the Boston Massacre. In 1773 Britain's Lord North imposed the Tea Act, which was a second tax on tea. Colonists responded by dressing as Indians and dumping the tea aboard a British East India Company ship into the harbor in an act that came to be known as the Boston Tea Party. Britain addressed the issue by passing the Coercive Acts of 1774. Parliament felt the acts would tame the rebellious colonists, but they instead infuriated the colonists. Colonists argued that the British Parliament had no right to enact such laws without consulting the local colonial assemblies. In April 1776, British and colonial tensions resulted in a call to arms and a declaration of revolution.

Women's participation in the American Revolution has often been largely overlooked. Their roles have often been considered less significant than those of male revolutionaries. However, women contributed on a large scale and in a variety of ways to the war effort. They did not hesitate to answer the call of patriotism. When demands on the homefront required the sacrifice of colonial women, they delivered. In a war that required them to portray the same level of bravery as men, revolutionary women did not disappoint. Colonial women were essential to ensuring an American victory over Great Britain.

Colonial women initially participated in the revolution by saying no to British goods. This boycott allowed women to incorporate political significance into everyday domestic behaviors. Because 18th-century women were expected to remain in the domestic sphere of colonial life, they found a boycott the most logical way to support the American cause. By refusing to purchase British goods and instead rely on American-made products, women began to find a political voice as they severely crippled British merchants and manufacturers. Revolutionary women denied their families a variety of British goods but mainly focused on tea and cloth.

In one of the most famous examples of coordinated political action by colonial women, 51 women gathered for a tea party in Edenton, North Carolina, on October 25, 1774. The organizer of the Edenton Tea Party, Penelope Barker, asked her female guests to stop drinking English tea and buying English cloth. After convincing her audience, Barker produced a petition. The document stated that the ladies would no longer indulge in British tea or cloth. It further stated that the members of the newly formed association intended to follow the example of their husbands. The document described the level of opposition that Britain could expect to receive. The ladies boldly sent their signed petition to the British newspapers. The published document shocked British people and Loyalists. The ladies of Edenton represented one of the first publicized political actions among women of the colonial era.

The Homespun Movement illustrated another way that colonial women boycotted British goods to promote the revolutionary cause. Such boycotts prompted a crusade in homespun clothing. By dressing themselves and their families in the clothing they made, women were able to display their sense of patriotism. The Homespun Movement also functioned as a means to provide the Continental Army with essential supplies like clothing and blankets. Items were generally created in spinning and quilting bees, popular events that colonial women attended with their spinning wheels.

In response to a call by Gen. George Washington for relief for the soldiers, Esther De Berdt Reed of Philadelphia published *Sentiments of an American Woman* (1780). The document encouraged women to become politically active through their domestic roles in order to boost the morale of Continental Army troops. *Sentiments* directly led to the establishment of the Ladies Association of Philadelphia, a nationwide fundraising organization run by women. It encouraged all to aid the war effort and received contributions from all classes of colonial citizens. The Ladies Association members went door to door to collect donations, often using their feminine charm to convince reluctant individuals to donate. By the end of the fund-raising campaign, the women had collected over $300,000 to improve the conditions of the soldiers. After communicating by letter with Washington, Reed honored his suggestion by using the funds to provide shirts for the troops. Rather than pay for another party to sew the purchased fabric into shirts, the ladies took on the task themselves by organizing numerous sewing bees. Reed died unexpectedly before seeing the

2,000 shirts delivered to Washington's troops.

Although women's public roles were limited in the period surrounding the American Revolution, some felt comfortable expressing their political beliefs to their husbands. In letters to her husband John, Abigail Adams encouraged this Massachusetts delegate to the First Continental Congress to support a revolution against Britain. She stressed the tyrannical ways that Britain governed the colonists and predicted that reconciliation was no longer possible. She believed that the colonists had no choice but to separate from Britain. In addition, Abigail often wrote of women's rights. She stressed that the property rights of women greatly needed reform. Although Abigail was not an aggressive suffragist, she urged powerful men like her husband to think about women's rights.

Other women also used writing to influence people during the Revolution. Famous American writer and playwright Mercy Otis Warren filled her writings with anti-British and anti-Loyalist messages. As a result, she has often been referred to as the Conscience of the American Revolution. Warren was most likely influenced by her father, a powerful and respected man of Massachusetts who was an outspoken opponent of British rule. In addition, she was close friends with women such as Adams and Martha Washington. A political meeting held in her home in 1772 resulted in the formation of the Committees of Correspondence. Warren's work was published anonymously until 1790. During that time, she produced several successful plays like *The Adulateur*, which foretold the Revolutionary War,

as well as *The Defeat* and *The Group*. In 1790 she published *Poems, Dramatic and Miscellaneous*, which listed her as the author. The book contained various works of a political nature. Warren used her writing abilities to share her political views as literary and theatrical entertainment.

The American Revolution could not have succeeded without the massive efforts of women on the homefront. Their sacrifices formed the backbone of the operation. With their husbands away at war, women had to continue doing their everyday domestic chores as well as the work of their husbands. Women found themselves becoming farmers, blacksmiths, weavers, and carpenters as well as slave managers. Women were responsible for meeting all the needs their families required. During times of scarcity and inflation, this task was difficult. Women also grew food for troops as well as sewed uniforms for the soldiers.

Because the Revolution was fought on American soil, women on the homefront worried about their safety and that of their families. Battles were fought in towns and throughout the countryside, causing a wave of destruction to homes, businesses, and farms. Opposing troops often raided homes in search of food or valuables, leaving the resident women and children with nothing to eat or wear. In addition, women faced the possibility of rape or even death. Despite the obstacles they faced, many women remained committed to the Patriots' cause.

Many women formed close bonds with the Continental Army as camp followers during the Revolutionary War. Women chose to follow the army for a variety of reasons. Some were lonely, others were trying to avoid poverty and starvation, and some were trying to avoid rape or death at the hands of the enemy. Still others attached themselves to the army to remain close to their husbands. These women served as cooks, washerwomen, seamstresses, nurses, scavengers for supplies, and sexual partners. Other camp followers aided the military as soldiers or spies. Women married to officers followed the troops seasonally to organize social gatherings like dances.

Camp followers were often a nuisance to military leaders but were essential to the successful operation of the army. The presence of the female camp followers reduced the number of deserters among the ranks. For example, troops were less likely to roam seeking sexual contact if women were among their group. Furthermore, female camp followers kept up the appearance of soldiers as well as maintained sanitary conditions in the camps. Many camp women became nurses who tended to the sick and wounded troops. Women's roles in sanitation were extremely important because poor sanitation in the camps often led to the spread of lice and communicable diseases like typhus and dysentery.

Camp followers received half of the rations of enlisted personnel. Although this allocation seemed unfair, it was a better alternative to starving. In addition, female camp followers were subject to military discipline if they disobeyed the rules and were required to perform tasks for the soldiers. Soldiers were required to pay women for performing various chores like laundry and had to report the women if they refused to perform these tasks. It was not unusual for tradeswomen and prostitutes to target the Continental Army. The services they provided were in high demand, and the army offered them an easy opportunity for profit.

Some colonial women served as spies during the American Revolution. Dicey Langston, also known as Laodicea Langston, lived on a farm in South Carolina surrounded by Loyalists. To aid the Patriots, she spied on Loyalists and often faced dangerous circumstance to convey intelligence to the Patriots. On one occasion she traveled over five miles in the middle of the night, crossing a swift, overflowing river to warn the Elder Settlement of South Carolina that a band of Loyalists was planning to attack at dawn. After nearly drowning, Langston arrived in time to warn her brother and his men. When the Loyalists arrived, they found the Elder Settlement abandoned. Langston's efforts saved many Patriots' lives.

Another spy, Philadelphia Quaker Lydia Darragh, overheard the British plans to launch a surprise attack on Washington's troops at White Marsh. After hearing these plans, Darragh told her husband she needed to travel to Frankfort to replenish their dwindling flour supply. She obtained a pass and traveled through the snow with her flour bag in hand. After trekking the four to five miles to the mill, Darragh proceeded to the outposts of the American army so that she could warn them. She revealed all that she had heard to Lt. Col. Craig and then returned home without incident. Upon their arrival to White Marsh, the British were greeted by a fully prepared American army. Darragh's efforts prevented what could have been a devastating attack on Patriot forces.

Other women acted as couriers for the American troops. For example, Emily Geiger served as a messenger for the Patriots. Gen. Nathaniel Greene needed to get word to Gen. Thomas Sumter that he needed backup. Greene could not find a man to deliver this message, so Geiger eagerly volunteered. Greene briefed the young lady and presented her with a letter containing the information. She immediately departed on horseback to reach Sumter. British Loyalists, their suspicions aroused because she was coming from the direction of Greene's army, intercepted Geiger. They detained Geiger until they could find a woman to search her body for any communication. While alone in a room, Geiger ate Greene's letter one piece at a time. As a result, upon the search, nothing suspicious was found on her body so Geiger was released. Geiger continued on a more concealed route to relay the memorized message to Sumter. Geiger's mission was a success that resulted in the joining of the two armies.

Some women chose a more aggressive method of aid by disguising themselves as men and engaging in battle. One of the most famous of these female soldiers was Deborah Sampson. Before announcing to friends that she was leaving town to find higher paying work, Sampson sewed together a man's outfit and hid it within a haystack. As she left town, she discreetly slipped into her new male attire. So convincing was Sampson's disguise that she was able to successfully enlist in the American army under the alias Timothy Thayer in early 1782. However, it did not take long for her fellow soldiers to discover her sex. Still determined to fight with the Patriots, Sampson enrolled in the army

yet again. This time she enlisted in Capt. George Webb's Company of the 4th Massachusetts Regiment under the name Robert Shurtleff. Enduring the same hardship as the other soldiers, Sampson fought bravely throughout the war. She was wounded twice, but her sex was not discovered until she fell ill with an ailing fever. While she was delirious, a physician treated her and discovered that Sampson was indeed a woman. Rather than revealing her identity, the physician took her to his home so that she could recover. Shortly after, Sampson was instructed to carry a letter to Washington, who honorably discharged her. Sampson returned to Massachusetts, where she was granted a pension by the Massachusetts legislature in 1804.

Another woman, Mary Ludwig Hays McCauley, was given the nickname Molly Pitcher as a result of her work on the battlefield. As a camp follower of the Continental Army, she stayed with her husband as he trained as an artilleryman. McCauley served as a water girl who carried water to drilling infantry troops during hot weather. In addition, she delivered water under heavy fire. During the Battle of Monmouth in June 1778, her husband collapsed next to the cannon he was manning. Without hesitating, Mary sprang to action as he was carried off the battlefield. She took over his position assisting the other artillerymen, spent the day loading the cannon, and helped the company secure a major victory for the Continental Army. Her bravery did not go unnoticed. In 1822 the Commonwealth of Pennsylvania awarded her a pension of $40 per year.

Margaret Cochran Corbin, the wife of John Corbin of Capt. Proctor's 1st Company of Pennsylvania Artillery, quickly gained the respect and admiration of the soldiers as she learned to load and fire cannons. As a sign of their affection, they began to refer to her as Captain Molly. In November 1776, she assisted on the front lines alongside her husband in the battle of Fort Washington. During the battle, she was seriously wounded in the arm. Captain Molly was later paroled in Philadelphia and eventually was awarded a disability pension from Congress that amounted to one-half a soldier's pay and one suit of clothes or the equivalent in cash. She also received the honor of being assigned to the Corps of Invalids at West Point. Captain Molly remained at West Point until her death and was buried at the United Stated Military Academy.

Another instrumental Patriot woman, Sybil Ludington, was 16 years old when she rode through the night on horseback to alert American forces that the British were approaching. She raced through Putnam County, New York, knocking on doors while yelling warnings to those inside. Her father, Col. Henry Ludington, had sent her to call colonial men to arms to defend the people of Danbury, Connecticut, from British attack. Along the route of her 40-mile journey, Ludington faced rain as well as an attack by a highwayman intending her harm. She courageously defended herself with her father's musket. Although the colonists suffered the loss of an arsenal, Sybil's ride rallied enough troops to successfully drive the British out of Danbury.

Black and Indian women also played limited roles in the American Revolution. Historically, their actions have not received as much attention as those of white colonial women. Free and enslaved black women were tired of the mistreatment they received from whites. Blacks feared the separation that slavery all too often caused among their families. The British were aware of black concerns and proceeded to provide an appealing alternative for blacks. The British promised that all enslaved persons who took up arms with the British would be freed. Although this attracted black men to fight for the British, it also encouraged desertion among portions of the slave population. The number of slaves that fled from their masters succeeded in creating economic hardships for colonists. They experienced a shortage of manpower that made it difficult to function as they had before the war.

Some female slaves became camp followers of the British. As such, they cooked, laundered, acted as nurses, and did other chores. However, the majority of female slaves chose to remain at home rather than to run away to an uncertain camp life. On the homefront, life often became difficult for these women as a result of the desertion of other slaves. Fewer field hands meant food shortages. In addition, many slaveholders chose to send their slaves south to ensure that they would not be lured to the British lines. This move separated many slaves from their loved ones. In addition, the slave women of Loyalists faced uncertain fates when captured by Patriots. Some were resold while others were forced to labor for the Continental Army. They were forced to perform tasks like building roads, cooking, and laundering without pay.

Like black women, Indian women made up a small portion of female participation in the American Revolution. Most Native Americans wished to remain neutral. When they were eventually forced to choose sides, many sided with the British. Indian women were concerned that an American victory would change social roles among their communities and that the great power those women held within their communities would be lost. They also believed that Americans would increase westward expansion if they won. Primarily, the American Revolution disrupted the agricultural lifestyle of Native American women. Farming was a woman's role in many Native American societies. The destruction of their land, crops, and livestock during the war greatly disturbed them and disrupted their lives. In addition, the war interrupted Indian trade with local whites, which prevented Native American women from obtaining many of the American and European goods to which they had become accustomed.

Some Indian women took an active part in the American Revolution. For example, Molly Brant, a Mohawk Indian, believed that whites and Native Americans lived more at peace under British rule. Brant married an Englishman, Sir William Johnson, and together they became a powerful political force in the Mohawk Valley. They kept open communications between the surrounding white and Indian societies. The American Revolution brought an end to Brant's influential position in the community. Her loyalties were with the British, and her actions infuriated the colonists. In one instance, Brant learned of reinforcements on the way to assist colonial troops at Fort Stanwix. She swiftly passed the information along to British troops. From that point forward, local residents refused to sell essential supplies to her. Furthermore, Patriots lashed out at her by slaughtering her livestock, murdering her overseer, and ransacking her home. Fearing for her life, she fled behind British lines for protection. Once wealthy and powerful, Brant was now destitute.

Loyalist women who chose to remain faithful to the British were a minority. Due to their affinity with the British, they often lacked support in their communities during difficult times. Many of these women were seen as Loyalists as a result of their husbands' political leanings, not their own. As a result of the attitudes toward them in Patriot strongholds, Loyalist women often felt the need to leave their community to ensure the safety of their families. They grabbed what they could carry and fled. Canada became a popular destination for Loyalists who left.

However, some Loyalist women turned to resistance. To show their political loyalties, they would often refuse to take loyalty oaths to the colonies. In addition, Loyalist women encouraged others to refuse oaths as well. In addition, at times Loyalist women were jailed for spying or providing aid to British troops. The actions of Loyalist women during the American Revolution proved to be problematic for the colonists.

Women participated in the American Revolution in various ways. Women's significant efforts on the homefront and on the battlefields helped to mold the events of the war as well as its outcome. The colonists could not have defeated the British without the participation of women. Revolutionary women took advantage of their domestic identities to express their political views, which they cautiously brought before the public eye. They consequently opened the door for future generations of American women to have a political voice.

Siobhan Elise Ausberry

See also: African American Women; Bache, Sarah "Sally" Franklin (1743–1808); Bailey, Anne Hennis Trotter "Mad Anne" (1742–1825); Bates, Ann (1748–1801); Brant, Mary "Molly" (1735–1796); Bratton, Martha Robertson [Robinson] (ca. 1749/1750–1816); Burgin, Elizabeth (n.d.–n.d.); Camp Followers; Champion, Deborah (1753–n.d.); Corbin, Margaret Cochran (1751–ca. 1800); Culper Spy Ring; Darragh, Lydia Barrington (ca. 1738–ca. 1790); Daughters of Liberty; Davis, Ann Simpson (1764–1851); Espionage; Fulton, Sarah Bradlee (1740–1835); Gay, Samuel [Ann Bailey] (n.d.–n.d.); Hart, Nancy Morgan (ca. 1735–1830); Indian Wars; Jemison, Mary (ca. 1742–1833); Ladies Association; Lane, Anna Maria (n.d.–1810); Ludington, Sybil (1761–1839); Mammy Kate (n.d.–n.d.); Martin, Grace Waring (n.d.–n.d.) and Martin, Rachel Clay (n.d.–n.d.); "Miss Jenny" (ca. 1760–n.d.); Motte, Rebecca Brewton (1737–1815); Native American Women; North American Colonial Wars (17th–18th centuries); Pitcher, Molly (n.d.–n.d.); Reed, Esther de Berdt (1746–1780); Rinker, Molly "Old Mom" (n.d.–n.d.); Ross, Elizabeth "Betsy" Griscom (1752–1836); Sacagawea (ca. 1787–1812); Samson [Sampson] (Gannett), Deborah [Robert Shurtliff] (1760–1827); Shattuck, Sarah Hartwell (ca. 1737/1738–1798); Strong, Anna "Nancy" Smith (1740–1812); "355" (n.d.–n.d.); Tyonajanegen (n.d.–ca. 1820); Ward, Nancy (ca. 1738–ca. 1824); Warner, Jemima (n.d.–1775); Wright, Prudence Cummings (1740–1823); Zane, Elizabeth "Betty" (ca. 1759–ca. 1847).

References and Further Reading

Berkin, Carol. *Revolutionary Mothers: Women and the Struggle for America's Independence.* New York: Alfred A. Knopf, 2005.

Bohrer, Melissa Lukeman. *Glory, Passion, and Principles: The Story of Eight Remarkable Women at the Core of the American Revolution.* New York: Atria Books, 2003.

Booth, Sally Smith. *Women of '76.* New York: Hastings House, 1973.

Freeman, Lucy, and Alma Halbert Bond. *America's First Woman Warrior: The Courage of Deborah Sampson.* New York: Continuum, 1992.

Gundersen, Joan R. *To Be Useful in the World: Women in Revolutionary America, 1740–1790.* Chapel Hill: University of North Carolina Press, 2006.

Loane, Nancy K. *Following the Drum: Women at the Valley Forge Encampment.* Dulles, VA: Potomac Books, 2009.

Marston, Daniel. *Essential Histories: The American Revolution, 1774–1783.* New York: Routledge, 2002.

Mayer, Holly A. *Belonging to the Army: Camp Followers and Community during the American Revolution.* Columbia: University of South Carolina Press, 1996.

Stuart, Nancy Rubin. *Muse of the Revolution: The Secret Pen of Mercy Otis Warren and the Founding of a Nation.* Boston: Beacon Press, 2006.

Ulrich, Laurel Thatcher. *The Age of Homespun.* New York: Alfred A. Knopf, 2001.

Young, Alfred F. *Masquerade: The Life and Times of Deborah Sampson, Continental Soldier.* New York: Vintage Books, 2004.

AMERICAN WOMEN'S VOLUNTARY SERVICES (AWVS)

Created in 1940 by Alice Throckmorton McLean, the American Women's Voluntary Services (AWVS) quickly grew in size and service, becoming one of the nation's largest female organizations devoted to home-front security and productivity. Despite its success during World War II, the pre–Pearl Harbor AWVS drew harsh criticism from various factions of the American public owing to the group's founders, mission, and egalitarian policy regarding membership. Although changed national

In 1942, American Women's Voluntary Services (AWVS) members pose in various uniforms. (Library of Congress)

priorities between 1941 and 1945 forced the AWVS to reevaluate its role in the wartime United States, the organization, to the credit of its members' dedication, managed to swiftly diversify and expand its contribution to the war effort.

Socialite McLean fashioned the AWVS after the British Women's Voluntary Services (BWVS) that proved useful during the London blitz. The growing war in Europe, reasoned McLean, would undoubtedly reach U.S. shores eventually, bringing with it the potential of German bombing raids comparable to those underway in Great Britain. Because of this fear, McLean created the AVWS in order to begin training volunteers who could both prepare for and act during enemy aerial

attacks against U.S. cities. Many of the organization's first members were close friends of its founder and shared a common social status as wealthy elites with ties to England and Europe in general.

The initial public reaction to the AWVS included a multitude of critiques. Because the majority of early members enjoyed an elevated social and financial rank, many Americans labeled the organization's membership as a frivolous band of socialites. This belief proved hard to alter, particularly after the media began jeering the women for wearing "decadent" uniforms that promoted style over practicality. In addition, the group's mission of preparing cities for possible air raids reinforced its negative public

image. American isolationists denounced the AWVS's call for preparation,
leveling accusations that members were
war hawks trying to drag the country into
a European war.

The strict social boundaries of the
prewar United States also hampered the
general population's acceptance of the
AWVS. Although it originated among
society's elite members, the organization's leadership believed that it must
extend membership and rank within the
group to all American women regardless
of social class or ethnicity. This open-
door policy, particularly as it pertained
to the recruitment of nonwhites, did not
sit well among the most fervent believers
in a segregated American society. As a
result, members in the AWVS endured
harassment from racially charged
groups, most notably the Ku Klux Klan
(KKK). Nonetheless, AWVS recruitment
efforts continued to break racial and economic barriers, establishing integrated
branch offices in cities such as Harlem,
Atlanta, New Orleans, Tucson, Chicago,
and Pittsburgh.

Much of the AWVS's early efforts to
fulfill its self-designated role in prewar
planning for enemy attacks limited the
group's activity to the eastern United
States. Members found themselves
employed in one of two types of sectors:
large cities or coastal communities.
Within cities such as New York, volunteers trained and readied themselves for
jobs associated with crisis management.
These positions ran the gamut from
directing crowds of panic-stricken citizens to bomb shelters, staffing emergency services' switchboards, and
driving ambulances in the midst of aerial
bombardment. Along the Atlantic seaboard, women in the AWVS assumed

the first roles as plane-spotters and
coast-watchers, whose job, in the event
of an emergency, required them to
quickly and accurately identify and
report the type, number, and heading of
enemy aircraft.

When such air raids failed to material-
ize throughout the mainland United
States during the war, and as the media
quipped that the organization did nothing
but prepare for an imagined enemy, the
AWVS began to adapt itself to the reality
of increased labor demands. Although
the AWVS found a limited number of
new positions available to those women
already in the organization, its well-
organized and thorough training program
continued to grow even after the group
began funneling new volunteers to sister
organizations, such as the Red Cross.
Records show that during the war over
325,000 women received training from
or worked through the AWVS. Most of
the volunteers who completed the
50 hours of training became drivers of
ambulances and motor pools for the
government and the military, staffed
mobile kitchens and hospitals, worked
for hospitality groups such as the
United Service Organizations (USO),
assumed clerical positions in the expan-
sive wartime bureaucracy, or kept communication networks operating around
the clock.

In addition to these jobs, members of
the AWVS worked throughout the war
to sustain U.S. agricultural production.
Most farmers initially resisted the use of
female labor in the fields, particularly
when most of that labor force came from
cities. As 1942 progressed, however, a
lack of labor began to threaten productivity. Traditional workers disappeared
as authorities sent West Coast Japanese

Americans to internment camps, migrants from the Great Depression and Dust Bowl began working in defense plants, the number of Southern sharecroppers dried up, and much of the Midwestern agricultural labor force enlisted in the military. With reservations reluctantly cast aside, farm owners began employing droves of available workers provided by the AWVS. Volunteers in California paid $1 a day for board, received the standard migrant worker salary, put up with cold camp showers, and endured radical temperature fluctuations between the day and night. Completely self-sustaining, AWVS farming camps provided their own kitchens, staffs, and pantry stores.

The AWVS began training willing women for the U.S. war effort before many Americans believed such preparations were necessary. During an age of racial segregation and social elitism, the organization gave thousands of women opportunities never afforded them in a peacetime nation. Despite an initial lack of public support, the women of the AWVS continued their training mission, ultimately helping to provide the wartime United States with a readily available workforce.

Matthew R. McGrew

See also: African American Women; American Red Cross; United Service Organizations (USO); World War II (1941–1945).

References and Further Reading

Heinemann, Sue. *Timelines of American Women's History*. New York: Penguin Group, 1996.

Litoff, Judy Barrett, and David Clayton Smith, eds. *American Women in a World at War: Contemporary Accounts from World War II*. Lanham, MD: Rowman and Littlefield, 1997.

Weatherford, Doris. *American Women and World War II*. New York: Facts on File, 1990.

Yellin, Emily. *Our Mothers' War: American Women at Home and the Front during World War II*. New York: Free Press, 2004.

ANDERSON, ELDA EMMA "ANDY" (1899–1961)

Elda E. Anderson was a remarkable physicist whose long career spanned the fields of spectroscopy, nuclear physics, and, most critically, health physics.

Born October 5, 1899, in Green Lake, Wisconsin, to Edwin A. and Lena (Heller) Anderson, Anderson earned a bachelor of science degree from Ripon (Wisconsin) College in 1922 and a master's degree in physics from the University of Wisconsin in 1924. Over the course of her long career as a scientist and educator she held several prominent professional positions. At Milwaukee-Downer College, she was promoted to chair of the Physics Department. She earned her PhD at the University of Wisconsin in 1941.

After the bombing of Pearl Harbor and the United States' entry into World War II, Anderson moved to Princeton University as a member of the science staff of the Office of Scientific Research and Development. She was among a number of prominent scientists at Princeton at the time, including Albert Einstein. In 1943, she became a member of the Manhattan Project and moved to Los Alamos Scientific Laboratory to work. Anderson was involved in the research for and advances in nuclear physics at Los Alamos that led to the atomic bomb. She was also present at the Trinity Event, the explosion of the first atomic bomb in the U.S. desert in 1945.

After the Japanese surrender in September 1945 ended the war, Anderson returned to Wisconsin with a continued passion for teaching and a commitment to protect people and the environment from the adverse effects of radiation. Four years later her research moved her to Tennessee and the Oak Ridge National Laboratory, where she became the first chief of education and training in the Health Physics Division at Oak Ridge National Laboratory. She retained that post until her death.

While active in Tennessee, she created a master's degree in health physics at Vanderbilt University. She further worked to ensure the safe use of radiation. From 1956 to 1958, working on behalf of the World Health Organization, she conducted courses on radiation protection and safety in Sweden, Belgium, and India.

A professional leader as well as respected scientist and educator, Anderson helped form the American Board of Health Physics and then served as its first chair. In that capacity she helped establish critical standards for professional certification in that field.

She was also a leader in the American Association for the Advancement of Science, the Health Physics Society (and was elected president of the organization in 1959), and the American Association of Physics Teachers.

Diagnosed with leukemia in 1956, Anderson died in Oak Ridge on April 17, 1961. The Health Physics Society still gives an annual award in her honor to outstanding professionals in the field of health physics.

Kathryn A. Broyles

See also: World War II (1941–1945).

References and Further Reading

Le-May Sheffield, Suzanne. *Women and Science: Social Impact and Interaction.* Santa Barbara, CA: ABC-CLIO, 2004.

Rossiter, Margaret W. *Women Scientists in America: Struggles and Strategies to 1940.* Baltimore, MD: Johns Hopkins University Press, 1984.

ANDREWS, ORIANNA MOON (1834–1883)

Dr. Orianna Moon Andrews, a Virginia native and 1857 graduate of the Female Medical College in Philadelphia, treated the wounded and supervised nurses in army hospitals in Virginia from 1861 to 1862. Andrews was the only Virginia woman to hold an MD and was likely the only Southern female physician who treated soldiers during the Civil War.

A native of Albemarle County, Virginia, Orianna Moon was born into a prominent planter family in 1834. She received her earliest education from tutors and decided to study medicine. To prepare for entry into the Female Medical College in Philadelphia, which opened in 1850, she matriculated at the

Troy Female Academy in Troy, New York, one of the few women's institutions that provided the necessary courses in mathematics and science. After spending a year at Troy, she returned to Virginia. At age 17, she was described as hostile to religion, an opponent of slavery, and a supporter of women's rights. The following year she entered the Medical College with its fourth group of students, becoming only the third Southern woman and the only Virginian to do so. She submitted her thesis in 1856 and graduated the following February. Her graduation made her part of an extremely small cohort of female physicians; only 38 women (including Moon) had received medical degrees by 1857.

After her graduation, Moon spent two years traveling abroad in the Middle East and Europe before returning home. In the spring of 1861 she saw a flyer recruiting doctors for the war effort. She began writing letters to Virginia's military commanders offering her services. In late spring, Gen. J. H. Cocke met with her at her home and then spoke about her to Brig. Gen. P. G. T. Beauregard, commander of the Northeast Virginia Army. Soon afterward Moon became superintendent of a ward of nurses at a makeshift hospital on the grounds of the University of Virginia in Charlottesville.

Moon hoped to be closer to the battlefield and in July 1861 informed Gen. Cocke that she was willing to forgo remuneration to follow the army and treat the wounded. Her sister—famous Southern Baptist missionary Charlotte "Lottie" Moon—also wrote to the general asking him to move Moon closer to the "action of the war." Moon was never sent to the front, but she continued working in Charlottesville. She left Charlottesville after marrying a hospital colleague, Dr. John Summerfield Andrews, in November 1861 and moving with him to Richmond. There they both worked in an army hospital. Andrews returned to Albemarle County in 1862 to give birth to her first son.

After the war, Andrews and her family moved to rural Tennessee, where she ran a school for the children of freed slaves. A nighttime visit from the local Ku Klux Klan soon prompted the family to relocate. In 1881, they moved back to Albemarle County, where she and her husband set up a joint medical office.

Orianna Moon Andrews died of cancer in 1883.

Regina D. Sullivan

See also: Civil War (1861–1865); Moon, Charlotte "Lottie" (1829–1895); Moon, Virginia "Ginne" (1844–1925); Nursing.

References and Further Reading

Sullivan, Regina Diane. "Woman with a Mission: Remembering Lottie Moon and the Woman's Missionary Union." PhD diss. University of North Carolina, Chapel Hill, 2002.

Warren, Edward. *A Doctor's Experiences in Three Continents.* Baltimore, MD: Cushings and Bailey, 1885.

ARMY-NAVY NURSES ACT OF 1947 (PUBLIC LAW 36-80C)

Passed on April 16, 1947, the Army-Navy Nurses Act established a permanent nurse corps in the Army and Navy and also established a Women's Medical Specialists Corps in the Army. The Act stipulated permanent commissioned rank and equal pay.

In November 1945, Surgeon General Norman T. Kirk sent Gen. Dwight D. Eisenhower a plan to gain Congressional approval of regular and reserve status for female nurses and specialists, establishing a new branch, the Women's Medical Service Corps. Eisenhower approved the plan three months later, in early February 1946. Immediately thereafter, Kirk and Col. Florence Blanchfield, then chief of the Army Nurse Corps (ANC), prepared a draft bill that won Army approval in June of that same year. The bill was introduced to the 79th Congress. However, it arrived too late for debate and vote before the July congressional adjournment.

In April 1947, the 80th Congress combined the bill with another bill that gave regular status to the women of the Navy Nurse Corps. On April 16, the act to establish a permanent nurse corps of the Army and Navy and to establish a Women's Medical Specialists Corps in the Army, known as the Army-Navy Nurses Act of 1947, became Public Law 36-80C. The Act stipulated permanent commissioned rank and equal pay.

On July 9, 1947, at the Pentagon in Arlington, Virginia, Eisenhower appointed Blanchfield to the rank of lieutenant colonel in the United States Army, making her the first woman in the U.S. history to hold permanent military rank.

Previously, Blanchard had held the ranks of first lieutenant, captain, and lieutenant colonel in the ANC; however, those ranks were only relative and did not afford her the same pay, rights, and privileges her male counterparts enjoyed. Blanchfield, appalled by these inequities, worked tirelessly to achieve full military rank for nurses.

Unfortunately, the passage of the Army-Navy Nurses Act did not give women complete equality with their male counterparts. Unlike men, an army nurse could not be married, nor could she have children who were under the age of 14 years. It would take additional time to erase the remnants of inequality for women who wanted to serve as nurses in the military.

Women's entry into the military was made additionally difficult because it required rigorous regulations, physical examinations, and a 150-item examination that assessed general nursing knowledge. The applicant seeking admission was also required to submit a biographical test and a self-analysis instrument that revealed personality traits and attitudes, and her personal references had to withstand intense scrutiny. She would appear before a board of five medical officers and present at least three previous documents that optimistically endorsed her skills as a nurse. The final decision was left to army nurse Maj. Frances Gunn, who served on the surgeon general's staff. Gunn rated each applicant's dossier and forwarded her recommendations to a medical board for final approval.

The efforts of Rep. Frances Bolton of Ohio led to the amendment of the Army-Navy Nurses Act of 1947 to include male military nurses. Nurse anesthetist Lt. Edward Lyon was the first man to receive a commission in the Army Nurse Corps in October of 1955.

Thomas E. Baker

See also: Army Nurse Corps (ANC); Bolton, Frances Payne Bingham (1885–1977); Navy Nurse Corps; Women's Medical Specialist Corps (WMSCP).

References and Further Reading

Amendments to Army-Navy Nurses Act of 1947: Hearings before the United States Senate Committee on Armed Services, 81st Congress, second session, February 6, 1950. Microfiche. Westport, CT: Greenwood Press, 1973.

Army-Navy Nurses Act of 1947: Bulletin 6. Washington, D.C.: War Department, May 5, 1947.

ARMY NURSE CORPS (ANC)

During World War II, approximately 59,000 women served in the United States Army Nurse Corps (ANC). Formed in 1918 as part of the Army Reorganization Act, the ANC helped mobilize women for the U.S. war effort. Approximately 32,500 members of the ANC served overseas during World War II. The ANC deployed nurses to North Africa, Italy, France, the Pacific, China, Burma, India, the USSR, Iran, Alaska, Iceland, Panama, and the South Atlantic. Although deployed close to the front lines from the beginning of their service, members of the ANC did not receive military training until July 1943.

On December 7, 1941, when the Japanese attacked the U.S. Pacific Fleet at Pearl Harbor, Hawaii, only 1,000 nurses served with the ANC. The surprise attack highlighted the lack of readiness for emergencies. The hospital at Hickam Field, Hawaii, was neither staffed nor supplied to handle such an emergency. Neither were the other area medical centers, Schofield and Tripler Army Hospitals. However, 1st Lt. Annie G. Fox worked tirelessly to treat the wounded soldiers and sailors at Hickam Field. For her dedication and actions, she became the first woman to be awarded the Purple Heart.

America's entry into the war spurred a steady swelling of the ranks in the ANC. Within six months of the attack on Pearl Harbor, the ranks of the ANC had grown to approximately 12,000. However, the initial rush to enlist was not sufficient. The demands of the war effort would not be easily solved, especially in terms of medical staffing. The demand for military and civilian nurses was so great that the U.S. government passed the Nurse Training Act, also known as the Bolton Act, in June 1943. This act created the Cadet Nurse Corps and subsidized nursing education for students who promised to serve out the duration of the war employed by the government either in a military or civilian setting. A civilian posting could include the Veterans' Administration, Bureau of Indian Affairs, or the Public Health Service. Two of the nursing training program specialties, nurse anesthetist and psychiatric nursing, were in high demand. Approximately 170,000 nurses joined the Cadet Nurse Corps by the war's close.

The dramatic increase in the need for military and civilian nurses opened up professional opportunities for women, including African American women. However, racial biases led the Army to restrict the participation of African American women in the ANC. Initially, approximately 2,000 African American women trained in the Cadet Nurse Corps. Throughout the course of the war, the number of African American nurses remained steady. By the end of the war, approximately 500 African American nurses had served in England, North Africa, and Southwest Asia. However, these nurses still experienced the sting of discrimination. African American nurses only served in segregated hospitals for African American soldiers, and they lived in segregated quarters.

ANC nurses first saw combat duty in Asia and North Africa. The military deployed the first units of nurses to the Philippines and Corregidor prior to their occupation by the Japanese Imperial Army early in the war. On the other side of the world, nurses accompanied the first wave of soldiers who landed in and captured Algeria in North Africa. As the theaters of operations expanded to include Europe and more of Asia, the nurses followed in lockstep with the troops.

Army nurses made giant gains for American women in a professional military context. Beginning with the North African theater of operations, nurses were integrated into the Army Medical Corps' newly created chain of evacuation. From evacuation hospitals to permanent medical-surgical centers situated at the rear, army nurses played a pivotal role in reducing the number of fatalities and decreasing the recovery time for wounded soldiers evacuated from the front lines.

Army nurses were not only on the cutting edge of new techniques and treatments for battlefield wounds, but they also became pioneers in technology and medicine. As part of the military's chain of evacuation, nurses became flight nurses who treated soldiers during air transportation. Women's duties focused on patient stabilization and comfort during the sometimes lengthy transport to military hospitals for further treatment. The high altitude and low temperatures increased the patients' discomfort. Nurses helped them deal with the pain by serving hot drinks. More importantly, these flight or evacuation nurses maintained vigilant watch for changes in the patients' conditions and for the warning signs of shock, a constant threat during transport. By the end of the war, 500 evacuation nurses accompanied over 1 million patients to hospitals. They only lost 46 patients en route. In addition, 17 flight nurses lost their lives while evacuating patients.

Despite serving only with relative rank until 1944, army nurses performed admirably. They faced dangerous conditions: 201 army nurses died and 83 were held as prisoners of war during World War II. Over 1,600 army nurses received medals and citations for their performance during the war. In June 1944, army nurses gained officers' commissions, equal pay, and the benefits granted to other military officers.

With the war over, the ANC reduced its numbers to prewar levels. ANC veterans returned home to a changed nation. Their valuable skills and priceless experience opened more opportunities in civilian nursing. Although gender discrimination was still prevalent in the medical field, few practitioners and administrators could argue with the solid self-confidence of these veteran nurses.

Ryan C. Davis

See also: African American Women; Army Reorganization Act (1920); Asian American

Women; Bolton, Frances Payne Bingham (1885–1977); Cadet Nurse Corps; Fox, Annie G. (1893–1987); Nursing; Prisoners of War; Women's Nursing Corps, Army; World War II (1941–1945).

References and Further Reading

Fessler, Diane Burke. *No Time for Fear: Voices of American Military Nurses in World War II*. East Lansing: Michigan State University Press, 1996.

Norman, Elizabeth M. *We Band of Angels: The Untold Story of American Nurses Trapped on Bataan by the Japanese*. New York: Random House, 1999.

Sarnecky, Mary T. *A History of the U. S. Army Nurse Corps*. Philadelphia: University of Pennsylvania Press, 1999.

Tomblin, Barbara Brooks. *G.I. Nightingales: The Army Nurse Corps in World War II*. Lexington: University of Kentucky Press, 1996.

ARMY REORGANIZATION ACT (1920)

On June 4, 1920, President Woodrow Wilson signed the Army Reorganization Act that provided for a regular army of 280,000 men and approximately 17,700 officers. Although it placed upon the War Department the responsibility of organizing the military establishment so as to be prepared for war, it did not provide for universal military training or for the application of the draft system in future emergencies, two items that many considered essential for the security of a country with so small an armed force. Nevertheless, it afforded a definite basis for proceeding with the reorganization of the Army, particularly with respect to the Army Nurse Corps.

During World War I, the suffragist attorney Helen Hoy Greeley lobbied Washington to grant military rank for nurses who were then serving both in the United States and overseas. As a champion of working women within the mainstream women's movement, Greeley was sensitive to the devaluation of women's work and the subjugation of women workers. She saw these problems particularly in the military, where women faced structural barriers to their advancement and their labor was taken for granted.

The Army Reorganization Act of 1920 provided the means to ostensibly address these inequities. Congress passed the Act at least in part in recognition of the services of more than 20,000 army nurses during World War I. The legislation granted army nurses the status of an officer with relative rank from second lieutenant through major. It also charged the secretary of war to make the necessary regulations prescribing the rights and privileges conferred by the relative rank. The Act additionally provided that, with respect to medical and sanitary matters and all other work within the line of their professional duties, nurses would hold authority in and about military hospitals, although after male officers of the Medical Department.

Although the Act suggested progress in addressing inequities in the military medical establishment, in practice it did not solve the problems. Although the Act permitted army nurses to wear the insignia of the relative rank, the secretary of war in fact did not prescribe full rights and privileges, such as base pay for nurses equal to that of an officer of comparable grade. Further, although the new system symbolically established a hierarchy among nurses and gave women formal authority over other women, it did not grant women formal authority over men.

After the Act was signed into law, the War Department turned its attention to other women's concerns, but efforts were focused almost exclusively on creating a positive image of the Army in the minds of female voters, partly in response to the reemergence of feminist pacifism in the wake of the war. The secretary of war appointed Anita Phipps director of women's relations for the army general staff and charged her with presenting the army as "a progressive, socially minded human institution." The secretary of war also wanted to ensure that women voters should not "fanatically demand the dissolution of a ruthless military machine." War Department officials intended to appeal to women as patriotic housewives, not as potential armed services personnel.

Phipps, however, prepared a comprehensive proposal for a Women's Army Corps, which projected a war emergency need for 170,000 women workers in a subsequent war. Phipps's plan was formally rejected by the general staff in August 1926, and her position was eliminated soon thereafter.

Brett F. Woods

See also: Army Nurse Corps (ANC); Phipps, Anita Evans (1886–1953); Women's Army Corps (WAC); World War I (1914–1918).

References and Further Reading

Feller, Carolyn M., and Debora R. Cox, eds. *Highlights in the History of the Army Nurse Corps*. Washington, D.C.: U.S. Army Center of Military History, 2001.

Treadwell, Mattie E. *The Women's Army Corps: United States Army in World War II*. Washington, D.C.: Office of the Chief of Military History, Department of the Army, 1954.

Zeiger, Susan. *In Uncle Sam's Service: Women Workers with the American Expeditionary Force, 1917–1919*. Ithaca, NY: Cornell University Press, 1999.

ARMY SIGNAL CORPS

The U.S. Army Signal Corps is a trained military signal service that develops and operates communications and information systems for the United States' military forces. During World War I, the Army Signal Corps played a vital role in the advancement of telephone, telegraph, radar, and radio technology. The international conflict also expanded the Army Signal Corps' operations as the military service recruited nearly 300 women to serve as bilingual telephone operators in Great Britain and France. Known as the "Hello Girls," the female switchboard operators improved communications and information operations along the Western Front.

At the onset of World War I, Allied forces and the Central Powers engaged in trench warfare, which hindered communications between the troops along the front lines and commanding officers at the rear of the battlefield. After the United States entered the conflict, Gen. John J. Pershing requested that bilingual female switchboard operators from the American Telephone and Telegraph Company (AT&T) volunteer for military service. Pershing maintained that the women could benefit the war effort by operating telephone exchanges while male soldiers remained in the trenches connecting and repairing necessary telephone lines. Following Pershing's recommendation, the Army Signal Corps published advertisements in major newspapers throughout the nation. The military service also recruited women from French-speaking communities in Louisiana and Canada. The Army Signal Corps stated that the recruitment process of female volunteers would be based upon specific criteria, which included a minimum age requirement of 25 years old and the ability to speak fluent English as well as French. Despite the Signal Corps' criteria, the U.S. military waived the age requirement for several of the applicants because few of the women volunteers spoke fluent French.

With over 7,000 applicants, the Army Signal Corps selected 450 women, who became the core of the Army Signal Corps Female Telephone Operators Unit. During the winter of 1918, the female recruits attended radio and switchboard operation classes at local telephone companies while they received basic military training at Fort Franklin in Maryland. By March 1918, the first detachment of female switchboard operators departed from New York City and arrived in Europe, where they supported communications between the Allied soldiers in the trenches and the commanding officers at the American Expeditionary Force's headquarters in Chaumont, France. Under the supervision of Chief Operator Grace Banker, other members of the Army Signal Corps Female Operators Unit were stationed at telephone exchanges throughout Western Europe including Paris, London, Southampton, and Winchester.

Even though the women switchboard operators observed army regulations and wore military uniforms, the Army Signal Corps considered them as civilian employees during World War I. Therefore, the women did not receive veteran status, medals, or honorable discharges when they concluded their military service. In 1978, the U.S. government recognized the contributions of the Army Signal Corps Female Telephone Operators Unit when President Jimmy Carter signed legislation that provided the former switchboard operators with veteran status.

Through the Army Signal Corps, nearly 450 female recruits served overseas during World War I. These women not only answered the United States' call to duty, but they also viewed their military service as an opportunity to accelerate social changes in the United States during the early 20th century.

Kevin M. Brady

See also: "Hello Girls"; World War I (1914–1918).

References and Further Reading

Marshall, Max L. *The Story of the U.S. Army Signal Corps*. New York: F. Watts, 1965.

Raines, Rebecca Robbins. *Getting the Message Through: A Branch History of the U.S. Army Signal Corps*. Washington, D.C.: Center of Military History, 1996.

Zeiger, Susan. *In Uncle Sam's Service: Women Workers with the American Expeditionary Force, 1917–1919*. Ithaca, NY: Cornell University Press, 1999.

ASIAN AMERICAN WOMEN

Asian American women have been an integral force of the United States military. Although Asian American men first served in the War of 1812, Asian American women entered military service during World War II, often in segregated units. The Women's Army Corps (WAC) recruited 50 Japanese American and Chinese American women and sent them to Fort Snelling, Minnesota, for training as military translators at the Military Intelligence Service Language School. Twenty-one were eventually assigned to the Pacific Military Intelligence Research Section at Camp Ritchie, Maryland, where they worked with captured Japanese documents, extracting information pertaining to military plans as well as political and economic information that impacted Japan's ability to conduct the war.

Other WAC translators assisted the U.S. Army in amalgamating with Chinese allies. Cpl. Helen M. Lee, who joined WAC in August 1943, was assigned as a Chinese translator of army training films at Lowry Army Air Field in California. A number of Asian American women also entered the Army Nurse Corps (ANC) during World War II. Helen Pon Onyett is perhaps one of the most notable nurses. After aiding wounded soldiers at the landing craft in North Africa, she was awarded the Legion of Merit. She later retired from the Army as a full colonel.

Not all Asian American women worked as translators and nurses. In 1943, before the Air Force became a separate branch, the WAC recruited a unit of Chinese American women to serve as "Air WACs." The Army lowered the height and weight requirements for the women of this particular unit, referred to as the Madame Chiang Kai-Shek Air WAC unit. Air WACs served in a large

variety of jobs, including those as parachute riggers, weather forecasters, and aerial photograph analysts. In some instances, female pilots trained male soldiers. Maggie Gee, for example, led qualifying flights for instrument ratings renewals and copiloted B-17 Flying Fortress bombers through mock dogfights staged to train bomber gunners.

The Women Air Force Service Pilots (WASPs) worked directly with the Army Air Forces on the homefront during World War II and performed dangerous assignments during the years when male pilots were needed in battle. They tested planes for perfunctory problems, towed targets for aerial gunnery students to practice shooting, and ferried planes from factories to air bases. During World War II, 38 WASPs died in the line of duty.

Although the Navy refused to accept Japanese American women throughout World War II, other Asian American women, including Lt. Susan Ahn Cuddy, a Korean American and the first female gunnery officer in the U.S. Navy, were allowed to serve. Numerous others volunteered for the Women Accepted for Volunteer Emergency Service (WAVES) program.

Overseas cooperation was also needed in the Japanese-occupied Philippines. Filipino American women served as members of the underground resistance movement to help U.S. forces in the Philippines. The women smuggled food and medicine to American prisoners of war (POWs) and carried information of Japanese deployments to Filipino and U.S. forces. One such woman was Florence Ebersole Smith Finch. After being captured and tortured by the Japanese for her efforts, she was later liberated by the U.S. military. She enlisted in the U.S. Coast Guard Women's Reserve (SPAR). Seaman 1st Class Finch was the first SPAR to receive the Asian-Pacific Campaign ribbon in recognition of her service in the Philippines. At the end of the war, she was awarded the civilian U.S. Medal of Freedom.

Josefina V. Geurrero, also a Filipino American, received the Medal of Freedom following the war. Geurrero drew a map of Japanese fortifications at the Manila waterfront that included information on secret tunnels, air raid shelters, and a number of other new installations in which the Allies were interested. Just before the U.S. invasion of Manila in 1945, Geurrero carried the map through Japanese-held territory showing the location of land mines along the planned U.S. invasion route. She reached the 37th Division with the map, enabling the Americans to avoid the land mines that had been positioned to destroy them.

After the war, many of the Asian American translators, including second-generation Japanese Americans who had trained at the Military Intelligence Service Language School, accepted assignments to the Allied Translator and Interpreter Section of Gen. Douglas MacArthur's headquarters for the Army of Occupation in Tokyo, Japan. There they worked as clerks, secretaries, and translators.

In subsequent decades, Asian American women have continued to serve in all branches of the military as officers, surgeons, advisors, and trainers, and they have served in each major U.S. war since World War II. Their valuable work as translators during the Korean War and Vietnam War was immeasurable.

The late 20th century also brought significant accomplishments. Capt. Alice K. Kurashige was the first Japanese American woman to be commissioned in the U.S. Marine Corps. Capt. Melissa Kuo spent a six-month deployment aboard the USS *Peleliu* as a member of the first Western Pacific (WESTPAC) Marine expeditionary unit to include women. During the Iraq War, Maj. Tammy Duckworth lost the lower part of both of her legs and partial use of one arm when a rocket-propelled grenade fired by insurgents hit the helicopter she was copiloting. Her military achievement led her to her current position as the assistant secretary of public and intergovernmental affairs for the U.S. Department of Veterans Affairs. Dr. Eleanor Concepcion Mariano, a physician, is the first Filipino American to reach the rank of rear admiral in the U.S. Navy, the first graduate of the Uniformed Services University of Medicine to reach flag officer status, and the first woman to be the director of the White House Medical Unit. Asian American women also reached unprecedented heights when, in 2001, Brig. Gen. Coral Wong Pietsch made history as the first Asian American woman general in the U.S. Army and the first woman general officer in the 230-year history of the U.S. Judge Advocates General Corps. With nearly 70 years of honorable service in a multitude of positions, Asian American women have made significant contributions to the U.S. military.

Ashanti White

See also: Afghanistan; Army Nurse Corps (ANC); Espionage; Finch, Florence Ebersole Smith (1915–); Gulf War (1991); Iraq War (2003–2011); Korean War (1950–1953); Nursing; Prisoners of War; United States Coast Guard Women's Reserve (SPAR); Vietnam

War (1965–1973); Women Accepted for Volunteer Emergency Service (WAVES); Women Air Force Service Pilots (WASP); Women's Army Corps (WAC); Women's Nursing Corps, Army; World War II (1941–1945).

References and Further Reading

Farolan, Ramon. "From Stewards to Admirals: Filipinos in the U.S. Navy." *Asian Journal*, July 21, 2003.

Oxtra, Cristina. "Asian-Americans Have Long, Proud History in U.S. Military." *US Air Force Press Releases*, May 28, 2002.

Williams, Rudi. "Asian Pacific American Women Served in World War II, Too." *American Forces Press Service*, May 27, 1999.

Williams, Rudi. "DoD's Personnel Chief Gives Asian-Pacific American History Lesson." *American Forces Press Service*, June 3, 2005.

Wong, Kevin Scott. *Americans First: Chinese Americans and the Second World War*. Cambridge, MA: Harvard University Press, 2005.

AYRES, CLARA EDITH WORK (1880–1917)

Enlisted in the military in May 1917 as an American Red Cross nurse, Clara Edith Work Ayres is a major figure in the history of U.S. military nursing. Her commitment to the medical front in World War I led her to embark on the USS *Mongolia*, where she was killed during target practice. She was one of the first two women of the U.S. military killed on duty.

Clara Edith Work was born on September 16, 1880, near Attica, Venice Township, Seneca County, Ohio. She was the daughter of James Clarkson Work, Venice Township city marshal and constable, and Mary Jane Work, born Smith. She was the eldest of the three Work children, with two brothers, Homer Carlton and Ross Burner. Clara Edith spent her childhood and early life in Attica, where she attended the Attica High School, from which she graduated on September 20, 1903.

On September 30, 1903, at age 23, she married Wayland D. Ayres, the owner of a grocery store in Attica. Soon after, in October 1906, her husband died from tetanus after a work accident, at age 26. After trying to run the store on her own, she worked as saleslady in a dry-goods store in Attica.

In 1910, she decided to leave Attica for Chicago, Illinois, to attend the nurses' training school. After graduation in 1913 and until 1917, she was an instructor at the Cook County Hospital in Illinois. Her military nursing career began early that same year as she responded to the American Red Cross call for nurses. After volunteering, Ayres was attached to Base Hospital number 12, due to head eastward toward France. Base Hospital number 12 enlisted personnel gathered at the Northwestern University of Chicago on May 16. From there, they were taken to New York, and they left New York Harbor a couple of days later onboard the *Mongolia*.

The following day around 2:00 p.m., when the ship was about 100 miles at sea, a practice drill was heard on the *Mongolia*. The gun crew followed the target practice procedure and fired both deck guns. A group of nurses and doctors were happily sitting watching the scene from the upper deck behind one of the two guns. As the practice was going on, three nurses were suddenly hit: Ayres, Helen Burnett Wood, and Emma Matzen. Ayres and Wood were instantly killed, but Matzen, who had been one of Ayres's classmates at the Chicago training school for nurses, survived with two flesh wounds. The nurses' injuries resulted from the explosion of one of the guns, which scattered shell fragments all over the deck but only hit the three nurses. The other members of the group remained safe. Ayres was struck in the temple and Wood in the heart. The ship went back to New York Harbor to bring the bodies of both killed nurses and to get Matzen to a hospital. Matzen was taken to Presbyterian Hospital in New York and soon recovered. She later rejoined the other unit nurses in France.

On their return, the Navy Department officers did not give extensive explanations of the accident. Their reluctance to reveal details largely contributed to a general misunderstanding of the drama, especially among the relatives of Ayres and Wood. The public similarly lacked a full grasp of the particular circumstances of this accident. In particular, two versions were reported in newspapers and official records. The first hypothesis was that a shell that allegedly ricocheted from the water killed the two nurses. The second account hinted at the fact that the gun fired was defective and prematurely exploded, or was faultily discharged. Both versions suggested the same possible origin, weapon deficiency,

but even today questions remain about the full details of the incident.

Ayres and Wood were the first women in the U.S. military killed on duty. The Red Cross held a memorial service in New York in the evening of May 23. Ayres's body was then shipped by the War Department to her home in Attica, Ohio.

On May 26, 1917, Ayres was buried with military honors at the Attica Venice Township Joint Cemetery. She had no children. A bronze tablet was placed at the Chicago Training School for Nurses on her memory.

Florence Dupré

See also: American Red Cross; McClelland, Helen Grace (1887–1984); Nursing; War of 1812 (1812–1815); World War I (1914–1918).

References and Further Reading

Committee of Naval Affairs, United States. *Casualties aboard Steamship "Mongolia."* New York: Government Printing Office, 1917.

Dock, Lavina L., Sarah Elisabeth Pickett, and Clara Dutton Noyes. *History of American Red Cross Nursing.* New York: The Macmillan Company, 1922.

Shrady, George Frederick, and Thomas Lathrop Stedman. *Medical Record 91.* New York: William Wood and Company, 1917.

Smith, Alfred Emanuel, Francis Rufus Bellamy, and Harold Trowbridge Pulsifer, eds. *The Outlook.* New York: Outlook, 1917.

B

BACHE, SARAH "SALLY" FRANKLIN (1743–1808)

American patriot Sarah Franklin Bache, the daughter of Benjamin Franklin, took an active role in the American Revolution. Unlike her brother William, the governor of New Jersey, she sided with her father and the American patriots. She served as her father's political hostess and proxy and did relief work throughout the war.

Sarah Franklin was born to Deborah Read and Benjamin Franklin on September 11, 1743. Called Sally for most of her life, she was educated as well as a woman could be in the 18th century and became an accomplished seamstress by the age of five. She mastered both domestic and academic learning. Her education included geography, history, grammar, French, drawing, dancing, and music. She excelled at the harpsichord. Her mother ran the family businesses so that her father could be freed to engage in his scientific work. Her mother modeled the dual roles of domestic and public work.

Against her parents' wishes, Sarah married Richard Bache in 1767. He was an importer whose business was ruined by all the boycotts the colonists engaged in as well as by lack of support from his investor in England. He acquired the lucrative position of postmaster general in 1776.

Bache served as her father's hostess for political and social functions after her mother had a series of strokes beginning in 1769. Her mother died from another stroke in 1774. After her father left the country in 1776 for France, Bache became his proxy. She sent a number of letters of introduction to her father concerning various visitors to their home. Bache also attended a number of society functions and entertained guests that included the Washingtons and a host of other colonial elite. She raised her eight children, overseeing their educations and battling their illnesses. She also had to flee the house twice, in 1776 and

Portrait sketch of Patriot Sarah Franklin Bache, January 2, 1784. (Kean Collection/Getty Images)

1777, when she faced threats from the British and from Loyalists. One of her sons spent nine years in France with his grandfather, Franklin.

With Esther de Berdt Reed, Bache founded the Philadelphia Ladies Association in 1780. Reed described the scope of the organization in a pamphlet that called for women to endure privations and willingly do all that was physically possible to aid the American war effort. The women created the Ladies Association to alleviate the deplorable condition of Continental Army soldiers. Bache had learned personally from Continental Army soldiers the difficulties that they faced. Some temporarily deserted because they could not survive without payment and clothing. Bache observed that the army did not lack patriotism, but it did lack money.

Reed and Bache called together three dozen women to organize a fund-raising drive to raise money for the troops. Bache's responsibility was to canvass an area in Philadelphia to ask for money and to write to friends requesting money for the troops. Their successful efforts resulted in $300,000 in Continental paper money from 1,600 individual donors. Although the women wanted to turn over the money directly to the soldiers, Gen. George Washington feared the soldiers would spend the money on rum and asked the women to instead give the money to Congress. The women refused. Washington then requested that they use the money to make shirts for the troops. This idea resonated with the women, and they began the project immediately. By the end of the war, they had produced 2,200 hand-sewn shirts for the American soldiers.

Bache wanted her father to approve of her work for the soldiers. A letter from Bache to Franklin detailed how much of her time was taken up cutting out and sewing together shirts and sending material to others to do the same. Their mutual acquaintance Francois Barbe de Marbois wrote to Franklin praising Bache's tireless efforts, her encouragement of others in the task, and her patriotism. He also sent newspapers with the account of her and the Philadelphia Ladies Association's efforts to produce the shirts. Franklin had the accounts published in a French paper, sent Bache a copy, and lavishly praised her in a letter.

By the middle of 1781, Franklin had officially asked Congress to relieve him of his post in France so that he could spend his retirement at his own home comforted by his daughter and entertained by his grandchildren. Franklin finally returned to Pennsylvania in 1785. He spent his declining years with Sally as the hostess of his house, entertaining both colonial and European elite. After his death in 1790, she inherited most of Franklin's estate. She moved to an estate outside of Philadelphia in the Delaware Valley but returned to the city in 1807. After her death in 1808, she was buried beside her parents.

Mark Anthony Phelps

See also: American Revolution (1775–1783); Ladies Association; Reed, Esther de Berdt (1746–1780).

References and Further Reading

Gunderson, Joan. *To Be Useful the World, 1740–1790*. New York: Twayne, 1996.

Oberg, Barbara, ed. *The Papers of Benjamin Franklin*, 39 vols. New Haven, CT: Yale University Press, 1999.

BAILEY, ANNE HENNIS TROTTER "MAD ANNE" (1742–1825)

A frontier scout and courier during the American Revolution, Anne Bailey was also an explorer and pioneer of the Kanawha Valley in present-day West Virginia.

Little is known of Bailey's life prior to her migration to America. She was born Anne Hennis in Liverpool, England, in 1742 to a family whose names are unrecorded. Her father was a former soldier in the service of Queen Anne, a fact many biographers have used to claim that she was named to honor the queen. Her parents saw that she attended school, learning to read and write. In 1761, when she was 19, both her mother and father died in unknown circumstances. This tragedy prompted Anne's move to Virginia. Whether she intended to join family or friends in the New World is unclear.

Four years later found her near Staunton, Virginia, and married to a local settler, Richard Trotter. Their union produced one son, William. Trotter enlisted in the Virginia militia under John Murray, the Earl of Dunmore, in a brief conflict known as Lord Dunmore's War that would last only one year (1774). This conflict was between the burgeoning body of white settlers and the local Shawnee and Mingo Indians. Trotter was part of this war's only large-scale action, the Battle of Point Pleasant on October 10, 1774. Trotter became one of the estimated 81 casualties of this battle.

Her husband's death is seen as the catalyst for Anne's decision to drastically alter her life. Leaving seven-year-old William in the care of a neighbor, she entered into service of the Patriot cause during the American Revolution (1775–1783). Her gender precluded entry into the militia and Continental Army ranks, so she vocally espoused the Patriot cause and encouraged those who could to enlist by traveling great distances to recruiting stations. She also served in an unofficial capacity as a scout and courier.

Anne continued acting as a courier and scout after the close of the Revolution. She also remarried, wedding another frontier scout, John Bailey, in 1785. Duty relocated the Baileys to Fort Clendenin, later renamed Fort Lee (present-day Charleston, West Virginia) in 1788. Both patrolled the wilds around the fort, reporting on Indian movements.

Bailey's most storied event occurred in 1791, when she was 49 years old. Warnings that Native Americans had targeted Fort Clendenin for a massive assault had been issued. Ammunition stores were low and in no shape for a sustained battle, so Bailey was tasked with securing more. She struck out from the fort, making a roughly 100-mile trek to Lewisburg, Virginia. Despite the harsh terrain, the dangerous conditions, and the looming attack, Bailey completed her mission, returning in time to resupply the fort. Thanks to Bailey's retrieval of ammunition, the next morning the defenders repulsed the attack. In gratitude, the garrison presented her with a black horse named Liverpool.

U.S. soldier Charles Robb immortalized this incident after he visited the area in 1861. His poem "Anne Bailey's Ride" saw publication first in an Ohio newspaper and was reprinted in several other places in the ensuing years. This poem added to the enduring myth.

The Baileys remained at their post until 1795 when the Greenville Treaty ended the constant warfare with the remaining Native Americans. They led a quiet frontier life during this period. After her husband died in 1802, Bailey spent more time with her son. Trotter, now 35, had married and settled in southeastern Ohio. In 1818, the reunited family relocated further north to Gallia, Ohio. Bailey visited Virginia several times afterwards but seemed to have finally settled in Gallia.

Some purport that Gallia settlers nicknamed her "Mad Anne" because they were taken aback by her frontier disposition. Other accounts claim that this nickname, along with the title "White Squaw of the Kanawha," was actually given to her by Native Americans during her earlier years.

On the eve of a trip in 1825, Bailey became ill and died suddenly. A memorial was placed for her at Point Pleasant Park in West Virginia. In addition, a Daughters of the American Revolution chapter in West Virginia bears her name as tribute.

Michael D. Coker

See also: American Revolution (1775–1783); Indian Wars; North American Colonial Wars (17th–18th centuries).

References and Further Reading

Green, Harry Clinton, and Mary Wolcott Green. *The Pioneer Mothers of America: A Record of the More Notable Women of the Early Days of the Country, and Particularly of the Colonial and Revolutionary Periods.* Whitefish, MT: Kessinger Publishing, 2007.

Lewis, Virgil Anson. *Life and Times of Anne Bailey: The Pioneer Heroine of the Great Kanawha Valley.* Charleston, WV: Butler Printing Co, 1891.

Vugt, William E. Van. *British Buckeyes: The English, Scots, and Welsh in Ohio, 1700–1900.* Kent, OH: Kent State University Press, 2006.

BAILEY, MARGARET E. (1915–)

The first black nurse in the United States Army to become lieutenant colonel and the first black to hold the rank of full colonel, Margaret E. Bailey was in the vanguard of the integration movement. She encouraged minorities to join the U.S. Army Nurse Corps (ANC).

Bailey was born December 25, 1915, in Selma, Alabama, the only child to Adam and Hailey Bailey. Her father died shortly after she was born, in a mining accident in Birmingham, Alabama.

Her mother eventually had three more children: Lucy, Hattie, and James.

In 1923, Bailey moved to Mobile, Alabama, to live with her relatives, Jeanette and Sam Green. In 1933, she graduated from Dunbar High School in Mobile. She moved back to Selma when she learned there was a black nursing school there and was disappointed when the school closed after the completion of the 1934 graduating class. However, Bailey soon discovered another black nursing school in Montgomery, Alabama.

In July 1935 she entered the Fraternal Hospital School of Nursing. She graduated on May 1, 1938. Bailey joined the U.S. Army on June 6, 1944, and reported to duty at Fort Huachuca, Arizona, on June 30, 1944. She received a telegram in July 1944 stating that black nurses would be accepted in the ANC without any limits imposed by a quota. The telegram further stated that black nurses could be stationed in the United States and overseas. Bailey joined the ANC and during World War II was stationed in Florence, Arizona, as a nurse at a German prisoner of war camp. On May 1, 1946, she was transferred to Halloran General Hospital in Staten Island, New York. Her duties in New York were her first experiences in the Army working with an integrated group of nurses.

Bailey was a specialist in medical and surgical nursing, but she wanted to continue her education. She was transferred on March 1, 1950, to the Medical Field Service School at Fort Sam Houston, Texas, to study psychiatric nursing. During her time in Texas, Bailey signed up for the Regular Army. On November 2, 1950, she was promoted to the rank of captain. She was transferred to Germany on January 22, 1951. She was one of only three black

officers in the area at the time. She was promoted to major on December 13, 1957.

Serving in the Army allowed Bailey to attend college courses only sporadically, but she was determined to finish her degree. She graduated on June 6, 1959, with a bachelor of arts degree from San Francisco State University. After graduation, she was transferred to the U.S. Army Hospital in Zama, Japan, on September 8, 1959, where she served as assistant chief nurse.

On November 9, 1962, Bailey was transferred to Fitzsimmons General Hospital in Denver, Colorado, and was assigned as the head nurse in the Department of Psychiatry. During her stay in Denver, the hospital was eager to recruit more nurses and developed the Nightingale Program; Bailey was appointed the chair of this program.

When on July 15, 1964, Bailey was promoted to lieutenant colonel, she became the first black U.S. Army nurse to achieve that rank. Following the promotion, she was elevated to supervisor of the neuropsychiatric section of Fitzsimmons General Hospital. On July 6, 1965, she was transferred to the 130th General Hospital in Chinon, France. At the 130th she was the first African American assigned as chief nurse of an integrated hospital. She left Europe on July 15, 1967, and became chief nurse at the United States Army Hospital at Fort Devens, Massachusetts. She also became the first black U.S. Army nurse to be promoted to colonel, in January 1970.

Bailey had served in the U.S. Army for 27 years when she retired on August 1, 1971. She was awarded the Legion of Merit for Exceptionally Meritorious Conduct for her service.

After retirement, she continued her contributions to the ANC. She became a consultant to the surgeon general and was charged with promoting minorities in the ANC recruitment program. She continued her affirmative action endeavors with Maj. Clara Adams-Ender as the two traveled around the United States promoting racial equality in the Corps. She also became a very active member of the Chi Eta Phi Sorority, Inc., Officers Wives Club and continued to be involved with the Job Corps.

Col. Margaret E. Bailey resides in Silver Spring, Maryland.

Paula L. Webb

See also: African American Women; Army Nurse Corps (ANC); Nursing; World War II (1941–1945).

References and
Further Reading

Bailey, Margaret E. *The Challenge: Autobiography of Colonel Margaret E. Bailey.* Lisle, IL: Tucker, 1999.

Sarnecky, Mary T. *A Contemporary History of the U.S. Army Nursing Corps.* Washington, D.C.: Government Printing Office, 2010.

Shields, Elizabeth A. *Highlights in the History of the Army Nurse Corps.* Washington, D.C.: Government Printing Office, 1981.

BAILEY, MILDRED "INEZ" CAROON (1919–2009)

Brig. Gen. Mildred Bailey served as director of the Women's Army Corps (WAC) from 1971 to 1975. She was one of the first women to be promoted to the rank of one-star general in 1971. She enlisted in the Army in 1942 and remained in service until 1975. Her friends knew her as Inez.

Born Mildred Inez Caroon in 1919, she lived most of her early life in Kingston, North Carolina, with her parents and four siblings. She attended Flora McDonald College in Red Springs, North Carolina, but transferred just over a year later to the Woman's College of the University of North Carolina–Greensboro. After graduating in 1940, she began a teaching career in North Carolina but joined the Women's Army Auxiliary Corps (WAAC, later the Women's Army Corps or WAC) in 1942 during World War II. She completed the third WAAC class of Officer Training School in Des Moines, Iowa. During the war, she served with the Army Air Corps in Daytona Beach, Florida; George Field Army Air Base, Illinois; and Walnut Ridge, Arkansas. In her final station at Craig Field, Alabama, she taught English to the French Air Force.

In 1943, she married Marine sergeant Roy Bailey. For the next two years, they lived apart while both completed their military assignments. When the war ended, Bailey traveled to California to be with her husband, who was still completing his military assignment.

Because they needed income, Bailey quickly requested to be reactivated to military duty. The Army stationed her in Florida, so she left her husband once again. Her job was to offer job guidance and counseling to veterans who were getting out of the service. She continued in this role after her husband's discharge, when he joined her in Florida to attend school and find a job.

When the Women's Armed Services Integration Act passed in 1948, Bailey elected to remain in military service and transferred to intelligence, hoping to stay in the position and the Florida area for two to three years while her husband finished school. Two months later, however, the Army transferred her to Germany. After she arrived in Stuttgart for her new position, she began investigating civil service jobs that might be available to her husband, who was pursuing an accounting career. He arrived soon after and found a job in Stuttgart, although military transfers soon left the couple living in two different locations in Germany.

In 1953, Bailey returned to the United States for an intelligence assignment in Washington, D.C. Upon completion of that job, she became head of recruiting at Fort MacPherson, Georgia, until 1961. Although Bailey preferred intelligence work, she adapted quickly to recruiting and would remain in that general arena of work until 1968. In 1961, she became head of the nation's largest WAC detachment, in Fort Myer, Virginia, and began work on the WAC traveling recruiting exhibit. The WAC planned for the exhibit to travel the nation, offering short, informative talks to educate Americans about women's opportunities in the military.

When the traveling exhibit went on the road in 1963, Bailey went with it as the head of the program. For the next five years, she and her staff traveled around the nation to promote women in military service. While on the road in 1966, she received news that her husband had died unexpectedly in an automobile accident.

Although she took a brief time off following his death, she soon returned to the exhibit team and remained with it until 1968.

After two years as the military's liaison officer to the Senate from 1968 to 1970, Bailey served briefly as deputy commander of the WAC training center in Fort McClellan, Alabama. While serving in this role during 1970 and 1971, she was told she would be the next director of the Women's Army Corps.

When she became director, Bailey also received a promotion to brigadier general, the third woman in the Army to attain that rank. During her time as director, the armed forces eliminated the draft, and this move led to the expansion of women's roles throughout the military. The number of women serving in the Army during those years tripled to become the highest level of women personnel since World War II. In addition to women's expansion into previously male jobs, women also began to command men, and the military eliminated all-female units.

After her retirement, Bailey continued to feel a connection to the Army and saw herself as a trailblazer for women in the military. In 1978, she completed an extensive oral history interview with the Army, and she completed another with the University of North Carolina–Greensboro Women Veterans Collection. She died at the age of 90 in 2009 of Alzheimer's disease at a military retirement facility. Bailey is buried in Arlington Cemetery.

Tanya L. Roth

See also: All-Volunteer Force (AVF); Espionage; Hoisington, Elizabeth P. (1918–2007); Women's Armed Services Integration Act of 1948 (Public Law 80-625); Women's Army Auxiliary Corps

(WAAC); Women's Army Corps (WAC); World War II (1941–1945).

References and Further Reading

Bailey, Beth. *America's Army: Making the All-Volunteer Force.* Cambridge, MA: Belknap Press of Harvard University Press, 2009.

Holm, Jeanne. *In Defense of a Nation: Servicewomen in World War II.* St. Petersburg, FL: Vandamere Press, 1998.

Holm, Jeanne. *Women in the Military: An Unending Revolution*, rev. ed. Novato, CA: Presidio Press, 1993.

Morden, Bettie J. *The Women's Army Corps, 1945–1978.* Washington, D.C.: Center of Military History, 1989.

BAKER (STEFFEN), CECILIA GENEVIEVE "LUCILLE" (1900–1968) AND BAKER (FRENCH), GENEVIEVE CECILIA (1900–1999)

Cecilia Genevieve Baker, commonly known as Lucille, and her identical twin Genevieve Cecilia Baker served as the first enlisted women in the Coast Guard.

Their parents, Chauncy and Bernice Waclawski, were Polish immigrants who settled in Brooklyn shortly before the birth of the twins on February 28, 1900. In order to more easily find employment, Chauncy Waclawski changed the family name to Baker.

By World War I, Lucille and Genevieve were already working in clerical positions at the Brooklyn Navy Yard. With two brothers in the family already serving as soldiers in France, the women were especially patriotic and eager to serve for the war cause. In April 1918, at 19 years old, the sisters applied at the Brooklyn Barge Office to enlist directly into the Coast Guard, asking to serve in the guard ranks. Newspaper accounts of the event note that the officer in charge feared that the job might be too strenuous for women, and he was unsure whether the Coast Guard was accepting women. Instead, the Baker twins enlisted in the Naval Coast Defense Reserve under the command of the Navy. When the Coast Guard was moved under Navy jurisdiction in 1919, Genevieve and Lucille were transferred together and became the first enlisted, uniformed women in the Coast Guard.

Struggling with personnel shortages in the administrative offices during World War I as the Navy sent enlisted men into combat, Secretary of the Navy Josephus Daniels authorized the enlistment of women into the Naval Coast Defense Reserve on March 19, 1917. Ultimately, over 12,000 women would enlist and serve. These women were popularly referred to as Yeomanettes in reference to the rating of yeoman (F) given by the Navy, short for yeoman female. Basic requirements for female recruits included that they be 18 to 35 years old, of good character and neat appearance, and able to pass a basic physical examination. Although there were no strict education requirements, there was a preference for high school graduates with business or office experience. Almost all of the enlisted women were given the rank of yeoman (F) but received no formal training from the military. Serving in the Navy, Marine Corps, and Coast Guard, these women worked exclusively in administrative, clerical, and supply positions.

Coast Guard records on the yeomen (F) are scant and show only a handful of women working in the Washington, D.C., headquarters. However, family records maintain that the twins continued to be based out of the Brooklyn Navy Yard and worked as bookkeepers and telephone operators. Though a uniform of dark blue tailored clothing eventually evolved, many yeomanettes adapted their civilian clothes into a uniform. The sisters were known for their matching dark dresses, collared shirts with neckties, and waist sashes.

At the time of their enlistment, articles about the Baker twins were published across the country. The twins received over 145 marriage proposals from readers of these articles. During the war, Lucille eloped with an army soldier named Edward Steffen, who was sent to France only three days later. Additionally, during her service in the Coast Guard, Lucille got a tattoo on her left bicep—an unusual action for young women of the time. Family lore remembers that it was either a ship or an American flag but that she kept it covered for the rest of her life.

In 1920, Genevieve married Harry E. French (1893–1957), a navy sailor she met in Prospect Park in Brooklyn during the war. After the war, Harry worked as a ticket agent in Penn Station for the Pennsylvania Railroad. They settled in Red Bank, New York, where they had two sons and four daughters.

At the end of the war, all yeomen (F) from the Navy, Coast Guard, and Marine Corps were mustered out of service. They received honorable discharges and full veterans' benefits, including preference for civil service ratings. However, neither Lucille nor Genevieve continued her career after her marriage. Once Lucille's husband returned from Europe, they settled in Long Beach, New York, where her husband worked as a fireman. They had one son.

It is notable that while the 1930 census indicates that their husbands were veterans, it does not indicate the same for Lucille or Genevieve. Though serving less than a year, Lucille and her twin sister Genevieve were proud and enthusiastic about their achievement as the first enlisted women in the U.S. Coast Guard.

Lucille Baker Steffen died in 1968 in Long Beach. Upon her death in 1999 on the day after her 99th birthday, Genevieve Baker French had 27 grandchildren, 50 great-grandchildren, and 16 great-great grandchildren.

Kate Wells

See also: World War I (1914–1918); Yeoman (F).

References and Further Reading

Ebbert, Jean, and Marie-Beth Hall. *Crossed Currents: Navy Women in a Century of Change.* Washington, D.C.: Brassey's, 1999.

Gavin, Lettie. *American Women in World War I: They Also Served.* Niwot: University Press of Colorado, 1997.

Tilley, John A. "A History of Women in the Coast Guard." *Commandant's Bulletin,* March 1996, insert.

Turner, Bernice. Interview by author. Savannah, GA, October 29, 2010.

BAKER, E. H.
(N.D.–N.D)

As a Union spy during the American Civil War, E. H. Baker successfully delivered intelligence about undersea vessels being developed by the Confederacy in the race for naval technologic superiority.

Little is known about E. H. Baker's early life. She had been employed by Allan Pinkerton's detective agency in Chicago prior to being dispatched as a spy to Richmond, Virginia, in November 1861. Pinkerton was Gen. George McClellan's secret service chief and had learned that the Confederates were developing torpedoes and submarine vessels in response to the Union blockade. Pinkerton believed that Richmond's Tredegar Iron Works was the leading producer of this technology, and he sent Baker to investigate.

Baker had once lived in Richmond and was acquainted with a captain in the Confederate navy. He took Baker to an exhibition along the James River of a submarine vessel intended for use against the Union fleet blocking the river's mouth. She recorded her observation of the submarine vessel that attached a floating magazine to the side of a ship. Baker watched as the submarine backed away and detonated the charge, sinking the ship in a large explosion.

Atwater also gave Baker a tour of Tredegar Iron Works, where she saw a much larger undersea vessel being produced, one she said was a larger version of the submarine used in the demonstration. Baker promptly returned north and reported her findings to Pinkerton, who then duly informed McClellan.

There is some speculation about what Baker saw. The submarine she saw demonstrated was likely that designed by William Cheeney, and the larger vessel at Tredegar might in fact have been a larger model. The armor plating for the CSS *Virginia* (also known as the *Merrimack*) was being produced at this time as well. Pinkerton claims that Baker's intelligence thwarted a submarine attack on the USS *Minnesota* in Hampton Roads, which captured a Confederate submarine using grappling hooks, although the capture took place a month prior to the time that Pinkerton reported that Baker was in Richmond.

Kristen L. Rouse

See also: Civil War (1861–1865); Espionage.

References and Further Reading

Coski, John M. *Capital Navy: The Men, Ships, and Operations of the James River Squadron*. Campbell, CA: Savas Woodbury, 1996.

Pinkerton, Allan. *The Spy of the Rebellion: Being a True History of the Spy System of the United States Army during the Late Rebellion*. New York: G. W. Carleton, 1883.

BAKER, JOSEPHINE
(1906–1975)

African American dancer and singer Josephine Baker became a Red Cross nurse and worked with the French Resistance movement during World War II.

Born Freda Josephine McDonald in St. Louis, Missouri, on June 3, 1906, to Carrie MacDonald, Josephine rarely

Dancer Josephine Baker became a Red Cross nurse and French Resistance spy during World War II. (Library of Congress)

saw her father. She left school early to work as a maid but later became a dancer. Although her marriage to Willie Baker in 1921 was a short one, she took her second husband's last name. She danced as a member of a troupe in Philadelphia and in shows on Broadway and on the floor of the Plantation Club.

In 1925, Baker traveled to Paris as part of Le Revue Negre by Caroline Dudley, a passionate Francophile and wife of an American foreign service officer. Baker was an immediate success in Paris and quickly became a headliner at the Folies Bergère. She introduced her *danse sauvage*, a number in which she danced semi-nude in a skirt of bananas, to France. She became a huge success and was very popular with French audiences.

The racism of the 1920s United States caught up to Baker in France. She was among the crowd at the fashionable restaurant L'Abbaye de Theleme to celebrate the arrival of Charles Lindberg

at Le Bourget and overheard a vicious racist comment from a compatriot. Shortly thereafter, Baker and her husband Pepito (alias the Count de Abatino) were refused a short-term lease on a suite of rooms at the Right Bank Hotel. According to the manager, the hotel's American clientele would resent the presence of an African American woman in the establishment.

Marcel Sauvage asked to coauthor Baker's memoirs. Although *Les Memoires de Josephine Baker* (1927) was a literary and commercial success, she made a dramatic blunder in her ruminations regarding World War I and its wounded soldiers. Much to the horror of her audience, she expressed her disgust for maimed veterans. Wounded veterans were held in high esteem in France. As a result, to avoid jeopardizing her popularity, Baker staged a gala benefit for France's war wounded. She became a French citizen in 1937.

During the early months of World War II, Baker served as a Red Cross nurse. After German troops entered Paris in 1940, she engaged in espionage work for Jacques Abtey, a former officer of the Deuxième Bureau of the French Resistance. Baker joined the Underground and declared that she would not perform "as long as there is a German in Paris." Wartime espionage may have been Josephine Baker's greatest role. She used her celebrity status to obtain exit visas for members of the Resistance. Furthermore, Baker was able to travel to the neutral countries of Spain and Portugal on her entertainer's passport, and when doing so she smuggled notes of invisible ink inside her underwear. She moved to an apartment in Montmartre located near the Gare St. Charles, and her quarters became a network center for exiles. Eventually, she took up residence in Morocco, the guest of Sheik Si Thami el Glaoui.

While in Casablanca, Baker initiated a service club for black GIs and was offered a contract to entertain U.S. troops. Although one of her goals was to unite black and white troops, she declined the offer because she considered herself a member of the Free French forces, where she held the rank of sublieutenant. After the liberation of Paris in 1944, she was commissioned by the French general de Lattre de Tassigny to follow the French First Army through the liberated countries and organize shows. The shows netted over two million francs for war victims.

Gen. Charles de Gaulle awarded to Baker the Croix de Guerre and the Légion d'Honneur for her wartime service. She was also awarded the Rosette of the Résistance. After the war, she changed the lyrics of her theme song "J'ai Deux Amours" from "mon pays et Paris" (my country and Paris) to "mon pays c'est Paris" (my country is Paris).

Baker retired to her estate Les Milandes in southwestern France and adopted children of many nationalities. She traveled to the United States and performed occasionally until her death in France on April 12, 1975.

Wendell G. Johnson

See also: African American Women; World War I (1914–1918); World War II (1941–1945).

References and Further Reading

Baker, Jean-Claude, and Chris Chase. *Josephine: The Hungry Heart*. New York: Random House, 1993.

Baker, Josephine, and Jo Bouillon. *Josephine*. Translated from the French by Mariana Fitzpatrick. New York: Harper & Row, 1977.

Wiser, William. *The Great Good Place: American Expatriate Women in Paris*. New York: W. W. Norton & Company, 1991.

BALCH, EMILY GREEN (1867–1961)

The second American woman awarded the Nobel Peace Prize, in 1946, Emily Green Balch was a leading 20th-century peace worker who was dismissed as professor of economics at Wellesley College because of her antiwar views during World War I. Although her peace activities defined her role in U.S. history, she was also involved in social causes such as poverty, child labor and education, and immigration, among other reform causes.

Balch was born on January 8, 1867, in Jamaica Plain, Massachusetts. The third child of Francis Balch, an attorney and former secretary to U.S. senator Charles Sumner, and Ellen Maria Noyes, a former schoolteacher from Illinois, Emily was a member of Bryn Mawr College's first graduating class in 1889. She did postgraduate work at Harvard and the University of Chicago. A product of Progressive Era reform policies, Balch was a major proponent of immigration reform in the United States. Her 1910 publication, *Our Slavic Fellow Citizens*, remains a frequently cited work on immigration histories.

In 1896, she began teaching economics at Wellesley College, devoting most of her studies to municipal reform and the treatment of minors. Her reservations about war as an extension of social oppression took root with the outbreak of world war in 1914. Balch joined Jane Addams and more than 40 other American delegates at the International Congress of Women at The Hague in an attempt to achieve peace through mediation. Her role as a peace ambassador is recounted in *Women at The Hague* (1915), coauthored with Addams and Alice Hamilton. In 1916, she participated in auto magnate Henry Ford's Stockholm Neutral Conference for Continuous Mediation, in which she published two studies calling for a postwar rehabilitation fund and the establishment of an international committee overseeing the administration of postwar colonies.

After the U.S. Congress declared war against Germany in April 1917, Balch's peace activities came under careful scrutiny by government officials and Wellesley administrators. Although she was on leave from her teaching position, Balch's participation in peace and antipreparedness groups such as the American Union Against Militarism, the Woman's Peace Party, the Emergency Peace Federation (which she personally established), and the left-wing People's Council of America for Democracy and Peace, as well as her public criticisms of the treatment of conscientious objectors proved embarrassing to Wellesley's trustees. Her contract as professor of economics was not renewed. The rest of her public life was devoted to the peace movement.

In 1919, Balch played an instrumental role in the transformation of the Woman's Peace Party into the Women's International League for Peace and Freedom (WILPF). She served as the league's first international secretary-treasurer and in 1931 was elected president of the U.S. branch. In 1926, critical of U.S. military involvement in Latin America, Balch, along with University of Chicago economist and later U.S. senator Paul Douglas and four others, investigated the U.S. military occupation of Haiti. Balch published a lengthy report, *Occupied Haiti* (1927), which called for an end to U.S. intervention. She also supported numerous disarmament agreements, endorsed the 1928 Pact of Paris, urged establishing an international administrative body to govern Manchuria after the Japanese invasion in 1931, and called upon the U.S. government to open its borders to European victims of fascist aggression.

Balch's antiwar convictions were sorely challenged during World War II. Without criticizing the Allied war effort, she continued working for the release of Japanese Americans interned in relocation camps, rejected the unconditional surrender policy, and supported the civil rights of conscientious objectors, who refused to work in government-run Civilian Public Service Camps. For her leadership role in the WILPF and in support of human rights, she received the Nobel Peace Prize in 1946, along with international Young Men's Christian Association leader John Mott. Although skeptical of world government, Balch supported the specialized agencies of the United Nations during the early years of the Cold War. Her hope for world peace, she insisted, remained in the international administration of atomic energy, aviation, agriculture, disarmament, refugee protection, waterways, polar regions, and economic aid to underdeveloped nations.

A master policy maker and skilled administrator, Balch died on January 9, 1961.

Charles F. Howlett

See also: Addams, Jane (1860–1935); World War I (1914–1918); World War II (1941–1945).

References and Further Reading

Addams, Jane, Emily G. Balch, and Alice Hamilton. *Women at The Hague: The International Congress of Women and Its Results, with Introduction by Harriet Hyman Alonso.* Urbana: University of Illinois Press, 2003.

Bussey, Gertrude, and Margaret Tims. *Pioneers for Peace: Women's International League for Peace and Freedom, 1915–1965.* Reprint. Oxford, UK: Alden Press, 1980.

Foster, Carrie. *The Women and the Warriors: The U.S. Section of the Women's International League for Peace and Freedom, 1915–1946.* Syracuse, NY: Syracuse University Press, 1995.

Foster, Carrie. *Women for All Seasons: The Story of the Women's International League for Peace and Freedom.* Athens: University of Georgia Press, 1989.

Gwinn, Kristen E. *Emily Greene Balch: The Long Road to Internationalism.* Urbana: University of Illinois Press, 2010.

Opfell, Olga S. *The Lady Laureates: Women Who Have Won the Nobel Prize.* Metuchen, NJ: Scarecrow Press, 1977.

Randall, Mercedes M., ed. *Beyond Nationalism: The Social Thought of Emily Greene Balch.* New York: Twayne Publishers, 1972.

Randall, Mercedes M. *Improper Bostonian: Emily Greene Balch.* New York: Twayne Publishers, 1964.

BALDENECKER, DONNA-MAE (1920–2010)

When she joined the Women's Army Auxiliary Corps (WAAC) Band in 1942, Donna-Mae Baldenecker became the first female bugler in the U.S. Army.

Baldenecker was born January 3, 1920, to Walter and Florence Baldenecker in Manly, Iowa. When she was 13, her family moved to St. Paul Park, Minnesota. She began her musical career singing in the church choir. She also joined her high school band as a trumpeter and played in local concerts. When she was a teenager, the Minnesota Mining and Manufacturing (3M) Company band, called the Payne Avenue and Brown and Bigelow Drum and Bugle Corps, recruited her. Baldenecker played trumpet with the group from 1935 until 1938. The Corps played for different local events including the St. Paul Winter Carnival Parade. After she graduated from high school in 1938, she won a singing scholarship to the Minneapolis School of Music.

Baldenecker originally hoped to become a music teacher, but when World War II began she felt compelled to assist in the war effort. Initially, Baldenecker took a position inspecting .30 caliber cartridges in a munitions factory. She found the noise of the factory jarring but continued to work there until she saw an advertisement in the newspaper for women to play in the WAAC Band. The male band members had largely been deployed overseas to work in foreign military bases. She quickly submitted an application, and the Army immediately responded, telling her to report for duty. Thus, in 1942 Baldenecker became a WAAC band member and the first female bugler in the U.S. Army.

The Army transported Baldenecker and other local recruits to Des Moines, Iowa, where they settled into their home, an old cavalry post. The women were afforded little pay, poor food, and no privacy, but Baldenecker was elated she could play her trumpet daily. The all-woman band, eventually comprising 80 women, practiced wherever they could find room in the tight barracks quarters. Fortunately, band members were spared from recruit training and many unpleasant base jobs because the Army feared they would injure themselves. Baldenecker maintained her position as first chair trumpet throughout the war, eventually rising to the rank of sergeant. The band traveled throughout the Midwest, marching in parades and working to recruit more women for the Army. In addition to her band responsibilities, Baldenecker had to wake the troops for reveille, sound the calls for the day, and play evening taps.

While in the military, Baldenecker met her future husband, Cpl. Robert M. Burr. They married in January 1943. Although she would have liked to remain in the Army, the military did not allow married women. She was discharged exactly one year and one day after joining the Army. Her husband remained in the military, and Baldenecker moved with him to several different assignments. They had their first child, a son named Craig, in March 1944. Burr left the military in 1945. The new family built a home in Minneapolis, Minnesota.

Baldenecker joined the Hormel Packing Company in 1945. She became leader of the Hormel's All-Girl Drum and Bugle Corps, serving as both director and housemother. Baldenecker eventually traveled with the drum and bugle corps to New York City for the American Legion Parade, where they earned second prize. At the conclusion of the parade, Jay Hormel asked Baldenecker to become a sales advocate for Hormel chili, and she accepted, touring across the South with her husband and son distributing chili samples. When the advertising junket ended, the family resettled in Minneapolis. In 1948, they had a second son, Kevin. In 1951, the family decided to move to the San Fernando Valley. Shortly thereafter, Kevin contracted leukemia and died at age seven.

Baldenecker held several jobs before her retirement and continued to be engaged in civic activities. In 1961 she became the senior financial manager at the Los Angeles Board of Education. She also established a successful fruitcake business, Donna's Delight. Her husband passed away in 1964.

She married Edgar H. Smith in 1969. The couple eventually moved to Oregon. She joined the Veterans of Foreign Wars (VFW) in Rosenburg, Oregon, and played trumpet for several VFW organizations in the area. She became a member of the American Legion, Post 15, serving as post commander. She was also a member of the American Women Veterans Association, American Veterans (AMVETS), and Eastern Star. After her 1992 retirement, she began to play taps for veteran funerals, Memorial Day, and Veterans Day commemorations throughout Oregon.

She was inducted into the Buglers Hall of Fame in 2009, the second woman to enter the group. Her grandson played bugle in the United States Air Force.

Donna-Mae Baldenecker Burr Smith died in Rosenburg, Oregon, on April 3, 2010.

Emily Meyer

See also: Women's Army Auxiliary Corps (WAAC); Women's Army Band; World War II (1941–1945).

References and Further Reading

Bjornstad, Randi. "Call of the Bugle: First Female U.S. Military Bugler Has a Place in the Hall of Fame." *The Register-Guard*, August 2, 2009.

Cavit, Christina M. "Donna-Mae Baldenecker Burr Smith, the U.S. Military's First Female Bugler." *Noteworthy: Official Newsletter of the IWBC, Lady Brass Series* 15, no. 2 (Winter 2009): 12–14.

Sullivan, Jill M. *Bands of Sisters: U.S. Women's Military Bands during World War II.* Lanham, MD: Scarecrow Press, 2011.

BARNWELL, BARBARA OLIVE (1928–)

In 1953, Marine Staff Sgt. Barbara Olive Barnwell became the first female Marine recipient of the Marine Corps Medal for heroism. She earned the award after she swam to the rescue of a fellow marine, Pvt. 1st Class Frederick H. Roman, to save him from drowning.

Born in 1928 in Kansas City, Missouri, Barnwell had served as a regular marine since May 1949. She was attached to the staff of the inspector-instructor, 1st Air and Naval Gunfire Liaison Company, at Fort Schuyler, New York, at the time of the incident and was stationed at Camp LeJeune. Barnwell was serving as a naval gunfire instructor at the time.

A strong swimmer, Barnwell had helped save several people from the water, and Roman's rescue was one of several that she was a part of throughout her life. When Barnwell herself was only a child, at around the age of 11, she saved a 7-year-old from drowning in Kansas City. Roughly five years later, she brought another young woman safely to shore.

In the course of rescuing her fellow marine, Barnwell struggled for 20 minutes. When she saw him struggling, Roman was swimming about 50 feet away from her and was caught in a heavy Atlantic Ocean undertow offshore from Camp LeJeune. The two were in deep water and about 120 yards offshore, so the rescue was not an easy one. Barnwell secured Roman and carried him back to dry land, struggling herself with the difficulties of the strong undertow. After she had him safely onshore, she saw that artificial respiration was successful and that Roman was going to live. Barnwell walked away without even providing her name.

For her actions, Barnwell received honors. The Navy and Marine Corps Medal ranks eighth in order between the Distinguished Flying Cross and the Bronze Star. The Marine Corps Medal is the Naval Service's highest award for heroism not involving combat. Barnwell received her medal in Washington, D.C., on August 7, 1953, from Gen. Lemuel C. Shepherd Jr., commandant of the Marine Corps. In addition to the medal presentation in the commandant's office, Barnwell was honored, along with six male officers, at a retreat ceremony at the Marine Barracks, Washington, D.C. It was the first time that a woman was so honored.

Rorie M. Cartier

See also: Women Marines.

References and Further Reading

Baron, Scott. *They Also Served: Military Biographies of Uncommon Americans.* Spartanburg, SC: Military Information Enterprises, 1998.

Read, Phyllis J., and Bernard L. Witlieb. *The Book of Women's Firsts: Breakthrough Achievements of Almost 1,000 American Women.* New York: Random House, 1992.

Sherrow, Victoria. *Women and the Military: An Encyclopedia.* Santa Barbara, CA: ABC-CLIO, 1996.

BARTON, CLARA HARLOWE (1821–1912)

Civil War battlefield nurse Clara Barton founded the American Red Cross. (National Archives)

A Union battlefield nurse during the Civil War, Clara Barton founded the American Red Cross.

Clarissa Harlowe Barton was born December 25, 1821, in North Oxford, Massachusetts, the youngest of five children of Capt. Stephen Barton, a prosperous farmer and former soldier. As a child she studied Latin, chemistry, and philosophy. In order to combat her natural shyness, Clara was sent away by her family at age 17 to become a teacher in Massachusetts's District 9, located in Worcester County. She became well known for her teaching skills and her disciplined classrooms. Barton would teach in several other local school districts for the next six years before finally establishing her own school in North Oxford.

Needing a change, she entered the Liberal Institute in Clinton, New York, an advanced school for female teachers, which placed her in a new pedagogical position in Hightstown, New Jersey, upon her graduation. Her success there inspired her to open one of the first free public schools in the state in nearby Bordentown. It successfully expanded to over 600 students by 1854. Unfortunately, the school board refused to offer Barton the high-paying position to head the school and hired a man instead.

Frustrated, Barton moved to Washington, D.C., where she worked as the first female clerk in the U.S. Patent Office. There she earned pay equal to that of her male counterparts. When she lost her position after the election of President James Buchanan in 1856, she returned home to Massachusetts. Once Abraham Lincoln entered the White House in 1861, Barton returned to Washington to work as a copyist.

When the 6th Massachusetts Infantry arrived in the capital after having been attacked by a pro-Confederate mob in Baltimore on April 19, Barton housed many of the wounded in her home. All of the regiment's baggage had been lost during the riot, so Barton rounded up clothing, food, and supplies from local merchants in order to provide for the troops whom she now considered "her boys." This experience inspired her to pursue a broader effort to improve the care for soldiers. After her experience with the Massachusetts troops, she wrote several letters home appealing to family and friends to send supplies for the army in Washington. When the wounded arrived after the July 21 Battle of Bull Run, she scoured the unprepared city for medicine, bandages, and proper food.

Her father's illness later that year forced Barton to return home briefly, but she came back to Washington in 1862 even more dedicated to serving the needs of the army and its soldiers. In August, she procured six wagons filled with supplies and personally drove them to the Union lines outside of Culpepper, Virginia. She remained with the army, which remained heavily engaged with Confederate forces for the remainder of that summer. Working in various field hospitals, Barton served as a nurse. She attended to the wounded from the Second Battle of Bull Run, Cedar Mountain, Chantilly, Harper's Ferry, and South Mountain. She worked so close to the fighting at the Battle of Antietam that a stray bullet allegedly passed through her sleeve and killed a man she was attending. Barton followed the Army of the Potomac back east towards the Rappahannock River and continued to tend to wounded soldiers in Falmouth after the Battle of Fredericksburg in December. Her bravery and tireless work, as well as her commitment to enduring the same conditions as the soldiers, earned her the affectionate moniker "Angel of the Battlefield."

In 1863, Barton left Virginia for South Carolina to be closer to her brother, Capt. David Barton, who was serving with Union forces at Hilton Head, outside of Charleston. The pace of military operations were slower in this theater, so Barton became actively involved in the work of fellow reformer Frances Dana Gage, who was educating former slaves who were left behind by their masters. Barton's involvement in this work ignited her commitment to the social equality of African Americans.

Barton's efforts to improve conditions for the troops, however, were undermined by the U.S. Sanitary Commission (USSC), which considered itself the sole agency of the Army's welfare and discouraged the participation of outsiders such as Barton. Barton continued her support as a nurse and a distributor of supplies for federal forces during the siege of Fort Wagner that summer but found continued resistance from both the military and the USSC in spite of all of her selfless efforts. During her time in South Carolina, Barton also allegedly had a romantic affair with a married Union officer, Col. John H. Elwell, which eventually soured. Barton would never marry.

Disillusioned with her experience in South Carolina, Barton returned to Washington, D.C., at the end of 1863. She spent the beginning of 1864 recovering from the Hilton Head trip and gathering supplies for the upcoming spring campaign of the Army of the Potomac.

Much as she had the two previous years, Barton traveled with Union forces, tending to the numerous wounded from Gen. Ulysses S. Grant's Overland Campaign. Although she avoided any official affiliation with the Army or the federal government, on June 23, 1864, the War Department named her head of diet and nursing of the X Corps Hospital under Gen. Benjamin Butler's Army of the James. Throughout the remainder of 1864, she served in this hospital as well as in those in both Fredericksburg and Petersburg, Virginia. At the end of the year, she returned home to Oxford to care for her dying brother Stephen. She remained there until the war's conclusion in April.

After the war, she committed herself to a nationwide campaign of searching for missing soldiers. Her work was highlighted by a visit to the former Union prison at Andersonville, Georgia, where she helped to locate and mark the graves of the nearly 15,000 federal soldiers who died there. In all, she located 22,000 of the nearly 62,000 missing soldiers missing during the conflict.

Barton also lectured in various cities about her wartime experiences and worked with the suffrage movement. During her lecture circuit, she gave over 200 speeches with such famous Americans as abolitionist William Lloyd Garrison, former slave and abolitionist Frederick Douglass, and author Mark Twain. Her busy lecture schedule and public appearance commitments drove Barton to ill health. In 1869, under doctor's orders, Barton traveled to Europe to rest and regain her health. During her visit, she found herself caught in the middle of combating European nations in the Franco-Prussian War of 1870–1871.

Much as she had during the Civil War, Barton performed nursing duties, establishing field hospitals and procuring medical supplies. It was through these efforts that she worked frequently with the International Red Cross and was urged by European patrons to establish a chapter in the United States.

By 1873, Barton had returned to Massachusetts to continue recovering from her poor health, but by 1876 she became active in the nation's capital once again. This time, she lobbied tirelessly for the United States to sign the Treaty of Geneva and for the nation to establish its own national Red Cross. Barton made her appeals directly to President Rutherford B. Hayes. Her efforts were finally rewarded in 1881 when the United States created the American Red Cross and made Barton its first president. A year later, the United States signed the Treaty of Geneva. Barton became the first female representative at the International Red Cross Convention. She was heralded as a hero for all of her efforts to officially include the United States.

As the head of the Red Cross, Barton approached her duties with the same indefatigable vigor she had shown during her work on the Civil War battlefields. She personally coordinated several major disaster relief efforts, including that launched after the historic 1900 Galveston, Texas, hurricane. Under Barton's tutelage, the organization provided food, clothing, shelter, and medical care to the victims of dozens of other emergencies throughout the United States, including floods, storms, epidemics, and other catastrophes.

In spite of all of its successes, the American Red Cross endured several growing pains such as disorganized bookkeeping and competition from rival organizations. Meanwhile, within the rank and file, many of Barton's subordinates viewed her leadership as inflexible and autocratic. Several argued that the organization had grown large enough for a more centralized, bureaucratic leadership rather than that of one individual. In 1904, Barton was forced to resign her position. She retired to Glen Echo, Maryland, where she published several books about her experiences and continued to support the causes of woman suffrage and civil rights.

Barton died on April 12, 1912, at her home in Glen Echo and was buried in the family cemetery plot in Oxford, Massachusetts.

Bradford A. Wineman

See also: American Red Cross; Civil War (1861–1865); Nursing; United States Sanitary Commission (USSC).

References and Further Reading

Barton, Clara. *The Story of My Childhood.* New York: Baker and Taylor Company, 1907.

Gilbo, Patrick F. *The American Red Cross: The First Century.* New York: Harper & Row, 1981.

Oates, Stephen B. *Woman of Valor: Clara Barton and the Civil War.* New York: The Free Press, 1995.

Pryor, Elizabeth Brown. *Clara Barton: Professional Angel.* Philadelphia: University of Pennsylvania Press, 1987.

BATES, ANN (1748–1801)

Schoolteacher, beekeeper, and Loyalist spy Ann Bates spent time in Pennsylvania, New York, and South Carolina during the American Revolution.

Details surrounding Bates's life before the Revolution are largely unknown. Bates's work as a schoolteacher suggests that she received some form of education as a child and gained proficiency in reading, writing, and arithmetic. Whether her training stemmed from a local school, hired tutor, or older family member is unknown. Like other girls in the mid-18th century, she likely received training in various household duties, such as cooking and sewing.

In addition to teaching, Bates supplemented her income through various other ventures, including bee keeping, managing a small shop, and tending animals. Her resourcefulness and self-sufficiency would prove indispensible during her stint as a spy for the British army.

Her loyalty to the British monarchy increased by way of her marriage to Joseph Bates, a British soldier who repaired faulty artillery. It is possible that the couple met, courted, and married during the British army's occupation of Philadelphia, which lasted from late September 1777 to June 1778. During this time, Ann made the acquaintance of John Cregge, an American Loyalist working for British intelligence. At Cregge's prompting, she agreed to work as a spy for the British.

Bates's residence in Philadelphia ended abruptly and roughly coincided with British general Sir Henry Clinton's order for British forces to vacate Philadelphia in June 1778. Upon reaching New York later that month, Bates met Maj. Drummond and was given her first assignment. Drummond ordered Ann to dress as a peddler and enter Gen. George Washington's camp, located at that time near White Plains, New York. Once inside the camp, Bates could expect to learn Washington's plans from another Loyalist spy positioned within the Continental Army. British intelligence agents used small, easily concealable tokens to identify one another.

Information about Bates and her work as an intelligence agent largely comes from her pension application to the British government and papers concerning Gen. Sir Henry Clinton's spy organization. Taken together, the documents provide a rough sketch of her participation in espionage activities in 1778. Using the last name of Barnes, Bates made a detour en route to New York, reaching White Plains on July 2 to inspect the Continental Army. Her disguise worked, and she gained entry into the camp, spending several days selling utilitarian items like thread and needles to soldiers. She was unsuccessful, however, in locating the Loyalist spy who had been serving in Washington's army as an officer. Unfazed by this development, Bates used her knowledge as wife to an artillery specialist to memorize the number of cannons in the camp. She also took note of the size and strength of the army before making her way back to New York City. Her first mission nearly ended in disaster, however. After leaving the camp, Bates was arrested and questioned for over a day. Her inquisitors, unable to find any incriminating evidence on her person, let her go free.

Bates completed three more missions in 1778, weaving in and out of Washington's camp with relative ease. In between selling her wares, she eavesdropped on soldiers' conversations, observed camp food provisions, learned of the Marquis de Lafayette's movements to Rhode Island, and counted artillery. Bates's luck ended in September when she came across a British deserter, a man named Smith, who recognized her as a spy. Though Bates could no longer navigate in and around American camps, she continued her work with British intelligence, conducting Loyalists through enemy territories.

Bates joined her husband and the British forces in Charleston, South Carolina, in 1780 before leaving for Britain in March 1781. Her marriage to Joseph Bates never produced any children. Sometime after their arrival in Britain, Joseph abandoned Ann, leaving her penniless and in poor health. She received a modest pension after much petitioning. Ann Bates died in 1801.

Carrie Glenn

See also: American Revolution (1775–1783); Espionage.

References and Further Reading

Bakeless, John. *Turncoats, Traitors, and Heroes*. Philadelphia: J.B. Lippincott Company, 1959.

Hastedt, Glenn P. *Spies, Wiretaps, and Secret Operations: A-J*. Santa Barbara, CA: ABC-CLIO, 2011.

BATTLE, MARY FRANCES "FANNIE" (1842–1924)

Mary Frances "Fannie" Battle was a scout and spy for the Confederacy during the American Civil War.

Battle was born in the Cane Ridge area near Nolensville, Tennessee, to Joel Allen Battle and Adeline Sanders Moseley Battle. As a teenager, she lived on the family plantation and attended Nashville Female Academy. When the Civil War broke out in 1861, the entire Battle family became directly involved in many aspects of the conflict. Battle's father organized a company, the Zollicoffer Guards, that eventually became Company B in the 20th Tennessee Infantry. He was captain of the company. He rose to the rank of colonel and gained command of the 20th Tennessee Regiment. During the Battle of Shiloh in April 1862, Fannie Battle's two brothers, Allen and William, were killed and her father was wounded and taken prisoner. En route to Nashville, Union troops came through Cane Ridge and burned the Battle family home. In March 1862, Fannie solidified her involvement in the war effort by joining a Confederate spy ring in Nashville.

From the time Union forces came through Tennessee in early 1862 through their occupation of Nashville, Fannie Battle served as a key link between the invading enemy and the Confederate troops. Battle and her sister-in-law, Harriet Booker, joined a group of scouts who attempted to gain information about the Union forces who occupied the city of Nashville. Many young women dated Union soldiers, so Battle easily obtained a pass to enter the city and did so several times to relay information about federal troop strength and position back to the Confederate lines. Sometimes, Battle would dress up as a boy in order to observe Union fortifications and talk to troops about campaign maneuvers. Her ability to penetrate the Union defenses and report inside information to Confederates was critical to the Southern war effort.

On December 7, 1863, Battle was stopped and searched by Union military police under the orders of Col. Truesdail. Battle was carrying documents intended for Confederate troops. Union soldiers arrested her with charges of spying, smuggling goods, and using a forged federal pass. Battle claimed she was indeed a Confederate and had forged a pass but that she was not a spy. The military police described Battle as attractive and well mannered, thus capable of luring Union soldiers into giving up army intelligence. Initially, federal troops imprisoned Battle at Camp Chase in Ohio, but when they learned of her father's rank in the Confederate army, they moved her to the Old Capitol Prison in Washington, D.C. Meanwhile, Col. Battle wrote Confederate secretary of war James Seddon for assistance in gaining his daughter's release. Seddon contacted Robert Old, the head of the Bureau of Exchange of Prisoners, to negotiate with Washington on a prisoner exchange. Old offered to exchange Battle and Booker in return for Union officers. On May 13, 1863, Old conducted the exchange through a flag-of-truce boat at City Point, Virginia. Battle returned to Nashville, where she lived for the remainder of the war.

After the war, Battle returned to a less-exciting life but continued to aid the people of her region. Battle taught arithmetic, geography, and spelling at Nashville public schools from 1870 to 1886. When the Cumberland River flooded in 1881, Battle helped the displaced victims through her leadership role in the Nashville Relief Society. Eventually, Battle became the leader of the Nashville Relief Society, later renamed the United Charities, where she served as secretary. Of the many groups Battle established through the United Charities, the most significant was a day-care facility for children of female cotton mill workers that opened in 1891. After her death, the Addison Avenue Day Home was renamed in her honor as the Fannie Battle Day Home for Children.

Battle died in 1924. She is buried in Mount Olivet Cemetery. Although Battle's career as a spy for the Confederate army ended with her capture, her activism and devotion for others remains a continuous legacy in Nashville. Every year since 1916, local children have continued the tradition of singing "Christmas Carols for Fannie Battle."

Lauren K. Thompson

See also: Boyd, Marie Isabella "Belle" (1844–1900); Civil War (1861–1865); Edmondson, Isabella "Belle" Buchanon (1840–1873); Espionage; Pigott, Emeline Jamison (1836–1919).

References and Further Reading

Bakeless, John. *Spies of the Confederacy.* Philadelphia: Lippincott, 1970.

Eggleston, Larry G. *Women in the Civil War: Extraordinary Stories of Soldiers, Spies, Nurses, Doctors, Crusaders, and Others.* Jefferson, NC: McFarland, 2003.

Lowry, Thomas P. *Confederate Heroines: 120 Southern Women Convicted by Union Military Justice.* Baton Rouge: Louisiana State University Press, 2006.

United States and Robert N. Scott. *The War of the Rebellion: A Compilation of the Official Records of the Union and Confederate Armies. Series II, Vol. 5.* Harrisburg, PA: National Historical Society, 1985.

BENJAMIN, ANNA NORTHEND (1874–1902)

During her short life, Anna Northend Benjamin, a pioneering American journalist, covered two major military conflicts: the Spanish-American War and the Philippine Insurrection. Her descriptive, lively, in-depth reports consistently provided a balanced view.

Benjamin was born in Salem, Massachusetts, on October 6, 1874. After graduating from St. Gabriel's School in Peekskill, New York, she began writing for periodicals. Among her earliest forays into journalism was a contribution to a paper published to raise funds for the Free Library of Orange, New Jersey. The "Woman's Edition of the Orange Chronicle" was issued in April 1895. It satirized editorial practice of the day by including a "Man's Page"—a counterpart to the "Woman's Page" on society and fashion in most contemporary newspapers. Though increasing numbers of women entered journalism in the late 19th century, their writing was usually confined to the women's pages, features, human interest stories, and stunt reporting rather than hard news.

Newspaper readership, already enormous in the 1890s, quadrupled during the Spanish-American War. Cuba's struggle for independence from Spain had begun attracting international attention in 1895. U.S. newspapers widely circulated sensationalist accounts of

Spanish brutality against the Cuban insurgents. Popular sentiment helped persuade the U.S. Congress to declare war on Spain on April 25, 1898. Hundreds of journalists from Great Britain, Canada, the United States, and Spain rushed to cover the ensuing conflict. Benjamin reported on the war for *Leslie's Weekly* even though the U.S. government banned women journalists from the war zone. Her first articles investigated conditions in Tampa and Key West as U.S. forces prepared to invade Cuba. Unlike the two other female correspondents working in Florida (Kathleen Blake Watkins for the Toronto *Mail and Express* and Katherine White for the Chicago *Record*), Benjamin focused directly on the military. She reported on inadequate troop rations and uniforms as well as the poor sanitation that later became a national scandal.

Rather than be left behind as the troops finally embarked for Cuba, Benjamin convinced the captain of a collier to transport her, along with his cargo of coal, to the U.S. Navy in Guantánamo. Cmdr. B. H. McCalla immediately sent her onward to Siboney and Santiago on the southeastern coast of the island. That proved fortunate because the decisive U.S. victory in the battle of Santiago was about to become a turning point in the war. Benjamin wrote several dispatches about the end of the siege and the city's surrender on July 17. The Armistice Protocol on August 12 ended hostilities very shortly thereafter.

In Cuba, Benjamin continued to write with a critical voice, exposing theft and intimidation of civilians by Theodore Roosevelt's celebrated Rough Riders regiment, the 1st United States Volunteer Cavalry, whom she called "Teddy's Terrors." She doggedly obtained information, from the pest house in Key West to Spanish trenches, interviewing Cuban residents as well as Americans. *Leslie's* proudly identified her as "our Special Correspondent at the Front."

Benjamin nursed troops and civilian passengers aboard the transport *Aransas* on their way back to New York. After her return, she gave illustrated lectures about her experiences. But a new war ignited in the Philippine Islands, which the United States had acquired from Spain under their peace treaty. Like Cuba, the Philippines had been in revolution against Spain; afterwards the Filipinos resisted the exchange of one colonial power for another. In May 1899, Benjamin headed to the Philippines to report on the insurrection for the *New York Tribune* and *San Francisco Chronicle*. She remained there for several months, avoiding the safety of Manila for rebel strongholds in the southern islands and Luzón. In one instance, she came under fire by rebels in an attack that killed two U.S. soldiers.

Though remembered principally as a war correspondent, Benjamin also wrote on other subjects, including on society and culture in Japan, Korea, China, and Russia, where she traveled extensively after her time in the Philippines. Her pieces, sometimes published with her own photographs, appeared in magazines such as *Outlook*, *Munsey's*, and *Ainslee's*, and (unsigned) in the *New York Tribune*. She died in January 20, 1902, of a tumor while on a visit to her sister in France.

Laura R. Prieto

See also: Spanish-American War (1898).

References and Further Reading

Berner, Brad K. *The Spanish-American War: A Historical Dictionary*. Lanham, MD: Scarecrow Press, 1998.

Brown, Charles B. "A Woman's Odyssey: The War Correspondence of Anna Benjamin." *Journalism Quarterly* (Fall 1969): 522–30.

Roth, Michael. *Historical Dictionary of War Journalism*. Westport CT: Greenwood Press, 1997.

BENTLEY, ELIZABETH TERRILL (1908–1963)

An American spy for the Soviet Union from 1938 to 1945, Elizabeth Terrill Bentley became an FBI informant who helped indict several prominent spies.

Born in New Milford, Connecticut, on January 1, 1908, Bentley graduated from Vassar College in 1930. While attending graduate school at Columbia University in 1933, she won a fellowship to the University of Florence. Returning to New York during the Great Depression in July 1934, Bentley experienced difficulty in obtaining employment. Her experience of living under Italian dictatorship prompted her to join the American League against War and Fascism in early 1935. The League was a communist underground group designed to develop and direct American opposition to authoritarian regimes in Europe. She joined the Communist Party (CP-USA) during the same period while working as an investigator with New York City's Emergency Home Relief Bureau, a Harlem-based welfare agency.

Elizabeth Bentley, an American spy for the Soviet Union, defected to the FBI in 1945 and passed information about the American Communist Party and the Soviet Union to the U.S. government. Her list of more than 100 suspected communists triggered the red scare and communist witch-hunt of the 1950s in the United States. (Library of Congress)

Bentley's first foray into espionage came in 1938 during her employment at the Italian Library of Information in New York. She discovered that the library was part of the Italian government's Ministry of Propaganda and was responsible for the production of anti-communist and anti-Semitic literature. She gathered information on pro-Fascist activity and reported it to her controller, Soviet secret police operative Jacob Golos. In 1940, he was forced to register as an agent of the Soviet government under the Foreign Agents Registration Act. Golos, by then in a romantic relationship with Bentley, used her to pass secret messages and documents from his contacts. Most of Bentley's interactions were with the Silvermaster group, a network of spies centered on Nathan Gregory Silvermaster, an economist with the U.S. War Production Board. This was one of the most important Soviet espionage operations in the United States, providing confidential data including U.S. munitions production levels and the Allies' schedule for opening a second front in Europe.

After Golos's death in November 1943, Bentley assumed his role as controller of the Silvermaster group and informant to her new contact in Soviet intelligence, Iskhak Akhmerov, an undercover spy chief working without diplomatic cover. Under pressure to relinquish the spy network to Akhmerov, Bentley initially defied this order and also took over as network handler of the Perlo group, which had sources in the U.S. Department of Treasury, the War Production Board, and the Senate La Follette Subcommittee on Civil Liberties. In June 1944, the KGB began to remove the spy networks from Bentley's control due to her excessive drinking and their desire to professionalize the spy network. In late 1944, Bentley was ordered to withdraw from the network completely.

In October 1945, CP-USA member Louis Budenz renounced communism and offered to provide the FBI with information on American communists. He knew about Bentley's activities, thereby placing her at risk of arrest by the FBI. One month later, she defected, undergoing a series of debriefing interviews in which she implicated more than 100 people in spying for the Soviet Union. Her defection severely disrupted Soviet espionage across the United States as Soviet intelligence services ordered a freeze of virtually all intelligence activities by the KGB until 1947. However, a security breach foiled the FBI's year-long attempt to employ Bentley as a double agent, and FBI surveillance of the people she accused revealed no evidence that could be used in prosecution. Attorney General Tom C. Clark presented Bentley's case to a grand jury. The communist-focused grand jury lasted from March 1947 until July 1948, failing to indict anybody named by Bentley, instead handing down sealed indictments against the 12 members of the national board of the CP-USA.

In 1948, Bentley testified before the Senate Permanent Subcommittee on Investigations and the House Un-American Activities Committee, describing her years as a communist and naming her undercover contacts. Bentley played a role in many important espionage trials of the early Cold War period, including those of William Remington and of Julius and Ethel Rosenberg. Initially dubbed the Red Spy Queen in newspaper headlines, she was increasingly attacked by critics who focused on her extramarital relationships and the inaccuracies contained in her 1951 autobiography *Out of Bondage*. The FBI provided her with financial assistance during the early 1950s, and despite periods of emotional instability, she supported herself through a series of teaching jobs. Bentley died in New Haven, Connecticut, on December 3, 1963.

Ruth E. Martin

See also: Cold War (ca. 1947–1991); Espionage; Rosenberg, Ethel Greenglass (1915–1953); World War II (1941–1945).

References and Further Reading

Bentley, Elizabeth. *Out of Bondage: The Story of Elizabeth Bentley.* New York: Ballantine Books, 1988.

Haynes, John Earl, and Harvey Klehr. *Early Cold War Spies: The Espionage Trials That Shaped American Politics.* New York: Cambridge University Press, 2006.

Kessler, Lauren. *Clever Girl: Elizabeth Bentley, the Spy Who Ushered in the McCarthy Era.* New York: Harper Collins, 2003.

Olmsted, Kathryn S. *Red Spy Queen: A Biography of Elizabeth Bentley.* Chapel Hill: University of North Carolina Press, 2002.

Mary McLeod Bethune fought to achieve social, economic, and educational opportunities for African Americans, especially for African American women. (Library of Congress)

BETHUNE, MARY McLEOD (1875–1955)

Social activist Mary McLeod Bethune fought for civil rights and founded the Daytona Normal and Industrial Institute for Negro Girls, better known today as Bethune-Cookman College.

Born on July 10, 1875, in South Carolina to parents who had been slaves, Bethune took an early and active interest in her education. Hoping to become a missionary to Africa, she attended the Institute for Home and Foreign Missions in Chicago. When told that there was no need for black missionaries, Bethune decided that she would teach. In 1904, she founded the Daytona Normal and Industrial Institute for Negro Girls in Daytona, Florida, with the goal of teaching skills that would allow women to find jobs. Although from the beginning the school accepted boys as well as girls, it did not officially become coeducational until 1923, when it merged with the Cookman Institute for Men.

In addition to running the school, Bethune worked towards gaining more rights for African Americans. Although Bethune initially did most of her work through the guise of women's associations such as the National Association of Colored Women's Clubs (NACW), she soon ventured out on her own and achieved national prominence. However, Bethune never left these women's organizations behind because she recognized their importance. In 1935, she created the National Council of Negro Women (NCNW). Her work in NCNW allowed Bethune to become close with First Lady Eleanor Roosevelt, who subsequently encouraged her husband to allow Bethune to become involved in his administration.

Consequently, some of Bethune's most important work occurred during Franklin Delano Roosevelt's presidency. As president of NCNW, Bethune was troubled by the lack of federal jobs available to African Americans, especially to black women. She constantly pushed the president and first lady to make changes so that more opportunities would be available. In 1936, Bethune was named head of the National Youth Administration (NYA), which served the dual purpose of giving part-time employment to students so that they could afford to continue their education and also to give jobs and training to youths who were not in school and were unemployed. President Roosevelt was so impressed with Bethune that she was given the title of director of Negro affairs for the NYA, becoming one of the few women to hold such power in his administration. While in this position, she was able to give help to over 600,000 African American youths.

When the United States entered into World War II on December 7, 1941, Bethune dedicated herself to the war effort. Her goal throughout the war was to advance the cause of civil rights while supporting her country. One of the ways in which Bethune wanted to help was by getting students at Bethune-Cookman involved with the war, whether it was by signing men up to be in the armed services or by encouraging her students to win the war from home by applying to take industrial jobs. With her position in the NYA, she was able to encourage African American youths throughout the country to become involved. One of Bethune's primary goals was working to ensure that the military, which was still segregated, gave blacks and whites equal treatment. She also became involved with the Women's Army Corps (WAC), serving as assistant director.

During World War II, the NYA was disbanded because so many African American youths were absorbed into the war effort, yet Bethune kept busy. Knowing that she could not keep up with all of her responsibilities, in 1942 Bethune resigned as president of Bethune-Cookman College so she could focus more on WAC and the NCNW. Although conditions were still not fair for blacks, Bethune remained encouraged by news such as when the Navy announced that it would allow black women to join Women Accepted for Volunteer Emergency Service (WAVES) and the Coast Guard accepted African American women for SPAR ("Semper Paratus—Always Ready"). She also strove to improve conditions on the homefront. She worked with Walter White, then head of the National Association for the Advancement of Colored People (NAACP), to help set up hospitals for returning veterans and was able to ensure that at least some of the hospitals would not be segregated. At the behest of Gen. George Marshall, Bethune went to inspect hospitals and reported to him on their conditions as well as on the morale of soldiers there. Bethune also worked to improve the spirits of troops stationed overseas. Although it was not publicized during the war, she wrote to thousands of servicemen and women, giving them advice and support.

When it came time to draw up the charter for the United Nations in 1945, a conference in San Francisco was planned to bring together delegates from 50 nations. Roosevelt wanted to use this conference to show off the United States to the rest of the world, and he wanted a wide range of delegates present to represent the country. Eleanor

Roosevelt insisted that Bethune be included, but she was not initially invited to participate. The NCNW was entirely excluded from the conference with the explanation that it was too new of an organization to get involved. Bethune was named an alternate for the NAACP so that she could attend. Roosevelt died before the San Francisco conference took place; however, Bethune still was present and was the only black woman in attendance. Bethune, along with Walter White and W. E. B. Du Bois, issued a plea calling for a World Bill of Rights, which was concerned with the status of colored people around the world. Their appeal is thought to have influenced the final charter of what was to become the United Nations. Bethune was especially elated three years later when the United Nations issued its Universal Declaration on Human Rights.

Throughout the 1940s, Bethune remained active, traveling to Haiti and Liberia. She also continued to fight for equal rights for blacks in the United States until her death on May 18, 1955, of a heart attack.

Elizabeth Ann Bryant

See also: African American Women; Roosevelt, Eleanor (1844–1962); United States Coast Guard Women's Reserve (SPAR); Women Accepted for Volunteer Emergency Service (WAVES); Women's Army Corps (WAC); World War II (1941–1945).

References and Further Reading

Hanson, Joyce. *Mary McLeod Bethune and Black Women's Political Activism.* Columbia: University of Missouri Press, 2003.

Long, Nancy Ann Zrinyi. *Life and Legacy of Mary McLeod Bethune.* Boston: Pearson, 2006.

Peare, Catherine Owens. *Mary McLeod Bethune.* New York: Vanguard Press, 1951.

BICKERDYKE, MARY ANN BALL "MOTHER" (1817–1901)

Mary Ann Ball Bickerdyke, a popular hospital administrator and nurse for Union soldiers during the Civil War, earned the nickname "Mother" from her patients.

Born on July 19, 1817, on a farm in Knox County, Ohio, Mary Ann Ball was the daughter of Hiram and Annie Ball. When she was 17 months old, her mother

Civil War nurse Mary Ann Ball "Mother" Bickerdyke organized Union military hospitals and worked to improve sanitary conditions. (Brockett, Linus Pierpont & Mary C. Vaughan, Woman's Work in the Civil War: A Record of Heroism, Patriotism and Patience, 1867)

died, and she went to live with her maternal grandparents. Upon their deaths, she lived with her maternal uncle on a farm near Cincinnati, Ohio. Self-taught in the field of herbal medicine, she assisted doctors in Cincinnati during the cholera epidemic of 1837. Ball married Robert Bickerdyke, a widower with three boys, in 1847. The couple moved to Galesburg, Illinois, in 1856. After her husband's death in 1859, Bickerdyke supported herself and her children by practicing botanic medicine.

In 1861, after hearing of the deplorable conditions at the military hospital at Cairo, Illinois, the members of Bickerdyke's church collected $500 worth of supplies for the wounded soldiers, many of whom were from Galesburg. Church officials charged Bickerdyke with personally delivering the supplies to Cairo. Sensing a need for her services, she remained in Cairo and served as a volunteer nurse. Bickerdyke's energy and concern for Union troops made her wildly popular with wounded soldiers, who fondly called her "Mother Bickerdyke." Her ability to organize military hospitals, especially her concern for their sanitary conditions, was promptly brought to the attention of Brig. Gen. Ulysses S. Grant.

Shortly after capturing Fort Donelson, Tennessee, in February 1862, Grant, now a major general, brought Bickerdyke and fellow nurse Mary Jane Stafford to the field hospital at Fort Donelson. Bickerdyke eventually worked on the hospital ships administered by the Western Sanitary Commission that transported wounded soldiers and supplies on the Mississippi River and its tributaries. By the beginning of 1863, Bickerdyke

was the chief of nursing for Grant's troops. From April to July 1863, she accompanied Grant during the Second Vicksburg Campaign.

Bickerdyke routinely led campaigns to solicit supplies from the civilian population for wounded Union troops. Unfortunately, officers and surgeons frequently expropriated supplies designated for the wounded soldiers. Bickerdyke openly criticized Union officers and surgeons involved in this activity and reported their actions to Grant. Although many of Grant's staff officers complained about the outspoken Bickerdyke's disregard of military protocol, Grant, who claimed that he was unable to force her to conform to military procedures, consistently supported Bickerdyke. A highly resourceful and energetic nurse and administrator, Bickerdyke believed that it was her Christian duty to help the wounded soldiers as efficiently and quickly as possible.

As Grant's forces plunged deeper into the Confederacy, Bickerdyke followed the troops and established hospitals along the way. By the end of the war, Bickerdyke had aided the wounded on 19 battlefields, participated in the establishment of hundreds of field hospitals, and proved instrumental in saving the lives of thousands of wounded soldiers, frequently searching battlefields at night with a lantern for wounded soldiers. Her popularity was so immense that soldiers frequently welcomed her with frenzied cheers rivaling those awarded to Grant. Bickerdyke's efforts even gained her the acclaim of Brig. Gen. William Tecumseh Sherman, a man who routinely excluded women from his camp. Popular legend holds that Bickerdyke was the only woman that Sherman ever welcomed into his camp. At the conclusion of the war, Sherman insisted that Bickerdyke ride at the head of the XV Corps during the Grand Review of the Armies in Washington, D.C.

Once the war ended, Bickerdyke settled in Salina, Kansas, with her sons and opened a boarding house and dining hall for war veterans moving to Kansas. She also assisted war veterans and volunteer nurses in their quest for pensions from the federal government. Bickerdyke eventually helped more than 300 female volunteer nurses earn federal pensions. Although she had been a volunteer for the duration of the Civil War, the U.S. Congress in 1886 awarded Bickerdyke a $25 annual pension. Bickerdyke died in Bunker Hill, Kansas, on November 8, 1901.

Michael R. Hall

See also: Civil War (1861–1865); Nursing.

References and Further Reading

Baker, Nina Brown. *Cyclone in Calico: The Story of Mary Ann Bickerdyke*. Boston: Little, Brown and Company, 1953.

De Leeuw, Adele. *Civil War Nurse Mary Ann Bickerdyke*. New York: Julian Messner, 1973.

Schultz, Jane E. "The Inhospitable Hospital: Gender and Professionalism in Civil War Medicine." *Signs* 17, no. 2 (Winter 1992): 363–92.

BLACKWELL, ELIZABETH (1821–1910)

The first female doctor to graduate from medical school in the United States,

Elizabeth Blackwell was responsible for training numerous women as nurses for the Union Army during the Civil War. She later cofounded and taught at the London School of Medicine for Women.

Blackwell was born on February 3, 1821, in Bristol, England. She was one of nine children born to sugar refiner Samuel Blackwell and Hannah Lane Blackwell. Her father was one of the founders of the Bristol Abolition Society and a devout member of the Society of Friends (Quakers), which directly influenced his children's own social activism. During the Bristol Riots of 1831, Samuel's business was destroyed by fire. In 1832, the family left Great Britain for the United States and established a refinery in New York City.

Elizabeth Blackwell was the first woman to receive a medical degree in the United States. During the Civil War, she helped to create the Women's Central Relief Association in New York City and helped to train nurses for the Union. (Library of Congress)

The Panic of 1837 hit Blackwell's business hard, and the family moved to Cincinnati in an effort to reestablish the refinery business. In 1838, only three months after arriving in Cincinnati, Samuel Blackwell died, nearly leaving the family destitute. Elizabeth, her mother, and two older sisters opened a small private school. For a few years, Elizabeth worked as a schoolteacher in Kentucky and North Carolina.

While teaching, Elizabeth became interested in the study of medicine. In 1845, she read medical works under the direction of Dr. John Dickson of Asheville, North Carolina, and his brother, Dr. Henry Dickson of Charleston, South Carolina. Rejected by medical schools in New York City and Philadelphia because of her gender, she finally was accepted by Geneva Medical College in upstate New York in 1847. Blackwell graduated at the top of her class in 1849 and became the first female medical doctor in the United States.

Upon graduation, she worked with patients at a Philadelphia almshouse, where she acquired a considerable amount of knowledge related to the study of epidemiology. She then moved to England, where she worked with Dr. James Paget in London, and where she developed a close relationship with Florence Nightingale and Elizabeth Anderson, pioneers in women's medicine in Great Britain. During this period, she also published her own observations on gender discrimination, *The Laws of Life* (1852). In 1853, she returned to the United States, where she was denied positions in New York City's hospitals. Along with her sister Emily, who had also received her medical degree, and

Dr. Marie Zakrzewska, she established the New York Infirmary for Indigent Women and Children. The infirmary became the focal point for the presentation of lectures on hygiene and preventive medicine, including the training and placement of sanitary workers in the city's slum areas.

In 1861, with the outbreak of the Civil War, Blackwell and other female reformers established the Women's Central Relief Association in New York City. The association set up an institute to train female nurses for the Union Army. The association was one of numerous local aid societies that came under the organizational structure of the United States Sanitary Commission (USSC). Blackwell gave nursing training to many socially connected women. These women served as volunteers aboard hospital ships such as the *Daniel Webster*, the *Ocean Queen*, and the *Spaulding* and subsequently as army nurses and sanitary relief workers. Blackwell, along with her sister Emily and with Mary Livermore, played an instrumental role in the development of the USSC during the conflict, which also built and ran hospitals and soldiers' lodging houses, provided blankets, and delivered letters and telegrams to men in the field. Although the USSC had male leadership, Blackwell served as one of its principal directors.

After the war, in 1868, she and Emily founded the Women's Medical College of the New York Infirmary, where Elizabeth taught as professor of hygiene. After returning to England the next year, Blackwell helped form the National Health Society, designed to promote educational awareness to health and hygiene issues, and the London School of Medicine for Women. From 1875 through 1907, she served as professor of gynecology at the medical college. Inspired by her father's own social justice activism, she also became involved in reform endeavors such as municipal reform co-op communities, prisoner rehabilitation, and the Garden City movement.

After suffering a fall in 1907, from which she never fully recovered, Blackwell died from a stroke on May 31, 1910, at her home in Hastings in Sussex.

Charles F. Howlett

See also: Civil War (1861–1865); Nursing; United States Sanitary Commission (USSC).

References and Further Reading

Baker, Rachel. *The First Woman Doctor: The Story of Elizabeth Blackwell, M.D.* New York: J. Messner, 1944.

Blackwell, Elizabeth. *Work in Opening the Medical Profession to Women.* London: Longmans, Green, 1895.

Frederickson, George M. *The Inner Civil War: Northern Intellectuals and the Crisis of the Union.* New York: Harper & Row, 1965.

Vietor, Agnes C. *A Woman's Quest: The Life of Marie E. Zakrzewska, M.D.* New York: D. Appleton & Co, 1924.

Wilson, Dorothy Clarke. *Lone Woman: The Story of Elizabeth Blackwell, the First Female Doctor.* Boston: Little, Brown, 1970.

Wright, Mary. *Elizabeth Blackwell of Bristol, The First Female Doctor.* Bristol, UK: Bristol Branch of the Historical Association, 1995.

BLAIR, LORINDA ANNA [ANNIE ETHERIDGE HOOKS] (CA. 1840–1913)

Annie Etheridge Hooks, born Lorinda Anna Blair, is best known for her bravery as a nurse in the Civil War, tending to wounded soldiers on the front lines of battle.

Lorinda Anna Blair was born in Detroit, Michigan, around 1840, with sources placing her year of birth anywhere between 1832 and 1844. After her mother died when Annie was young, she moved with her father, a merchant, to Milwaukee.

In 1860, Annie married James Etheridge. She returned to Detroit, where she enlisted as a regimental nurse when her husband joined the 2nd Michigan Infantry in 1861. After training for six weeks, the regiment left for Washington, D.C. By this point, she was the only woman left out of the 20 women who had enlisted with her.

Named the Daughter of the Regiment, she served with the 2nd Michigan Infantry for three years. On July 18, 1861, her regiment first engaged in war at Blackburn's Ford, with the Union troops losing 78 men and the Confederates 68. A few days later, on July 21, 1861, at the First Battle of Bull Run (Manassas), her regiment was ordered to guard an escape route to Washington. Shortly after this battle, her husband deserted, but she stayed on with the regiment.

In the spring of 1862, Blair left the 2nd Michigan Infantry to work on hospital ships, transporting wounded soldiers to hospitals in New York, Washington, and Baltimore. In August 1862, she returned to regiment work, this time with the 3rd Michigan Infantry Regiment. That month, her regiment was involved in the Second Battle of Bull Run (Manassas), and Blair was on the front lines tending to the injured.

Throughout the war, Blair aided the wounded, serving in 32 battles, including the Battle of Antietam, the Battle of Fredericksburg, the Battle of Gettysburg, and the Battle of Chancellorsville. Besides providing medical care, there are accounts of her cooking and serving food to the soldiers. Even though she bravely served on the front lines of many of the war's bloodiest battles, the only wound she ever received was a shot to the hand.

In June 1864, the veterans of the 3rd Michigan Infantry, including Blair, were transferred to the 5th Michigan Infantry Regiment, with which she served from 1864 to July 5, 1865, when it was mustered out of service. During this time, she also worked in a Union military hospital in City Point, Virginia, during the winter.

After the war, Annie worked as a clerk in the U.S. Pension Office in Washington. In 1870, she married Charles E. Hooks, a Civil War veteran of the 7th Connecticut Infantry. In 1886, Congress authorized her to receive a $25-a-month pension acknowledging her military service. She died in 1913 and was buried with honors in Arlington National Cemetery.

Sigrid Kelsey

See also: Civil War (1861–1865); Nursing; Vivandieres.

References and Further Reading

Eggleston, Larry G. *Women in the Civil War: Extraordinary Stories of Soldiers, Spies, Nurses, Doctors, Crusaders, and Others.* Jefferson, NC: McFarland, 2003.

Leonard, Elizabeth D. *All the Daring of the Soldier: Women of the Civil War Armies.* New York: W. W. Norton, 1999.

Schultz, Jane E. *Women at the Front: Hospital Workers in Civil War America.* Chapel Hill: University of North Carolina Press, 2004.

BLAKE, ESTHER McGOWIN (1897–1979)

Often referred to as the first woman in the Air Force, Esther M. Blake enlisted on July 8, 1948, on the first minute of the first hour of the first day that women were allowed to join the Air Force. Prior to her enlistment in the Air Force, she worked in the Miami Air Depot during World War II and served in the Women's Army Corps (WAC).

Born in 1897, she was a young woman during World War I. By the time the United States entered World War II in December 1941, Blake was a widow and the mother of two grown sons who both joined the military and fought during wartime.

Blake's active military service began originally in March of 1944. Up until then, she had been supporting the war effort working at the Miami Air Depot as a civilian employee. When her oldest son, Lt. Julius Blake, was reported missing, she ended her service as a civilian. Instead, she decided to enlist in the U.S. Army Air Forces as a member of the WAC. Her younger son reported that her reason for joining was that she hoped by her service to free a solider from clerical work in order to fight so that the war could end more swiftly.

Women had already been supporting the military, especially the war effort, in many capacities. In fact, at least 350,000 women served in the U.S. armed forces, both at home and abroad, during World War II. Blake served in the WAC for one year in the Alaskan division, being assigned to several bases including in the Yukon Territory near the Aleutians. She was discharged in 1945. By then, there were more than 100,000 women in the WAC and 6,000 female officers serving in the Army Air Forces. Blake did not end her military service in 1945 with the end of the war but, after a short return to her civilian job in Miami, answered a call back to service in the WAC in 1947, this time at Fort McPherson near Atlanta.

Eventually, both of Blake's sons—Lt. Julius Blake, who had been shot down over Belgium flying a B-17 Flying Fortress out of England, and Lt. Tom Blake, who had been shot down while serving in B-25 Mitchell medium bombers in Italy—returned home from combat safely. They were heavily decorated with service medals.

It was while Blake was serving at Fort McPherson that the National Security Act of 1947 established the U.S. Air Force as separate branch of military service distinct from the U.S. Army (September 18, 1947). The government soon followed this act with one integrating the military. Blake was serving her second enlistment in the WAC, when President Truman signed into law the Women's Armed Services Integration Act on June 12, 1948, paving the way for women like Blake to expand their service to the regular armed forces. Blake enlisted in Miami, Florida, for regular Air Force duty in the first minute of the first hour it was legal for women to do so. She remained active with the Air Force until 1954, when she took up a civil service post at the Veterans Regional Headquarters in Montgomery, Alabama.

Blake died on October 17, 1979. Her achievements were honored in 1987 when the Air Force Senior Non-Commissioned Officer Academy at Maxwell Air Force Base in Alabama named one of its student dormitories in her honor.

Kathryn A. Broyles

See also: Women in the Air Force (WAF); Women's Armed Services Integration Act of 1948; Women's Army Corps (WAC); World War I (1914–1918); World War II (1941–1945).

References and Further Reading

Holm, Jeanne. *Women in the Military: An Unfinished Revolution*. Novato, CA: Presidio Press, 1992.

Merry, Lois K. *Women Military Pilots of World War II: A History with Biographies of American, British, Russian and German Aviators*. Jefferson, NC: McFarland & Company, 2010.

Schwartz, Heather E. *Women of the U.S. Air Force: Aiming High*. North Mankato, MN: Capstone Press, 2011.

BLALOCK, SARAH MALINDA [SAMUEL BLALOCK] (1839–1903)

Malinda Blalock was one of only two women known to have fought for both the Confederacy and the Union during the Civil War.

A product of backwoods Appalachia, much of Blalock's life story is missing from the historical record, and some of what can be reconstructed is based on the tenuous information gathered from local folklore and oral traditions. Malinda Blalock was born Sarah Malinda Pritchard in Alexander County, North Carolina. According to her gravestone, she was born on March 10, 1839. While attending school in Watauga County, she met William "Keith" Blalock, a neighbor who was 10 years Pritchard's senior. Despite the age difference and a multigenerational feud that existed between the Pritchards and the Blalocks, the two married in either 1856 or 1861.

The couple resided in the Grandfather Mountain area of western North Carolina, where Keith was a farmer. The residents of this area—like those of many mountainous regions of the South—contained disproportionately large numbers of Union sympathizers. Despite Keith's Unionist leanings, he soon enlisted in the 26th North Carolina Regiment, a unit commanded by Col. Zebulon B. Vance, the state's future governor. Although Keith's enlistment may seem at odds with his political ideology, he planned to defect to the Union army once his unit reached the battlefront. It is also possible that Keith wished to deceive some secessionist neighbors into believing he was a loyal Confederate.

Malinda Blalock, despite some Southern sympathies, was unwilling to be separated from her husband. She cut her hair and stole some of Keith's clothing to disguise herself as a man. Claiming to be Keith's younger brother, Malinda assumed the name Samuel Blalock and enlisted in her husband's regiment. Unfortunately for the couple's duplicitous scheme, the regiment was not transferred to the front in Virginia but headed to eastern North Carolina. Malinda continued to march and drill with the men in the unit. The Blalocks fought together in a handful of minor engagements during the war's early months. It is not known why Keith and Malinda never defected during these battles.

In spring 1862, the unit was involved in a skirmish near the Neuse River. During this action, Malinda was wounded in the shoulder. While the regimental surgeon was operating on Malinda's wound, her true sex was revealed. His wife's ruse now over, Keith knew she would soon be discharged. Apparently every bit as committed to his wife as she was to him, Keith disrobed and rolled around in a batch of poison ivy. Afraid that he had some sort of contagious illness, Keith's superiors allowed his discharge as well. The Blalocks returned to Grandfather Mountain.

Fearing that Keith would be conscripted back into the Confederate Army once his outbreak subsided, the Blalocks absconded deep into the North Carolina mountains and eventually into Tennessee. On June 1, 1864, Keith joined the command of notorious Union partisan Col. George W. Kirk. Keith and Malinda Blalock were soon leading Union raids and partaking in other guerilla activities in their native state. With her loyalty now shifted to the Union, Malinda became one of only two women known to have fought for both sides during the Civil War, the other being Mary Ann Pitman.

Initially the couple's partisan band targeted their secessionist counterparts. As often occurred with guerilla units in the Civil War, however, Keith and Malinda Blalock and their comrades soon degenerated into bandits and marauders. Similar to more famous groups in Kansas and Missouri, such as those led by William Clarke Quantrill and William "Bloody Bill" Anderson, the Blalocks began thieving and murdering for their own motives. It is also possible that their partisan activities gave the Blalocks the opportunity to settle prewar grudges.

Although they were both wounded during their wartime activities, Malinda and Keith Blalock survived the Civil War. They returned to their home, where Keith resumed his career as a farmer.

Malinda Blalock died on March 9, 1903. Keith survived his wife by 10 years, dying in 1913. The couple is buried in Montezuma Cemetery in Avery County, North Carolina.

Robert L. Glaze

See also: Civil War (1861–1865).

References and Further Reading

Blanton, DeAnne, and Lauren M. Cook. *They Fought Like Demons: Women Soldiers in the Civil War.* New York: Vintage Press, 2003.

Hall, Richard. *Women on the Civil War Battlefront.* Lawrence: University Press of Kansas, 2006.

Hardy, Michael C. *Remembering Avery County: Old Tales From North Carolina's Youngest County.* Charleston, SC: History Press, 2007.

Stevens, Peter F. *Rebels in Blue: The Story of Keith and Malinda Blalock.* Dallas, TX: Taylor, 2000.

BLATCH, HARRIOT EATON STANTON (1856–1940)

Harriot Eaton Stanton Blatch was a leader in the suffrage campaign and strong advocate for women workers.

Harriot Eaton Stanton was born on January 20, 1856, in Seneca Falls, New York. She was the sixth of seven children of Elizabeth Cady Stanton, a leader in the women's suffrage movement, and

Harriot Stanton Blatch brought fresh energy to the feminist movement through her work with the Women's Political Union from 1910 to 1915. During World War I, she highlighted the opportunities that wartime work offered to women. (Library of Congress)

Henry Brewster Stanton, a lawyer, state senator, and fervent abolitionist. Harriot was educated in private schools and graduated with honors from Vassar College in 1878. She also attended the Boston School of Oratory and traveled to Germany as a tutor from 1880 to 1881. Upon her return, she contributed a chapter on Lucy Stone's American Women Suffrage Association to *History of Women Suffrage*, a work written by her mother and Susan B. Anthony.

In 1882, she married British business-man William Henry Blatch and moved with him to England. They had two daughters, although one died in early childhood. While in England, Blatch grew increasingly politically active. She joined the socialist Fabian Society, Women's Liberal Federation, and Women's Franchise League. She formed a close friendship with Emmeline Pankhurst, founder of the British Women's Social and Political Union.

Blatch returned to the United States with her family in 1902 after her mother became ill. Upon her mother's death, Blatch attempted to reinvigorate the suffrage movement, which she believed had gotten stale and too conservative. The core of Blatch's philosophy was that suffrage would only be won by economically independent working women.

From 1907 to 1910, she launched and led the Equality League of Self-Supporting Women, an organization to support women's economic independence and unionization for women workers. Blatch's opinionated and aggressive approach included open-air rallies, suffrage parades, and marches. Aggravating several conservative leaders in the suffrage movement, Blatch was known for her skilled use of political theater and publicity stunts. When the League was dissolved in 1910, she created the Women's Political Union (WPU) to work more actively with politicians on women's issues. In 1917 Blatch merged the WPU with the more militant Congressional Union led by Alice Paul. This joint organization later became the National Woman's Party.

In 1915, upon her husband's death, Blatch returned to England to address his affairs. During her time abroad, she observed the war in Europe and became convinced that the United States should join with the Allies to fight Germany and that the war could advance the feminist cause. She returned to the United States in 1917. When the United States entered the war, Blatch's focus on suffrage shifted towards one on women's war work. Arguing that when men went to war, women went to work, Blatch broke with many of the more conservative suffragettes serving on the advisory Women's Committee.

She published *Mobilizing Woman-Power* in 1918. In it Blatch emphasized her support of the war and the opportunities that it could afford to women. She described mobilization efforts of European women and urged that American women follow suit by working on farms and in factories. However, rather than expecting women to go back home at the conclusion of the war, Blatch hoped that the experience of wartime work would spark a revolution for women.

During World War I, Blatch campaigned for the professionalization of women workers involved in the war effort. She became head of the Food Administration's Speakers Bureau and a leader of the Women's Land Army of

America. In addition, she urged the military to provide military rank to nurses in military service and chaired the New York arm of the Committee to Secure Rank for Nurses in 1918. She argued in front of the House Committee on Military Affairs in April 1918 in favor of changing military regulations to allow all nurses to receive officer commissions.

After the war, Blatch continued to write. She published *A Women's Point of View: Some Roads to Peace*, a study of the causes and effects of World War I and American women's wartime employment, in 1920. With her brother, she coedited and published her mother's biography and papers in 1922. She published her own memoirs, *Challenging Years*, in 1940.

Blatch worked for the remainder of her life as a staunch advocate for women's rights. She aligned with the National Woman's Party and served as chairman of their congressional committee in the campaign for the Equal Rights Amendment. She joined the Socialist Party but was never content with its treatment of female workers. She worked for the League of Nations and a variety of other liberal causes.

Blatch died on November 20, 1940, in Greenwich, Connecticut.

Kate Wells

See also: Women's Land Army; World War I (1914–1918).

References and Further Reading

Blatch, Harriet Stanton, and Alma Lutz. *Challenging Years: The Memoirs of Harriot Stanton Blatch*. Westport, CT: Hyperion Press, 1976.

Dubois, Ellen Carol. "Harriot Stanton Blatch and the Transformation of Class Relations among Woman Suffragists." *Gender, Class, Race, and Reform in the Progressive Era*. Lexington: University Press of Kentucky, 1991.

Dubois, Ellen Carol. *Harriot Stanton Blatch and the Winning of Woman Suffrage*. New Haven, CT: Yale University Press, 1997.

Jensen, Kimberly. "A Base Hospital Is Not a Coney Island Dance Hall." *Frontiers: A Journal of Women Studies* 26, no. 2 (2005): 206–35.

BLODGETT, KATHARINE BURR (1898–1979)

A highly respected research physicist, Katharine Burr Blodgett became a prominent scientist at a time when few women were accepted in the profession. She is credited with the invention of nonreflective glass and made major advancements related to the technology of gas masks, smoke screens, and other military equipment.

Blodgett was born in 1898 in Schenectady, New York. Her father, an employee with General Electric (GE), died only weeks before her birth. Blodgett's mother moved with her and her siblings first to New York City and later to France for several years. After a brief return to the United States, Blodgett's mother once again took the children to Europe. This time they settled in Germany; Blodgett's early experience with the German language proved highly useful in her future academic career. Throughout her time in Europe and the United States, Blodgett received an excellent education at private primary and secondary schools. At only 15 years of age, she won a scholarship contest and began attending Bryn Mawr College.

In 1917, after graduating second in her class with a degree in physics, Blodgett began working on her master's degree in the University of Chicago's Department of Physics. She wrote her master's thesis on the effect of certain gases in gas masks, a subject that had recently attracted major interest as a result of the chemical warfare used in World War I. In 1918, after receiving her master's degree, Blodgett returned to Schenectady to work in GE's labs. She started out as a lab assistant to Dr. Irving Langmuir, a renowned physicist who would go on to win the Nobel Prize in 1932. During her early years at GE, Blodgett and Langmuir jointly published important several papers.

Langmuir quickly recognized Blodgett's enormous potential and encouraged her to pursue a doctorate. With his recommendation, she was accepted into Cambridge University's PhD program in physics. There, she studied under such illustrious figures as Nobel Prize–winning physicist Sir Ernest Rutherford. In 1926, Blodgett became the first woman to receive a PhD in physics from Cambridge.

After receiving her doctorate, Blodgett returned to Schenectady and again began collaborating with Langmuir. For several years, she worked on research related to the tungsten filaments used in electric lamps. She then began to assist Langmuir on the projects that would eventually win him the Nobel Prize. Among other things, they discovered a way to create a chemical film with a thickness of only one molecule. Blodgett improved upon this molecular film technology, applying it to the development of nonreflecting glass.

After the United States entered World War II, Blodgett turned her attention to research relevant to the war effort. One of her most important contributions was the development of new ways to de-ice airplane wings in freezing weather. She also conducted research that improved military smoke screens; these screens were employed in both the Italian and North African campaigns and saved thousands of American lives. Shortly after the war, in 1947, the military began using her molecular films on its weather balloons.

While Blodgett continued to refine her molecular film projects, she also branched out into other areas of research. She and Langmuir built GE's first analog computer in order to run simulations on the growth of ice crystals. She also studied ways to conduct electricity with glass and the use of gas molecules to clean solid surfaces. Today, both of these areas of research have applications for the design and improvement of semiconductors.

During the first half of Blodgett's career, the media and the public largely ignored her achievements. She was rarely mentioned in news articles or stories related to GE's labs, for example. After 1938, however, she began to receive recognition for her accomplishments. She was profiled in *Independent Woman*, *Current Biography*, and *Chemical and Engineering News*, among other publications.

Blodgett never married or had children, but she lived for many years with a woman named Gertrude Brown. She was known to have many hobbies, including gardening and community theater. In addition, she served as president of GE's professional women's club.

In 1951, Blodgett received the American Chemical Society's Garvan Medal, an award given to outstanding female chemists.

Blodgett retired from GE in 1963. In 1979, she died of cerebral thrombosis at the age of 81.

Jamie Stoops

See also: World War I (1914–1918); World War II (1941–1945).

References and Further Reading

MacDonald, Anne M. *Feminine Ingenuity: Women and Invention in America.* New York: Ballantine Books, 1992.

Williams, Gary A. "Katharine Burr Blodgett (1898–1979)." In *Out of the Shadows: Contributions of Twentieth-Century Women to Physics*, edited by Nina Byers and Gary Williams, 149–57. New York: Cambridge University Press, 2006.

Yost, Edna. *American Women of Science.* Philadelphia: J.B. Lippincott, 1943.

BOLTON, FRANCES PAYNE BINGHAM (1885–1977)

Congresswoman Frances Payne Bolton's volunteer work with the Visiting Nurses Association (VNA) led to the creation of the Case Western Reserve Nursing School and the 1944 Bolton Bill, which established the United States Cadet Nurse Corps.

Born on March 29, 1885, in Cleveland, Ohio, Frances Payne Bingham had a privileged childhood. Her parents, Charles W. and Mary Perry Payne Bingham, raised her to understand the potential and responsibility that came with wealth and advantage. These ideas influenced her work throughout her personal life and professional career. As a young woman, nursing provided her with the first venue in which to convey these principles.

As a young woman, Bingham's first introduction to health care and its relation to Cleveland society came through a community service group made up of her and her friends, known as the Brownies. In one of their first projects, the young women cut, rolled, and donated bandages to the VNA. Director Matilda Johnson encouraged the Brownies to do more, so they began to travel and assist some of the nurses in their work. This experience proved to be foundational for Bingham, and after her marriage to Chester C. Bolton in 1907 she decided to increase her involvement in the field of nursing. She became a member of the Lakeside Nursing School board, where she advocated for nurses and the importance of their work and the need for proper education. She continued her volunteer work locally over the next few years while the Boltons added three sons to their young family.

As a result of her husband's appointment to the War Industries Board during World War I, the couple began a political career that gave them a voice on the national stage. While Chester worked with Assistant Secretary of War Benedict Crowell, Frances served on a committee that represented three national nursing organizations. She used her Cleveland connections to Secretary of War Newton Baker, going so far as to sit outside the secretary's office until he signed documents that established an army school of nursing. After the war, the family moved back to Cleveland. Bolton continued her commitment to the profession when she used her family money to provide an endowment for the Frances Payne Bolton School of Nursing at Case Western Reserve University.

In 1928, Chester Bolton was elected to Congress, and the family returned to the nation's capital. He was reelected to Congress five times, and during his tenure Frances increased her own political agenda. She became active in the Republican National Committee. She served as the vice chairman of the Program Committee from 1937 to 1940 and on the Ohio Republican State Central Committee from 1938 to 1940. During this time, illness and heart ailment gradually weakened Chester Bolton, and by 1939, amid the tensions of World War II in Europe, Frances took over her husband's congressional seat. Since her introduction to nursing in 1904, Bolton had steadily increased her knowledge and influence at the local, state, and even national level. Yet none of the work she had done before her husband's death could compare to the task she now faced. Ultimately, on February 27, 1940, Bolton was elected in a special election to fill her husband's unexpired term. As a freshman in Congress, the same values that influenced Bolton as an advocate for nurses would continue to influence her on a new stage.

Bolton asserted that the return to war for the American people had consequences that touched every aspect of their lives, nursing included. She supported the efforts of the Red Cross to meet the increased needs for medical professionals and the home courses created for women of all ages who wanted to become nurses. However, she only partially applauded the president's approval of an appropriation bill that allotted $1.2 million for nursing schools across the country. She felt it did not provide enough to assist the women whom she called on to enlist in the war effort. At this early point in Bolton's legislative career, she already recognized that more than legislation was necessary to make real changes.

Bolton called on the government to increase support for the training of nurses, and by 1942 she had authored legislation to create the U.S. Cadet Nursing Corps. The proposal called for $5 million for the creation and training of the corps. The program provided scholarships, stipends, and uniforms in order to rapidly increase the "nurse-power" of the country. After she received congressional approval in 1944 for the legislation, President Franklin Delano Roosevelt signed the Bolton Act into law. By 1945, the program had prepared 124,000 nurses for service, and in exchange for their training these women committed to tours of duty in the armed services and at essential civilian posts. The Bolton Act contributed to the war effort and more importantly to the eventual permanent establishment of nurses in the U.S. armed forces.

For many years Bolton served on the House Foreign Affairs Committee. When she traveled to the Middle East in 1947, she became the first female member of Congress to head an official mission overseas. She became a congressional delegate to the United Nations in 1953.

After she lost her bid for reelection in 1968, she returned to Lyndhurst, Ohio, where she continued to support programs in nursing as well as those that helped children.

Frances Payne Bolton died on March 9, 1977.

Bailey L. Trenchard

See also: American Red Cross; Cadet Nurse Corps; Nursing; World War I (1914–1918); World War II (1941–1945).

References and Further Reading

Bolton, Frances P. "Nursing Answers." *American Journal of Nursing* 42, no. 2 (February 1942): 138–40.

Gurin, Patricia, and Louise Tilley, eds. *Women, Politics and Change*. New York: Russell Sage Foundation Publication, 1992.

Loth, David. *A Long Way Forward: The Biography of Congresswoman Frances P. Bolton*. New York: Longmans, Green and Co., 1957.

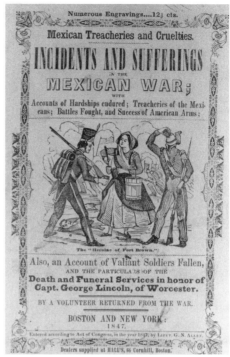

In the years following the Mexican War, American Sarah Borginis, who cared for soldiers on the battlefield and took supplies south to Mexico, was celebrated in books and newspaper accounts as the "Heroine of Fort Brown." (Bettmann/Corbis)

BORGINIS, SARAH [SARAH A. BOWMAN] (1812–1886)

Sarah Borginis became an American heroine for her bravery during the Mexican War. She took supplies south to Mexico and cared for soldiers during the heat of battle.

Borginis was born in Clay County, Missouri, in 1812. Married to a soldier by 1840, she worked for the U.S. Army as a laundress. Her duties included washing clothes and cooking for officers as well as caring for the sick and wounded.

Strong, athletic, and graceful, she stood over six feet tall with an hourglass figure. Borginis's striking appearance brought her much attention. Her nickname, the Great Western, was inspired by the largest steamer afloat in her day.

In 1845, anticipating trouble over the U.S. annexation of Texas, President James K. Polk authorized Gen. Zachary Taylor to assemble the largest number of military troops since the Revolutionary War. Borginis and her husband joined Taylor's forces in Corpus Christi, Texas. Borginis, who idolized Taylor, was outspokenly confident in the general's leadership ability. When orders came from

Washington for Taylor's forces to move into Mexico, Borginis drove her donkey cart full of supplies south with great skill. On the Rio Grande River opposite Matamoras, Mexico, Taylor hurriedly constructed Fort Texas. After the war officially began, Taylor maneuvered to protect his supply base, leaving Maj. Jacob Brown in charge of the fort and its 500 inhabitants. In May 1846, the Mexicans laid siege to Fort Texas for seven days. Borginis frequently exposed herself to danger as she served meals, dressed wounds, and loaded rifles. Brown was killed before Taylor returned to save Fort Texas, which was renamed Fort Brown in his honor.

Borginis achieved national attention when word of her courage and composure under attack appeared in U.S. newspapers. The Great Western became a notable part of western lore as the heroine of Fort Brown. Borginis maintained her reputation, accompanying Taylor's forces in several battles. After her first husband was killed in combat, she had several other male companions and husbands. Borginis, a woman of great business acumen despite being able neither to read nor write, managed two hotels, both called the American House, in the Mexican cities of Saltillo and Monterrey. The hotels provided soldiers with entertainment, food, lodging, liquor, and women.

The war's end in early 1848 coincided with the discovery of gold in California. Borginis eventually moved to what became El Paso, Texas, where federal troops were ordered to protect westward-migrating Americans. Borginis is remembered as El Paso's first Anglo female resident as well as its first madam. After a few years in El Paso, Borginis headed west with a new man, Albert Bowman, a European immigrant and Mexican War veteran. They settled in Fort Yuma, Arizona, where Borginis, Yuma's first Anglo female resident, started a business cooking and cleaning for officers while her husband pursued mining. Soon she was running a restaurant, bar, boarding house, and brothel across from the fort. Her final years were spent managing her various businesses in Arizona, most of them in Yuma. Borginis, the only woman laid to rest in Fort Yuma's cemetery, was buried with full military honors in 1866. Her body and others there were reinterred at San Francisco National Cemetery, where her gravestone is marked Sarah A. Bowman.

David M. Carletta

See also: Republic of Texas.

Reference and Further Reading

Sandwich, Brian. *The Great Western: Legendary Lady of the Southwest*. El Paso: Texas Western, 1921.

BOSIN, (MARGARET) SIDONIE SANSOM (CA. 1960–)

U.S. Coast Guard search-and-rescue pilot Lt. Cmdr. Sidonie Sansom Bosin made history when she became the first female aviation officer in charge of air crews deployed to the Coast Guard cutter *Polar Sea* in the Antarctic. She also commanded the first all-female Coast Guard air crew in the Antarctic.

Before joining the U.S. Coast Guard in her early twenties for the express purpose of learning to be a pilot, Bosin earned a bachelor of arts degree in history from Rhodes College in Memphis, Tennessee, in 1982. She also attended Saint Mary's College of California and the University of St. Andrews in St. Andrews, Scotland. She completed U.S. Navy flight training at Naval Air Station Pensacola and Whiting Field, Florida.

During her long career, she served in many situations requiring skill, bravery, and extreme competence under pressure. While serving as senior aviator and assistant division chief of the Polar Operations Division, Bosin made two Antarctic trips. It was during that time that she also headed up the first all-female helicopter flight crew in Antarctica. Her three-person flight crew included aviation technician Dani Keating and Lt. Kelly Larson.

After serving for more than 22 years, Bosin retired from her work as a search-and-rescue helicopter pilot in the U.S. Coast Guard. She then went to work as an emergency planner at San Francisco International Airport. Her training and experience in the Coast Guard planning and leading flight operations throughout the world and conducting missions involving high-latitude science, law enforcement, and terrorism response expertise prepared Bosin well for the new shape of her career. On December 17, 2003, the First Flight Centennial Commission's 100 Heroes Committee named Bosin one of the top 100 aviators of all time. Among the top 100 aviators on stage with Bosin were several people whose careers had inspired her to start flying in the first place: Neil Armstrong, Buzz Aldrin, and Chuck Yeager.

Bosin was 43 years old when she was honored as one of the nation's top aviators. At the time, she was serving under the 11th Coast Guard District, headquartered in Alameda and stationed in San Francisco. She had already been in the U.S. Coast Guard for 16 years and was admired by those she worked with for bravery and professionalism in addition to unequaled piloting skills.

Bosin joined the Port of San Francisco as director of homeland security in July 2005. Her current responsibilities include readying and, when necessary, implementing emergency plans and procedures on behalf of the Port of San Francisco for man-made emergencies as well as natural disasters.

Kathryn A. Broyles

See also: War on Terror (2001–).

References and Further Reading

Bender, Kristin. "Woman Aviator among the Best Ever." *Oakland Tribune* (Oakland, CA), January 20, 2004.

U.S. Department of Homeland Security. "Women & the U.S. Coast Guard." http://www.uscg.mil/history/uscghist/womenchronology.asp.

Yount, Lisa. *American Profiles: Women Aviators*. New York: Facts on File, 1995.

BOURKE-WHITE, MARGARET (1904–1971)

A photojournalist, foreign correspondent, and industrial photographer, Margaret Bourke-White was among the

Photojournalist and war correspondent Margaret Bourke-White pioneered the photo-essay as she documented wars and humanitarian issues. (Library of Congress)

first to capture the people and places of World War II. Her pioneering work in the development of the photo essay set the standard for detailed achievement and artistic expression.

The second child of Joseph Edward White, an industrial photographer, inventor, and engineer, and teacher Minnie Bourke White, Margaret was born June 14, 1904, in the Bronx, New York. Following high school in New Jersey, she began her education at age 17 at Rutgers University, and then studied photography while a student at Columbia University in 1922 and 1923. At the University of Michigan from 1923 to 1925, she took pictures for the yearbook. Her first marriage, to Everett Chapman, a graduate student at Michigan, lasted only one year. In 1926, following the divorce, she began using the hyphenated compound of her mother's maiden name and her last name.

Bourke-White also attended Western Reserve University in Cleveland. She received her BA at Cornell in 1927 and while there made a photographic record of the campus for the alumni newsletter. She moved back to Cleveland following graduation and became a commercial photographer specializing in architecture and industry.

In 1929, she was named associate editor and the first photographer for Henry Luce's *Fortune* magazine. In 1930, she was the first Western photographer given permission in the Soviet Union to chronicle its Five-Year Plan, and the resulting pictures were published as *Eyes on Russia* (1930). In 1935, Bourke-White, along with Alfred Eisenstaedt and other prominent photographers, joined Henry Luce's newly founded *Life* magazine, a vehicle he created to showcase photojournalists. It was Bourke-White's photograph of a dam under construction in New Deal, Montana, that became the cover of its premiere issue on November 23, 1936.

In 1935, Bourke-White and writer Erskine Caldwell documented the poverty and abysmal living conditions of sharecroppers in the South in *You Have Seen Their Faces* (1935). She and Caldwell married in 1939 but divorced three years later. Their collaboration on two other books, *North of the Danube* (1939) and *Say, Is This the U.S.A.?* (1941) set the stage for the kind of panoramic study of life in both Europe and the United States before and during World War II that was to be her signature contribution to photojournalism.

During World War II, Bourke-White became a part of one of the first groups of women who covered the war on the front lines. In October 1939, *Life* sent her first to London, where she photographed the blackouts and Winston Churchill, and then to Romania, Turkey, and Syria. In Egypt she photographed French and British troops and the king of Egypt.

In May 1941, following Germany's breaking of its nonaggression pact with the Soviets, she arrived in the Soviet Union, the only foreign photographer in the country. She was allowed to photograph the Soviet dictator Joseph Stalin and was the only foreign photographer present when the first bombs fell on Moscow on July 22.

At the beginning of 1942, as an official Air Force photographer, Bourke-White was named the first female correspondent in uniform. On January 22, 1943, she was the first woman allowed to go on a bombing mission, and she flew on a mission over a German airfield in North Africa. After a brief return to the United States, she was again at the front, this time photographing artillery action in Italy.

As Germany was collapsing, Bourke-White accompanied Gen. George Patton's Third Army along the Rhine. When she arrived at the concentration camp at Buchenwald in 1945, she photographed the dead and dying. Her photograph "The Living Dead at Buchenwald" became a classic. Her adventures and diaries during the war were compiled in *Shooting the Russian War* (1942) and *Dear Fatherland, Rest Quietly* (1946), the latter an attempt to deal with the German atrocities she witnessed.

Following the war, Bourke-White was sent by *Life* to cover social causes and humanitarian issues around the world. She met with Gandhi in India on January 30, 1948, just hours before he was assassinated. In 1950 she documented labor and racial unrest in South Africa and was the first woman to go below ground into the gold mines.

Bourke-White was a UN correspondent and the first to reach the foremost outposts of the Korean War, though she covered the war from the perspective of the Korean people. When she returned to the United States, she was an international star, and her autobiography, *Portrait of Myself* (1963), became a bestseller.

After a 19-year struggle with Parkinson's disease, Margaret Bourke-White died of respiratory failure on August 27, 1971, in Stamford, Connecticut.

Gary Kerley

See also: Korean War (1950–1953); World War II (1941–1945).

References and Further Reading

Bourke-White, Margaret. *Portrait of Myself*. Boston: G. K. Hall & Co., 1985.

Brown, Theodore M. *Margaret Bourke-White, Photojournalist*. Ithaca, NY: Cornell University Press, 1972.

Callahan, Sean. *Margaret Bourke-White, Photographer*. Boston: Little, Brown and Company, 1998.

Goldberg, Vicki. *Margaret Bourke-White: A Biography*. New York: Harper & Row, 1986.

Silverman, Jonathan. *For the World to See: The Life of Margaret Bourke-White*. New York: Viking Press, 1983.

BOWSER, MARY ELIZABETH (CA. 1839–N.D.)

Little is known of Union spy Mary Elizabeth Bowser's life before or after the Civil War. During the war, she worked with Elizabeth Van Lew in Richmond to get information on Confederate war operations.

She was born a slave on the Richmond, Virginia, plantation of John Van Lew. Upon his death, probably in 1851, his wife and daughter freed their slaves and purchased and manumitted a number of their former slaves' relatives. The daughter, Elizabeth Van Lew, became well known as an abolitionist in Richmond during the 1850s. She arranged for Mary to be educated at the Quaker School for Negroes in Philadelphia. Mary returned to Richmond in 1861, and at the outbreak of the Civil War she married Wilson Bowser, a free black man.

During the Civil War, Mary's former owner, Elizabeth Van Lew, operated a Union spy ring in Richmond. Van Lew was able to allay suspicion by affecting an attitude of eccentric behavior, coming to be called Crazy Bet. Van Lew arranged for Bowser's employment as a servant in the household of Confederate president Jefferson Davis. There Bowser posed as a dull but hardworking slave and gained access to both conversations and documents concerning the most sensitive activities of the Confederate government and military. Bowser would repeat what she learned to Van Lew or to Thomas McNiven, the Union's Richmond spymaster, who operated a bakery that became a major information clearinghouse. McNiven credited Bowser with being one of his best sources of wartime intelligence because of her photographic memory. It became obvious to Confederate authorities that there was a leak in the Davis household, but suspicion did not fall on Bowser until January 1865, when she chose to flee from Richmond to the North. Some reports indicate that her last act as a Union spy and sympathizer was an unsuccessful attempt to burn down the Confederate White House.

The specific details of Bowser's activities and the exact information she passed to the Union will never be known. After the war, the federal government destroyed its records on McNiven, Van Lew, and their agents to protect them from retaliation by Confederate sympathizers.

Bowser dropped out of sight after the Civil War. Nothing is known about where she went or what she did, and the date and place of her death are unknown. Papers believed to have been Bowser's diaries were apparently discarded by family members in the 1950s. Her descendants rarely talked about Bowser's work out of the same fear of retaliation that prompted the government to destroy the records of her activities.

The U.S. government honored Bowser's contributions in 1995 by inducting her into the Military Intelligence Corps Hall of Fame at Fort Huachuca, Arizona.

Robert D. Bohanan

See also: African American Women; Civil War (1861–1865); Espionage; Van Lew, Elizabeth (1818–1900).

References and Further Reading

Coleman, Penny. *Spies!: Women in the Civil War.* White Hall, VA: Shoe Tree Press, 1992.

Ryan, David D. *A Yankee Spy in Richmond: The Civil War Diary of "Crazy Bet" Van Lew.* Mechanicsburg, PA: Stackpole Books, 1996.

Varon, Elizabeth. *Southern Lady, Yankee Spy: The True Story of Elizabeth Van Lew, a Union Agent in the Heart of the*

Confederacy. New York: Oxford University Press, 2003.

BOYD, MARIE ISABELLA "BELLE" (1844–1900)

A Confederate spy during the American Civil War, Boyd has often been referred to by the sobriquets "Belle Boyd" and the "Cleopatra of Secession." She authored an autobiographical account of her clandestine services, worked a short stint as actress, and toured as a lecturer in the latter part of the 19th century.

Mary Rebecca Glenn and Benjamin Reed Boyd, a successful businessman, welcomed Marie Isabella Boyd, the first of their eight children, into their family

Confederate spy "Belle" Boyd provided critical information about Union troop movements during the Civil War, most notably during the Shenandoah Valley Campaign in 1862. (Library of Congress)

on May 9, 1844. She lived in her hometown of Martinsburg, Virginia (which became part of West Virginia on June 23, 1863) and attended Mount Washington College for Young Ladies in Baltimore, Maryland, at the age of 12. After four years, Boyd completed her education and relocated to Washington, D.C., for the winter of 1860–1861.

Boyd returned to her family in Martinsburg in time for Virginia's secession from the Union. Many of the Boyd clan enlisted in the Southern cause, several specializing in irregular warfare and espionage, which may have influenced her later actions. Boyd's espionage career began in early July 1861, when she was 17 years old. Retreating from the Battle of Falling Waters, on July 2, 1861, Thomas "Stonewall" Jackson and his Confederate troops passed through Martinsburg. The Federal Army in pursuit arrived to occupy Martinsburg on July 3. On July 4 the Union soldiers celebrated both their recent victory and Independence Day. Word had filtered through their ranks that Boyd's bedroom was decorated with rebel flags. Determined to burn these offending banners on their day of revelry, a party of soldiers raided her home, only to find them already hidden.

Against the protests of its occupants, the soldiers decided to raise a Union flag over the Boyd household instead. Incensed at the Union flag and a soldier's threat to her mother, Boyd drew the pistol she carried and shot the soldier dead. The victim's superior officer reviewed the case, passing the verdict that Boyd had been justified in her actions and would not face charges.

Despite this incident, Boyd befriended many of the federal troops. She exploited their trust and friendship to gather information about troop strength, positions, and other military matters. She then carried this intelligence across the lines to the Confederates personally or sent it by a trusted courier. In addition, she lifted numerous weapons, including sabers and guns, from unsuspecting federal troops and then transported those into the hands of their enemies. Generals P. G. T. Beauregard and Jackson began to regard Boyd as a valuable resource.

At the close of 1861, Union forces intercepted one of Boyd's communiqués. Alerted to her activities, federal officials arrested Boyd. Again, she escaped a harsh sentence; she was simply warned and let go. Although Boyd was now under surveillance, she was free to resume her work.

In May of 1862, the federal troops were also in possession of Front Royal, Virginia, roughly 45 miles south of Martinsburg. Boyd relocated to Fort Royal and engaged in her proven tactics of befriending and romancing Union soldiers for information. In addition, Boyd gained one of her most crucial bits of information in Front Royal by hiding in a closet during a war council. This key bit of intelligence, supplied to Jackson on May 23, 1862, permitted the Confederates to briefly retake the captured town. Northern newspapers covered this event, referring to Boyd as the "Secesh' Cleopatra."

Roughly two months later, Boyd was arrested and sent to serve a term in the Old Capitol Prison in Washington, D.C. She was part of a prisoner exchange in December 1862 and was sent to the Confederate capital. A parade was held in her honor in Richmond, where Confederates gave her the honorary title of "Captain."

A second arrest followed in the spring of 1863. Boyd had returned to Martinsburg, only to be deported to Washington, D.C., for her suspicious behavior. She remained in Carroll Prison, an annex of the Old Capitol Prison, until December 1863. Officials commuted her prison sentence and replaced it with a more ominous sentence: if she was again apprehended on federal soil she would face execution.

Six months later Boyd, now 20 years old, volunteered to carry dispatches across the Atlantic to Confederate agents in Europe. Running the federal blockade was a dangerous endeavor, especially when encumbered with sensitive documents. In early May 1864, her transport, the *Greyhound*, attempted to bypass the blockade. However, a Union vessel captured it and steered it to Boston. One of the Union officers, Samuel W. Hardinge, became deeply enamored with Boyd during this return voyage, reputedly proposing to her twice. Boyd accepted his proposal with several caveats, one of which required him to join the Confederate service.

Through the intercession of her fiancé, Boyd was banished to Canada rather than executed. Hardinge was discharged from the U.S. Navy under charges of neglect. The two were reunited in London in late August 1864 and were married. Federal officials arrested Hardinge a few months later in Baltimore and ultimately transferred him to Fort Delaware. It was during this period that the pregnant Boyd penned her two-part autobiography, *Belle Boyd in Camp and in Prison*, which would see publication in 1865.

Her husband was released in early 1865. His health had suffered during his captivity, leading to his death within the year. Grace Hardinge, their daughter, was also born during this period. After Hardinge's death and the end of the Civil War, Boyd became a actress, performing in England and in the United States.

In 1869, Boyd remarried to former British officer John Hammond. This union produced three children, Byrd Swainston Hammond, Marie Isabella Boyd Hammond, and John Edmond Swainston Hammond. The two divorced in 1884, and Boyd married a third time, this time to actor Nathaniel Rue High.

Boyd went on the lecture circuit for the next 16 years, giving lively accounts of her career as a Confederate spy.

While on tour, Belle Boyd died of a heart attack in June 1900 at the age of 56. She was buried at her last stop in the town of Kilbourn, Wisconsin (now Wisconsin Dells).

Michael D. Coker

See also: Civil War (1861–1865); Espionage.

References and Further Reading

Axelrod, Alan. *The War between the Spies: A History of Espionage during the American Civil War*. New York: Atlantic Monthly Press, 1992.

Bakeless, John. *Spies of the Confederacy*. Mineola, NY: Dover, 1970.

Boyd, Belle. *Belle Boyd in Camp and Prison*. London: Saunders, Otley, and Co., 1865.

Markle, Donald E. *Spies and Spymasters of the Civil War*. New York: Barnes and Noble, 1994.

Scarborough, Ruth. *Belle Boyd: Siren of the South*. Macon, GA: Mercer University Press, 1983.

BRADLEY, AMY MORRIS (1823–1904)

Amy Morris Bradley served as a nurse during the Civil War. As a nurse with a Maine regiment, she served in field hospitals and on a hospital ship. She also served as a special relief agent for the U.S. Sanitary Commission (USSC).

Bradley was born on September 12, 1823, in Vassalboro, Maine. She was educated in local public schools and at the age of 15 began teaching at private schools and summer country schools to earn money for her tuition at the East Vassalboro Academy. When she was 21, she was named principal of the grammar school at Gardiner, Maine. Health problems, however, compelled her to move to more southern climes, and she subsequently relocated to North Carolina and lived with a brother. In 1853, she went to Costa Rica, where she taught English to wealthy Costa Rican children and opened an English school. When her father died, she returned to Maine.

When the Civil War erupted in 1861, Bradley volunteered as a nurse and was attached to the 5th Maine Infantry Regiment. During the war, she earned a reputation as a tireless and dedicated worker, having served in field hospitals, on a hospital ship, and at a convalescent facility in northern Virginia. She also supervised a soldiers' convalescent home in Washington, D.C. Her dedication and organizational skills led her to the USSC, where she ultimately became a special relief agent. In that role, she almost singlehandedly transformed numerous filthy, ill-run army hospitals into modern, clean, and well-run facilities. By war's end, she had won the respect and admiration of many U.S. leaders, both political and military.

When the war ended, Bradley settled in Wilmington, North Carolina, to help educate impoverished white students there. In 1867, she established a school in Wilmington, and five years later she opened the Tileston Normal School to train teachers for work in primary and secondary schools in the greater Wilmington area. She remained the chief administrator of the school until ill health forced her to retire in 1891.

Bradley died on January 14, 1904, in Wilmington, North Carolina.

Paul G. Pierpaoli Jr.

See also: Civil War (1861–1865); Nursing; United States Sanitary Commission (USSC).

References and Further Reading

Cashman, Diane Cobb. *Headstrong: The Biography of Amy Morris Bradley, 1823–1904.* Wilmington, NC: Broadfoot, 1990.

Sudlow, Lynda L. *The Fifth Maine Regiment Community Building: A History.* Portland, ME: Arlington Street Press, 1992.

BRANT, MARY "MOLLY" (CA. 1735–1796)

The daughter of a Mohawk woman, Mary Brant played a substantive role in support of the British during the American Revolution.

Brant was born in Canajohanie, a Mohawk village in Albany County, New York. She was baptized in 1735 and was likely born in the same year. Her mother, Margaret, was a Mohawk. Mohawk status was derived matrilineally, through the mother's bloodline, but Brant was born into a clan that was not significant in terms of kinship status or power.

When Brant was born, the Mohawk world was in upheaval. Traditionally, Mohawks had lived in longhouses, multi-family dwellings that were organized along matrilineal lines. However, by the middle of the 18th century, single-family dwellings replaced these longhouses. In addition, colonial governments shifted the ownership of land to men rather than women, who had always determined land distribution and usage in Mohawk culture. Further, European efforts to sedentarize native populations limited the hunting cycles that played a role in Mohawk interaction, peaceful and otherwise, with other native peoples. In an era of declining power for women and declining unity for the Iroquois Nation, Brant's influence was remarkable.

Brant evidently attended school, given she could read, write, and speak English. William Johnson, an Irish immigrant who became a successful trader, impregnated her during his stay at her parents' house in 1753, not an uncommon thing for him to do on his travels. Johnson's ties to the Mohawk community resulted in his being named an honorary *sachem* (tribal leader) and eventually the second largest landholder in the colonies, surpassed only by the Penn family. Upon the death of his German wife, Catherine Weisenberg, Johnson welcomed Brant as his new wife, according to Mohawk standards. She bore him nine children, of which eight survived infancy.

Brant's prestige grew, not only because of her husband's reputation but also as a result of her liberal gifting of clothing, rum, and blankets to the Mohawks, which built status in the Mohawk world. She was the estate's hostess, as well as its manager while William was away, which was a frequent occurrence. She also played a role in the negotiations with the tribes. Her husband secured a number of governmental and military posts. He became the superintendent of Indian affairs for the northern colonies in 1756, a post that made him answerable only to superiors in London. In this post, he made Iroquois concerns the cornerstone of British policy, further endearing himself to the nations. In 1756, he was made a baronet, henceforth known as Sir William Johnson.

Mary and William never married in a European sense. However, after he died in 1774, all of Brant's children (as well as Catherine's) were considered legitimate in his will, and all of them inherited property. The will, however, repeatedly referred to Mary as his "housekeeper" or "present housekeeper." After William's death, Brant returned to Canajohanie with her children and with four slaves. His title and the bulk of his estate went to his eldest son, John. She filled her house with oriental porcelain and expensive furniture and opened a trading store with her brother Joseph.

Not surprisingly, given her ties to the Crown, Brant emerged as a staunch Loyalist with the advent of the war for independence. She provided supplies, ammunition, food, and shelter to Loyalists. She also hid fugitives. Though most Loyalists had fled the region by 1776, Brant remained.

British and native forces laid siege to Fort Stanwix in 1777. When she learned of a rebel attempt to reinforce the besieged, she sent word to her brother Joseph at Stanwix. An ambush was planned near Oriskany. The ambush was successful, and Brant had to flee immediately. Her house was plundered by a band of Oneida (an Iroquois tribe) and rebels in revenge for her role in the battle. Brant retreated west and sought shelter with her kin among the Cayuga. When Cayuga chief Sayenquagyta appealed to the people to seek peace with the rebels, he was strongly rebuked by Brant. He relented, acknowledging that she was the "relict" of William, and they should do what she said.

Later that year, Lt. Col. John Butler, the commandant at Fort Niagara, asked Brant to come to help him maintain ties with the native populations in the region, in particular with the Iroquois. She accepted and worked throughout the remainder of the war in this capacity. Daniel Claus, William Johnson's son-in-law, noted that one word of hers was superior to a thousand from any white man.

After the war, Mary Brant applied for compensation for war losses and for a pension. She received £1,200 in compensation and an annual pension of £100. Both numbers were the most awarded by the Crown to a single Native American. She died in Kingston, Ontario, in 1796.

Mark Anthony Phelps

See also: American Revolution (1775–1783); Native American Women.

References and Further Reading

Berkin, Carol. *Revolutionary Mothers: Women in the Struggle for American Independence.* New York: Alfred Knopf, 2005.

Gunderson, Joan. *To Be Useful to the World: 1740–1790*. New York: Twayne, 1986.

Thomas, Earle. *The Three Faces of Molly Brant*. Kingston, ON: Quarry Press, 1996.

BRATTON, MARTHA ROBERTSON [ROBINSON] (CA. 1749/1750–1816)

South Carolinian Martha Bratton sent information to her husband's militia that helped the Patriot forces defeat the British at the battle of Huck's Defeat.

As is far too common for this period, reliable documentation on this Southern woman's early life is scarce. According to family tradition, Bratton was born to her Scots-Irish parents, the Robertsons or Robinsons, at sea during their Atlantic migration to the American colonies. The transplanted family most likely settled in Rowan County, North Carolina. It is believed she married William Bratton in this county, but the date and the definitive details of this union have yet to be verified. Her husband seems to have been at least modestly wealthy. William Bratton purchased several hundred acres of land in the early 1770s.

In 1775, the Brattons relocated to part of their property held in South Carolina, in what is now York County. The area would later become known as Brattonsville because of the large number of extended Bratton family members residing in close proximity.

By 1780, the couple was living in a substantial home and had five children. William Bratton served in several significant posts in the community, including justice of the peace in 1776 and tax collector in 1777. The Brattons were also one of the few slaveholding families in this region of South Carolina at the time. As was typical for someone of his standing, William Bratton was elected officer in the local militia. He continued in this capacity, serving the Patriot colonists in rebellion against the Crown, often serving with partisan fighters such as Thomas "the Gamecock" Sumter.

While her husband was active on the battlefield, Martha Bratton managed family affairs. The war in the backcountry of South Carolina during the American Revolution impacted many communities, and the conflict came to her doorstep. A band of Loyalists, those colonists who remained loyal to British rule, under the command of Capt. Christian Huck arrived at Bratton's home on July 11, 1780. Huck demanded she divulge her husband's whereabouts. When Huck's appeals failed, one of his troopers brandished a reaping hook at Martha and threatened her for information. Some accounts state the blade was placed across her throat; another claims it was a noose around her neck. Regardless of the implement, Bratton refused to reveal her husband's whereabouts, and another trooper interceded on her behalf.

After the British left her house, Bratton sent a family slave named Watt to warn her husband. This intelligence helped Patriot forces secure the victory at the resulting battle the next day (July 12, 1780) at an engagement called Huck's Defeat. This small battle energized Patriot resistance, providing a needed link in a chain of eventual victories that would lead to British defeat in the region. Bratton and her family nursed the wounded from both sides in the aftermath of the battle.

One possibly apocryphal story is also attributed to Bratton. A cache of gunpowder, a prized commodity during the American Revolution, was supposedly entrusted to the Brattons for safekeeping. With her husband in the field, Bratton was left to tend to the security of the powder. British supporters learned of the existence of the depot and alerted the royal authorities. Bratton purportedly detected the betrayal and detonated the gunpowder just as the redcoats appeared. This story further states that she proudly took responsibility for this act in the face of a hostile inquiry. No other details, such as the date, the British parties involved, or why Bratton escaped punishment, have yet to surface, rendering this tale suspect. Nonetheless, it is often used to exemplify the valor of Southern women during the Revolution.

Bratton died on January 16, 1816, at the age of 66. She was laid to rest in Bethesda Presbyterian Church Cemetery in York, South Carolina. Her former home and a marker chronicling her wartime actions still stand at the Historic Brattonville site in York County, South Carolina.

Michael D. Coker

See also: American Revolution (1775–1783); Nursing.

References and Further Reading

Berkin, Carol. *Revolutionary Mothers: Women in the Struggle for America's Independence.* New York: Alfred A. Knopf, 2005.

Edgar, Walter B. *Partisans and Redcoats: The Southern Conflict That Turned the Tide of the American Revolution.* New York: Harper Perennial, 2003.

Ellet, Elizabeth Fries. *The Women of the American Revolution.* 1848; reprint Charleston, SC: Nabu Press, 2010.

Scoggins, Michael C. *The Day It Rained Militia: Huck's Defeat and the Revolution in the South Carolina Backcountry, May–July 1780.* Charleston, SC: History Press, 2005.

BRECKINRIDGE, MARGARET E. (1832–1864)

During the Civil War, Margaret Breckinridge worked as a nurse for Union soldiers and served as a member of the U.S. Sanitary Commission (USSC).

Breckinridge was born on March 24, 1832, in Philadelphia. Her cousin was former U.S. vice president and Confederate

During the Civil War, Margaret Breckinridge served as a nurse through the U.S. Sanitary Commission. (Brockett, L. P., "Woman's Work in the Civil War," 1867)

major general John C. Breckinridge. Her parents had died by the time she was six years old, and she went to live with her grandparents in Princeton, New Jersey, where she was educated in local schools and by a private tutor.

After the Civil War began, Breckinridge decided to take up nursing. The fact that she was not married and had independent means of support bolstered her decision. In 1862, she traveled to Lexington, Kentucky, where she took up nursing duties at Union Hospital. During her tenure there, Confederate troops occupied the city for several weeks, and the ensuing fighting resulted in many casualties. When the Confederates withdrew in the fall of 1862, Breckinridge took on work on a relief boat sponsored by the USSC. On it she cared for wounded troops being transported from Vicksburg, Mississippi, to St. Louis, Missouri.

Although she served on just two boat trips, her heroism and connection to John C. Breckinridge captured headlines through the North. By March 1863, however, the ailing Margaret, overcome by exhaustion, returned east to her family. She spent a number of months convalescing in Philadelphia and then trained as a surgical nurse in Philadelphia's venerable Episcopal Hospital.

In the early summer of 1864, her illness, which to this day is unknown, returned, and she died on July 27, 1864, in Niagara Falls, New York. It is believed that she contracted a communicable disease while caring for troops, probably typhoid or some similar illness.

Paul G. Pierpaoli Jr.

See also: Civil War (1861–1865); Nursing; United States Sanitary Commission (USSC).

References and Further Reading

Favor, Lesli J. *Women Doctors and Nurses of the Civil War.* New York: Rosen, 2004.

Holland, Mary Gardner. *Our Army Nurses: Stories from Women in the Civil War.* Roseville, MN: Edinborough, 1998.

Leonard, Elizabeth D. *Yankee Women: Gender Battles in the Civil War.* New York: W. W. Norton, 1994.

Schultz, Jane E. *Women at the Front: Hospital Workers in Civil War America.* Chapel Hill: University of North Carolina Press, 2007.

BREWER, LUCY [LOUISA BAKER, GEORGE BAKER, LUCY WEST, ELIZA BOWEN]
(CA. 1793–N.D.)

Lucy Brewer disguised herself as a man to serve as a marine sharpshooter during the War of 1812.

Known only through a popular series of autobiographical pamphlets, Brewer was an ex-prostitute who reputedly served in disguise for three years as a Marine sharpshooter on board the USS *Constitution* during the War of 1812. According to the pamphlets published in 1815 and 1816 by Nathaniel Coverly, Brewer was born in Plymouth County, Massachusetts. At 16 she became pregnant. With no hope of marriage and determined not to bring disgrace on her family, Brewer fled to Boston, where her child was born and soon died; she subsequently worked in a brothel.

When the War of 1812 broke out three years later, Brewer determined to leave the brothel and see the world. One of her clients, apparently a lieutenant on board the U.S. frigate *Constitution*, encouraged her to join the crew. Brewer was inspired by the story of Deborah Samson, who had served for three years in disguise as a soldier during the Revolutionary War. Brewer disguised herself as a man and, with her lover's assistance to avoid the usual physical examination, enlisted under the name George Baker. Assigned to the fighting troops as a sharpshooter, Brewer participated in the victories over the British frigates *Guerriere* and *Java*. She served on the *Constitution* throughout the war and was discharged in 1815. Brewer returned to her parents' farm and published her experiences in a series of pamphlets, later collected and published as "The Female Marine; or, Adventures of Miss Lucy Brewer." Her later experiences are unknown.

Some authorities dispute that Lucy Brewer ever existed as there is no independent confirmation of her exploits. Alexander Medlicott Jr. and Daniel Cohen claim to have checked records throughout Plymouth County and can find no record of a Lucy Brewer (or any of her aliases), and the muster rolls of the *Constitution* do not reveal a George Baker.

Her memoirs, however, were very popular at the time among women and served as an inspiration to other women of what they could accomplish. The U.S. Marine Corps itself, while producing a report that denied Lucy Brewer's existence, later realized the value of a woman serving in a nontraditional role. Lucy Brewer is now commemorated as the "first girl marine," and a street at Camp Lejune, North Carolina, is named for her.

Tim J. Watts

See also: Samson [Sampson] (Gannett), Deborah [Robert Shurtliff] (1760–1827); War of 1812 (1812–1815).

References and Further Reading

Cohen, Daniel A., ed. *The Female Marine and Related Works: Narratives of Cross-Dressing and Urban Vice in America's Early Republic.* Amherst: University of Massachusetts Press, 1998.

Medlicott, Alexander Jr. "The Legend of Lucy Brewer: An Early American Novel." *New England Quarterly* 39, no. 4 (December 1996): 461–73.

West, Lucy Brewer. *The Female Marine, or Adventures of Miss Lucy Brewer.* Boston: n.p., 1817; reprint 1966.

BREWER, MARGARET A. (1930–)

Margaret Brewer was the first woman Marine to attain flag rank. She served as the seventh director of Women Marines (1973–1977) and became the director of Information, which made her the public face of the Marine Corps.

Born in Durand, Michigan, in 1930, Brewer spent her childhood in Michigan. She attended a one-room elementary school in Swartz Creek. She graduated from Baltimore's Catholic High School and then returned to her home state to enroll in the University of Michigan at Ann Arbor. While at Michigan, she participated in a summer reserves program. She was also a member of the Zeta Tau Alpha sorority.

Upon her January 1952 graduation from Michigan as a geography major and a conservation geology minor, she received her commission from the Marine Corps. She had to decide whether to accept it or to remain a civilian. The Korean War had begun, so accepting her commission would mean that she would immediately be ordered to active duty. Although she had planned to continue her studies in conservation geology in graduate school, Brewer accepted her commission. She joined the U.S. Marine Corps and, in March, was commissioned as a second lieutenant.

Brewer's first assignment was at the Marine Corps Air Station El Toro, California, as a communications watch offer. As such, she helped coordinate the data coming in and out of the base. She remained in that post until June 1953, when she was reassigned to Brooklyn, New York, as inspector-instructor of a Women Marine Reserve unit.

Brewer excelled in her leadership positions, all of which put her in charge of other female marines. After her post in New York, she served as commander of female Marine companies at Norfolk, Virginia, as well as at Camp Lejeune, North Carolina. She also served as a platoon commander for women officer candidates at Virginia's Woman Officer School at Quantico. She was also a mess officer at Camp Pendleton, California.

In September 1961, while at Camp Pendleton, Brewer earned promotion to major. She was subsequently posted back to Quantico's Woman Officer School. She initially served at the school as executive officer but later became its commanding officer. Next Brewer became the public affairs officer for the 6th Marine Corps District Headquarters in Atlanta. In December 1966, while stationed in Atlanta, Brewer was promoted to lieutenant colonel.

Brewer continued to rise up through the ranks. She served as the deputy director of Women Marines at Headquarters Marine Corps from March 1968 until March 1971. While serving in this position she earned promotion to colonel in December 1970. After her time as the deputy director, she became the special assistant to the director, Marine Corps Education Center. She then became the chief of the unit's support detachment.

Brewer is perhaps best known for her position as the director of Women Marines. Brewer became the seventh woman to hold this post as well as the last. She began this post on February 1, 1973. This position, which put Brewer in charge of all female marines, was abolished on June 30, 1977, when the Marine Corps fully integrated women into all of its training programs.

Her department reorganized and became the Division of Public Affairs, so Brewer's next assignment was as the deputy director of the Division of Information, Headquarters Marine Corps. During this post Brewer was nominated for promotion. The Marines promoted Brewer to brigadier general on May 11, 1978, making her the first woman to achieve this rank in the Marine Corps. Her appointment brought the Marine Corps in line with the other branches of service, which had earlier named women to equivalent ranks. With her promotion, she also became the director of information. As the head of this division, Brewer became the chief public spokesperson for the Marine Corps.

The incorporation of women into the ranks led to the change in the Marine Corps' famous slogan "A Few Good Men." With women integrated and a female brigadier general, the branch changed its slogan to one with no mention of men, "The few, the proud, the Marines."

Brewer left active duty in July 1980. By the time of her retirement, she had earned a Legion of Merit Medal with a Gold Star, a Navy Meritorious Unit Commendation, and a National Defense Service Medal with a service star for her outstanding service. In addition, the University of Michigan's Board of Regents honored her with an Outstanding Achievement Award.

Lisa Tendrich Frank

See also: Women Marines.

References and Further Reading

Holm, Jeanne M. *Women in the Military: An Unfinished Revolution*. Novato, CA: Presidio Press, 1992.

Milks, Keith A. "Brewer Made Corps History When She Made General." *Army Times*, May 21, 2003.

Monahan, Evelyn M., and Rosemary Neidel-Greenlee. *A Few Good Women: America's Military Women from World War I to the Wars in Iraq and Afghanistan*. New York: Alfred A. Knopf, 2010.

Stremlow, Mary V. *U.S. Marine Corps Women's Reserve: A History of the Women Marines, 1946–1977*. Washington, D.C.: U.S. Marine Corps, History and Museums Division Headquarters, 1986.

Tufty, Esther Van Wagoner. "Durand's Margaret Brewer will Retire from Marines." *The Argus-Press*, June 9, 1980, 13.

BRION, IRENE (1920–)

Irene Brion was a member of the Women's Army Auxiliary Corps (WAAC) and the Women's Army Corps (WAC) who served during World War II in the Pacific Theater.

Brion was born in 1920, one of five sisters. In 1943, Brion was working as a teacher in Friendship, a small town in western New York near Buffalo. While shopping in Rochester with her mother and sister, Brion took a brochure from WAAC recruiters and decided that the military offered educational and social opportunities that she did not want to pass up. One of her sisters, Ann, would later join her in military service.

Brion applied to the Navy in March 1943 but was rejected. She then applied and was accepted into the WAAC (later changed to the Women's Army Corps). She reported to duty on July 1, 1943, under the serial number Auxiliary Basic A-217606, and underwent training at Fort Devens, Massachusetts. One of Brion's teaching friends was in the same unit.

After basic training, Brion was sent to Fort Carson, Colorado. In summer of 1944, she underwent signal corps training at Vint Hill Farms in Virginia. Part of her training included an introduction to the Japanese language and familiarization with Hepburn Kana, a system devised to convert Japanese characters into syllables. In fall of 1944, the WAC sent her to Fort Olgethorpe, Georgia, for eight more weeks of instruction. The extended field-service program trained Brion in the survival skills needed for her eventual overseas deployment to the Pacific Theater. Brion never received firearms instruction because WACs were not allowed to use them.

Brion's last stop in the United States before her overseas deployment was Camp Stoneman, near Pittsburg,

California. She shipped out on October 11, 1944, on board the *Luline*, a luxury liner with the Matson Line that had been converted into a troop transport ship. The transpacific journey to Milne Bay, Papua, New Guinea took three two weeks.

By late 1944, the South Pacific had become a secondary theater of operations as the Allies' offensive against the Japanese Empire shifted to the Philippines and the Central Pacific islands. A sign of Japan's fading power in the South Pacific, the WAC housing in Oro Bay in Papua New Guinea had previously been a Japanese base. Brion recalled finding a GI's dog tag as she walked along the beach, a poignant reminder of the deadly business of war that had raged throughout the South Pacific only months before. She and 17 other WACs lived in small huts with dirt floors and worked in Quonset huts decoding Japanese messages.

In November, Brion was moved to the headquarters section in Hollandia in Dutch New Guinea, where she would remain until June 1945. Her duties there included decoding and signals intelligence. While in Hollandia, Brion learned of her mother's death. Further tragedy struck the family when her sister, Mary, died in the spring of 1945.

In June 1945, Brion deployed to the Philippines Islands. Her flight included a layover on Peleliu, in the Palau Islands, which had been seized from the Japanese by U.S. forces in a bloody two-month battle in the fall of the previous year. Compared to the relative rural isolation of her previous post on Papua New Guinea, life in bustling wartime and war-torn Manila proved a change of pace for Brion and her fellow WACs. Brion was serving in the Philippines when the atomic bombs were dropped on Japan and when the Japanese government surrendered. Spontaneous celebration broke out at her post at San Miguel.

Brion and other WACs shipped out from Manila on the *Lurline* in November 1945. She was discharged at Fort Des Moines, Iowa, at the end of the month. By the time she completed her service, her decorations included the American Campaign Medal, the World War II Victory Medal, the Philippine Liberation Ribbon, the Asiatic Pacific Campaign Medal, the Good Conduct Medal, and the WAAC Service Medal.

After the war, the G.I. Bill helped to pay for Brion's college education. After she received her bachelor's and her master's degrees at the University of Colorado, she taught special education classes. She retired in 1981, having served 22 years with the Palo Alto school district. Her memoir of her wartime service, *Lady GI: A Woman's War in the South Pacific*, was published in 1997.

L. Bao Bui

See also: Espionage; Women's Army Auxiliary Corps (WAAC); Women's Army Corps (WAC); World War II (1941–1945).

References and Further Reading

Bergerud, Eric M. *Fire in the Sky: The Air War in the South Pacific*. Boulder, CO: Westview Press, 2001.

Brion, Irene. *Lady GI: A Woman's War in the South Pacific: The Memoir of Irene Brion*. Novato, CA: Presidio Press, 1997.

Howton, Elizabeth, "Page 4: One Woman's War." *Palo Alto Online*, August 9, 1995. http://www.paloaltoonline.com/weekly/morgue/page4/1995_Aug_9.NOTES09.html.

BROWN, MONICA LIN (1988–)

Army combat medic Monica Lin Brown received the Silver Star for combat bravery in Afghanistan. She became the second woman to receive the medal for her actions in combat.

A native of Lake Jackson, Texas, Brown was born on May 24, 1988. Inspired by her older brother, Justin Brown, who had long dreamed of being an infantryman, she began her military career in November 2005 at the age of 17. Having graduated from high school a year and a half early, and legally underage at the time, Monica joined the U.S. Army with her grandmother's consent, enrolling in basic and advanced individual training (AIS) as an army combat medic. Once enlisted, Brown was assigned to the 782nd Brigade Support Battalion, 4th Brigade Combat Team, 82nd Airborne Division. By February 2007, she was deployed to a military outpost in Khost Province, Afghanistan.

After a short stay in Khost, Private 1st Class Brown was informed in March that she was to be attached to an infantry unit in need of a female medic in an isolated military stronghold situated near the Afghan-Pakistani border. In Afghanistan in particular, female medics are often brought to remote regions to provide health services for local women—a task that cultural sensitivity dictates could not be performed by a male health professional. Although Pentagon policy decrees that female soldiers are forbidden to serve in combat roles on the front lines, the absence of conventional warfare and the guerrilla tactics often invoked by the enemy meant that there was a high probability that Brown and her unit could be engaged by enemy activity. With the unit's only male combat medic on leave, Brown was thrust into the position.

Due to the increasing presence of Taliban forces in the region and a renewed offensive on the part of the insurgents, Brown's participation in village patrols became more frequent and more necessary. Bomb-making cells were suspected to be operating in the region. Accompanying her all-male combat unit, the 4th Squadron, 73rd Cavalry Regiment's Troop C, Brown and her team repeatedly ventured into enemy territory on four- to five-day missions before returning to base to rest and resupply.

During one such operation on August 25, 2007, one month shy of her 19th birthday, Brown and her squadron came under fire after nearly three days of routine patrol in the Jani Khail District, located in Afghanistan's remote Paktika Province. Traveling through a dried *wadi* (riverbed) in a convoy of humvees, the rear vehicle was struck by an improvised explosive device, which almost instantaneously triggered a barrage of small-arms fire from a group of Taliban insurgents. Brown and her platoon sergeant, Staff Sgt. Jose Santos, exited their vehicle and made their way to their injured comrades a few hundred yards to the rear. Reaching the burning humvee, Brown and Santos immediately began medical treatment on the five injured soldiers, two of whom had been badly burned and sustained life-threatening injuries. While her other uninjured counterparts laid down suppressive fire, Brown treated the wounded men despite a barrage of mortar fire that had commenced shortly after she and Santos had reached the crippled vehicle.

Shielding their bodies with her own, Brown maintained her position until Santos was able to retrieve an operational vehicle to transport the group to a safer location, approximately 500 yards away from the initial ambush site. Nearly two hours after the attack had begun, Brown remained by the side of her disabled companions, prepping them for evacuation until they could be transported by air to a base hospital.

Within a week of the assault, Brown was recalled to the U.S. base in Khost. However, her maturity, heroism, and poise under fire did not go unrecognized. In March 2008, credited with saving the lives of her comrades, Brown became the first woman in Afghanistan and only the second woman since World War II to receive the Silver Star, the United States' third highest medal for bravery. Her award, presented by Vice President Dick Cheney, marked only the 15th occasion in U.S. history in which a woman earned such a military honor. In addition, she became the second woman to receive the medal for action in direct combat operations.

Beyond her outstanding military service, Brown's actions have raised further questions concerning the role of women in combat. In particular, the Pentagon's 1994 combat exclusion policy, which prohibits female soldiers from engaging in direct combat in war zones and other areas of conflict, has been scrutinized by both internal and external sources. Since 2007, many have argued that the actions of Brown and others have demonstrated that female soldiers can adequately manage the hardships of close-combat operations.

Blake A. Duffield

See also: Afghanistan; Campbell, Kim Reed (1975–); Hester, Leigh Ann (1982–); War on Terror (2001–).

References and Further Reading

Alfonso, Kristal L. M. *Femme Fatale: An Examination of the Role of Women in Combat and the Policy Implications for Future American Military Operations.* Maxwell Air Force Base, AL: Air University Press, 2009, 56–57.

Clare, Micah E. "Face of Defense: Woman Soldier Receives Silver Star." *American Forces Press Service*, March 24, 2008.

Tyson, Ann Scott. "Woman Gains Silver Star—and Removal from Combat." *Washington Post*, May 1, 2008.

BROWNELL, KADY (1842–1915)

A markswoman with the First Rhode Island Infantry volunteer unit during the Civil War, Kady Brownell proudly carried her unit's colors and fought openly as a woman in several battles alongside her husband Robert.

Born in 1842 in an army camp along the African coast, this daughter of a Scottish soldier in the British army grew up in the military life. Brownell was 19 years old, living in Rhode Island, and recently married when Fort Sumter was surrendered to Confederate forces in May 1861. The following day, Brownell and her husband Robert signed up for a three-month enlistment with the Rhode Island Infantry, one of the earliest regiments to respond to the call for volunteers.

While in camp, Brownell became known as the "Daughter of the Regiment."

Kady Brownell served in the Union Army beside her husband with the Rhode Island Volunteers. (Library of Congress)

She also gained skills as a sharp-shooter and a sword handler, items she carried as a symbol of her position as sergeant and color bearer. In the middle of July, when her regiment moved south of the Potomac River and headed toward Richmond, Brownell carried the flag. Her company came under fire, and she was separated from her husband, but she maintained the colors throughout the skirmish. As her regiment retreated and Brownell found herself in the woods, she found a horse and rode to nearby Centreville to learn of Robert's fate.

After Brownell found Robert unhurt, the pair returned to Providence, where they were discharged following the completion of their three-month term. They immediately joined the Fifth Rhode Island Infantry and participated in the January 1862 campaign for Roanoke Island. Brownell became the regiment's acting nurse and Daughter of the Regiment. Soon thereafter she again carried the flag. During a friendly fire incident with Union soldiers, Brownell ran to the front and waved the flag to stop it.

Another battle flared up soon after at New Bern, North Carolina, during which Robert sustained injuries. Brownell tended to him and the other wounded soldiers on the field. She even helped a badly wounded Confederate soldier who insulted her after regaining consciousness, which prompted Brownell to grab a bayonet and plunge it at his chest. A nearby Union soldier stopped her from hurting the Confederate.

Brownell spent the next six weeks nursing her husband and other Union soldiers back to health in New Bern. She continued to help a nearby Confederate hospital by bringing coffee and soup to the doctors, nurses, and patients. By late April, the Brownells were transferred by steamship to New York, where Robert spent several months recuperating in the Soldier's Relief Hospital. They were both discharged in the winter of 1863.

Robert's wounds prevented him from enlisting again, so the Brownells adopted a civilian life. Kady kept her colors, which had been signed by Gen. Ambrose Burnside. Beginning in 1884, Kady received a veteran's pension of $8 per month.

Brownell died in a Women's Relief Corps Home in Oxford, New York, in January 1915.

Eloise Scroggins

See also: Civil War (1861–1865); Nursing.

References and Further Reading

Leonard, Elizabeth D. *All the Daring of the Soldier: Women of the Civil War Armies.* New York: W. W. Norton, 1999.

Moore, Frank. *Women of the War; Their Heroism and Self-Sacrifice.* Hartford, CT: S. S. Scranton & Company, 1866.

BURGIN, ELIZABETH
(N.D.–N.D.)

Elizabeth Burgin operated an escape line for American prisoners of the Revolutionary War in 1779. After the war, Burgin, alternatively spelled "Bergen," became one of the few women granted a pension by Congress in recognition of her service.

Little is known about Burgin's early life. Burgin never set out to be a heroine. A widow with Patriot sympathies, she volunteered to bring baskets of food and supplies to captured American soldiers held in British prisons in and around New York. In the summer of 1779, George Higday, a member of the Culper Spy Ring, recruited her in a plan to facilitate the escapes of American prisoners of war. Together, Burgin and Higday smuggled out approximately 200 prisoners, mostly of officer rank. How Burgin went about this work is unknown, though she probably exploited her familiarity with the prisons gleaned from her charity work. Further, Burgin's gender allowed her to maneuver without arousing the suspicions of prison guards. In 18th-century America, men generally did not expect women to participate in such dangerous and sophisticated operations.

Burgin did not avoid detection for long, however. British counterintelligence officials intercepted a letter written by Gen. George Washington to the head of the Culper Spy Ring, Maj. Benjamin Tallmadge, which implicated Higday in espionage. On July 13, 1779, British troops broke into Higday's home and arrested him. Perhaps in exchange for a lesser punishment for her husband, Higday's wife betrayed Burgin to British authorities. James Pattison, major general of British forces and commandant of the city and garrison of New York, sent for Burgin on July 17, 1779. When Pattison was unable to find her, he announced a substantial bounty of £200 for her capture. Burgin fled first to Long Island and then to American-held Connecticut. She finally reached relative safety in Philadelphia.

A political exile, Burgin lost everything, including her children, her home, and all of her possessions. In September or October of 1779, she obtained a flag of truce from the Board of War to travel safely to New York to retrieve her three small children but was forced to leave her belongings behind. Upon her return to Philadelphia, Burgin was left destitute and with few options. The Continental and Confederation congresses had no relief policy for women who had served the Patriot cause, and ration lines were open only to former soldiers and the widows of officers. The only hope for women Patriots like Burgin to receive recompense was to directly petition policy makers.

Burgin appealed to Washington in a letter on November 19, 1779. After retelling her saga, she requested permission to draw rations for herself and her children in Philadelphia. Washington was impressed. On Christmas Day, 1779, he personally directed Philadelphia's commissary to furnish her with rations. Washington assigned further action on her case to Congress, writing a strong letter in her favor. Congress heard Washington's letter on December 30 of that year and referred the matter to the Board of War. There, Burgin's case was tabled and forgotten.

Burgin continued to petition Congress for what she felt she was entitled to receive. Eighteen months later, in a letter dated July 2, 1781, Burgin described her trouble obtaining the rations Washington had permitted her. To make ends meet, she was forced to sell much of what little property she had left. Burgin asked Congress to consider granting her full employment as a seamstress for the Army. Once again, Congress referred her case to the Board of War. This time they acted. On August 10, 1781, the Board of War advised that she should receive a pension, though they ignored her application for employment. The congressional committee assigned to her case concurred with the Board's judgment and granted Burgin an annuity in the sum of $53.30 on August 24, 1781. Treasury records show that Burgin drew from these funds at least through 1787.

The success of Burgin's petitioning, though belated, can be seen as a small victory for female Patriots of the Revolutionary period. The struggles Burgin encountered along the way, however, reveal just how difficult it remained for women in a patriarchal society with few avenues for political representation.

Sonia Hazard

See also: American Revolution (1775–1783); Culper Spy Ring; Espionage; Prisoners of War.

References and Further Reading

Chalou, George C. "Women in the American Revolution: Vignettes or Profiles?" In *Clio Was a Woman: Studies in the History of American Women*, edited by Mabel E. Deutrich and Virginia C. Purdy, 73–90. Washington, D.C.: Howard University Press, 1980.

Gunderson, Joan R. *To Be Useful to the World: Women in Revolutionary America, 1740–1790*. Chapel Hill: University of North Carolina Press, 2006.

Kerber, Linda K. *Women of the Republic: Intellect and Ideology in Revolutionary America*. Chapel Hill: University of North Carolina Press, 1980.

C

CADET NURSE CORPS

The U.S. Cadet Nurse Corps was established by an act of Congress in 1943 in order to address the precarious situation of nurse shortages caused by World War II. Congresswoman Frances P. Bolton, a Republican representative from Ohio, introduced a bill to establish the corps on March 29, 1943. The Bolton Act or Nurse Training Act was voted unanimously through the 78th Congress and signed into law by President Franklin D. Roosevelt on June 15, 1943. The act was one of the largest and most successful pieces of public health legislation passed during the war, and the Cadet Nurse Corps was officially founded on July 1, 1943.

Wartime demand for nurses was felt immediately after the Japanese attack on Pearl Harbor. As a result, Congress passed the Labor-Security Agency Appropriation Act of 1942, which provided funding for nursing schools. The U.S. Public Health Service (USPHS) was placed in charge of the monies, but

the funds did not go far enough, and an organized recruiting effort never took shape. The Bolton Act once again placed the USPHS in charge, but this time a formal administrative structure was created.

A Nurse Education Division was set up and headed by a committee of at least five members that would advise the surgeon general, Dr. Thomas Parran. This division formulated the rules and regulations for the new corps and dispersed the federal funds to the appropriate institutions. The main purpose of this advisory board was not to revamp or standardize nursing education but rather to utilize the school systems already in place. It was also clearly understood that the qualified nurses were to serve where needed in both civilian and military capacities. The board's chief dilemma was to accelerate training while still holding institutions to the highest standards of the nursing profession.

Regulations for schools and eligibility requirements for cadets were quickly established. Nursing schools applying for federal aid were required to graduate nurses within a range of 24 to 30 months. Cadets were to be between 17 and 35 years of age, high school graduates, and in good health. They signed on for civilian or military service for the duration of the war, and if the war ended those enrolled 90 days prior to the final surrender would be eligible for full aid. Married women and African Americans were allowed to join the corps, and women already enrolled in schools (those enrolled after January 1, 1941) were also eligible for financial aid. In order to maintain high academic standards, funds were allocated for postgraduate education, refresher programs, and supervisory and instructor training courses.

Qualified nurse cadets were designated into three distinct classes based on the amount of training they had received. Precadet nurses were those candidates within the first nine months of their studies. During this period, cadets learned the fundamentals of their new profession and were strictly supervised. Junior cadets fell into the 15- to 20-month range of instruction, while senior cadets spent their last months of training in local hospitals to gain clinical experience and supplement nurse shortages. Scholarships provided for tuition, uniforms, and books. Stipends were granted based on class rank: precadets received $15 per month, junior cadets received $20 per month, and senior cadets earned $30 per month. The cadet uniforms were gray, and the corps' insignia, a white Maltese cross placed in a red circle, was worn on the left shoulder. The eight points of the Maltese cross represented the eight beatitudes: spiritual joy, to live without malice, to weep over thy sins, to humble thyself, to love justice,

to be merciful, to be sincere and pure of heart, and to suffer persecution.

Once the qualifications were established, a national recruitment campaign was launched to attract able-bodied women, many of whom were lured to higher-paying jobs in the factories. Over 300 national radio stations played ads for the new corps daily. Newspaper and magazines ads appealed to patriotism as well as the prospect of a free education. A 10-minute film was shown in movie theaters before main features, and cadet nurse characters began appearing in popular films. Leaflets were placed in local stores and hospitals, and cadets participated in parades and bond rallies. This marketing campaign succeeded. It resulted in exceeded quotas for both 1943 (quota goal 65,000) and 1944 (quota goal 60,000). The 1945 quota of 60,000 was reduced to 50,000 after V-E Day in May, and 40,000 had signed up by the time of the Japanese surrender in August.

The Cadet Nurse Corps proved to be extremely successful. By February 1945, 60 percent of the corps were serving or applying to serve in the military. Of the 1,300 nursing schools operating during World War II, 1,125 participated in the federal program. An estimated 179,000 women entered nursing institutions during the war with 169,443 enlisting in the Cadet Nurse Corps, 3,000 of whom were African Americans.

The final date for admission into the corps was October 15, 1945, with the last candidates graduating in 1948. The Cadet Nurse Corps not only succeeded in augmenting the nursing personnel in both the military and civilian sectors, which were dangerously low during the war, but also produced many long-term benefits. It helped foster a greater public awareness of the need for a strong nursing profession. A more academic approach to nurse training was adopted nationwide. Nursing schools, libraries, and graduate programs were expanded, as was integration, with more African Americans entering the field. The corps established a standard of excellence that is still felt today through highly trained health-care professionals.

William E. Whyte

See also: African American Women; Army Nurse Corps (ANC); Bolton, Frances Payne Bingham (1885–1977); Navy Nurse Corps; Nursing; Women Accepted for Volunteer Emergency Service (WAVES); World War II (1941–1945).

References and Further Reading

Kalisch, Philip A. "Why Not Launch a New Cadet Nurse Corps?" *American Journal of Nursing* 88, no. 3 (March 1988): 316–17.

Petry, Lucile. "The U.S. Cadet Nurse Corps: A Summing Up." *American Journal of Nursing* 45, no. 12 (December 1945): 1027–28.

Petry, Lucile. "The U.S. Cadet Nurse Corps: Established under the Bolton Act." *American Journal of Nursing* 43, no. 8 (August 1943): 704–8.

Robinson, Thelma M. *Your Country Needs You: Cadet Nurses of World War II.* Bloomington, IN: Xlibris Corporation, 2009.

Willever, Heather, and Parascandola, John. "The Cadet Nurse Corps: 1943–48." *Association of Schools of Public Health* 109, no. 3 (May–June 1994): 455–57.

CADORIA, SHERIAN GRACE (1940–)

Sherian Grace Cadoria became the U.S. Army's first black female general.

When she retired as a brigadier general in 1990, she was the highest-ranking woman in the Army. She was also the first woman to serve as a military police officer, to command an all-male battalion, to lead a criminal investigation brigade, and to be admitted to the U.S. Army Command and General Staff College and the Army War College.

Born January 26, 1940, in Marksville, Louisiana, to Joseph and Bernice (McGlory) Cadoria, she was one of three children. Because their father had chronic health problems, she and her siblings picked cotton with their mother to support the family. Her mother's example instilled in her strength and moral character. To avoid the humiliation of segregated bus seating, she and her siblings walked five miles each day to attend school at Holy Ghost Elementary. Cadoria knew that she did not want to stay in the small town as a tenant farmer.

Brig. Gen. Sherian Cadoria became the Army's first black female general. (Russel Roederer, U.S. Army)

With the encouragement of her mother and a high school English teacher, Cadoria enrolled at Southern University in Baton Rouge, Louisiana. Always looking for the next opportunity, Cadoria joined the Women's Army Corps (WAC) College Junior Training Program during her junior year at Southern. Programs such as WAC were often the best way for African Americans to secure some type of stability in a racially divided United States.

Upon graduation from Southern in 1961 with a degree in business education, she enlisted in the Army. The newly commissioned Cadoria went to Fort McClellan in Alabama for further training in 1962. Although the Army had been integrated, the Jim Crow laws in Alabama did not allow Cadoria much freedom. Ku Klux Klan members often stood outside the gates of the base to harass African American soldiers. In addition, black officers were not allowed to take white solders off base and could also be refused service at local restaurants.

Cadoria served in Vietnam from 1967 until 1969. By the time she returned to the United States in October 1969, she had been promoted to major. She was selected to attend the U.S. Army Command and General Staff College at Fort Leavenworth, Kansas, the first African American woman to be given that opportunity. She graduated in 1971. She earned a master's degree in human relations from the University of Oklahoma in 1974. She served as a White House social aide to President Gerald Ford from 1975 to 1976. Then, in 1978, she became the first African American woman to study at the U.S. Army War College in Pennsylvania.

After the disbandment of the WAC and the integration of women into the Regular Army, Cadoria earned promotion to colonel on September 1, 1980. In August 1985, she became the first African American woman appointed director of manpower and personnel for the Joint Chiefs of Staff. Then, on October 1, 1985, Cadoria earned promotion to brigadier general. She later became deputy commanding general of Total Army Personnel Command at Alexandria, Virginia.

In recognition of her service, she has received the Legion of Merit, three Bronze Stars, two Meritorious Service Medals, the Air Medal, and four Army Commendation Medals. She has also received honors from Southern University, the NAACP, the Louisiana Black History Hall of Fame, and the Louisiana Justice Hall of Fame. Ohio Dominican College and Benedictine College have both awarded honorary doctorates to her.

After her retirement in 1990 at the rank of brigadier general, Cadoria became the founder and CEO of Cadoria Speaker and Consultancy Service. She also serves as volunteer principal of her elementary school in Marksville, Louisiana.

Aineshia Carline Washington

See also: African American Women; Vietnam War (1965–1973); Women's Army Corps (WAC).

References and Further Reading

Hine, Darlene Clark, ed. *Black Women in America*, Vol. 1. New York: Oxford University Press, 2005.

Lanker, Brian. *I Dream a World: Portraits of Black Women Who Changed America.* New York: Stewart, Tabori & Chang, 1989.

CAMMERMEYER, MARGARETHE (1942–)

Military nurse Margarethe Cammermeyer was discharged from the military after 26 years of exemplary service when she admitted her homosexuality in a security clearance interview. She successfully sued the Department of Defense. She was reinstated at her former rank of colonel in 1994.

Margarethe "Grethe" Cammermeyer was born in Nazi-occupied Norway on March 24, 1942. Her parents supported the Norwegian resistance. The Cammermeyers immigrated to the United States in 1951, and she became a citizen in 1960. She enlisted in the Army Student Nurse Program at age 19, earning her bachelor's degree from the University of Maryland in 1963. While serving in Germany, she met Harvey Hawken, whom she married in 1965. She volunteered for nursing duty in Vietnam and served for 14 months at the 24th Evacuation Hospital at Long Binh, earning a Bronze Star. After the war, the couple lived in Washington state and had four sons.

In 1972, when the regulation barring women with dependents from military service ended, Cammermeyer joined the Army Reserve. She obtained a master's degree (1976) and a doctorate (1991) from the University of Washington's School of Nursing. Specializing in

After her discharge for homosexuality, Army nurse Margarethe Cammermeyer successfully sued the Department of Defense and won her reinstatement in the military. (Kim Komenich/Time Life Pictures/Getty Images)

neuroscience and sleep disorders, she has coauthored nursing textbooks and research articles. Amid growing dissatisfaction with her personal life, Cammermeyer divorced Hawken in 1980. In 1985, the Veterans Administration selected her as Nurse of the Year from a pool of 34,000 candidates. The National Organization of Women named her a Woman of Power in 1985.

Cammermeyer struggled with awareness about her sexual identity for years, but in April 1989, when asked about her orientation during a security clearance interview, she answered honestly that she was a lesbian, saying the words for the first time. She later learned that her children had known she was a lesbian before she had realized it. Military policy at the time stipulated that statements acknowledging homosexuality were sufficient grounds for discharge. The military began discharge procedures, ending her ambition to become a general and chief nurse of the Army Nurse Corps. When she lost her Washington State National Guard position on June 11, 1992, after 26 years of exemplary service, she became the highest-ranking officer to fall victim to the military's antigay policy. Due to her outstanding service record and reputation, the Department of Defense was unable to make a case that gay people are less qualified for military service than heterosexuals.

Although devastated, Cammermeyer did not quietly disappear. She sued the Department of Defense in civil court. While the Military Law Task Force, Lambda Legal Defense and Education Fund, and the Northwest Women's Law Center participated in her legal efforts, she worked at the Veterans Administration Hospital near Tacoma, Washington, and wrote an autobiography, *Serving in Silence*, which was published in 1994. The American Nurses Association awarded her its Honorary Human Rights Award in 1994 for fighting discrimination against gays and lesbians in the military.

On June 1, 1994, U.S. District Judge Thomas Zilly rescinded her ouster, ordering the clearance of her record. He ruled that the military's policy on gays was unconstitutional and based only on prejudice, violating her rights to due process and equal protection under the law. She was reinstated on July 8, 1994, to her former rank as colonel and her position as chief of nursing services for the 164th Mobile Army Surgical Hospital. Analysts viewed the outcome of Cammermeyer's case as a potential threat to the new "Don't Ask, Don't Tell" policy regulating homosexual service in the military. Cammermeyer became an honorary cochair of the Servicemembers Legal Defense Network, which was established to provide legal support for gays and lesbians serving under the "Don't Ask, Don't Tell" policy.

The TV movie *Serving in Silence: The Margarethe Cammermeyer Story* aired in 1995, winning three Emmys, a Peabody Award, and the Gay and Lesbian Alliance Against Defamation (GLAAD) Media Award. In 1997, when Cammermeyer retired after 31 years of service, she operated a sleep lab and seizure clinic in Washington and made an unsuccessful congressional bid in 1998. She was a radio talk show host for the pioneering GayBC Radio Network from November 1999 to December 2001.

Cammermeyer operates an adult-care home on Whidbey Island, Washington, where she lives with her partner, artist Diane Divelbess. In 2010, the Department of Defense appointed Cammermeyer to the Defense Advisory Committee on Women in the Services. In 2011, Cammermeyer received the Point Foundation's Point Legend Award for lifetime achievement and support for the LGBT community.

Betty J. Glass

See also: Army Nurse Corps (ANC); Defense Advisory Committee on Women in the Services (DACOWITS); Mobile Army Surgical Hospital (MASH); Nursing; Vietnam War (1965–1973).

References and Further Reading

Cammermeyer, Margarethe, with Chris Fisher. *Serving in Silence*. New York: Penguin, 1994.

Serving in Silence: The Margarethe Cammermeyer Story. Culver City, CA: Sony Pictures Home Entertainment, 2006.

Shilts, Randy. *Conduct Unbecoming: Lesbians and Gays in the U.S. Military—Vietnam to the Persian Gulf*. New York: St. Martin's Press, 1993.

Zilly, Thomas. "Cammermeyer v. Aspin," 850 *Federal Supplement*. 910, 924 (Washington, D.C.: June 1, 1994).

CAMPBELL, KIM REED (1975–)

A fighter pilot in the U.S. Air Force, Maj. Kim Reed Campbell achieved international fame in 2003 when she successfully landed a plane that had sustained heavy fire in Iraq. Despite flying without a functioning hydraulics system, Campbell landed the plane safely and subsequently received the Distinguished Flying Cross for her actions.

Kim Reed was born on June 6, 1975, in Honolulu's military hospital to Chuck and Paula Reed. Her father was as an officer in the U.S. Air Force. Shortly after Kim's birth, the family moved to northern California. She spent most of her childhood in San Jose. From an early age, she displayed notable athletic abilities, competing in track and soccer. In the seventh grade, Reed joined the Civil Air Patrol (CAP). This experience gave her early training in military discipline and paved the way for learning to fly aircraft.

On her 16th birthday, Reed began flying lessons. Two years later, she joined the U.S. Air Force Academy. She proved to be an excellent student and stood out among her peers. Her CAP experiences and background as an athlete helped her to achieve an outstanding score of 478 out of 500 on the Academy's rigorous Physical Fitness Test. Air Force officials identified her exceptional potential early in her first year when she was profiled in *Checkpoints*, the Academy's alumni magazine.

In 1993, Kim met Scott Campbell, one of the sergeants who supervised her basic training. While she disliked him upon their first meeting, they eventually became friends and began dating. They married in 1999.

At the Academy, Reed majored in space operations and minored in French. In her senior year, she achieved the status of cadet wing commander, a position that placed her in a leadership role above her fellow cadets. In 1997, she graduated from the Air Force Academy first in her class and as cadet wing commander. This achievement was particularly notable because her father had graduated with the same honors in 1970. Their similar accomplishments marked the first time in Air Force Academy history that a father and daughter graduated with the same titles and rank.

After Reed graduated from the Air Force Academy, she attended the University of Reading in the United Kingdom, earning a master's degree in international security studies. One year later, she began studying for her master's of business administration (MBA) degree at Imperial College, London. As part of her degree program, she completed an internship with the National Air and Space Administration (NASA). While in Houston, she undertook advanced pilot training that she had been unable to complete at the Academy due to medical issues.

In 2002, Reed Campbell completed her A-10 flight training and was assigned to a flight squadron at Pope Air Force Base in North Carolina. For the first time since their marriage more than two years earlier, Kim and Scott moved in together. Only a few months later, however, both of them were deployed to Afghanistan. In March of 2003, the United States began its second war in Iraq, and both of them became involved in combat operations.

In April of 2003, Campbell survived the incident that would propel her into the international spotlight. While flying over Baghdad in order to provide air support to ground troops, her A-10 was damaged by enemy fire. The A-10's hydraulics system failed immediately, nearly sending the plane out of control. Rather than ejecting over Baghdad,

Campbell switched the plane to manual reversion mode, which does not require hydraulics. With the advice of a fellow pilot, she flew the damaged plane back to the base; because the plane lacked functioning hydraulics, the return flight had to be accomplished without effective landing gear, brakes, and a variety of other components that keep the A-10 stabilized while in the air. Despite these dangers, Campbell landed safely. For this remarkable feat, she received the Distinguished Flying Cross.

After returning from her tour of duty in Iraq, Campbell gave several interviews and talks relating to her experiences in the war. In addition, she participated in an Air Force Academy program intended to reduce sexual harassment and assault of female cadets.

As of 2009, Reed Campbell had flown 55 missions in Iraq and 66 in Afghanistan. During her tours of duty in both wars, she was known by the call sign "Killer Chick." While she remains a pilot in the U.S. Air Force, she has stated that she would eventually like to become an astronaut for NASA.

Jamie Stoops

See also: Civil Air Patrol (CAP); Iraq War (2003–2011).

References and Further Reading

Douglas, Deborah G., and Amy Foster. *American Women and Flight since 1940.* Lexington: University Press of Kentucky, 2004.

Hoppin, Christopher J. *Same Date of Rank: Grads from the Top and Bottom from West Point, Annapolis, and the Air Force Academy.* Bloomington, IN: Xlibris, 2009.

CAMP FOLLOWERS

As long as there have been armies there have been civilians who, for various reasons, attached themselves to the troops. Young and old, slave and free, male and female, these people followed the soldiers, becoming unofficial members of the military community. By the early 19th century they became known as camp followers. Some went willingly, including entrepreneurs hoping to make money by providing goods and services to the soldiers. Some were family members accompanying their loved ones either from a sense of duty, loyalty, or desperation. Then there were individuals with little or no choice in the matter. These were the slaves and servants who frequently accompanied their masters, usually officers, and provided the same types of domestic services in camp that they had at home. The number of camp followers varied depending upon the time period in history, the type of conflict, the season of the year, and the location of the army.

During the American Revolution, many small merchants set up stalls near military encampments. If officially sanctioned by the army, they were known as sutlers. They sold a wide assortment of goods, from alcohol and tobacco to needles and thread. The majority of these vendors were male, but many women also took advantage of the economic opportunities offered by war. Some worked with their husbands and if widowed continued the businesses by themselves. Other women defied convention and set out on their own as peddlers. However, most women camp followers who worked for food or money did so in more traditional feminine roles as laundresses, nurses, cooks, seamstresses, and prostitutes. Although in more recent years, for reasons that are unclear, the term *camp follower* has often been used synonymously with *prostitute*, the number of women working as prostitutes constituted only a small percentage of the total female population of camp followers. Most of the working women were mothers, wives, sisters, and daughters of the soldiers.

Although the majority of army officers came from the upper socioeconomic levels of society, soldiers usually did not. When a man was recruited, drafted, conscripted, or pressed into military service, family members left behind frequently lost their means of support. Desperate to survive, they often had little choice but to follow along, hoping to pick up work and rations (food) from the army. The army considered these women and children necessary nuisances. They overburdened often scarce resources and slowed down the movement of troops. Forced to travel with the baggage wagons, the women and children were forbidden to ride and were made to walk alongside the carts and horses. Frequently they hopped on board, catching illegal rides. Either way, walking or riding, they encumbered the troops. On the other hand, they provided essential services that the army did not. They washed the laundry, nursed the sick and wounded, and repaired torn and worn-out clothing. In addition, they sometimes cooked not only for their own men but also for other soldiers. Just as importantly, they provided a sense of domestic life for the weary soldiers. A soldier who had his family with him was less likely to desert than one without his family.

Officers' wives were usually not in the same dire financial straits as soldiers' families. They frequently remained at home tending to viable businesses or farms. Yet when the army settled down into winter encampments, they, too, often joined their husbands for a few months, swelling the ranks of camp followers. Their presence in camp provided a semblance of domesticity for the officers that included dinner parties, balls, and other social engagements. These activities also provided soldiers' wives with the opportunity for additional employment as laundresses, cooks, and maids in officers' households.

By the 19th century, the army had codified the employment of laundresses, allowing rations, bedding straw, and wages for one laundress per 17 men but capping the number at four per company. The laundresses were usually soldiers' wives but sometimes were single women or widows. In addition to these sanctioned women, other soldiers' wives, daughters, and mistresses trailed along, sharing food and cramped living space with their men and often finding work as domestic servants for the officers. Officers' wives did not work for pay but performed the same sorts of domestic duties as their civilian counterparts, raising children, overseeing the running of the household, and planning parties, dances, theatricals, and other social entertainments.

Nineteenth-century army officers were allotted quarters (living space) based upon rank. The higher the rank, the more space was allowed. If an officer brought his wife and family with him, they shared whatever space he was assigned. A general might rattle around in a large house all by himself while a lieutenant's wife and four children squeezed into one room. Unlike soldiers' wives who worked as laundresses, an officer's family received no rations, and technically they were not even eligible for medical services from the army doctor. If a laundress's soldier husband died, she could continue her employment with the army. If an officer died, his wife lost not only her husband but also her income, her social standing, and her home. She needed to vacate the quarters almost immediately.

Although generally viewed as a bastion of masculinity, the 18th- and 19th-century army community teemed with women and children. They performed valuable services and provided the officers and men the trappings of domestic life.

Robin D. Campbell

See also: African American Women; American Revolution (1775–1783); Civil War (1861–1865); Indian Wars; North American Colonial Wars (17th–18th centuries); Nursing.

References and Further Reading

Campbell, Robin D. *Mistresses of the Transient Hearth: American Army Officers' Wives and Material Culture, 1840–1880*. New York: Routledge, 2005.

Mayer, Holly A. *Belonging to the Army: Camp Followers and Community during the American Revolution*. Columbia: University of South Carolina Press, 1996.

Stallard, Patricia Y. *Glittering Misery: Dependents of the Indian Fighting Army*. Norman: University of Oklahoma Press, 1991.

CARACRISTI, ANN ZEILINGER (1921–)

The first woman to serve as deputy director of the National Security Agency (NSA) (1980–1982), Ann Zeilinger Caracristi is known for her inspired leadership and pioneering cryptologic efforts in both World War II and the Cold War.

Born in Bronxville, New York, on February 1, 1921, she graduated from Russell Sage College in 1942 with a bachelor's degree in English and history. That same year she joined the U.S. Army's Signal Intelligence Service (SIS), later to be called the Signal Security Agency (SSA) and then the Army Security Agency (ASA). She was first an assistant cryptologic specialist, sorting raw traffic for the team studying Imperial Japanese Army enciphered messages, but she quickly became a cryptanalyst and rose to the ranks of supervisor before the end of the war.

Caracristi left government service briefly at the conclusion of the war and worked in an advertising position with a New York–based newspaper. She returned to cryptology in late 1946, first with ASA and then with the Armed Forces Security Agency (AFSA), which would become the NSA in 1952. Her expertise and professionalism responding to tough intelligence problems brought her rapid advancement at NSA.

From 1952 to 1959, she served as chief of several operations elements. In 1959, she became one of the first women at NSA to be promoted to supergrade rank, the equivalent of today's senior executive service. Caracristi directed several major research and operations efforts from 1959 to 1975. She graduated from the Federal Executive Institute in 1969. In 1975, she was the first woman at NSA to be promoted to GS-18, and she became the first woman to be chief of a major operations group. Under her leadership, the group enjoyed numerous technical breakthroughs and became noted for its dedication to the needs of intelligence consumers, both areas Caracristi emphasized.

Caracristi was an early advocate of automated techniques, pioneering in the application of computers and mechanized processing. She played an important role in establishing a laboratory facility to study and begin to exploit new technologies. In January 1980, the director of NSA, Vice Adm. Bobby Ray Inman, selected her to be the agency's sixth deputy director, the first woman to serve in that position. As deputy director, the agency's highest civilian post, Caracristi's duties involved broad responsibility for agency operations and for establishing and monitoring NSA policies for recruiting, training, and assigning civilian and military personnel. She was an advocate of good customer support and community relations long before these terms came into general use. Caracristi retired from NSA in August 1982.

Since her retirement, Caracristi has continued to serve on a number of boards and committees that have shaped not only cryptologic policies but also the relationships between the various parts of the intelligence community. Among her many positions have been the Chief of Naval Operations (CNO) Executive Panel (1982–1991), chairperson of a director of central intelligence (DCI) task force on the intelligence community (1992–1993), the President's Foreign Intelligence Advisory Board (PFIAB) (1993–2001), the Intelligence Oversight Board (1993–2001), the DCI/Secretary of Defense Joint Security Commission, the Commission on the Roles and Capabilities of the United States Intelligence Community, the National Research Council's Committee to Study National Cryptography Policy, the Naval Intelligence Foundation's Board of Advisors, and the NSA Scientific Advisory Board. She was president of the Association of Former Intelligence Officers (AFIO) from 1989 to 1991 and has served on the Board of Directors of the National Cryptologic Museum Foundation.

Among Caracristi's many honors are the Federal Woman's Award (1965), the NSA Meritorious Civilian Service Award (1966), the NSA Exceptional Civilian Service Award (1975), the National Intelligence Distinguished Service Medal, the National Service League Career Service Award (1978), and, in 1980, the Defense Department's highest civilian honor, the Distinguished Civilian Service Award. Since her retirement, she has received the National Security Medal (1982) and the William Oliver Baker Award from the Intelligence and National Security Alliance (INSA) (1999). In 2002, the National Defense Intelligence College (NDIC)—now the National Intelligence University (NIU)—established the Ann Caracristi Award to recognize postgraduate academic excellence in the field of intelligence at the school.

Caracristi's achievements in her nearly 40 years of government service and in the decades since her retirement were exceptional, and she is remembered as an outstanding manger and mentor. Her service contributed to the security of the United States during both World War II and the Cold War and inspired countless employees, both male and female.

Betsy Rohaly Smoot

See also: Cold War (ca. 1947–1991); Espionage; World War II (1941–1945).

Reference and Further Reading

O'Toole, G. J. A. *The Encyclopedia of American Intelligence and Espionage: From the Revolutionary War to the Present.* New York: Facts on File, 1988.

CARROLL, ANNA ELLA (1815–1894)

Political pamphleteer and military strategist Anna Ella Carroll, the daughter of Maryland governor Thomas King Carroll, is best known for her claim to have devised the so-called Tennessee Plan for the Union Army's invasion in February 1862. Carroll wrote a series of pamphlets that laid out the legal rationale for using the army to enforce federal laws in the Southern states.

Carroll wrote a number of pamphlets in support of the Union in 1861 and 1862. The most important of these, "Reply to Breckinridge" (1861), detailed the arguments that President Abraham Lincoln and Attorney General Edward Bates made that, as commander-in-chief, Lincoln could use the armed forces to perform his duties as chief enforcement officer of the United States. In other words, he could call for volunteers, suspend the writ of habeas corpus, institute a naval blockade, and use the army to put down a domestic rebellion. Lincoln employed this legal tactic throughout the course of the war.

Carroll's pamphlet was so clearly written that Secretary of State William Henry Seward ordered it distributed to Congress. The legal rationale Carroll described was later delineated by notable lawyer Horace Binney and published more widely, but Carroll provided the earliest explication of the legal basis for Lincoln's actions in the first months of the war.

Later pamphlets by Carroll criticized the president's actions, particularly regarding the Union's confiscation of slaves as contraband of war, arguing the border states would rebel. She also promoted colonization efforts by Aaron Columbus Burr to settle ex-slaves in Central America in what he named the Lincoln Colony.

Carroll's claim to fame rests not on her writings but on her claim that she created the Tennessee Campaign. She approached the War Department in 1861 after she met riverboat captain Charles Scott in St. Louis, Missouri. As Carroll wrote to the Washington, D.C., *National Intelligencer* shortly after the Confederate surrender in 1865, Scott pointed out the strategic value of using the Tennessee and Cumberland Rivers, which flowed north, instead of the Mississippi River, to invade the Confederacy via Tennessee. Neither river was strongly fortified, and controlling them would relieve Union loyalists, particularly in eastern Tennessee. Any gunboats damaged by Confederate fire would float northward, back into Union territory, and the Tennessee was navigable clear to Alabama, providing excellent ingress to the heart of the Confederacy.

Carroll presented Scott's information to Assistant Secretary of War Thomas Scott in November 1861. Her plan duplicated others, including the overall strategy of the Union army under Gen. Ulysses S. Grant, who had captured towns at the mouths of the rivers and was waiting for Union gunboats before venturing farther inland. In February 1862, the Union invaded Tennessee up the rivers, taking Forts Henry and Donelson.

Shortly after the war, Carroll began petitioning Congress to pay her as a strategist. Her claim was adopted by the suffragists Susan B. Anthony, Sarah Ellen Blackwell, and Elizabeth Cady Stanton, for whom Carroll became a symbol of the military's disregard for women when it came to the work of the war. Her role as a symbol endures in her continuing appearances in Civil War historiography as an unsung female hero. Her legal acumen, while widely respected by politicians, including Lincoln, has drawn less attention than her legendary status as military strategist.

Janet L. Coryell

See also: Civil War (1861–1865).

References and Further Reading

Carroll, Anna Ella. *Reply to the Speech of Hon. J. C. Breckinridge*. Washington, D.C.: Henry Polkinhorn, 1861.

Carroll, Anna Ella. *The War Powers of the General Government*. Washington, D.C.: Henry Polkinhorn, 1861.

Coryell, Janet L. *Neither Heroine nor Fool: Anna Ella Carroll of Maryland*. Kent, OH: Kent State University Press, 1990.

Williams, Kenneth P. "The Tennessee River Campaign and Anna Ella Carroll." *Indiana Magazine of History* 46 (1950): 221–48.

CARY, MARY ANN SHADD (1823–1893)

The activist daughter of free black parents, Mary Ann Shadd Cary worked as a recruiting officer of black troops for the Union army from 1863 to 1864. Cary was a paid organizer of the 29th Regiment Connecticut Volunteers and later of the 28th Colored Infantry (Indiana). Working from a base in New Albany, Indiana, she used her considerable ties among networks of abolitionists and her skill at public speaking to muster in both enslaved and free African Americans. She also organized aid to contraband families. In her lifetime, Cary was an antislavery lecturer; a proponent of black nationalism; a participant in black emigration to Canada; an opinionated editor, teacher, writer, and lawyer; and a women's rights advocate.

Mary Ann Shadd was born in Wilmington, Delaware. Her father, Abraham Shadd, worked with the Underground Railroad and was an agent for abolitionist William Lloyd Garrison's *The Liberator*. Mary Ann attended a Quaker school in Pennsylvania and soon became a teacher of free black children. With the 1850 passage of the Fugitive Slave Law, she joined other family members as they immigrated to Canada. She established an integrated school there through the auspices of the American Missionary Association. She also began publishing accounts that encouraged black migration to the Canadian West and was the strongly opinionated editor of the *Provincial Freeman* newspaper (ca. 1854–1860).

Shadd was attracted to the African colonization ideas of Martin Delany but criticized the James Redpath and Haitian emigration schemes. She married Thomas F. Cary of Toronto in 1856 but was widowed in 1860. Thwarted in her bid to become a missionary in Africa, she left her two young children with family and returned to the United States to work as Delany's agent, traveling across the Midwest speaking in churches and other venues and canvassing possible recruits. The work was dangerous in states with black codes and in those where conservative Democrats feared an influx of African Americans as a result of the Emancipation Proclamation. Cary made her base in New Albany, a steamboat-building center on the Ohio River with a proportionately high population of black residents and at the Kentucky state line—a good spot not only to recruit but also to aid runaways in their journey to Canada.

Cary's recruitment of African American soldiers for the Union army bore fruit in 1864. The 29th Colored Infantry was mustered in Connecticut in March 1864 and sent to the Department of the South for active duty. Cary continued working as a recruiter for Connecticut and Indiana. She was also an agent for the Chicago-based Colored Ladies' Freedmen's Aid Society (CLFAS), which gathered and sent supplies to former slaves living on the front lines. She also raised funds for her Mission School in Chatham, Canada. She returned to Chatham in the last months of the war.

Cary later moved to Washington, D.C., where she attended Howard University Law School and earned her law degree in 1870, becoming the first black female lawyer in the United States. She was a strong advocate of women's rights, including the right to vote. She organized the Colored Women's Progressive Franchise Association in 1880.

Barbara Bair

See also: African American Women; Civil War (1861–1865).

References and Further Reading

Bearden, Jim, and Linda Jean Butler. *Shadd: The Life and Times of Mary Shadd Cary.* Toronto: N. C. Press, 1977.

Rhodes, Jane. *Mary Ann Shadd Cary: The Black Press and Protest in the Nineteenth Century.* Bloomington: Indiana University Press, 1998.

CAZNEAU, JANE McMANUS STORMS [CORA MONTGOMERY] (1807–1878)

Journalist Jane McManus Storms Cazneau coined the term *Manifest Destiny* and argued for the annexation of all Mexican territory in the aftermath of the Mexican-American War. At a time when women were excluded from public affairs, she helped shape history through her written articles and association with influential policy makers.

Jane Maria Eliza McManus was born on April 6, 1807, in Troy, New York. Educated at an all-girls academy in Troy, she married Allen Storms in 1825. Facing economic hardship after her divorce from Storms in 1831, she investigated land speculation opportunities in Texas. In 1832, she traveled to Texas, then still Mexican territory, with her brother and acquired a land grant in Matagorda.

In 1835, Storms openly supported Texan independence from Mexico and advocated annexation to the United States. She subsequently published numerous articles supporting her position in American newspapers and journals, often using the pseudonym "Cora Montgomery." In the March 1845 issue of *The United States Magazine and Democratic Review*, she wrote an article in which she coined the term *Manifest Destiny*. Although the term was initially credited to the journal's editor, John L. O'Sullivan, recent historical research has revealed that the unsigned article in question was most likely written by Storms.

During the Mexican War, Storms served as the first female war correspondent, providing American readers with coverage of the conflict from behind enemy lines. In November 1846, President James K. Polk authorized *New York Sun* editor Moses Yales Beach to initiate a secret mission to investigate the terms of a possible peace treaty with Mexico. Assisted in his efforts by Storms, Beach returned to the United States in April 1847; his mission was unsuccessful. Regardless, Storms can be considered the first unofficial female diplomat in U.S. history. Publishing numerous articles as Cora Montgomery, Storms insisted that the United States annex all Mexican territory in the aftermath of the war. As such, she became one of the most vocal champions of the "All-Mexico" movement in the United States. She was especially interested in acquiring the Isthmus of Tehuantepec in Oaxaca as a possible rail and canal route to connect the Gulf of Mexico with the Pacific Ocean. Northern abolitionists who feared the potential expansion of slavery into Mexican lands and others who believed that it would be impossible to incorporate the culturally diverse Mexicans into mainstream U.S. society, however, successfully countermanded Storms's insistence on annexing all of Mexico.

In 1849, Storms married Texan businessman and politician William Cazneau. From 1850 to 1852, the couple lived at Eagle Pass, Texas. Jane Cazneau now devoted herself to writing and furthering the cause of U.S. territorial and commercial expansion. Her efforts to reconcile sectional attitudes toward U.S. expansion exemplified the desires of nationalistic Democrats. Motivated by a complex combination of altruistic ideological justifications and self-serving economic imperatives, following the Mexican-American War Cazneau supported the expansion of U.S. political and economic hegemony in Mexico, the Dominican Republic, Cuba, and Nicaragua. Interested in transit routes across Nicaragua, Cazneau wrote articles supporting the activities of American filibuster William Walker in Nicaragua during the 1850s. Cazneau spent most of the 1850s living in the Dominican Republic, where her husband served as a special U.S. agent investigating the possibility of acquiring Samaná Bay as a coaling station for U.S. ships. In addition to frequent newspaper and journal articles supporting the expansion of

U.S. hegemony in the Caribbean Basin, Cazneau also wrote lengthy letters supporting her convictions to prominent members of the Democratic Party, including presidents Franklin Pierce and James Buchanan. The issue of slavery, however, stymied all attempts at U.S. expansionism during the 1850s.

Following the Civil War, U.S. interest in acquiring territory in the Caribbean Basin, especially the Dominican Republic, was reinvigorated. President Ulysses S. Grant used the influence of the Cazneaus in his unsuccessful attempt to annex the Dominican Republic in 1870.

Sailing from New York to Santo Domingo onboard the *Emily B. Souder*, Cazneau died when the steamship sank in a storm off the coast of North Carolina on December 10, 1878.

Michael R. Hall

See also: Civil War (1861–1865).

References and Further Reading

Cazneau, Jane Maria McManus. *Eagle Pass: Or, Life on the Border*. Austin, TX: Pemberton Press, 1966.

Hudson, Linda S. *Mistress of Manifest Destiny: A Biography of Jane McManus Storm Cazneau, 1807–1878*. Austin: Texas State Historical Association, 2001.

CHAMPION, DEBORAH (1753–N.D.)

Patriot Deborah Champion delivered important dispatches to Gen. George Washington at the beginning of the

American Revolution. She recorded her actions in a letter to a friend.

Born May 3, 1753, in Colchester County, Connecticut, Deborah was the daughter of Deborah and Henry Champion, a commissary general of the Continental Army.

In a letter she later wrote to a friend, Champion detailed the event that would qualify her as a patriot of the American Revolution. The letter has provided the most information on her mission from her home to Washington's headquarters. As she told it, in 1775, the year that Paul Revere rode through the area to give messages to the patriots, Henry Champion sent his daughter Deborah on a mission from Wenchester, Connecticut, to Boston. A young man brought dispatches to the Champion home and let the general know that the dispatches needed to be carried undercover to Washington as quickly as possible.

Her father tasked Deborah, instead of her brother, with carrying the dispatches because he knew that a young woman would be less likely to be questioned than a man. The British soldiers would not see her as suspicious, although they might suspect her brother of illicit activities. She also carried with her money to pay the soldiers who had fought at Bunker Hill months before. The next morning Deborah willingly stashed the dispatches and money under her bodice and dressed as an older lady in out-of-fashion clothing. Accompanying her was a family slave, Aristarchus, with whom Deborah had been close since she was a child. The two set out early in the morning.

She arrived at Providence, Rhode Island, where she stayed the night at an uncle's house. The following morning,

after being provided a new horse, Champion set out for Boston once again. In her letter, Deborah recalled that many men, women, and children were along the roads and that although they loved their mother country, they still wanted their rights. She specifically stated in her letter that she was not offered imported tea but rather milk or local tea made out of raspberry leaves. At this time, she moved the dispatches from her bodice to a compartment in the horse's saddlebags.

At the end of her second day of riding, Champion and Aristarchus decided to ride through the night. After the morning had settled in, Deborah grew tired. Suddenly a man called for her to halt. The soldier, wearing the traditional red coat of the British, said she would have to be sent to the captain for a search. Champion talked her way out of the search by saying that she was in a hurry to see a needy friend. He agreed to let her pass, assuming from her appearance that she was an old woman. Champion continued her journey to deliver the dispatches to Washington.

As she wrote the letter to her friend, her father interrupted her to caution her about disclosing important information about Washington and his whereabouts. Consequently, in her letter, she skipped the part about arriving at Washington's headquarters. She did, however, give many details about meeting him. As she recorded, she crossed the grounds to where he was and handed the dispatches to him personally. He complimented Deborah on her courage and patriotism. Her mission accomplished, Champion headed back home.

Later that year, Champion married Judge Samuel Gilbert of Connecticut.

Known as the "female Paul Revere," Champion was recorded in history as a courageous woman willing to undergo a dangerous mission for her country.

Rebecca E. Price

See also: American Revolution (1775–1783); Espionage.

References and Further Reading

Carbaugh, Marsha Wilson, and Lorraine Cook White. *The Barbour Collection of Connecticut Town Vital Records*, Vol. 1. p. 119, Vol. 2. p. 34. Baltimore, MD: Genealogical Pub., 1999.

Fennelly, Catherine. *Connecticut Women in the Revolutionary Era*. Chester, CT: Pequot, 1975.

Grunwald, Lisa, and Stephen J. Adler. *Women's Letters: America from the Revolutionary War to the Present*. New York: Dial, 2005.

CHARETTE, HOLLY A. (1983–2005)

Lance Corporal Holly A. Charette, of Cranston, Rhode Island, was the first female marine killed in Operation Iraqi Freedom. She was killed in action on Thursday, June 23, 2005, by a suicide car bomber in Fallujah, Iraq. At the time, Charette was 21 and was at least the seventh Rhode Islander to die in Iraq.

Charette was born September 27, 1983, in South Kingstown, Rhode Island, to Raymond Charette and Virginia Wheetman (Roberts). She lived in Coventry for most of her life. Charette graduated from Cranston High School East in 2001. While in school, she played field hockey and participated on the hockey cheerleading team, where she was remembered as being a popular member. Charette was known for her love of dancing and had expressed a desire to become a child psychologist.

She completed half a year at Community College of Rhode Island before enrolling with the Marine Corps after the September 11, 2001, terrorist attacks. Her family had a strong connection with both the Marines and September 11. A relative, Mark Charette, had died on the 100th floor of the World Trade Center when the hijacked Boeing 767 jet hit it. In addition, Charette's grandfather, Hank Charette, was a marine.

At the time of her deployment to Iraq, Charette was based out of Camp Lejeune, North Carolina, where she worked delivering mail. Once in Iraq, she was assigned to Headquarters Battalion, 2nd Marine Division, II Marine Expeditionary Force.

Official Pentagon policy excluded women from serving in traditional front-line combat roles found in the infantry, armor, or artillery branches. However, the nature of insurgency warfare in Iraq ensured that coalition female servicemembers would be exposed to combat and direct enemy action.

Charette was assigned to checkpoint searches of local Iraqi women. Local sensibilities forbade men from touching women who were not related to them in public; hence, female marines had been assigned to work the checkpoints in and around Fallujah. Regulations prohibited female marines from spending the night at their checkpoint stations, so each morning and evening an armed convoy would carry a contingent of female American soldiers between their home base and the various checkpoints in the city.

Shortly after 7:00 p.m., on June 23, 2005, Charette's convoy came under attack by a vehicle-borne improvised explosive device outside of Fallujah, Iraq, a hotbed of insurgent activity that saw heavy fighting between coalition forces, local insurgents, and Al Qaeda operatives. Charette was one of over a dozen female soldiers in the truck that was struck by the suicide bomber. Six marines died either immediately or as a result of injuries sustained by the bombing and subsequent small-arms fire. Although she survived the attack with burns and other wounds, she died on the operating table. Three U.S. servicewomen died in the attack, making it one of the costliest incidents for American military women in U.S. history. Of the 13 wounded personnel, 11 were female. The terror group Al Qaeda in Iraq claimed responsibility for the bombing. The attack constituted one of the single deadliest attacks against the Marines—and against female American soldiers—during the war.

Two days after her death, Rhode Island governor Don Carcieri ordered state flags lowered in honor of Charette's sacrifice and flown at half-staff until her internment. Her funeral service, with full military honors, was held on Saturday, July 2, 2005, in the Rhode Island Veterans Cemetery, Exeter, in Washington County.

Later that year, Rhode Island senator Jack Reed introduced a bill to rename a local post office to honor Charette, who had worked in the mail while in the Marines. Reed's bill passed the Senate on November 18, 2005. Following passage by the House of Representatives, the bill was sent to the president and signed into law on February 27, 2006. Public Law 109-175 designated the facility of the U.S. Postal Service located at 57 Rolfe Square in Cranston, Rhode Island, as the Holly A. Charette Post Office. About 150 marines, several of whom had served with Charette, attended the dedication ceremony on Sunday, October 15, 2006.

Her family helped establish the Cpl. Holly Charette Scholarship Fund, which presents two scholarships each year to local high students to further their education.

L. Bao Bui

See also: Clark, Regina Renee (1962–2005); Iraq War (2003–2011); Valdez, Ramona M. (1984–2005); War on Terror (2001–).

References and Further Reading

Tucker, Eric. "Rhode Island Marine Killed in Iraq Bombing." Associated Press. Available at http://militarytimes.com/valor/marine-lance-cpl-holly-a-charette/941127.

Wise, James E. Jr., and Scott Baron. *Women at War: Iraq, Afghanistan, and Other Conflicts.* Annapolis, MD: Naval Institute Press, 2006.

CHILD, JULIA McWILLIAMS (1912–2004)

Although best remembered as a television chef, Julia McWilliams Child served with the Office of Strategic Services (OSS, the precursor to the CIA) in Washington, D.C., and then later in Ceylon and China during World War II. She was awarded the Emblem of Meritorious Civilian Service for her work with the OSS.

During World War II, long before she became a famous chef, Julia McWilliams Child worked for the Office of Strategic Services (OSS) in Washington, D.C., and overseas. (AP/Wide World Photos)

Born in Pasadena, California, on August 15, 1912, to John McWilliams Jr. and Julia Carolyn Weston, Julia McWilliams grew up with a privileged lifestyle. She was an athletic girl who earned a B.A. in history from Smith College and hoped to become an author. She had experience working as a copywriter in advertising and other areas of publishing, but in 1941 she was living the life of an idle socialite in Pasadena, California. When the United States entered the war, McWilliams sought to be of service to her country and applied to join the Women's Army Auxiliary Corps (WAAC) and the Navy's Women Accepted for Volunteer Emergency Service (WAVES). Like many women, McWilliams saw the war as an opportunity to escape a boring life while aiding her nation. Unlike many women, McWilliams was rejected by

both services because, at 6 feet 2 inches, she was considered too tall.

Like thousands of American women, McWilliams took advantage of new opportunities during World War II. Instead of military service, McWilliams found herself in Washington, D.C., using her copywriting skills to type index cards for the Office of Wartime Intelligence. Although she quit this tedious job after three months, it provided McWilliams with the experience necessary to apply for and receive a job with the newly formed OSS, an intelligence agency being organized by William Donovan. McWilliams worked for Donovan as a file clerk until 1944, when she volunteered to serve the OSS overseas. In March 1944, the OSS sent McWilliams to India. While on the way to India, she was transferred to Ceylon (now

Sri Lanka), an island off the coast of India. At the headquarters of the South East Asia Command, McWilliams was put in charge of the Registry, a compilation of all the highly classified documents sent by and to OSS agents in the China-Burma-India theater. McWilliams developed the system used to keep track of the materials the Registry contained. Maintaining the Registry was a huge undertaking, and McWilliams did it alone for many months until she received an assistant. Ten months after arriving in Ceylon, the OSS base was moved to Kunming, in southern China. McWilliams followed with the Registry and finished out the war in China. For her work as head of the Registry, McWilliams was awarded the Emblem of Meritorious Civilian Service.

Life on the OSS bases in the Pacific proved a huge change from the life McWilliams had lived in Pasadena. In Ceylon, the quarters were grass-thatched huts surrounded by barbed wire, and the residents had to suffer tropical heat and heavy rains through the 10 months that they were based on the island. The flight from Ceylon to Kunming, over the Himalayas and through frequent bad weather, was notoriously dangerous. The conditions in Kunming were slightly better than those in Ceylon, but they were more dangerous as the base there was closer to the front lines than the one in Ceylon. Despite the conditions, McWilliams thrived, enjoying the differences and the freedom from her old life.

It was not only the living conditions that McWilliams found different. The sort of people who were attracted to and recruited by the OSS were not at all like the sort of people she had grown up with.

Overseas service during the war exposed McWilliams to an entirely different set of ideas and ideals than those of her parents. Notably, it was while serving in Ceylon that McWilliams met her future husband, Paul Child. Julia and Paul married in 1946. In 1948, he was assigned to the U.S. Information Service at the U.S. Embassy in Paris, so the couple moved to France. In Paris, Julia learned French cooking, began cowriting *Mastering the Art of French Cooking* (1961), and set the foundations for her later fame as a television chef.

Child died of kidney failure in Montecito, California, on August 13, 2004.

Mike Timonin

See also: Espionage; United States Coast Guard Women's Reserve (SPAR); Women Accepted for Volunteer Emergency Service (WAVES); Women Air Force Service Pilots (WASPS); Women's Army Auxiliary Corps (WAAC); Women's Army Corps (WAC); Women Marines; World War II (1941–1945).

References and Further Reading

Fitch, Noel Riley. *Appetite for Life: The Biography of Julia Child.* New York: Doubleday, 1999.

Shapiro, Laura. *Julia Child.* New York: Lipper, Viking Group, 2007.

CIVIL AIR PATROL (CAP)

The Civil Air Patrol (CAP) is an organization of civilian pilots that acts as an auxiliary to the U.S. Air Force. Founded on December 1, 1941, the CAP had a membership of over 43,000 by May of 1943, and members were known as the "Minute-men of the Air." From the beginning, the CAP was gender integrated, and it is estimated that approximately 20 percent of the membership was female. Women held nearly every position in the CAP, including pilot, ground technician, squadron leader, and flight instructor. After the war, the CAP continued to flourish and today provides one of the primary opportunities for young women to get involved in aviation.

During the 1930s, the federally funded Civilian Pilot Training Program (CPTP) provided free pilot training to men and women through college campuses around the United States. Before the CPTP, the opportunities for female pilots were quite limited; aside from wealthy women who took private flying instruction, few women could get flight experience. The small Army Air Force did not admit women, and no airline would allow them to fly, believing that passengers would not feel comfortable with a female pilot. The CPTP was the first large-scale opportunity for pilot training. The program was not entirely gender neutral, but it did admit women. Women comprised up to 10 percent of every training class. By January of 1940, the number of qualified female pilots in the United States had jumped from approximately 500 to approximately 3,000, largely as a result of this program.

Once the United States entered World War II in December 1941, the federal government imposed a blanket ban on all civilian flying activities within the country. If pilots wanted to continue flying, they had to join an organized group, either the Army Air Force or the CAP.

Although the number of male pilots trained by the CPTP was quite large, all of those pilots had been required to sign a pledge that, in the event of war, they would volunteer for the Army Air Force. Women, however, were not required to sign such a pledge. As a result, women made up a large portion of the trained civilian pilots available to staff the CAP in its early days.

The initial suggestion for the formation of the CAP came from the editor of *Flying Magazine*, Gill Robb Wilson. He and his wife were both pilots and believed that civilian aviators could make an important contribution to the war effort. His suggestion led to the formation of the CAP under the auspice of the Office of Civil Defense, led by Fiorello La Guardia and Eleanor Roosevelt.

After it was organized, the CAP took on all duties that the Army Air Force was unable or unwilling to do. In the early days of the war, the Air Force was stretched thin, and the CAP filled in the gaps. CAP pilots helped fight forest fires, ferried parts and supplies around the country, transported troops from base to base, and helped patrol the coast for enemy submarines. This last duty was not officially open to women because of its close relationship to combat, but several CAP fliers reported that women occasionally participated anyway.

Like their male counterparts, women of the CAP wore uniforms, held ranks, and trained with small arms. Many women joined alongside their husbands, and tales of husband-and-wife flying teams are commonplace. The participation of women in the CAP received positive press coverage in a number of national periodicals, and female fliers were featured on the front page of the *New York Times Magazine* in 1943. Several advertising campaigns, most notably those run by Camel cigarettes and Norge appliances, featured female pilots in the CAP. The CAP also began training younger cadets in high school and college, and several groups of female cadets began training by 1942.

In 1942, pilot Jacqueline Cochran began working to form the Women Air Force Service Pilots (WASP), which would become the official women's auxiliary to the Army Air Force, analogous to the Women's Army Corps (WAC) or the Women Accepted for Volunteer Emergency Service (WAVES). Many of the pilots that Cochran recruited were from the CAP and had gotten much of their flight training on CAP missions. When the WASP program was disbanded in 1944, most of these women returned to the CAP to continue flying.

After the war ended, the CAP continued its efforts to promote civilian aviation. After the CPTP ended, the CAP was the easiest place for civilians to receive free pilot training. Because many CAP-trained men could get jobs as professional pilots after the war, although women were still barred from the commercial aviation world, the gender balance of the CAP continued to equalize. By 1947, there were at least four female state wing commanders and a female regional commander, and by the mid-1950s, the CAP was almost 40 percent women. Today, local CAP wings actively recruit female cadets, and in 2008 Maj. Gen. Amy Courter became the national commander, the first woman to hold that post.

Anthony Todd

See also: Campbell, Kim Reed (1975–); Cochran, Jacqueline (ca. 1910–1980); Roosevelt, Eleanor (1844–1962); Women Accepted for Volunteer Emergency Service (WAVES); Women Air Force Service Pilots (WASP); Women's Army Corps (WAC); Women's Flying Training Detachment (WFTD); World War II (1941–1945).

References and Further Reading

Glines, Carroll V. *Minutemen of the Air: The Valiant Exploits of the Civil Air Patrol in Peace and War*. New York: Random House, 1966.

Merryman, Molly. *Clipped Wings: The Rise and Fall of the Women's Airforce Service Pilots*. New York: New York University Press, 1988.

Neprud, Robert E. *Flying Minute Men: The Story of the Civil Air Patrol*. New York: Dell Sloan and Pierce, 1948.

Pisano, Dominick. *To Fill the Skies with Pilots: The Civilian Pilot Training Program, 1939–46*. Urbana: University of Illinois Press, 1993.

Pope, Virginia. "Out of Uniform . . . " *New York Times*, November 8, 1942, SM30.

Wilson, Gill Robb. *I Walked with Giants*. New York: Vantage Press, 1968.

CIVIL WAR (1861–1865)

The American Civil War was an armed conflict between the United States of America and the Confederate States of America, which consisted of 11 Southern states that had seceded from the United States. One of the most influential events in the history of American women, the Civil War brought women from all walks of life into an unprecedented degree of involvement with military operations on their home soil. Women served both the Union and the Confederacy as soldiers, spies, nurses, washerwomen, seamstresses, and bushwhackers. Many women held these roles informally, and all faced considerable challenges in their efforts to contribute to their respective causes. Countless other women who remained on the homefront provided essential resources to the troops. Women who lived near battle zones witnessed the war's death and destruction firsthand, and many of these women became refugees with their families. As the war progressed and the Union army occupied growing areas of the Confederacy, both black and white Southern women experienced ongoing and often contentious interactions with Northern soldiers. In the decades after the conflict, many women maintained a strong link to the war as they organized memorial activities and received pensions as individuals or as widows of deceased soldiers.

Without a doubt, 19th-century Americans viewed war as a man's business. Two popular Civil War songs make this clear. The Confederate favorite "The Bonnie Blue Flag" is written for a "band of brothers," while the Union song "The Battle-Cry of Freedom" urges the "boys" to rally around the flag. Women who wanted to muster in and fight therefore had to blend in with the "boys."

About 250 women are known to have fought in the Civil War, although the actual number is certainly larger. Most of them disguised themselves as men, drawing on a European tradition that their American foremothers had followed during the Revolutionary War. However, as the Confederacy grew short on recruits, some female rebel soldiers no longer bothered to hide their identities. A handful of female soldiers had begun dressing as men before the war began so that they could earn better incomes, but most women soldiers took this bold step for the first time during the war. Many joined the ranks with their husbands, brothers, or fiancés so they had some assistance in keeping their sex a secret. That many Civil War soldiers wore ill-fitting uniforms and few bathed with any frequency aided women's efforts to appear as men. Amazingly, at least six women are known to have served as Civil War soldiers while pregnant. Some women, especially among the Confederate forces, simply looked like the underage boys who fought alongside them. Many female soldiers drew upon their hard work on farms and factories to keep up with male soldiers. Perhaps more than anything else, women soldiers benefited from the very mindset that forced them to disguise themselves: few officers or soldiers expected to find women in the ranks.

Like their male fellow soldiers, women joined the armed forces for a variety of reasons: devotion to the cause, the desire for excitement, an opportunity to travel beyond the confines of their communities, and the simple need for a job. Rosetta Wakeman, for example, an unmarried young farm woman who joined the 153rd New York State Volunteers as Lyons Wakeman in 1862, had initially left home to help her family climb out of debt. Dressed as a man, she worked as a coal handler on a canal boat but soon signed on with recruiters for the 153rd. Wakeman regularly sent home significant amounts of money until her death from illness at a military hospital in New Orleans in 1864.

Women fought in every major battle of the war. In carrying out their duties as soldiers, they apparently differed little from their male comrades. Historians have yet to find any case of a woman whose identity was revealed based on her performance on the field. When a soldier was discovered to be a woman, it was usually because she had been injured or killed. No officers initiated courts-martial against women found in the ranks.

When the war ended, few women shared stories about their combat experiences; like many male veterans, they simply wanted to return to the normalcy of civilian life. During and after the war, journalists who learned about women soldiers celebrated them in print, often to the point of romanticizing them. After World War I, the image of female Civil War soldiers changed, and for many years historians portrayed them as either immoral or mentally unstable. More recently, women who fought in the Civil War have taken their place among important historical precedents for the participation of women in combat.

Alongside women disguised as men in the ranks were women designated as "daughters of the regiment." Although demeaned as camp followers in some postwar accounts of the war, such women performed a variety of quasimilitary tasks and were usually related to men in the regiments to which they were attached. For example, youthful Arabella "Belle" Reynolds served as a daughter of the regiment for the 17th Illinois Infantry, to which her husband, John, belonged. Reynolds, who sometimes carried a musket as she marched, cooked meals and cared for the sick and wounded. At the Battle of Shiloh (April 6–8, 1862), she stood onboard a Union hospital ship with a revolver to keep men who were retreating from the battlefield off of the ship's decks. In acknowledgement of her service, the governor of Illinois gave her an honorary major's commission.

Women willing to take up arms on the front lines also proved adept at assisting the military in other ways, including spying and nursing. Several women who did stints in the ranks disguised as men are known to have also served as spies, including Loreta Velazquez of New Orleans; Sarah Emma Edmonds of New Brunswick, Canada; and Mary Ann Pitman of Tennessee. Just as women succeeded in melting into the ranks of male soldiers because no one expected them to be there, women initially thrived as spies because few thought that members of their sex had the political awareness or gumption to undertake passing secrets.

Yet pass secrets they did—on both sides of the conflict. They carried messages written on silk, buttons, and tissue; some used special ink to conceal secret notes within everyday letters. Women hid such missives beneath their hoop skirts and corsets or within their parasols, accurately gauging—at least during the war's early years—that officers would be reluctant to search women carefully. If captured, female spies were usually imprisoned and then sometimes exchanged and banished from their areas of operation. Union officials gave some Confederate women the opportunity to take the oath of allegiance to the United States and go on their merry way.

Some female spies became famous during the war when they penned their memoirs or journalists uncovered their feats. Several of these women remain well known today: Harriet Tubman, who provided Union general David Hunter information that she gathered from former slaves while serving as a scout in South Carolina and Florida; Belle Boyd, a flamboyant Confederate spy in the Shenandoah Valley of Virginia who received an honorary commission as captain and aide-de-camp from Gen. Thomas "Stonewall" Jackson; Rose Greenhow, who is credited with passing key information to Confederate generals before the First Battle of Bull Run (July 21, 1861); the aforementioned Sarah Emma Edmonds, who, already passing as a man, disguised herself as a slave to get behind Confederate lines; Pauline Cushman, an actress captured twice by Confederate troops; and Elizabeth Van Lew, who not only spied but also helped Union soldiers escape from Libby Prison in Richmond.

Other spies garnered less attention. Mary Louveste worked at a navy yard in Norfolk and funneled information to Gideon Welles, the U.S. secretary of the navy. Mary Elizabeth Bowser, freed from slavery in the 1850s, worked in the Confederate White House in Richmond and secreted information to Union authorities without arousing suspicion until she fled to the North in January 1865. E. H. Baker translated her work for Allen Pinkerton's detective agency before the war into wartime service as a spy. Some women, such as Confederate spy and smuggler Mary Frances "Fanny" Battle of Nashville, consciously chose not to discuss their spying activities after the war.

Considerably less glamorous than spying, nursing attracted women who wanted to assist the troops and who needed gainful employment. Thousands of women served as nurses, both formally and informally; at least 21,000 are known to have worked for the Union. Many women volunteered as nurses, and numerous others received pay and depended on the work. Widow Phoebe Yates Pember, for example, served as chief matron of the second division of Chimborazo Hospital in Richmond and scoffed at the idea that her job was a choice rather than a necessity for her to be independent. Although she took pride in her work and firmly supported the Confederacy, she also felt the burden of spending her days among dying men. What is more, Pember supplemented her income by writing for magazines and doing copying for the Confederate government at night.

Pember held no illusions about her status within the military hospital where she worked. In her memoir, she acknowledged her low rank and then described how she proceeded to exercise the little power that she had. Other matrons and nurses fared similarly. Women had to prove that they could do the hard, often gruesome work of nursing and that they belonged among soldiers. Most male surgeons did not welcome female nurses, especially at the start of the war. Mary Ann Ball Bickerdyke, whom soldiers in Cairo, Illinois, dubbed "Mother," is said to have told a dubious army surgeon that she derived her authority to feed wounded men from none other than God above.

Many Union nurses like Bickerdyke served the troops under the auspices of the U.S. Sanitary Commission (USSC) and its state branches. Civilians created the USSC to care for men in the field when it became apparent that the military infrastructure was not adequate to support a conflict of the scope of the Civil War. At first, military authorities looked askance at USSC nurses and other workers, as when Gen. Henry W. Halleck complained in May 1862 that the commission was depleting his forces unnecessarily by taking away men who were not really very sick. Soon, however, commanders acknowledged the contributions of the commission and its workers.

North and South, nurses did far more than the relatively specialized tasks associated with that profession today. Civil War nurses' various responsibilities included writing letters for patients, changing bandages and washing wounds, cooking meals and feeding the men, cleaning and laundering, reading the Bible aloud and passing out sermons, dispensing medicine, and procuring and distributing supplies. Phoebe Pember described many of these functions in her memoir. She noted, for example, the challenges of feeding the men—especially when she and the hospital's cooks also had to battle opportunistic rats in the kitchen. Pember also showed how the seemingly straightforward task of distributing supplies could become quite contentious. She engaged in a constant struggle with male surgeons and other staffers over her efforts to regulate the distribution of whiskey to patients.

Just as woman nurses performed a multitude of tasks, they did so in a variety of situations. Women served in field hospitals and urban military hospitals, onboard hospital ships, and on the battlefield itself. By far the most famous Civil War nurse, Clara Barton demonstrated her courage by ministering to wounded men on the battlefield rather than waiting

for them to be brought to the rear. Known as the "Angel of the Battlefield," Barton worked among flying bullets at the battles of Antietam and Fort Wagner. Although well disposed toward the military based on her father's experiences in the Indian wars in the Northwest Territory, Barton did not hesitate to criticize Union officials for inefficiency and neglect of the wounded. Although this did not make her popular among military leaders, she received an appointment as superintendent of nurses in the Army of the James in June 1864. Her experiences during the Civil War and her distress over the suffering of the wounded on the battlefield led her to found the American Red Cross in 1881.

Regardless of where they served, most nurses came face to face with the horrors of war and described their experiences as unforgettable and even life changing. During the Army of the Potomac's Peninsular Campaign of 1862, women served as both nurses and superintendents of nurses on board hospital ships sponsored by the USSC. Drawing on their organizational abilities, the middle-class female superintendents, who were volunteers, oversaw the work of nurses, orderlies, and former slaves— and felt superior to them. When the fighting grew intense, however, the superintendents also cared for the wounded and dying. Like female nurses throughout the conflict, these women did what they had to do as their situation evolved.

Other female workers who served the armies in the field had to be similarly flexible. Susie King Taylor, a former slave who had fled with relatives to the Sea Islands off the coasts of Georgia and South Carolina in the spring of 1862, enrolled as a laundress for her husband's regiment, the 1st South Carolina Volunteers (later the 33rd Regiment, U.S. Colored Troops). She ended up performing a variety of tasks, including nursing sick soldiers, teaching soldiers to read, searching for food, and cleaning guns. As she wrote in her 1902 memoir, by war's end she had done little washing. In addition to laundresses, regiments had cooks and matrons; like Taylor, women who filled these positions were often the wives of men in the regiment.

Away from the battlefront, women remained intimately tied to the men who took the field. In 1861, many white women had encouraged their husbands, fiancés, and brothers to enlist. Groups of women feted the local boys with flags they had made—sometimes from their own clothing. These spirited send-offs were repeated later in the war by African American women sending their men into the ranks of the U.S. military. Despite such demonstrations of enthusiasm, all women made sacrifices when sending their loved ones off to fight. Families on the homefront suffered, often acutely, without their primary breadwinners. As the war dragged on, more and more women had second thoughts about mobilization. Some Northern women both individually and collectively assaulted or tried to chase away enrollment officers; similarly, some former slave women violently protested impressment and conscription of their husbands. Women in the North participated in mob violence through draft riots, the largest of which took place in New York City and Boston in 1863. Especially in areas of the Confederacy and the border states torn by guerilla warfare, some women pressed their husbands to desert and return home to take care of their families.

From the homefront, women both North and South furnished supplies and raised funds that literally sustained the armies in the field. As individuals, as well as through soldiers' aid organizations and sewing societies, women made and donated clothing, bandages, blankets, and other linens as well as all manner of foodstuffs. In the South, slaveholding women compelled their enslaved workers to assist with the support of Confederate troops. In addition, some Northern and Southern women held jobs that directly supported the war effort, from clerking in government treasury departments to working in munitions factories. When the fighting came to their communities, many women on the homefront became impromptu nurses and cooks for the men in the field. If women could depend on anything amid the war's chaos, they knew that soldiers would be hungry.

On the Confederate homefront, scattered groups of women took up arms to defend their communities. Most who did so joined local militia units that were predominately male. Under the leadership of Nancy Morgan, however, a group of about 40 women in LaGrange, Georgia, organized themselves into a company of soldiers in 1862. Naming themselves the Nancy Harts after Georgia's Revolutionary War heroine, the women drilled and took target practice regularly. Ready to defend their town against an approaching column of Union cavalry in April 1865, the women did not have to fire any shots after the Union commander complimented them on their readiness and promised not to destroy any homes in the town.

Some women joined the ranks of guerilla fighters on the homefront. The group of bushwhackers who attacked the Union hospital in Ketesville, Missouri, in April 1862 included a handful of women, for example. Unionist Malinda Blalock and her husband, who had once enlisted in a Confederate regiment as brother and sister with plans to desert to the other side, later participated in the partisan warfare that ravaged the mountains of North Carolina.

Women were far more likely to suffer from guerilla attacks than to participate in them. Because irregular fighting left few distinctions between civilians and soldiers, violence came to many homes in areas of the South and trans-Mississippi West. Women suffered by association when guerillas targeted their male relatives and then came to their homes to inflict violence on the men or their property. Some—but certainly not all—guerillas stopped short of harming white women physically but would often treat black and Indian women brutally. As a result of guerrilla warfare, many women and children became refugees.

Beginning in the winter and spring of 1862 until the end of the war, the Union Army occupied significant population centers within the Confederacy. Women responded to this occupation according to their political affiliations. Union supporters, including many free black people and enslaved workers, cheered the coming of federal troops and sought to support, feed, nurse, and entertain them. Too often, these women discovered that occupying soldiers had no compunction about stealing from them or otherwise mistreating them, regardless of their Unionism.

Former slave women had an especially complex relationship with Union military forces. The arrival of federal troops in areas of the Confederacy served as a catalyst for the emancipation of hundreds of thousands of enslaved people as the war raged. Men, women, and children took to their feet for federal lines as soon as troops gained a toehold in an area, and occupation forces regularly assisted their flight. Gender, however, played an influential role in how Union commanders greeted former slaves. Valued for their labor and, beginning in 1863, for their potential as soldiers, able-bodied men who had escaped slavery were generally welcomed by the federals. On the other hand, Union officers usually defined women, especially those with young children, as an unwanted burden. Many officers initially tried, unsuccessfully, to keep women and children out of Union lines; later, officers of U.S. colored troops sought to limit soldiers' wives' access to their husbands. The army had no precedent for dealing with such a large number of refugees, and many ex-slave women suffered as a result.

When they realized that it was futile to try to stop the outpouring of escaping slaves, Union authorities worked with Northern aid societies, such as the American Missionary Association and the Western Freedmen's Aid Commission, and the former slaves themselves to create temporary way stations within Union-held territory. In such places as Beaufort, South Carolina; Craney Island, Virginia; and Corinth, Mississippi, women erected shanties or used tents or former army barracks to house themselves and their children. Many of these contraband camps, as they were called, became breeding grounds for deadly diseases that killed scores of newly freed people. Settlements of former slaves also drew the attention of immoral officers and soldiers who viewed black women as promiscuous and abused them accordingly. Women and children, including families of soldiers whose pay was tardy, also suffered for want of enough warm clothing, medicine, and even food. In addition, women discovered how fragile contraband camps could be when military authorities might at any time decide to scuttle the settlements, as happened disastrously in November 1864 at Camp Nelson in Kentucky.

At the same time, African American women drew on the resilience they had developed under slavery to begin new lives for themselves. Former slave women and their children took advantage of the opportunity to learn to read and write in the schools established in Union areas. To make ends meet, women and children raised crops on government farms, grew food in garden plots, and raised chickens and hogs. As individuals or at army wash houses, many former slave women washed uniforms and other clothing for the troops. Others sewed for the army on their own or at industrial schools established by military officials, worked as military hospital attendants, or became personal servants of officers. Women also sold soldiers cakes, pies, fruits, vegetables, eggs, milk, and butter.

Women who supported the Confederacy also had unprecedented interaction with Union forces under occupation. These women demonstrated a range of responses. Some Confederate women socialized with Union troops even as they held firm to their support for the rebellion.

Many of these women enjoyed the opportunity to debate the merits of secession and the conduct of the war with the enemy. Other Confederate women unloaded their anger on the occupying soldiers. Eager to be known as "secesh," some female Confederates hurled insults at Union troops, accusing them of being hirelings of President Lincoln and thieves of the South's slaves. Other women avoided the occupying forces at all costs, refusing to speak to them or share a sidewalk with them. Many female Confederate supporters wore apparel, ribbons, bows, and flowers that reflected their loyalties—and that Union commanders sometimes tried to prohibit.

Confederate-leaning women in New Orleans, frustrated that their city had fallen so easily to the federal troops, instigated one of the most notorious occupation controversies of the war in May 1862. Gen. Benjamin F. Butler, shocked at the contempt demonstrated by women who supported the Confederacy toward his officers and soldiers in the Crescent City, issued General Orders No. 28, known unofficially as the Woman Order. In this short directive, Butler stated that any woman, even one claiming to be a "lady," who insulted Union troops would be subject to being treated by the authorities as a prostitute. The order gained the general lasting infamy throughout the Confederacy. Unmoved, Butler backed up his bluster by arresting women for sedition and other offenses, such as displaying secession flags. Butler's order underscores the intense conflict generated by Union occupation of the Confederacy.

Of course, actual prostitutes did flock to New Orleans and other occupied urban areas. In some of these places, including Nashville and Memphis,

Tennessee, and Charleston, South Carolina, the Union army initiated a revolutionary program of inspecting and licensing prostitutes so as to keep venereal disease at bay among the officers and soldiers. Nashville women, at first so reluctant to participate in the program that they had to be rounded up at bayonet point, responded positively once they found that the doctor in charge treated them decently. The women took pride in the program and soon voluntarily turned themselves in when they became ill.

Like urban women, many women in rural areas of the Confederacy saw their world change dramatically with the arrival of Union troops. As the hard hand of war began to fall on areas of the Deep South late in the war, women decried the destruction caused by Union forces. Gen. William T. Sherman's March to the Sea from Atlanta to Savannah created havoc as the 60,000 soldiers lived off the land and destroyed personal property in an attempt to deprive the state's inhabitants of sustenance and crush their spirits. Youthful Eliza Frances Andrews lamented in her journal the wanton killing of livestock so that Georgians would not be able to make crops in the spring.

After the war ended in 1865, American women's engagement with military operations and interaction with military personnel persisted, though at a reduced level. U.S. forces occupied some areas of the former Confederacy until 1877. Congress established the Bureau of Refugees, Freedmen, and Abandoned Lands, or Freedmen's Bureau, as a unit of the War Department in March 1865 to ease the transition from slavery to freedom. Former slave women regularly interacted with agents of the bureau, many of whom had served in the Union Army, to sign labor contracts, claim rations and wood, file complaints about mistreatment by employers, attempt to find family members separated under slavery, and participate in marriage ceremonies and Emancipation Day celebrations.

Former Confederate women chafed under ongoing military occupation even as they focused on honoring their war dead, transforming soldiers' aid societies into ladies' memorial associations dedicated to creating Confederate cemeteries, erecting monuments, and holding Memorial Day commemorations. Northern women also became active in the public remembrance of fallen soldiers. During the 1870s, Southern Unionist women whose homes and property had been confiscated or destroyed by the Union army during the war applied to the Southern Claims Commission for reimbursement. Widows of Union soldiers received pensions from the federal government, and many Confederate widows got small payments from their state governments. Some Civil War widows chose to be buried at military cemeteries. Finally, some women, including Bickerdyke, Edmonds, and Tubman, received pensions from the U.S. government for their efforts on behalf of the war effort.

Antoinette G. van Zelm

See also: African American Women; American Red Cross; American Revolution (1775–1783); Andrews, Orianna Moon (1834–1883); Baker, E. H. (n.d.–n.d); Barton, Clara Harlowe (1821–1912); Battle, Mary Frances "Fannie" (1842–1924); Bickerdyke, Mary Ann Ball "Mother" (1817–1901); Blackwell, Elizabeth (1821–1910); Blair, Lorinda Ann [Annie Etheridge Hooks] (ca. 1840–1913); Blalock, Sarah Malinda [Samuel Blalock] (1839–1903);

Bowser, Mary Elizabeth (ca. 1839–n.d.); Boyd, Marie Isabella "Belle" (1844–1900); Bradley, Amy Morris (1823–1904); Breckinridge, Margaret E. (1832–1864); Brownell, Kady (1842–1915); Camp Followers; Carroll, Anna Ella (1815–1894); Cary, Mary Ann Shadd (1823–1893); Clalin, Frances Louisa [Francis Clayton] (n.d.–n.d.); Cushman, Pauline [Harriet Wood] (1833–1893); Divers, Bridget (ca. 1840–n.d.); Dix, Dorothea Lynde (1802–1887); Edmonds (Seelye), Sarah Emma [Franklin Thompson] (1841–1898); Edmondson, Isabella "Belle" Buchanan (1840–1873); Espionage; Ford (Willard), Antonia (1838–1871); Government Girls; Greenhow, Rose O'Neal (ca. 1814–1864); Hart, Nancy (ca. 1843–1902); Hodgers, Jennie [Albert D. J. Cashier] (1844–1915); Moon, Charlotte "Lottie" (1829–1895); Moon, Virginia "Ginnie" (1844–1925); Mountain Charley [Elsa Jane Guerin a.k.a. Charles Hatfield] (n.d.–n.d.); "Nancy Harts"; Native American Women; Nursing; Pigott, Emeline Jamison (1836–1919); Prisoners of War; Ratcliffe, Laura (1836–1923); Reynolds, Arabella "Belle" (1843–1930); Tompkins, Sally Louisa (1833–1916); Tubman, Harriet [Araminta Ross] (ca. 1820–1913); Turchin, Nadine [Nedezhda] Lvova (1826–1904); United States Sanitary Commission (USSC); USS *Red Rover*; Van Lew, Elizabeth (1818–1900); Velazquez, Loreta Janeta [Harry T. Buford] (1842–1897); Vivandieres; Wakeman, Sarah Rosetta [Lyons Wakeman] (1843–1864); Walker, Anna Nancy Slaughter (n.d.-n.d.); Walker, Mary Edwards (1832–1919); Williams, Cathay [William Cathey] (ca. 1844–n.d.); World War I.

References and Further Reading

Berlin, Ira et al., eds. *Free at Last: A Documentary History of Slavery, Freedom, and the Civil War*. New York: The New Press, 1992.

Blanton, DeAnne, and Lauren M. Cook. *They Fought Like Demons: Women Soldiers in the American Civil War*. Baton Rouge: Louisiana State University Press, 2002.

Burgess, Lauren Cook, ed. *An Uncommon Soldier: The Civil War Letters of Sarah Rosetta Wakeman, alias Private Lyons Wakeman, 153rd Regiment, New York State Volunteers*. New York: Oxford University Press, 1994.

Clinton, Catherine, and Nina Silber, eds. *Divided Houses: Gender and the Civil War*. New York: Oxford University Press, 1992.

Faust, Drew Gilpin. *Mothers of Invention: Women of the Slaveholding South in the American Civil War*. New York: Vintage Books, 1996.

Giesberg, Judith. *Army at Home: Women and the Civil War on the Northern Homefront*. Chapel Hill: University of North Carolina Press, 2009.

Leonard, Elizabeth D. *All the Daring of the Soldier: Women of the Civil War Armies*. New York: W. W. Norton & Co., 1999.

Pember, Phoebe Yates. *A Southern Woman's Story: Life in Confederate Richmond*. Edited by Bell Irvin Wiley. Marietta, GA: McCowat-Mercer Press, 1954.

Schultz, Jane E. *Women at the Front: Hospital Workers in Civil War America*. Chapel Hill: University of North Carolina Press, 2004.

Taylor, Susie King. *Reminiscences of My Life in Camp*. New York: Arno Press and The New York Times, 1968.

Whites, LeeAnn, and Alecia P. Long, eds. *Occupied Women: Gender, Military Occupation, and the American Civil War*. Baton Rouge: Louisiana State University Press, 2009.

CLALIN, FRANCES LOUISA [FRANCIS CLAYTON]
(N.D.–N.D.)

Frances Louisa Clalin disguised herself as a man to serve as a Union soldier. One of approximately 400 women soldiers who served in the Civil War, Clalin left behind photographs showing her as herself and disguised as Francis Clayton, Civil War soldier.

Little is known about her life outside the Civil War, and there is also uncertainty about her name, which is sometimes spelled Clalin, Clatin, Claytin, or Clayton. The first known accounts of her life place her in Minnesota, living with her husband John in 1861. When the war began, John enlisted in the Minnesota State Militia Cavalry. Frances enlisted alongside him, disguised as a man, possibly by the name of Francis Clayton. There is doubt surrounding not only her name and pseudonym but also her military service. What little is known about Clalin is from the accounts about her published in the papers at the time and from an interview she gave after her military service ended.

Shortly after enlisting, Frances and John moved on to another regiment, most likely because the cavalry enlistment expired. Frances continued to act the part of a man, keeping her hair short, drinking, chewing tobacco, swearing, smoking cigars, and even gambling. A tall and masculine-looking woman, Frances was considered a good soldier by her comrades. There are varying reports of her military service after the cavalry enlistment, some placing her with Missouri regiments and others presuming she stayed with Minnesota units. Altogether, Frances and her husband fought side by side in 18 battles. When her husband John was killed at the Battle of Stone's River, just a few feet in front of Frances, accounts record that she bravely stepped over his body and continued to fight. Because the only Minnesota military unit at Stone's Rives was the 2nd Minnesota Battery, this may have been her regiment.

Some sources record that she was shot in the hip at Stone's River and that it was while being treated for her injury that her sex was discovered. A *Fincher's Trades' Review* reporter who talked with Frances in November 1863 gave another account, claiming that Frances was not discovered while she was in the service, nor was she wounded at Stone's River. Instead, this reporter wrote, she was wounded at Fort Donelson.

On January 3, 1863, Clalin was discharged from the regiment, and she returned to Minnesota to recover from her injury. Upon recovering, Frances tried to return to the army, ostensibly to get money in back pay and bounty money that she and John had earned, but perhaps to seek another position in the army. In Louisville, the provost marshal intercepted her, ordering her to return home. Clalin was last reported going to Washington, D.C., but there are no records of what happened to her thereafter. Some sources speculate that she may have continued her masquerade in another section of the military.

Sigrid Kelsey

See also: Civil War (1861–1865).

References and Further Reading

Eggleston, Larry G. *Women in the Civil War: Extraordinary Stories of Soldiers, Spies, Nurses, Doctors, Crusaders, and Others.* Jefferson, NC: McFarland, 2003.

Leonard, Elizabeth D. *All the Daring of the Soldier: Women of the Civil War Armies.* New York: W. W. Norton & Company, 1999.

CLARK, REGINA RENEE (1962–2005)

Regina Clark was a naval reservist who served in Operation Iraqi Freedom. She, along with several others, was killed by a suicide bomber on June 23, 2005. On her last tour of duty, Clark held the rank of Navy culinary specialist 1st class. She was the first female service member from the state of Washington to be killed in the line of duty during the Iraq War. She was 43 at the time her death.

Clark was born in Kassel, Germany, on January 26, 1962. She attended college on softball scholarships and joined the naval reserves. Her decision to enlist was not a surprising one to those who knew her. She came from a family with strong naval traditions; both her brother and her father had served in the Navy. Clark worked for several years in the deli and bakery at Fuller's Market Basket grocery store in Centralia. She played on the store's softball team as a short-stop. In between her tours of duty in the Middle East and her leaving her job at Market Basket, Clark worked at Cedar Creek Correction Center near Littlerock, Washington. Her son, Kerry, was born in the 1980s.

Clark was a veteran of Operation Desert Storm. After she returned to civilian life, she continued to serve in the naval reserves as a mess cook, where she held the rank of petty officer 1st class. She was called up for active service shortly after the terrorist attacks of September 11, 2001. In March 2003, she deployed to Kuwait for a six-month tour. In addition to her land assignments, she spent four months on the aircraft carrier USS *Nimitz*.

In early 2005, she deployed for what would be her third and last tour of duty in Iraq. She shipped out with the Naval Mobile Construction Battalion 18, based out of Tacoma, Washington. Once in Iraq, she served with the Naval

Construction Region Detachment 30 (Navy Reserve), based out of Port Hueneme, California. She was temporarily assigned to II Marine Expeditionary Force with a unit out of Camp Lejeune, North Carolina.

In her previous assignments in the Middle East, Clark had worked as a mess hall cook; but in this deployment, she did checkpoint searches. Local sensibilities forbade men from touching women who were not related to them in public, so female marines were assigned to work the checkpoints in and around Fallujah. Regulations prohibited female marines from spending the night at their checkpoint stations. Consequently, each morning and evening an armed convoy carried a contingent of female American soldiers between their home base and the various checkpoints in the city.

On the evening of June 23, 2005, as the military women were being taken back to their base at Camp Fallujah, a nearby car exploded. The improvised explosive device caused the death or injury of many in the military vehicle. Six marines died either immediately or as a result of injuries sustained by the bombing and subsequent small-arms fire. Clark was the only non-Marine woman in the truck that was struck by the suicide bomber. Three servicewomen died in the attack, making it one of the costliest incidents for American military women in U.S. history. Of the 13 wounded personnel, 11 were female. The attack, for which Al Qaeda claimed responsibility, constituted one of the single deadliest attacks against the Marines—and against female American soldiers—during the war.

Clark had planned to retire from the military after this tour of duty and spend more time at home with her son. Clark's military benefits helped her 18-year-old son to go to college. He received his associate's degree at Centralia College and then majored in humanities with a history minor in Washington State University's online program. He hopes to pursue a postgraduate degree in history.

L. Bao Bui

See also: Charette, Holly A. (1983–2005); Gulf War (1991); Iraq War (2003–2011); Valdez, Ramona M. (1984–2005); War on Terrorism (2001–).

References and Further Reading

Ballard, John R. *Fighting for Fallujah: A New Dawn for Iraq.* Westport, CT: Greenwood Publishing Group, 2006.

Mosher, Andy. "Blast Kills at Least 2 Marines, Injures 13." *Washington Post*, June 25, 2005, A16.

Ryan, Cheyney. *The Chickenhawk Syndrome: War, Sacrifice, and Personal Responsibility.* Lanham, MD: Rowman & Littlefield, 2009.

CLARKE, MARY E. (1924–)

Maj. Gen. Mary E. Clarke served in the U.S. Army from 1945 to 1981. She spent the majority of her service career within the Women's Army Corps (WAC), the women's component of the Army, until the dissolution of the WAC in 1978. Most significantly, Clarke was the last officer to serve as director of WAC (1975–1978). In 1978, Clarke became the first woman in the Army to receive a promotion to the rank of two-star general. Her career spanned a variety of transitional periods from the end of World War II through the integration of women into the Regular Army after the elimination of the WAC.

Clarke was born December 3, 1924, and raised in Rochester, New York. There she attended Immaculate Conception Grammar School and graduated from West High School. Clarke joined the WAC as an enlisted woman in August 1945, shortly before the end of World War II. As an enlisted member of the WAC, she completed basic training at Fort Des Moines, Iowa, before being assigned as a supply sergeant to facilities in Camp Stoneman, California, and Berlin, Germany. During her time in Berlin, she served with the Berlin Brigade in the midst of the Berlin Airlift efforts of 1948 and 1949.

In 1949, Clarke attended Officer Candidate School and became a commissioned WAC officer. Following this career transition, Clarke went on to serve at the U.S. Army Chemical Center, Valley Forge General Hospital; completed one year as a recruiter; and served for two years as commanding officer of a WAC detachment in Tokyo, Japan.

Between 1958 and 1972, she held a number of roles in Texas, Maryland, California, Washington, D.C., and Alabama. As she progressed from the rank of captain to colonel during these years, her job positions included work in the Office of Equal Opportunity, the Deputy Chief of Staff for Personnel, and leadership roles in WAC training and advisement.

After her promotion to colonel in 1972, Clarke became the commander/commandant of the U.S. WAC Center and School in Fort McClellan,

Alabama. At that time, Fort McClellan was the location where all WACs completed basic training. In 1974 and 1975, just before her appointment as director of WAC, Clarke served as chief of the WAC Advisory Branch and chief of the WAC Advisory Office.

Clarke became the final director of the WAC in August 1975, receiving a promotion to brigadier general at the same time. During Clarke's three years as director of WAC, the military continued to expand women's opportunities exponentially. In 1976, President Gerald Ford signed legislation that admitted women to the military academies. To support this move, Clarke helped secure spaces for women in a special course at the U.S. Military Academy Preparatory School in 1976. This course helped prepare women to attend the academies.

In general, the final years of the WAC under Clarke's leadership included the transition to ensure men and women participated on a more equal basis within the military. Women began to serve for the same length of time in overseas assignments as men, and women started to receive weapons training as well in 1976. The following year, men and women began to complete identical basic training programs. In 1977, women also participated in war games in Germany.

An act of Congress in 1978 led to the disestablishment of the WAC in early 1978, and by October 1978 women were considered members of the Regular Army. Along with this transition, the Army combined men and women for basic training within the same companies to ensure unified, equal training processes. In a number of speeches and articles, Clarke expressed continued commitment to ensuring women's

equality and equal opportunity as members of the U.S. military. She saw the disestablishment of the WAC as an important step to ensure women's complete integration within the Army, in particular. Clarke also encouraged women to demonstrate their ability to combine motherhood and a career, believing that women's capacity to have children should not limit their job opportunities.

With the end of the WAC in 1978, the military also eliminated the position of director of WAC. Clarke received a new assignment as commander of the U.S. Army Military Police School and Training Center, which took over the former WAC facilities at Fort McClellan. On November 1, 1978, Clarke received her final promotion, to major general.

In mid-1980, Clarke accepted her final career assignment as director of the Human Resources Directorate in the Office of the Deputy Chief of Staff for Personnel at the Pentagon. On October 31, 1981, Clarke retired from active military service. She received the Distinguished Service Medal at that time. She received a number of military awards, including the Legion of Merit, Army of Occupation Medal, World War II Victory Medal, National Defense Service Medal, and the Army Commendation Medal. In addition, Norwich University in Northfield, Vermont, granted Clarke an honorary doctor of military science degree. Clarke relocated back to Alabama after her retirement.

Tanya L. Roth

See also: Bailey, Mildred "Inez" Caroon (1919–2009); Hoisington, Elizabeth P. (1918–2007); Military Police; Milligan (Rasmuson), Mary Louise (1911–); Women's Armed

Services Integration Act of 1948 (Public Law 80-625); Women's Army Corps (WAC); World War II (1941–1945).

References and Further Reading

Bailey, Beth. *America's Army: Making the All-Volunteer Force*. Cambridge, MA: Belknap Press of Harvard University Press, 2009.

Holm, Jeanne. *In Defense of a Nation: Servicewomen in World War II*. St. Petersburg, FL: Vandamere Press, 1998.

Holm, Jeanne. *Women in the Military: An Unending Revolution (Revised Edition)*. Novato, CA: Presidio Press, 1993.

Morden, Bettie J. *The Women's Army Corps, 1945–1978*. Washington, D.C.: Center of Military History, 1989.

Witt, Linda, Judith Bellafaire, Britta Granrud, and Mary Jo Binker. *"A Defense Weapon Known to Be of Value": Servicewomen of the Korean War Era*. Hanover, NH: University Press of New England, 2005.

In 1943, U.S. pilot Jackie Cochran was appointed to lead the Women Air Force Service Pilots (WASP). Cochran set over 200 flying records and helped to erase gender barriers in aviation. (Library of Congress)

COCHRAN, JACQUELINE (CA. 1910–1980)

Accomplished female aviator, director of the Women Air Force Service Pilots (WASP) during World War II, and lieutenant colonel in the U.S. Air Force Reserve, Jacqueline "Jackie" Cochran set over 200 aviation records, including becoming the first woman to fly a bomber across the Atlantic Ocean and the first woman to fly faster than the speed of sound. At the time of her death, she held more aviation records than any other pilot.

Although her exact birth date is unknown, Cochran was born sometime around 1910 in a sawmill town in northern Florida. Many historians argue she was born on May 11, 1906, in Muscogee, Florida, as Bessie Pittman, although Cochran never verified this in her autobiography. She claimed that she picked her name out of a phonebook, but some suggest Cochran was the last name of an ex-husband.

Growing up in an impoverished family with no formal education, Cochran worked in a cotton mill at the age of eight. She left her family during her teenage years to become a nurse. Unsatisfied with the career, she decided to work as a beautician. In the early 1930s, she moved to New York and worked at Antoine's, a prominent beauty salon. This position gave her the opportunity to associate with well-connected people, and she eventually started her own cosmetics line. Her aviation career began shortly after she met millionaire Floyd B. Odlum, who suggested she get a pilot's license to better advertise her potential cosmetics line.

After earning her pilot's license in less than three weeks in 1932, Cochran was fascinated with flying and sought to become the nation's top pilot. She flew in her first air race just days after receiving her pilot's license. In 1936, Cochran married Odlum. Throughout her life, Odlum provided some of the financial resources and political connections she needed to achieve her aviation goals. During the 1930s, Cochran won a series of important awards. She received the 1938 Gen. William E. Mitchell Award for her aviation contributions, earned first place in the 1938 Bendix Transcontinental air race, and broke international speed records in 1939. She then proposed a women's military pilot program for the United States.

Despite rejections at first, Cochran soon succeeded in making a place for American women pilots in wartime military service. In 1941, Army Air Force general Henry H. "Hap" Arnold asked Cochran to select and supervise a group of American women to fly in the British Air Transport Auxiliary (ATA), a branch of the Royal Air Force. Later, in 1942, the Army Air Force organized two women's pilot programs, the Women's Auxiliary Ferrying Squadron (WAFS) and the Women's Flying Training Detachment (WFTD). The purpose of these programs was to free men for combat. Nancy Harkness Love directed the WAFS program, which was comprised of 25 to 50 highly experienced women pilots assigned to the task of ferrying

aircraft. Cochran was in charge of the WFTD, a program designed to train up to 1,500 women in military aircraft flying. These two programs combined in 1943 to become the WASP. Arnold named Cochran director of WASP, a position she held until the WASP program ended in December 1944. Cochran placed the WASP in various Army Air Force assignments, including towing targets and testing aircraft returned from overseas duty.

After World War II, Cochran spoke publicly and used her connections to argue that the Air Force should become a separate branch of the military apart from the Army. In 1945, she received the Distinguished Service Medal for her work as director of the WASP. Later, in 1948, she became a lieutenant colonel in the Air Force Reserve. She was also one of a few women to fly military jets in the postwar period.

During the late 1950s and early 1960s, Dr. William Randolph Lovelace began testing women's potential abilities as astronauts. Cochran and her husband provided funding for Lovelace's Woman in Space Program. Although Cochran wanted to be a candidate for the program, she did not meet the age or health requirements. After the conclusion of the women's training, Cochran was appointed as a special consultant to the National Aeronautics and Space Administration (NASA), a position she held for a few years.

Cochran continued to set aviation records throughout the 1960s, but by the 1970s health problems forced her to give up piloting. In 1971, she was inducted into the Aviation Hall of Fame in Dayton, Ohio. Throughout her lifetime, Cochran continually searched for ways to pursue aviation during a time when the number of women pilots and the opportunities for an aviation career were limited.

Cochran died on August 9, 1980, in Indio, California. She was posthumously awarded the Congressional Gold Medal on March 10, 2010, for her work as director of the WASP.

Sarah Parry Myers

See also: Love, Nancy Harkness (1914–1976); Lovelace's Woman in Space Program (WISP); Women Air Force Service Pilots (WASP); Women's Auxiliary Ferrying Squadron (WAFS); Women's Flying Training Detachment (WFTD); World War II (1941–1945).

References and Further Reading

Cochran, Jacqueline, and Floyd Odlum. *The Stars at Noon*. Boston: Little, Brown and Company, 1954.

Douglas, Deborah G. *American Women and Flight since 1940*. Lexington: University Press of Kentucky, 2004.

Rich, Doris L. *Jackie Cochran: Pilot in the Fastest Lane*. Gainesville: University Press of Florida, 2007.

Weitekamp, Margaret A. *Right Stuff, Wrong Sex: America's First Women in Space Program*. Baltimore, MD: Johns Hopkins University Press, 2004.

COLD WAR
(ca. 1947–1991)

The Cold War was a complex ideological conflict. A long-term global struggle of power between the United States and the Soviet Union that led to a tense world where all lived under the shadow of nuclear destruction, the Cold War was not a traditional conflict—although the proxy wars it provoked are—for which one can precisely define the number of women involved, their role, their agency, or the evolution of their situation.

The Cold War lasted for over 40 years, from the post–World War II era (1947 is the most commonly used starting point) to the collapse of the Soviet Union in 1991. During this period, the U.S. military repeatedly reorganized to adapt to new developments. Accordingly, the place of women in the military dramatically evolved from a struggle to maintain full military status in peacetime to the complete integration in the armed forces and the dissolution of separate female organizations. As a conflict with not only military ramifications but also ideological, political, economic, and scientific ones, the Cold War affected women in all spheres of U.S. society. As women's situation evolved, their image was forged both by the need for propaganda against Soviet communism and by the society's internal evolution and demands for equal rights.

After World War II, the public generally expected the 280,000 women who had served in uniform to be dismissed, except perhaps for those who served as military nurses. These expectations were not unreasonable as many of the women's branches had been formed as temporary answers to the war's drain on manpower and the need for women to fulfill duties that freed men to go to the battlefront. For example, the Women's Army Corps (WAC), the women's reserve of the Navy (WAVES), the Marine Corps Women's Reserve (Women Marines), and the women's reserve of the Coast Guard were only supposed to function during the war and the following six months.

However, the emergence of international tensions over nuclear power, the Cold War, helped the military to overcome public and political reluctance to establishing a permanent military status for women. Indeed, the Soviet threat in Europe and growing influence in the Third World led Americans to commit to peacetime alliances, to accept a sizeable military sustained by a peacetime draft, and to increase the level of military involvement in traditionally nonmilitary sectors from government and diplomacy to science and technology. Despite the initial belief that the atomic age would reduce the number of military forces needed, the early Cold War situation proved otherwise: occupation forces in defeated countries (Japan, Germany, and Austria) and deterrent forces to avoid the spread of communism became the means of a greater scale of foreign policy, including the new 1949 North Atlantic Treaty Organization (NATO). The Korean War (1950–1953) would prove that the U.S. military also needed to fight traditional wars to support its global Cold War foreign policy. As a result, U.S. military leaders did not want to lose all their uniformed women and searched for ways to enable women to serve in the armed forces on a permanent basis. At the same time, the postwar era witnessed a return of women to the home, a drop in women's ages at marriage and childbearing, and an unfavorable climate and public opinion to women in the workforce.

Initiated and supported by Gen. Dwight D. Eisenhower, the Women's Armed Services Integration Act passed easily in the Senate in 1947, although the House of Representatives preferred a reserve-only policy for women in the military. The worsening world situation in early 1948 precipitated the decision on integrating women into the military. Cold War tensions intensified as the Soviet Union consolidated its hold on Eastern Europe, gained control of Czechoslovakia, and blocked rail and highway traffic from West Germany to West Berlin. In response to the military's inability to recruit male volunteers, President Harry S. Truman asked for an unpopular peacetime draft. The possibility of a draft forced politicians to show their constituents that they had not turned down a potential source of volunteer women and therefore to accept the Women's Armed Service Integration Act on June 12, 1948, which established both regular and reserve women in each of the military services, with the restriction that they could not command men, be subject to combat, or represent more than 2 percent of the total forces. Women's authority and promotions were also strictly limited.

Despite the advances in women's position in the military, female recruits were still held to gender-specific standards. Women who wished to enlist were required to fit the late 1940s and 1950s image of women in U.S. society. The recruits had to be between 18 and 35 years old (those under 21 needed the consent of a legal guardian), to be single with no dependent children under the age of 18, to possess a high school diploma, and to pass a mental alertness test and a physical examination. These restrictions reflected the idea that women, as docile housewives, belonged in the home, an ideal that was extremely strong at the time and that diametrically contrasted with McCarthyism's demonization of Soviet women, who were allegedly equal to men in freedom and education. To highlight the cultural differences between democracy and communism, propaganda pointed out that Soviet women worked in factories and on collective farms and served in the Soviet armed forces just like Soviet men. As a result, women's integration into the U.S. armed forces was a tricky process.

Intelligence agencies grew during the Cold War. As a result, as early as 1949 the growth of covert operations might have given women opportunities in intelligence agencies, especially the Central Intelligence Agency (CIA) operating overseas. However, during the first four decades of its existence, the CIA mostly employed female recruits for secretarial or support tasks; those rarely sent in the field were drawn from these staffs. Only the gutsiest, smartest, and most persistent women managed to obtain opportunities in the field. However, many women served as spies and code breakers, some of whom had done so during earlier wars. In the mid-1980s, President Ronald Reagan's military buildup forced the agency to loosen its recruitment policy and to hire women as active agents.

Throughout the Cold War women in the military worked toward equality with their male peers. The late 1950s and 1960s saw an increasing acceptance of women in the labor force in U.S. society, which in the military translated into the idea that some military occupation specialties (MOSs) could be performed interchangeably by men or women. In addition, the "space race" between the United States and the U.S.S.R. opened up avenues for women. Female scientists

played a role in creating new military technologies such as weapons, modes of transportation, and communications systems that required more complex training and management. Military women took this opportunity to expand their role and, therefore, their numbers. In 1967, President Lyndon B. Johnson eliminated the restrictions on percentages and promotions of women in the armed forces. However, most men still viewed the military as their arena; in order to gain acceptance in the ranks, women had to be efficient and exemplary. Female leadership imposed on their enlistees a code of behavior much stricter than that expected of men.

In the meantime, renewed Cold War tensions in the early 1960s, including the Second Berlin Crisis in 1961 and the Cuban Missile Crisis in 1962, provoked a wave of patriotism and led to a surge of female recruits. However, the question of women's participation in the growing confrontation in Vietnam arose with the influx of female volunteers. The realities of the Vietnam War posed some problems, the most important one related to combat restriction, which could not be totally guaranteed in Vietnam. In addition, officials worried about the logistical problem of the cost of procuring safe housing for women in Saigon. Meanwhile, the increase in combat action, draft calls, and death tolls, combined with the lack of important victories, contributed to a loss of public support for the war. In this context, President Richard Nixon was elected primarily on the basis of ending both the war and the draft.

For this purpose, the military had to be reorganized and to be able to attract enough volunteers, men and women, to fill its ranks. Nixon participated in making the armed forces appealing to women by appointing the first female generals in 1970. The changes in the military also reflected the resurgence of the women's rights movement. Liberal ideas about women's status and moral standards led to a reexamination of the role of women, and enlistment restrictions based on private life began to fade. Although women still faced rejection from the military for having illegitimate children or venereal disease (which did not bar men from enlistment) as well as discharge for marriage or pregnancy, beginning in 1971 they could apply for a waiver to retain their military status. The strongest opposition to these revised policies came from the military leadership's women, who argued that these changes would jeopardize the quality of women recruits.

Nonetheless, the new traditional and untraditional opportunities, the elimination of restraints, and the multiplication of meritorious service awards for women's contributions in Vietnam encouraged new enlistments as well as reenlistments. In addition, these advances eventually forced the women in the military out of their conservative patterns and led military leadership to amend the restrictions. In 1969, the Air Force started to enroll women in its Reserve Officer Training Corps, followed in 1972 by the Navy and the Army. In 1972, women could be trained as noncombat aviators, and the Air Force allowed them to command some mixed male and female units. The Navy and Army soon followed with similar command rules.

In December 1972, Nixon announced the end of the draft, leading to the first all-volunteer armed forces since World War II. In this context, the Department of Defense asked the Army, Navy, and Air Force to double their 1972 womanpower by 1977—the Women's Army Corps would reach 23,800, the women in the Air Force 22,800, and the women in the Navy 11,400—and the Marines to increase it by 40 percent, up to 3,100. Initially created to provide trained women in case of mobilization, the female military strengths eventually blossomed in peacetime. Women's success in the military made it easier for the women's rights movement to insist on an equality of criteria between men and women. Women pushed for admission to the service academies, removal of combat restrictions, and dissolution of the separate women's organizations. With the integration of the sexes in training, the elimination of dual enlistment standards, and the progressive merger of female and male units, the abolition of separate women's organizations within the military appeared as the logical following step. The Navy in 1972, the Marine Corps in 1975, the Air Force in 1976, and the Army in 1978 integrated their women as full partners in their activities, with full progress opportunities, and eventually dissolved their separate women's organizations. Alongside the evolution of women's situation in the wider society, during the Cold War women in the military had achieved equality in the military, except for combat restrictions.

In the wake of the U.S. military withdrawal from Vietnam and the failure of détente, Americans had lost faith in their armed forces; by contrast, their new ally's military, the Israeli Defense Forces, appeared efficient, determined, and bold. Far from the 1950s portrayal of purportedly manly Soviet women, in the 1970s, influenced by the women's rights movement and attracted by the Israeli example, Americans conceived of women in the military as the image, and maybe even the means, of the armed forces' rejuvenation. On this basis, Reagan undertook a massive military buildup that eventually led to the economic exhaustion of the Soviet Union. After the rapprochement initiated in the mid-1980s by the new Soviet leader Mikhail Gorbachev, the Soviet Union disintegrated in December 1991. Its dissolution opened a new era for women in the U.S. military that the first Gulf War had inaugurated in January 1991.

Sarah J. Gavison

See also: Espionage; Gulf War (1991); Korean War (1950–1953); Reserve Officer Training Corps (ROTC); United States Coast Guard Women's Reserve (SPAR); Vietnam War (1965–1973); Women Accepted for Volunteer Emergency Service (WAVES); Women in the Air Force (WAF); Women Marines; Women's Armed Service Integration Act of 1948 (Public Law 80-625); Women's Army Corps (WAC); World War II (1941–1945).

References and Further Reading

Barkalow, Carol. *In the Men's House*. New York: Poseidon Press, 1990.

Godson, Susan. *Serving Proudly: Women in the Navy*. Annapolis, MD: Naval Institute Press, 2002.

Holm, Jeanne M. *Women in the Military: An Unfinished Revolution*, rev. ed. Novato, CA: Presidio Press, 1992.

Morden, Bettie J. *The Women's Army Corps, 1945–1978*. Washington, D.C.: Center of Military History, 2000.

Stremlow, Mary V. *U.S. Marine Corps Reserve: A History of the Women Marines, 1946–1977*. Washington, D.C.: U.S. Marine Corps, 1986.

COLE, MARY ANN
(N.D.—N.D.)

An American medical nurse during the War of 1812, Mary Ann Cole is known for her dedication to the wounded and dying during the siege of Fort Erie.

Although many of the details of Cole's life are unknown, she appears in the historical record as a paid contract nurse during the War of 1812. As a nurse, Cole cleaned wounds, changed bandages, and cared for recently injured soldiers in addition to completing a variety of other duties. Successful nurses in the War of 1812 were courageous and not easily flustered, for they faced many of the same dangers as men. While serving on the battlefield, nurses could be wounded or killed by stray bullets and explosions, just like the male soldiers they were trying to save.

From July through November 1814, Cole worked as a hospital administrator, or "matron," inside Fort Erie. Fort Erie, located near Buffalo, New York, had been a military site since 1764 and was the first permanent fort built by the British in Ontario. By 1812, the fort had two bastions and two barracks. During the War of 1812, the fort changed hands several times. On July 3, 1814, under the command of Maj. Gen. Jacob Brown, approximately 4,000 U.S. soldiers surrounded the British fort and captured it. After expanding the size of the fort, the Americans used it as a base for their surrounding operations. On August 15, the British launched a four-pronged attack against the fort. As the British bombarded the fort, the American soldiers worked to maintain their defenses. Over the course of four months, over 1,800 Americans were wounded or killed in action. In the fort's makeshift hospital, Cole and other nurses cared for sick, wounded, and dying soldiers. Chronic diarrhea and typhus frequently afflicted soldiers, and amputations remained a common solution and surgery in the fort.

In addition to performing the duties of a medical nurse, Cole completed additional tasks. She helped prepare meals to feed the men inside the fort, whose number would rise to approximately 6,000 towards the end of the occupation. Although the fort almost always had food, it was poor in quality and consisted primarily of hard bread and salted pork. This diet would be supplemented by vegetables and dairy, which occasionally became available through trade or purchase. The shortage of soap in the fort also contributed to the spread of disease. Cole also distributed medications and maintained the medical records for the regimental surgeon. Though they did not know it at the time, the siege on Fort Erie would be the longest siege of the war.

As Cole worked, Congreve rockets, shell fragments, and cannon balls landed around her. The siege would last for over a month, and with each day that passed, food and medical supplies grew shorter and the number of wounded and sick increased. On September 17, the U.S. army launched a full-scale attack into the British siege lines. Both sides suffered a combined total of 1,000 casualties that day, a total that would keep Cole extremely busy. The Americans were unaware that the day before the attack,

the British had already decided that they would cease the siege and withdraw. The British began pulling back their siege guns on September 18 and 19. In late October, with winter approaching and news that the eastern seaboard of the United States was under attack, American officers began to consider abandoning the fort. On November 5, 1814, the American occupants destroyed the fort so it would not be of use to the British and formally withdrew.

Cole left the fort with the troops, heading for Buffalo, New York, and once again disappeared from the historical record. On December 24, 1814, the Treaty of Ghent was signed and the War of 1812 officially ended. As of 2012, the Fort Erie site remains the bloodiest battlefield in Canada. Old Fort Erie, which is owned and operated by the Niagara Parks Commission, honors the work of Cole in an exhibit. Though not much is known about her, Cole's experiences remind us that women participated and risked their lives during the War of 1812. Like male soldiers, female nurses also emerged as veterans of war, taking their stories, and sometimes their secrets, with them to the grave.

Angela Esco Elder

See also: Nursing; War of 1812 (1812–1815).

References and Further Reading

Barbuto, Richard V. *Niagara 1814: America Invades Canada*. Lawrence: University Press of Kansas, 2000.

Bellafaire, Judith. *Women in the United States Military: An Annotated Bibliography*. New York: Rutledge Press, 2011.

Pfeiffer, Susan, and Ronald F. Williamson, eds. *Snake Hill: An Investigation of a Military Cemetery from the War of 1812*. Toronto: Dundurn Press, 1991.

Whitehorne, Joseph. *While Washington Burned: The Battle for Fort Erie 1814*. Baltimore, MD: Nautical and Aviation Publishing Company of America, 1992.

COLLINS, EILEEN MARIE (1956–)

In 1995, U.S. Air Force colonel and astronaut Eileen Collins became the first woman to pilot a space shuttle. Four years later, she also became the first female commander of a shuttle mission.

One of four children, Collins was born on November 19, 1956, in Elmira, New York. Both of her parents were immigrants from County Cork, Ireland. The Collins family struggled financially during Eileen's childhood, receiving food stamps and living in government-subsidized housing for six years. As early as the fourth grade, Eileen developed a fascination with flight. However, as a result of their financial difficulties, her parents were unable to pay for flight lessons. To raise the money, Collins worked a series of odd jobs through her

Astronaut Eileen Collins, the nation's first female space shuttle pilot, also became the first woman to lead a U.S. space mission. (AP/Wide World Photos)

teenage years. By her 19th birthday, she had raised $1,000 and was able to sign up for flying lessons.

Collins attended Corning Community College before receiving her bachelor's degree in mathematics and economics from Syracuse University in 1978. Shortly after graduating from college, Collins joined the Air Force. She was one of only four female students in Vance Air Force Base's pilot training program, in the first class to admit women. Despite the challenges inherent in being one of the few women in a largely male environment, Collins succeeded in completing her pilot training in 1979.

After the completion of her training, Collins flew C-141 Starlifter airplanes and worked as a flight instructor at California's Travis Air Force Base. She met her future husband, Pat Youngs, while both of them were flying C-141s. In 1986, she became a T-41 flight instructor and mathematics professor at Colorado's Air Force Academy. While still an officer and instructor, Collins attended graduate school at Stanford University, earning a master's degree in operations research in 1986. She then went on to earn a second master's degree in space systems management from Webster University.

After her time as a graduate student and flight instructor, Collins was accepted into the Air Force Test Pilot School. In 1990, she became only the second woman in Air Force history to graduate as a test pilot. Shortly thereafter, at the age of 33, Collins applied to become an astronaut for the National Aeronautics and Space Administration (NASA). Two months after completing the rigorous six-day testing and interview process, she became an astronaut.

In 1995, Collins was selected to pilot the *Discovery* shuttle on NASA's STS-63 mission. Two years later, she piloted the shuttle for the STS-84 *Atlantis* mission. Collins achieved another milestone in 1999, when she became the first female shuttle commander, for the *Columbia* orbiter's STS-93 mission. During this mission, she and her crew launched NASA's new Chandra X-Ray Observatory.

Between flight missions, Collins performed a variety of tasks at NASA headquarters. She provided engineering support to the orbiter, worked in mission control, and served in a number of positions, including chief information officer and shuttle branch chief. She also briefly took time off to give birth to her two children, Bridget and Luke.

In February 2003, as Collins prepared for her final mission, the *Columbia* shuttle disintegrated upon reentering Earth's atmosphere. The accident killed all seven of the astronauts onboard. As a result, all scheduled space flights were cancelled until investigators could determine the cause of the accident. After a two-year delay, Collins flew her last shuttle mission in 2005. It was the first mission to space since the *Columbia* disaster. NASA had determined that the accident had been the result of defective tiles in the heat shield. To ensure that this disaster did not reoccur, Collins and her crew had to perform a new maneuver while piloting the shuttle. This involved "flipping" the shuttle midflight to allow outside observers to photograph the heat shield; they performed the maneuver successfully, allowing engineers to detect and fix a potentially disastrous flaw in the shield.

Collins retired from the U.S. Air Force in 2005. One year later, she announced her retirement from NASA. Since that time, she has worked as a public speaker and news analyst for stories related to space flight and NASA projects.

Over the course of her career in NASA, Collins flew four space flights and logged over 870 hours in space. She contributed to a number of vital missions, including trips to the International Space Station and Mir. She has received numerous awards and military commendations, including the Distinguished Flying Cross, the Defense Meritorious Service Metal, the French Legion of Honor, the NASA Outstanding Leadership Metal, and the National Space Trophy.

Jamie Stoops

References and Further Reading

Colonel Eileen M. Collins: Leadership Lessons from Apollo to Discovery. Video. Chicago Humanities Festival, 1998.

Ellis, Lee. "Collins, Eileen Marie (Colonel, USAF), NASA Astronaut." In *Who's Who of NASA Astronauts*, 46–47. River Falls, WI: Americana Group Publishing, 2004.

O'Neill, Ann Marie, et al. "Collins, Eileen (Eileen Marie), 1956." *People* 49, no. 18 (May 1998): 225.

COOK, CORDELIA ELIZABETH "BETTY"
(N.D.–N.D.)

First Lt. Cordelia Elizabeth Cook served in the U.S. Army Nurse Corps (ANC) during World War II. Cook received the Purple Heart and became the first American woman to receive the Bronze Star. As the recipient of the Purple Heart and the Bronze Star, Cook became the first American woman to receive multiple awards for her service during World War II.

Cook was born in Fort Thomas, Kentucky. She graduated from the Christ Hospital School of Nursing located in Cincinnati, Ohio, in 1940. She married Army officer Capt. Harold E. Fillmore.

During World War II, Cook served overseas, along with nine other surgical nurses, in the 11th Field Hospital located in the Presenzano sector along the Italian front. Cook and her fellow nurses worked closer to the battlefront than any other American women had ever worked before. When U.S. troops were fighting their way through the lowlands of the Cassino corridor in southern Italy, Cook and the 11th Field Hospital nurses were stationed ahead of the American heavy guns. The advanced position of the field hospital allowed the nurses to save many of the severely wounded soldiers. Cook, also known as "Betty," carried out her hospital duties at the 11th Field Hospital from November 1943 until January 1944.

Cook was nursing wounded soldiers when her field hospital in Italy was bombed in 1943. Despite being wounded by artillery fire, Cook continued to fulfill her duties as a nurse and looked after the wounded soldiers under her care.

As a result, Cook was awarded the Purple Heart in 1944 for the wounds she received when her field hospital was bombed in the Presenzano sector of the Italian front. In 1944, Cook also received the Bronze Star, the fourth highest award given in the military for any servicemember who distinguishes himself or herself through heroic actions or meritorious achievement or service. Cook received the Bronze Star for her service in the U.S. Army Nurse Corps because she provided direct support of combat operations even when wounded by artillery fire. She was the first American woman to receive the award.

Rorie M. Cartier

See also: Army Nurse Corps (ANC); Nursing; World War II (1941–1945).

References and Further Reading

Baron, Scott. *They Also Served: Military Biographies of Uncommon Americans.* Spartanburg, SC: Military Information Enterprises, 1998.

Bourke-White, Margaret. *They Called It "Purple Heart Valley": A Combat Chronicle of the War in Italy*, 1st ed. New York: Simon and Schuster, 1994.

Gruhzit-Hoyt, Olga. *They Also Served: American Women in World War II*. Secaucus, NJ: Birch Lane Press, 1995.

Jackson, Kathi. *They Called Them Angels: American Military Nurses of World War II.* Lincoln: University of Nebraska Press, 2006.

Read, Phyllis J., and Bernard L. Witlieb. *The Book of Women's Firsts: Breakthrough Achievements of Almost 1,000 American Women.* New York: Random House, 1992.

CORBIN, MARGARET COCHRAN (1751–CA. 1800)

A camp follower who took up her husband's post on the battlefield after his death, Margaret Cochran Corbin was honored for her wartime service during the American Revolution and given a soldier's pension.

Margaret Cochran was born in 1751 near Chambersburg, Pennsylvania, on what was then the frontier. Her parents were killed in 1756 in the course of a Native American attack on the small blockhouse and stockade known as Fort Bigham. She was raised by a maternal uncle and married John Corbin from Virginia in 1772.

When her husband enlisted in the 1st Company of Pennsylvania artillery as a matross, who loaded the cannon for firing and then sponged it clean in preparation for the next load, Margaret accompanied him. She joined him on military campaigns as a camp follower. In addition, she is rumored to have worn men's clothing while assisting the men on the artillery line.

On November 16, 1776, John was manning a cannon at Fort Washington at the northern tip of Manhattan in the wake of the crippling defeat at White Plains. Some 4,000 Hessians under British command were in the process of storming this high point. The cannoneer of John's gun was killed, and he stepped up to aim and fire the cannon. As he changed positions, Margaret filled John's role of matross. After a musket ball hit her husband, Margaret took over his role firing the cannon. She continued firing until enemy fire hit her with grapeshot and musket balls in the arm, jaw, and chest. She and the other survivors were captured and paroled, and she found her way to a hospital in Philadelphia.

She survived her wounds but never regained the use of her left arm. She was assigned to the Corps of the Invalids, a unit created in 1777 for soldiers who were wounded and incapable of serving in the front lines. These soldiers supplied a number of services that freed up able soldiers for front-line duty. Corbin was formally discharged from the army in 1783 and was granted both state and federal pensions in 1779. The Pennsylvania state resolution recognized her duty, wounds, and bravery. The federal finding similarly recognized her role as a soldier and highlighted her entitlement to a monetary pension and clothing allowance. She served at West Point until her death.

In 1782, she married another member of the Corps of the Invalids. He succumbed to his wounds a year later. Local oral traditions painted her as rude, drunken, vulgar, and quick-tempered after the war. A tradition holds that the Philadelphia Women's Society wanted to erect a monument to her, but the members were horrified by her drunken disposition when they met her and subsequently withdrew the offer. She died around 1800 in relative obscurity, buried in a grave that was soon forgotten.

Corbin's story was rediscovered in the early 20th century, and she was further recognized for her bravery. After having an army surgeon confirm her identity by her war wounds, the Daughters of the American Revolution disinterred her body and reburied her at West Point in 1926. She is the only Revolutionary soldier buried there. In further tribute to her, the entry to Fort Tryon Park (the name given to Fort Washington after its fall) is named Margaret Corbin Circle. Further, the Margaret C. Corbin Award is given by the military to civilian spouses of soldiers whose volunteer efforts have a substantive effect on soldiers and their families. Two hundred

years after she became a legend, the military created a vehicle for the assimilation of women into West Point in 1976, named the Margaret Corbin Forum. Finally, the U.S. Naval Academy hosts the Margaret Corbin Leadership Summit, an annual meeting that focuses on various human relations issues.

Mark Anthony Phelps

See also: American Revolution (1775–1783); Camp Followers.

References and Further Reading

Berkin, Carol. *Revolutionary Mothers: Women in the Struggle for American Independence*. New York: Alfred Knopf, 2005.

Department of the Army. *Margaret C. Corbin Award*. TRADOC Regulation 672-8. Fort Monroe, VA: United States Army, 2008.

Wensyl, James. "Captain Molly." *Army* 31 (November 1981): 48–53.

CORNUM, RHONDA (1954–)

Physician and army officer Rhonda Cornum was one of two U.S. service-women captured by Iraqi forces during the 1991 Persian Gulf War. During her captivity, Cornum was sexually assaulted by an Iraqi guard. This revelation, and the way in which Cornum handled it, helped to change American attitudes towards women in combat roles and opened more duties to women.

Cornum was born on October 31, 1954, in Dayton, Ohio. She earned a

PhD in biochemistry from Cornell University in 1978. Cornum joined the U.S. Army that same year and conducted medical-related research in San Francisco. Later, Cornum went to medical school at the Uniformed Services University of the Health Sciences in Bethesda, Maryland, earning an MD in 1987. Later that year, she was a finalist for selection as an astronaut. Although she was disappointed when she was not selected, Cornum became a flight surgeon at Fort Rucker, Alabama.

In 1990, Cornum deployed to Saudi Arabia as a flight surgeon with the 101st Airborne Division as part of Operation Desert Shield. On February 27, 1991, three days after the commencement of ground operations in Desert Storm, a Lockheed Martin F-16 Fighting Falcon flown by Capt. William Andrews was shot down during fighting near Basra. Andrews successfully ejected, although he suffered a broken leg. An initial rescue attempt failed to locate Andrews. A second rescue mission by the 101st Airborne, which included Cornum, flew in a Sikorsky UH-60 Black Hawk helicopter to Andrews's last reported position.

Despite the overall destruction of Iraq's air defenses, Iraqi ground forces still retained significant antiaircraft capabilities. The Black Hawk in which Cornum was flying was shot down and crashed. Five of the eight team members were killed in the crash, and Cornum was severely injured. She had taken a bullet in one shoulder, and both her arms were broken. Iraqi soldiers pulled Cornum and other survivors from the wreck and threatened to shoot them. Instead, the Iraqis placed them in a truck and drove them to a prison in Basra. During the transit, Cornum was sexually assaulted by one of the Iraqi soldiers guarding her. Because of her injuries, Cornum was unable to resist the assault.

The Iraqis held Cornum prisoner for the next eight days. She later reported that she was treated well by the other Iraqi guards; they helped her with personal hygiene and other matters that she was not able to perform for herself because of her injuries. Although she was interrogated, she was not tortured or physically beaten like some other American prisoners of war (POWs). Cornum and the other American POWs were released on March 5, 1991. Cornum and Melissa Rathbun-Nealy, an army enlisted woman, were the only female POWs in the group.

Some who opposed American women in combat cited Cornum and Rathbun-Nealy's experiences as POWs as evidence proving why women did not belong on the battlefield. In the spring of 1992, a congressional committee held hearings on the question of women's roles in the military. Cornum testified and revealed that she had been sexually assaulted. Although this experience was precisely what those who did not want women in combat had warned about, Cornum's testimony helped convince most Americans that women could and should play a more central role in the military. She argued that military women should be treated according to their talents and abilities. The fact that she had been assaulted, she declared, was not relevant. According to Cornum, everything that happens to a POW is essentially nonconsensual, so her sexual assault was only one part of the experience.

Cornum's arguments helped sway opinion in favor of greater opportunities for women in the military. In April 1993, Secretary of Defense Les Aspin announced that more duties in the military, including some that might include combat, would be opened to women. That policy has continued to the present, as more and more tasks and roles have been opened to both sexes.

Cornum remained in the Army. Promoted to colonel, she subsequently commanded a medical unit in Tuzla, Bosnia. She also trained in urology and was named a staff urologist at the Eisenhower Medical Center in 1998. In 2003, she assumed command of the Landstuhl Military Hospital in Germany, the largest U.S. military facility outside the United States. During her tenure, the hospital treated many American soldiers wounded in the 2003 invasion of Iraq. Cornum was often found working with the wounded, encouraging them and treating their wounds. She has since been promoted to brigadier general and was appointed assistant surgeon general for force protection.

Tim J. Watts

See also: Gulf War (1991); Rathbun-Nealy (Coleman), Melissa (1970–).

References and Further Reading

Cornum, Rhonda, and Peter Copeland. *She Went to War: The Rhonda Cornum Story.* Novato, CA: Presidio Press, 1992.

Stiehm, Judith. *It's Our Military, Too!: Women and the U.S. Military.* Philadelphia, PA: Temple University Press, 1996.

CRAWFORD v. CUSHMAN (1976)

In 1976, the Second Circuit Court ruled it was unconstitutional to automatically discharge pregnant servicewomen. On February 5, 1968, 21-year-old Stephanie Crawford joined the Marines for a term of four years and worked as a secretary at the Marine Corps Air Station in El Toro, California. In March 1970, Crawford became pregnant out of wedlock. Upon learning of her pregnancy, Gen. Robert E. Cushman Jr. discharged Crawford on May 27, 1970. In January 1971, Crawford attempted to reenlist in the Marines but was refused because she had a child.

Crawford filed a lawsuit. The U.S. District Court for the District of Vermont ruled in favor of the Marines. However, Crawford appealed the District Court's ruling, and the U.S. Court of Appeals for the Second Circuit overturned the original ruling. On February 23, 1976, the Second Circuit Court determined that automatic discharge for pregnancy violated the Fifth Amendment's due process clause. The Second Circuit Court ruled that pregnancy was the only temporary disability that the Marine Corps considered an automatic discharge. The Marine Corps evaluated all other temporary disabilities—such as illness or injury—on an individual basis, and a marine most often returned to his or her unit after treatment. The Second Circuit Court determined that pregnant women could perform their duties for most of the term of their pregnancies and that childbirth did not negatively affect the rest of their military careers. Pregnancy, the court concluded, must be treated like all other temporary disabilities.

On April 27, 1951, President Harry Truman had established the military's family and pregnancy policy when he signed Executive Order 10240. The order gave each branch of the service the option to discharge any female soldier who was the parent of a child under 18 years of age, who had custody of a child under 18 years of age, who was the step-parent of a child under 18 years of age, who was pregnant, or who gave birth to a living child while serving. Although this policy was optional, the military chose to enforce it as mandatory. Women could apply for a waiver, but very few waivers were granted.

The military maintained that pregnancy and parenthood were grounds for automatic discharge because of readiness. A soldier who was a mother or who was pregnant, the services contended, would not be ready to perform her duties or deploy at the military's discretion. Furthermore, many in the military and in civilian society believed women's role was to give and nurture life, not take life.

On the other hand, those who challenged the military's policy argued that women actually lost very little time while pregnant. In fact, they demonstrated that men lost more time from their service due to greater disciplinary problems such as substance abuse or being absent without leave than did women for pregnancy. Moreover, such a restrictive family policy prevented women from advancing their careers in the military.

Crawford v. Cushman was one of several important court cases during the 1970s to dismantle discrimination against women in the military. In 1973, the Supreme Court ruled in *Frontiero v. Richardson* that it was unconstitutional for servicewomen, as opposed to servicemen, to have to prove that their civilian spouses were dependent on them to receive medical benefits and on-base family housing. Additionally, in 1978, *Owens v. Brown* allowed Navy women to serve aboard all Navy ships except battleships.

These court cases came amid larger changes granting women more equality in the military during the 1970s. President Richard Nixon's decision to create an all-volunteer force in 1973 opened up opportunities for women when a manpower-starved military needed volunteers. Additionally, in 1973 Congress passed the Equal Rights Amendment (ERA), which would have made discrimination based on sex illegal. Although the ERA ultimately failed to pass, during the 1970s the military expected enough states to ratify the amendment. Finally, the feminist movement of the late 1960s and 1970s made it more socially acceptable for women to enter traditionally male fields. *Crawford v. Cushman* helped establish women's permanent place in the military.

Lia D. Winfield

See also: All-Volunteer Force (AVF); *Frontiero v. Richardson* (1973); *Owens v. Brown* (1978).

References and Further Reading

Boumil, Marcia Mobilia, Stephen C. Hicks, and Joel Friedman. *Women and the Law.* Littleton, CO: Fred B. Rothman & Co., 1992.

Feinman, Ilene Rose. *Citizenship Rites: Feminist Soldiers and Feminist Anti-militarists.* New York: New York University Press, 2000.

Holm, Jeanne. *Women in the Military: An Unfinished Revolution*, revised edition. Novato, CA: Presidio Press, 1993.

Stiehm, Judith Hicks. *Arms and the Enlisted Woman.* Philadelphia: Temple University Press, 1989.

CREA, VIVIEN S.
(1952–)

Vice Adm. Vivien Crea was the first female aircraft commander in the Coast Guard, the first woman to command an air station, and the first woman from any service as well as the first from the Coast Guard to serve as a presidential military aid. In addition, she was the first woman to obtain flag rank in the Coast Guard and the first woman in any branch of the armed forces to be appointed second in command of an entire service. Her remarkable accomplishments are a testament to her determination, perseverance, courage and leadership.

Born in 1952 at Fort Belvoir, Virginia, and a direct descendant of Nathaniel Bowditch, credited as a founder of modern maritime navigation, Crea's father served in the U.S. Army. As a result of his extensive billets, Crea travelled the world and graduated from Seoul American High School in 1968. At the time, the U.S. Coast Guard Academy was not open to women, but inspired by the stories of Women Air Force Service Pilots's (WASP) service during World War II, she began to consider a military career. She graduated with a BA in biology from the University of Texas at Austin in 1972, earned a

master's degree from Central Michigan University, and was then commissioned an ensign in the U.S. Coast Guard Reserve upon graduation from Officer Candidate School at the Reserve Training Center, Yorktown, Virginia, in December 1973.

She told one of her first Coast Guard bosses that she wanted to become an aviator, but at the time women were barred from flight school. Her commanding officer promised to help her, and in 1975 Crea became one of the first two female aviators to enter flight school at Pensacola, Florida. During her time there, some students were transferred to the Air Force Navigation School because the naval facility closed down, and as a result Crea earned both her Navy/Coast Guard pilot wings and her Air Force navigator's wings. Her first air station assignment was at Barbers Point, Hawaii. There she flew the C-130 Hercules turboprop and the HH-65 Dolphin helicopter.

Crea was on the verge of becoming aircraft commander of the station's Gulf Stream jet when she was offered the opportunity to interview for a job as military aide to President Ronald Reagan. Her commanding officer, Capt. Kwang-Ping Hsu, encouraged her to take the interview. Crea described this as one of the turning points in her career. Promoted to lieutenant commander, Crea carried the "nuclear football" for President Reagan for three years. After this her assignments included chief, Office of Programs, at Coast Guard headquarters in Washington, D.C., where she coordinated bilateral exchanges with the French and the Soviet Union on marine environmental protection. She then became commanding officer of Air

Station Clearwater, executive assistant to the commandant of the Coast Guard, and commanding officer, Air Station Detroit. She also became a Sloan Fellow and graduated from the Massachusetts Institute of Technology with an MS in management in 1992.

She served as director of information technology of the Coast Guard; as chief information officer, she oversaw the Coast Guard's Research and Development Program, and as commander, First Coast Guard District, she led all Coast Guard operations from the Canadian border to New Jersey. On February 5, 2004, Crea was promoted to rear admiral and was given command of the Coast Guard Atlantic Area. This post was the operational command for all Coast Guard activities in an area of responsibility spanning five Coast Guard districts, over 14 million square miles, covering the Eastern and Midwestern United States from the Rocky Mountains to Mexico, out across the Atlantic, and through the Caribbean Sea. She was responsible for over 33,000 military and civilian employees and 30,000 Coast Guard auxiliary personnel. She served concurrently as commander, Coast Guard Defense Force East. During this time she led the Coast Guard through significant changes in its mission and priorities following 9/11 and the Hurricane Katrina recovery efforts. In addition to overseeing modernization efforts, Crea demonstrated an unrelenting commitment to improving the quality of life for service members and their families.

On June 2, 2006, the Senate confirmed her as the 25th vice commandant of the U.S. Coast Guard under Adm. Thad W. Allen. Finally, before retiring in August 2009, at a ceremony at the Coast Guard Air Station in Elizabeth City, New Jersey, on June 26, 2008, Crea became the "Ancient Albatross" for the Coast Guard, the longest serving active-duty Coast Guard aviator. This honor placed her in what the Coast Guard affectionately refers to as the Group of Ancients—the Gold Ancient Mariner, the Silver Ancient Mariner, the Ancient Albatross, the enlisted Ancient Albatross, and the Ancient Keeper. Crea was the first woman to receive this honor.

Her many military awards include the Homeland Security Distinguished Service Medal, the Coast Guard Distinguished Service Medal, the Legion of Merit with three awards stars, the Transportation 9/11 Ribbon, the National Defense Service Medal with one service star, the Special Operations Service Ribbon with two service stars, and the Humanitarian Service Medal with two service stars. She was honored by the Woman's International Center, served on the Board of Trustees of the Coast Guard Academy, and was the Massachusetts Maritime Academy Maritime Person of the Year.

Vice Adm. Crea is married to Ronald Rutledge. They live in Beverly, Massachusetts.

Thomas Francis Army, Jr.

See also: War on Terror (2001–); Women Air Force Service Pilots (WASP); World War II (1941–1945).

Reference and Further Reading

Merryman, Molly. *Clipped Wings: The Rise and Fall of the Women Airforce Service Pilots (WASPs) of World War II*. New York: New York University Press, 1998.

CUBERO, LINDA GARCIA
(1958–)

Former Air Force officer Linda Garcia Cubero was part of the first class of women to graduate from the Air Force Academy. After a successful military career, she became an engineer in the private sector.

Capt. Cubero is a former U.S. Air Force officer of Mexican-American and Puerto Rican descent. She was born in 1958 in Shreveport, Louisiana. Her mother was an airman second class, and her father was a pilot in the U.S. Air Force. At the age of 18, Cubero graduated from Chicopee Comprehensive High School in Massachusetts. She graduated 25th out of 485 students and was a member of the National Honor Society.

On October 7, 1975, President Gerald R. Ford signed legislation that allowed women to enter U.S. military academies. In June 1976, the first group of women entered the U.S. Air Force Academy. Cubero was among the 157 women who entered the U.S. Air Force Academy in El Paso County, Colorado. She was also the first woman in Massachusetts to receive an appointment to any military academy.

Cubero had trouble with the mental and emotional challenges of being part of the first class of women in the U.S. Air Force. This first class of women cadets constantly had to prove that they belonged, trying to convince their peers that allowing women into the academy did not lower the academy's standards. Additionally, the process of becoming a leader while also learning to be part of a team was extremely challenging for Cubero. However, her experience at the Air Force Academy gave her the self-confidence necessary for success in the Air Force and in the corporate world.

In 1980, Cubero was a member of the first class of women to graduate from the Air Force Academy. She was also the first Hispanic woman graduate of the Air Force Academy and the first Hispanic woman to graduate from any service academy. Cubero graduated with a bachelor of science degree in political science and international affairs and earned her free-fall parachute wings.

Upon her graduation, she was commissioned a second lieutenant in the Air Force. Cubero spent seven years in the Air Force, serving as a command briefer to a four-star general and on national-level task forces at the Pentagon. Cubero served as special assistant to the Deputy Secretary of Defense. She also served as a liaison to the White House, supervising the development of a U.S. commemorative postage stamp designed by the 10 surviving Hispanic Congressional Medal of Honor recipients. On October 31, 1984, President Ronald Regan unveiled the stamp at the White House. Cubero also served four years at the Pentagon with the Defense Intelligence Agency and three years at the Tactical Air Command at Langley Air Force Base in Virginia. Cubero earned her master's degree in systems engineering from Virginia Polytechnic Institute and State University. Cubero was honorably discharged from the Air Force with the rank of captain in 1987. During her career in the Air Force, Cubero completed five tours of duty in Cuba, Latin America, Grenada, and the Falkland Islands.

After leaving the Air Force, Cubero's career shifted from air intelligence to engineering in private industry. She began working for General Electric Aerospace, becoming its senior systems engineer in 1991. From 1995 to 1998, Cubero served as the director of Global Supplier Relationships. From 1998 to 2003, she served as the director of Hardware and Telecommunications Procurement for Electronic Data Systems (EDS). From 2003 to 2006, Cubero served as the IT client director for Hewlett-Packard. From 2006 to 2011, she served as the president of Falcon Cash Investors, LLC. Cubero is currently the executive services manager at the NCR Corporation.

Cubero received the Joint Service Commendation Medal (1982) and the National Defense Medal (2003). She also earned a Parachutist Badge and an Office of the Joint Chiefs of Staff Identification Badge. Cubero also won several awards and honors, including the Hispanic Engineer National Achievement Pioneer Award (1991) and Women of Color Technology Award in Managerial Leadership (1998). *Dollars & Sense Magazine* awarded her a Distinguished Career Achievement Award in Corporate America in 2002. Several magazines included her in their list of influential Hispanic women; she appeared in *Hispanic Engineer & IT Magazine*'s "Top 50 Hispanic Executives in Engineering and IT" (2000) list and *Hispanic Business Magazine*'s "Top 100 Most Influential Hispanics in the United States" (2002) list. In 1998, she was inducted into the National Hispanic Engineering Hall of Fame and was featured in a cover story profiling

"Innovative Minds" in *Women Engineer Magazine*.

Estefania Ponti

See also: Espionage; Hispanic American Women.

References and Further Reading

Palmisano, Joseph M. *Notable Hispanic American Women*. Farmington Hills, MI: Gale Research, 1998.

Stanton, Edward F. *Contemporary Hispanic Quotations*. Westport, CT: Greenwood Publishing Group, 2003.

CULPER SPY RING

In November 1778, Gen. George Washington authorized Benjamin Tallmadge, a dragoon officer in the American Continental Army, to establish an intelligence service within the British-controlled New York City. Known as the Culper Spy Ring, the covert network provided Washington with vital information about British installations and troops in New York City and the surrounding areas. Local female residents supported the spy network. During the remainder of the American Revolutionary War, Tallmadge and members of the Culper Spy Ring utilized invisible ink, aliases, signals, encryptions, and secret codes to pass along information about the British operations in the New York area to Washington.

Following the Battle of Monmouth, Tallmadge received orders from Washington to recruit individuals who could gather intelligence on British activities and operations in New York City. In the fall of 1778, Tallmadge enlisted the services of Robert Townsend, Abraham Woodhull, Austin Roe, and Caleb Brewster. By November, the Culper Spy Ring had developed a discreet operation, which collected information about British troops and fortifications. For instance, Townshend, who owned a dry-goods store in New York City, talked with British soldiers, while Roe placed written dispatches in drop-boxes, which belonged to Woodhull. After Woodhull received the various messages, he transported them to an awaiting Brewster, who delivered the secret letters to Washington in upstate New York.

Local female residents from the New York area also participated in the Culper Spy Ring. For example, Anna Smith Strong signaled members of the spy ring about incoming messages by hanging laundry in her backyard. If Strong's laundry included a black petticoat and a white handkerchief, it indicated that Brewster had arrived from Connecticut and he was waiting in a hidden cove at Conscience Bay. Strong's signals enabled Woodhull and other spies to pass along dispatches about the British activities in New York City to Brewster, who would transport them to Washington's Continental Army.

The Culper Spy Ring also recruited a mysterious lady, who was known only as "Agent 355." It is believed that the female spy came from a prominent New York family, which enabled her to gather vital information from Maj. John Andre and other British commanders. In the fall of 1780, Brig. Gen. Benedict Arnold believed that Agent 355 had informed Washington about his treasonous plot to surrender West Point to the British forces, so he imprisoned her in the

Jersey, which was a British prison ship stationed in New York. The female spy remained a prisoner aboard the ship for three months before she died in January 1781. However, Agent 355 passed away without incriminating the other members of the Culper Spy Ring.

The Culper Spy Ring played a vital role in American success. Despite the danger involved in gathering intelligence about British soldiers in New York City and the surrounding areas, American women collaborated with the Culper Spy Ring to supply Washington's Continental Army with valuable information about British activities and military operations during the American Revolutionary War.

Kevin M. Brady

See also: American Revolution (1775–1783); Espionage; "Miss Jenny" (ca. 1760–n.d.); Strong, Anna "Nancy" Smith (1740–1812); "355" (n.d.–n.d.).

References and Further Reading

Groh, Lynn. *The Culper Spy Ring*. Philadelphia: Westminster Press, 1969.

Rose, Alexander. *Washington's Spies: The Story of America's First Spy Ring*. New York: Bantam Books, 2006.

CURTIS, NAMAHYOKE SOCKUM (1861–1935)

Namahyoke Sockum Curtis served as a nurse and helped recruit African American female nurses during the Spanish-American War in 1898.

Namahyoke Sockum was born in California in 1861 to Hamilton Sockum, a Native American of the Acoma Pueblo tribe. Her mother, whose name is unknown, was the daughter of German and African American parents. Namahyoke received her primary education in San Francisco and later graduated from Snell Seminary in Oakland in 1888. On May 5, 1888, Namahyoke married Austin Maurice Curtis, who graduated from Lincoln University in Pennsylvania that year. After the marriage, they settled in Chicago, where Austin attended the medical school of Northwestern University and earned a medical degree in 1891. In Chicago, Namahyoke joined a movement for the establishment of a hospital in which African American patients could receive advanced medical treatment. With Daniel Hale Williams, a noted African American surgeon, and Rev. Louis Reynolds, whose sister was refused admission to training schools for nurses because of her race, Curtis played an active role in collecting donations for their hospital venture from both wealthy white elites and African American residents in the city. On January 22, 1891, Curtis and other advocates succeeded in establishing Provident Hospital, and her husband, Austin, became the first intern and later the visiting surgeon there. In 1898, when Austin was appointed surgeon in chief of Freedmen's Hospital (later the medical school of Howard University, where Austin worked as a professor for the following 40 years) in Washington, D.C., the couple left Chicago and moved to the nation's capital.

During the Spanish-American War in 1898, Curtis traveled to the South as a recruiter of female nurses for the U.S. Army. Beginning in late April, Army Surgeon General George M. Sternberg had detailed women nurses to the army hospitals through the examining board supervised by Anita Newcomb McGee, a woman physician who became the acting assistant surgeon general of the Army during the war. In the summer months, the rampancy of infectious diseases among American soldiers seriously undermined the physical strength of the U.S. Army and consequently generated huge demand for women army nurses. Typhoid fever struck army soldiers at camps and hospitals, and yellow fever assaulted the regiments in Cuba and Puerto Rico.

At army hospitals, where yellow fever raged severely among their patients, the care for sick and wounded soldiers often required caregivers to be immune to the epidemic through their previous experiences of infection. However, McGee could not always secure enough immune nurses to satisfy requests from army hospitals. When yellow fever appeared among American soldiers in Santiago, Cuba, in early summer, McGee failed to dispatch the required number of immune nurses there. To meet this urgent need, Sternberg decided to detail Curtis to the South to recruit nurses who were immune to yellow fever. On July 13, Curtis began her search for immune nurses in New Orleans and other Southern cities that had previously experienced outbreaks of yellow fever. She subsequently secured 32 African American nurses immune to the epidemic for army service. At least two of these nurses, T. R. Bradford and Minerva Trumbull, died from typhoid fever during their service. Throughout the war, a total of 80 African American women joined the military nursing service. Although McGee critically viewed the professional efficiency of these African Americans as army nurses, Curtis received official commendation for her work, which brought her a lifetime government pension after the war.

After the war with Spain, Curtis continued her nursing service, especially in the rescue activities during natural disasters. In 1900, when a hurricane and consequent flood devastated Galveston, Texas, Curtis volunteered for the relief squad of the American Red Cross organization under the direction of Clara Barton. During the San Francisco earthquake in 1906, Curtis received a commission from William H. Taft, the secretary of war at that time, and engaged in relief activities for the victims of the disaster and the following fire in the city. Through these nursing services both on the battlefields and in disaster-stricken areas, Curtis attempted to show the public usefulness of African American nurses for the advancement of their social status.

Curtis died on November 25, 1935. She is buried in Arlington National Cemetery for her military services.

Yoshiya Makita

See also: African American Women; American Red Cross; Barton, Clara Harlowe (1821–1912); McGee, Anita Newcomb (1864–1940); Native American Women; Nursing; Spanish-American War (1898).

References and Further Reading

Carnegie, Mary Elizabeth. *The Path We Tread: Blacks in Nursing Worldwide, 1854–1994*, 3rd ed. New York: National League for Nursing Press, 1995.

Cirillo, Vincent J. *Bullets and Bacilli: The Spanish-American War and Military Medicine*. New Brunswick, NJ: Rutgers University Press, 1999.

Hine, Darlene Clark. *Black Women in White: Racial Conflict and Cooperation in the Nursing Profession, 1890–1950*. Bloomington: Indiana University Press, 1989.

Sarnecky, Mary T. *A History of the U.S. Army Nurse Corps*. Philadelphia: University of Pennsylvania Press, 1999.

CUSHMAN, PAULINE [HARRIET WOOD] (1833–1893)

Famous for both her antebellum acting career and her role as a spy for the United States during the American Civil War, Pauline Cushman employed her talents for both verbal and physical disguises.

Cushman was born Harriet Wood in New Orleans on June 10, 1833, but spent most of her childhood in Michigan. She changed her name when she began her acting career in the 1850s. In 1853, she married a musician, Charles Dickinson, who later served in the 41st Ohio's regimental band. He died in 1862.

Cushman's espionage career began in Louisville, Kentucky, in 1863. During a performance at Wood's Theater, a group of Confederate officers dared Cushman to offer a toast in Jefferson Davis's honor. Cushman took this challenge and an unusual idea to the city's Union provost marshal, Col. Moore, suggesting that she offer the proposed toast to convince Confederates in Louisville that she supported their cause. Doing so,

Actress Pauline Cushman feigned Confederate sympathies to spy for the Union. Her 1863 arrest by Confederates ended her career in espionage. (Library of Congress)

Cushman continued, would allow her to carry out activities on behalf of the Union without discovery. The provost marshal agreed, providing Cushman would take an oath of loyalty to the United States. She took the oath. At her performance the next evening, Cushman offered praise of Davis and the Confederacy to her shocked audience. The Northern theater company expelled her and sent her to Nashville. Once in occupied Nashville, Cushman reported to the Union's chief of army police to get her instructions.

In Nashville, Cushman cultivated her reputation as an ardent secessionist and Confederate. This image allowed her inside access to valuable details about Confederate fortifications and operations. As part of her intelligence operations, Cushman also made lists of people who harbored what she considered dangerous anti-Union sentiments. She passed this list, as well as the names of local Confederate spies, on to Union officials. In addition, she served as a federal courier, moving information through Kentucky, Tennessee, Georgia, Alabama, and Mississippi. Cushman successfully passed through enemy lines, using her acting skills, disguises, and the enemy's assumption that she supported the Confederacy. The Union army valued Cushman's assistance and awarded her an honorary military commission.

Cushman's activities on behalf of the Union did not go unnoticed. Late in the spring of 1863, Confederate general John Hunt Morgan arrested Cushman on suspicion of espionage. After questioning Cushman, Gen. Nathan Bedford Forrest and Gen. Braxton Bragg gave her a death sentence. The hanging was not carried out, perhaps because it was interrupted by the sudden arrival of Union troops. The publicity surrounding Cushman's arrest by Morgan, however, brought her espionage activities to a halt.

President Abraham Lincoln officially recognized Cushman's contributions to the Union, awarding her an honorary commission as a brevet major. After the Civil War, Cushman went on a speaking tour. In addition, a biography celebrating Cushman's role on behalf of the United States was published in 1865.

In the late 1860s, she moved to California, where she again found work as an actress. In 1872, she married August Fictner. He died before their first anniversary. After she married Jere Fyer in 1879, the couple moved to the

Arizona Territory. They separated in 1890, and she returned to San Francisco.

Cushman died on December 2, 1893, from an overdose of morphine. Local Civil War veterans gave her a full military burial.

Lisa Tendrich Frank

See also: Civil War (1861–1865); Espionage.

References and Further Reading

Leonard, Elizabeth D. *All the Daring of the Soldier: Women of the Civil War Armies*. New York: W. W. Norton, 1999.

Sarmiento, Ferdinand L. *Life of Pauline Cushman, The Celebrated Union Spy and Scout*. Philadelphia: John E. Potter and Company, 1865.

D

DARRAGH, LYDIA BARRINGTON
(CA. 1728–CA. 1790)

Irish-born Lydia Barrington Darragh was an American patriot and a spy during the Revolutionary War.

She was born in Dublin, Ireland, around 1728. She moved to Philadelphia, Pennsylvania, with her husband William soon after they married in 1753. She bore nine children, five who lived to adulthood. The family lived on Second Street, nearly directly opposite of the home owned by John Cadwalader.

During the British occupation of the city in 1777, Cadwalader's house became the headquarters of the British commander, Thomas Howe. Cadwalader's house was seized because of his commission as a general in the Continental Army. The British requisitioned the Darragh house as well. Lydia went across the street to Howe's headquarters to seek reconsideration. A fellow Dubliner who was a British officer struck up a conversation as the pair discovered they were both Barringtons and were related. His pleading is credited with the compromise that the Darraghs would supply the British with their spacious upper room for meetings. The two youngest children of the Darraghs would stay with relatives in the country outside of Philadelphia while the rest of the family would stay in their home.

Unbeknownst to the British, Darragh and her husband engaged in intelligence gathering. Their typical activities began with William transcribing messages in shorthand. These messages would be hidden inside the buttons of the coat of their 14-year-old son, John. Lydia would then cover the buttons with cloth matching the coat. The son would then visit their eldest son, Charles, who was a lieutenant serving with Washington. He and the army were roughly 13 miles away at White Marsh. Charles would remove the material from his family, transcribe it, and pass it on to his superiors. What sort of information they passed on is not known.

Patriot and spy Lydia Barrington Darragh aided the Continental Army by passing information to officers. (Library of Congress)

Darragh's biggest espionage feat occurred on December 2, 1777. She was warned that a meeting was to be held that evening and that the family needed to be in bed early. She slipped out of bed, listened to the summary of the meeting while secreted in an adjacent closet, separated by a board wall covered with wallpaper. She learned that 5,000 troops, 13 cannons, and 11 wheeled boats were to launch a surprise attack on Washington's forces on the morning of December 5. She returned to bed and feigned deep sleep. She did not answer until the third knock of the officer who was informing her that the meeting was over and that she could lock up the house after they left.

She secured a pass for the 4th, ostensibly to see her youngest children and get a bag of flour from a mill outside the city. Darragh walked through the miserably cold day until she happened to meet an acquaintance, Lt. Col. Thomas Craig, to whom she told the information. He escorted her to a home to be fed and then left to deliver the information.

With this information, Washington was able to harass the British forces as they approached White Marsh. The British feebly tried to attack at one point but were routed. They retreated, as it was evident that their plans had been compromised. When interviewed by the officer who had knocked on her door that night and asked if anyone had been awake, Lydia insisted that all were asleep. He commented that it was clear that she had been asleep, given the effort it took to wake her up. As a result, neither she nor her family remained under suspicion.

Lydia's daughter Ann, who was 21 in 1777, preserved her mother's account, as did some contemporaries and more distant descendants. Darragh's story was first published in 1827. Although it was seriously challenged 50 years later, nearly all of the challenges proposed are readily deflected. The most significant challenge was that a Washington staffer, Gen. John Armstrong, credited multiple sources with betraying the British movements in letters dated from the end of November.

The papers of the commissary general of prisoners for the Continental Army, Elias Boudinot, were published in 1896. Boudinot had also been involved in espionage activities during the Revolution. In his journal, he recorded a story of sitting at the Rising Sun Tavern, which was likely Darragh's destination when she met Craig, when a slight, shabby woman who matched Darragh's description gave him a needle book, which contained a message in a pocket. This information proved to be decisive. Boudinot's journal seems to confirm Lydia's story, regardless of some discrepancies.

Through her actions, Darragh saved the lives of many Americans, including her son. Her Quaker church barred her from fellowship for her activity in the war. Darragh ran a store after the war until she died in 1790.

Mark Anthony Phelps

See also: American Revolution (1775–1783); Espionage.

References and Further Reading

Berkin, Carol. *Revolutionary Mothers: Women in the Struggle for American Independence.* New York: Alfred Knopf, 2005.

Bohrer, Melissa Lukeman. *Glory, Passion, and Principle: The Story of Eight Remarkable Women at the Core of the American Revolution.* New York: Atria, 2003.

Darrach, Henry. *Lydia Darragh: One of the Heroines of the Revolution.* Philadelphia: City History Society, 1916.

DAUGHTERS OF LIBERTY

In Revolutionary America, women's activities, especially spinning bees, increased and became more politicized. The women involved in these activities, often referred to as the Daughters of Liberty, played pivotal roles in American society both before and during the American Revolution. The ways in which women participated in the American struggle for independence were highly significant and instrumental

The Daughters of Liberty actively participated in the conflict against the British by organizing spinning bees so that the colonists could become independent of foreign-made goods. (North Wind Picture Archives)

to the successful outcome of the struggle. Daughters of Industry, young women, and the Daughters of Liberty not only made homespun items for patriots but also boycotted British goods.

Resistance to the Stamp Act of 1765, a direct tax imposed by the British Parliament on the American colonies, resulted in petitions to the King and Parliament, the refusal to use stamps or stamped paper, and tea and textile boycotts, among other things. Although traditional gender ideas portrayed women as uninformed politically, they proved otherwise through their knowledge and involvement during the Revolutionary period.

Women's contributions during this period were vast and varied. They raised funds, collected materials, made items, engaged in public protests, and wrote documents, as well as participated in fund-raising activities and street protests. In some cases, their efforts included going to the battlefield. Though some women saw actual combat and recognition for their valor, cooking, laundry, and nursing formed their primary duties. Despite the additional responsibilities on the home-front due to the absence of men, the Daughters of Liberty are recognized for their patriotic organization and involvement in boycotts.

In particular, Daughters of Liberty gathered at spinning bees to collectively produce homespun cloth or wool as well as to maintain morale. Their spinning-bee efforts further allowed Patriots to free themselves from their dependence on British textiles. The work of the group revealed that women's involvement in political matters could be beneficial both for the current cause of the war as well as for the future. The production of homespun goods allowed self-sufficiency and helped to change public opinion. Consequently, women's domestic activities became charged with a political agenda and created a new mindset of how women were viewed. Society recognized the Daughters of Liberty as patriotic heroines.

Gustavo Adolfo Aybar

See also: American Revolution (1775–1783).

References and Further Reading

Branson, Susan. "From Daughters of Liberty to Women of the Republic: American Women in the Era of the American Revolution." In *The Practice of U.S. Women's History*, edited by S. Jay Kleinberg, Eileen Boris, and Vicki L. Ruiz, 50–66. New Brunswick, NJ: Rutgers University Press, 2007.

Jakobson, Pia Katarina. "Daughters of Liberty: Women and the American Revolution." In *Perspectives in American Social History:* *Women's Rights People and Perspectives*, edited by Christa DeLuzio, 35–56. Santa Barbara, CA: ABC-CLIO, 2010.

Norton, Mary Beth. *Liberty's Daughters: The Revolutionary Experience of American Women, 1750–1800*. Boston: Little, Brown and Company, 1980.

Ulrich, Laurel Thatcher. "'Daughters of Liberty': Religious Women in Revolutionary New England." In *Women in the Age of the American Revolution*, edited by Ronald Hoffman and Peter J. Albert, 211–43. Charlottesville: University Press of Virginia, 1989.

DAVIS, ANN SIMPSON (1764–1851)

As a teenager, Ann Simpson served as a courier for Gen. George Washington and his officers' corps during the crucial war years of 1777 to 1778.

The daughter of William and Nancy Hines Simpson, she was born in Buckingham Township, Pennsylvania, on December 29, 1764. Her father was an Irish immigrant, and her mother's family came from New Britain. Simpson reached adolescence as the Declaration of Independence was being signed in Philadelphia and the American Revolution was beginning. Pennsylvania society was filled with both supporters of independence as well as Tories, who not only verbally supported the continuation of British rule but also actively worked to assist the British military, which captured Philadelphia a little over a year after that auspicious event at Independence Hall. The territory between the Schuylkill and the Delaware Rivers, where Simpson resided, was contested as both military and civilian actions ravaged the area. Shortages of supplies for both the British and American forces made activities such as illicit sales of goods to the enemy, Tory raids on Patriot storehouses, and the reporting of American military movements by these colonists who were loyal to Great Britain to the British military common. As a result, violence and danger cast a shadow over the area.

The outcome of the Revolutionary War during the years 1777 to 1778 was far from certain. In 1776, British general William Howe defeated Washington's troops in the Battle of White Plains and subsequently the Battle of Fort Washington in New York. Although the Battle of Long Island was less decisive or spectacular than the others, it resulted in a hollow victory and a midnight retreat of the Continental Army. Washington took his troops south through New Jersey to Pennsylvania. There, his forces engaged the British army in numerous battles, with American losses taking a heavy toll on the revolutionary effort.

Washington and his troops spent a brutally cold winter in Valley Forge in 1777 and 1778 as the Continental Army sought to liberate Philadelphia from British control. During this period, Simpson proved invaluable to the American military. She acted as a courier, delivering messages to and from the general staff and officers and other contacts in locations as widespread as Bucks County and Philadelphia. This period of the war was especially precarious; American troops suffered from numerous deprivations, ranging from a shortage of food and arms to widespread dissatisfaction at the lack of funds to pay their salaries. Despite these difficulties, Washington promoted an illusion of strength that made the

American forces seem fearsome to the British. The communications that Washington maintained with his widespread forces and the spy network buttressing his efforts supported this image of strength.

In this environment, Simpson's skills as a horsewoman and her image as an innocent young girl made her invaluable to Washington and the military. In her home territory, Tory and Patriot locals thought nothing of seeing her crisscrossing the various fields and roads on horseback. Her familiarity in the community, as well as her age and skills, allowed her a plausible cover as she carried important messages on behalf of Washington. She also undertook missions to Philadelphia, where she carried the secret communications in sacks of grain as well as beneath her dress. In these situations, her age and gender again proved a valuable cover. British sentries and soldiers, desperately searching for information on the Patriots' movements and plans, never noticed the young girl or suspected her of carrying secret missives. Had she been caught as a spy, she could have faced death by hanging.

After the war, Simpson married her childhood friend John Davis, a veteran of the Continental Army. During the war, Davis served under Washington and fought in battles including those at Trenton and Brandywine. He had also survived the harsh winter of 1777–1778 in Valley Forge. The couple eventually moved to Ohio, where they settled on a land claim granted to John as a Revolutionary War veteran. In 1832, on his death, Ann received a pension as a veteran's widow. On June 6, 1851, Ann passed away and was buried next to her late husband in the family cemetery in Perry Township, Ohio.

Leonard H. Lubitz

See also: American Revolution (1775–1783); Espionage.

Reference and Further Reading

Davis, William Watts Hart. *History of Bucks County, Pennsylvania: From the Discovery of the Delaware to the Present Time, Volume 3.* New York: Lewis Historical Publishing Company, 1905.

DAVIS, WILMA ZIMMERMAN (1912–2001)

Wilma Zimmerman Davis was an early American code breaker who worked in the U.S. Army's Signal Intelligence Service, the precursor to the National Security Agency. She worked on the Japanese codes during World War II and later on the Chinese code and the VENONA project.

Born in West Virginia in 1912, Davis grew up in her home state and then went to Bethany College, where she graduated in 1932 with a degree in mathematics. She became a teacher for several years. After moving with her first husband to Washington, D.C., and with the help of her brother-in-law, she enrolled in U.S. Navy correspondence courses that focused on cryptology. After passing the civil service exam, Davis was hired by William Friedman to work as a cryptanalyst in the Army's Signal Intelligence Service. Throughout her career, Davis

left the cryptologic field a few times, but she always returned until her retirement in 1973.

Her first assignment as a prewar cryptanalyst was working with the Italian diplomatic codes. Davis was assigned to the team attacking and deciphering the Italian diplomatic codes, which Davis later recalled as enjoyable because they were easily exploitable. She continued to work on the Italian diplomatic codes until 1942 when she was reassigned to work on Japanese codes.

Within two years, in 1944, Davis was head of Department A, the group of cryptanalysts responsible for attacking and solving Japanese Army coded messages. Davis remained in her position as head of Department A throughout World War II, collecting and processing all of the Japanese Army's coded messages for the duration of the war. At the end of World War II, Davis left her position and was reassigned to the Chinese problem. Davis only worked on deciphering Chinese codes for a short time when she was once again reassigned, this time to the Russian problem.

While on the Russian cryptanalysis team, Davis began working on VENONA. The task of project VENONA was to examine and exploit Soviet diplomatic communications, but soon after the program began the message traffic included espionage efforts as well. American cryptologists, including Elizebeth Friedman, worked on the project for almost two years before they were able to break the encryptions of the KGB. The VENONA project is famous for exposing Julius and Ethel Rosenberg, and the information gained from VENONA provided indisputable evidence of their treasonous involvement with a Soviet spy ring. Although the Rosenberg case proved to be the most famous aspect of project VENONA, the information that was gained through the project by cryptanalysts such as Davis provided the United States government with important insights into Soviet intentions and government activities during the Cold War up until project VENONA was cancelled in 1980.

Davis herself worked on the VENONA project until 1949, when she moved to Canada after marrying her second husband, John Manson. In 1952, after Manson's death, Davis returned to the U.S. Army's Signal Intelligence Service at the request of the man who originally hired her, Friedman. Once again, Davis was assigned to the VENONA project. Davis remained on the project for several years before marrying a third time. Her third husband, Lt. Gen. John L. Davis, served as the assistant director for production, the equivalent of today's signals intelligence director. Again Davis left her cryptanalyst position in 1960, this time to deal with family problems.

Davis returned once again to the Army's Signal Intelligence Service, this time using her codebreaking skills to support the United States in a new military conflict, the Vietnam War. From the beginning of her career as a codebreaker, when Davis was hired by Friedman in the 1930s, she worked for the National Security Agency and its predecessor, the United States Army's Signal Intelligence Service, through World War II up until the Vietnam War with two breaks, until her retirement in 1973.

After her retirement, Davis remained in the area where she had worked for so long, living in Fairfax, Virginia. In 1982, Davis gave an oral interview in which she reminisced about her days as a codebreaker for the U.S. government. Davis

recalled her work fondly, mentioning that she could not think of another line of work that would have been so interesting.

Davis died on December 10, 2001, at the age of 89. She was buried at Arlington National Cemetery next to her third husband.

Rorie M. Cartier

See also: Cold War (ca. 1947–1991); Espionage; Friedman, (Clara) Elizabeth Smith (1892–1980); Korean War (1950–1953); Vietnam War (1965–1973); World War II (1941–1945).

References and Further Reading

Budiansky, Stephen. *Battle of Wits: The Complete Story of Codebreaking in World War II*. New York: Free Press, 2000.

Frahm, Jill. *Venona: An Overview (Cryptologic Almanac 50th Anniversary Series)*. N.p.: National Security Agency, 2000.

Frahm, Jill. *Wilma Davis (Cryptologic Almanac 50th Anniversary Series)*. N.p.: National Security Agency, 2000.

Lewin, Ronald. *The American Magic: Codes, Ciphers, and the Defeat of Japan*. New York: Farrar Strauss Giroux, 1982.

Wilcox, Jennifer. *Sharing the Burden: Women in Cryptology during World War II*. Fort George G. Meade, MD: Center for Cryptologic History, National Security Agency, 1998.

DEFENSE ADVISORY COMMITTEE ON WOMEN IN THE SERVICES (DACOWITS)

The Defense Advisory Committee on Women in the Services (DACOWITS) is a civilian group that advises the Department of Defense on policies related to servicewomen, including women's employment in the military, recruiting and retention, and other related topics. Founded in 1951, members serve terms of approximately three years. Representatives from the Department of Defense and the military branches also serve on DACOWITS. As of 2008, the committee included 15 civilian representatives, but in the late 20th century DACOWITS included up to 50 civilian members at any time.

DACOWITS began in 1951 when Secretary of Defense George Marshall and Assistant Secretary of Defense Anna Rosenberg gathered a group of 50 women from across the United States to discuss women in the military. Marshall and Rosenberg wanted to understand how to best recruit and utilize women in national defense. The women at that meeting became the first members of DACOWITS, and Marshall charged them with advising the Department of Defense on how to best recruit, retain, and utilize women. DACOWITS members were women of influence in their own communities, highly respected for their work in civic organizations and the private employment sector. Marshall and Rosenberg hoped that DACOWITS members could use their standing in their communities to convince Americans that military service offered young women a respectable, important career with many benefits, including equal pay.

Because the Department of Defense hoped DACOWITS members would convince families and young women in their communities of the need for womanpower in national defense, through the 1970s DACOWITS member rosters included prominent women in business and education, including television producers, magazine editors, and deans of colleges and universities. Industrial engineer Dr. Lillian Gilbreth of *Cheaper by the Dozen* served in the first member group, as did retired colonel Ruth Cheney Streeter, who directed the Women Marines during World War II. In the 1960s, Esther Pauline Friedman Lederer, better known as advice columnist Ann Landers, also participated in the group. Civil rights activist Dorothy Height was a DACOWITS member, as were Mary Rockefeller and Democratic National Committee member India Edwards. State legislators and state supreme court justices contributed to the organization, and U.S. Supreme Court Justice Sandra Day O'Connor served on DACOWITS from 1974 to 1976. Currently, DACOWITS members represent a mix of civilian and former military personnel.

Following the first meeting in 1951, members advocated a massive recruitment drive to increase publicity and awareness of the nation's need for women in uniform during the Korean War. Members gave speeches and presentations at organizations in their communities, often working directly with servicewomen who could serve as examples of what the military offered women. This community-based activism, the Department of Defense and DACOWITS members believed, would offer one of the best ways to attract women to military service. Major DACOWITS issues during the 1950s included housing improvements, evaluation of servicewomen's training, and work on diet and health issues, such as expanding access to healthier foods in military mess halls.

During the 1960s, DACOWITS members worked to expand their influence even further. In 1962 and 1963, the organization teamed with President John F. Kennedy's Commission on the Status of Women to provide information on military women's needs and status. Working together, the two groups of women recommended that the Department of Defense remove rank limitations that prohibited women officers from being promoted above the rank of lieutenant colonel or lieutenant commander on a permanent basis. For four years, DACOWITS members fought for such legislation, which finally passed in 1967. Public Law 90-130 made it possible for women to be promoted to any rank and also removed a regulation that required that women comprise no more than 2 percent of the total military force.

The 1970s were a decade of major change throughout the military, and the women of DACOWITS continued to fight for servicewomen's equal opportunity. In particular, DACOWITS members petitioned the Department of Defense to admit women to the military academies (West Point, the Naval Academy, and the Air Force Academy). DACOWITS also recommended allowing Navy women to serve on ships and that the services remove prohibitions that kept women from filling combat roles. Additionally, DACOWITS recommended that the military review its policies and practices for handling rape. The organization opened its meetings to the public for the first time and allowed external groups such as the National Organization for Women (NOW) and the American Civil Liberties Union (ACLU) to attend proceedings and offer their own ideas on how to improve women's status in the military.

By 1978, the military had dissolved the women's service components that had existed since World War II. Following the disestablishment of the Women's Army Corps in 1978 and the formal end of the Women Marines, WAVES (Women in the Navy), and Women in the Air Force during the 1970s as well, DACOWITS had to refocus its mission in light of the military's new emphasis on full sexual integration.

Opening DACOWITS to male membership in the 1980s helped signify a gender balance and men's interest in sexual integration, while focus remained on women in the services. Since 2002, DACOWITS has grown smaller as a committee but has maintained its focus on women. It has added a new element of also considering issues related to families within the military and continues to address sexual harassment topics.

DACOWITS's major contributions as an organization have been to draw attention to issues related to utilization and recruitment of women, particularly since the end of the women's service components in the 1970s. In the late 1980s and early 1990s, DACOWITS members successfully campaigned to repeal laws prohibiting women from serving in combat. Although those laws no longer exist, Department of Defense policies often limit women's access to formal combat participation. DACOWITS members monitor ongoing issues of sexual and workplace discrimination in the military. During the 1990s, DACOWITS recommendations began to move beyond its traditional concerns such as training and utilization to also begin pressing for changes in child care and family living arrangements.

Tanya L. Roth

See also: Holm, Jeanne M. (1921–2010); Public Law 90-130 (1967); Streeter, Ruth Cheney (1895–1990); Women Accepted for Volunteer Emergency Service (WAVES); Women in the Air Force (WAF); Women Marines; Women's Army Corps (WAC).

References and Further Reading

Holm, Jeanne. *Women in the Military: An Unending Revolution (Revised Edition)*. Novato, CA: Presidio Press, 1993.

Katzenstein, Mary F. *Faithful and Fearless: Moving Feminist Protest inside the Church and Military*. Princeton, NJ: Princeton University Press, 1999.

Morden, Bettie J. *The Women's Army Corps, 1945–1978*. Washington, D.C.: Center of Military History, 1989.

Witt, Linda, Judith Bellafaire, Britta Granrud, and Mary Jo Binker. *"A Defense Weapon Known to Be of Value": Servicewomen of the Korean War Era*. Hanover, NH: University Press of New England, 2005.

Jane Arminda Delano served as superintendent of the Army Nurse Corps (ANC) from 1909 to 1912 and was a founding chair of the American Red Cross (ARC) Nursing Service. (Library of Congress)

DELANO, JANE ARMINDA (1862–1919)

Jane Arminda Delano, a registered nurse, served as the second superintendent (1909–1912) of the Army Nurse Corps (ANC), established in 1901, following Dita H. Kinney (1901–1909). Delano was also a founder of the American Red Cross Nursing Service, which soon was accepted as the official recruiting arm of the War Department for nurses and nursing reserves. Delano is credited with keeping the ANC viable and ready to serve when needed in World War I.

Delano was born March 12, 1862, in Schuyler County, New York, to George and Mary Ann Wright Delano. Her father died in Louisiana while serving in the Union Army during the Civil War; thus she never had contact with him. Little is known about her childhood and upbringing, but she must have had some primary education. Before attending and graduating from the Bellevue Hospital Training School for Nurses in 1886, she taught school for two years.

Following graduation, she traveled to Jacksonville, Florida, where she served as superintendent of nurses at Sandhills Hospital during the yellow fever epidemic. It was here that she employed the innovative idea of using window screens and netting to keep the patients' and the nurses' areas free of mosquitoes. Next, Delano journeyed to Bisbee,

Arizona, where she spent three years nursing copper miners who had typhoid.

For five years, beginning in 1891, Delano served as superintendent of nurses at the University of Pennsylvania Hospital School of Nursing. She then decided to move to Buffalo, New York, to attend medical school. Delano eventually decided against becoming a physician and instead went next to New York City, where she worked in nursing while studying for an advanced degree. About the same time, Delano began her long association with the American Red Cross, joining the New York chapter during the Spanish-American War (1898). Her next position was that of superintendent at New York City's House of Refuge on Randall's Island. Then, in 1902, she moved on to the position of superintendent at the Bellevue Hospital, a well-respected school of nursing. She left that position in 1906 to care for her ailing mother in Charlottesville, Virginia.

Joining the ANC Reserve in 1905, Delano became a strong advocate for the need of the United States to have a reserve of army nurses. Somehow, the officials did not notice that she was over the maximum ANC age limit of 45. In 1908, she took on the dual position as president of the Board of Directors of the American Journal of Nursing and president of the Nurses Associated Alumnae. The following year she became chair of the American Red Cross Nursing Service as well as superintendent of the ANC, with an office in that of the surgeon general of the United States. Her efforts in establishing a nursing corps proved to be vital to the war effort when the United States entered the war in April 1917. From

1912 on she concentrated strictly on American Red Cross work, which was closely aligned with that of the U.S. Army. During this period, the American Red Cross was the only agency that the U.S. government allowed to recruit nurses for the ANC. As a result of her work, Delano deserves much of the credit for the recruiting of the over 21,000 American army nurses who served in World War I.

While on a postwar inspection tour of hospitals in France during the spring of 1919, Delano became ill with an ear infection that proved to be fatal. Although it was thought she was improving when she briefly rallied, the infection worsened into mastoiditis, and she died on April 15. Delano was buried in the American Military Cemetery at Savenay, France. She was posthumously awarded the Distinguished Service Medal. In 1920, her body was exhumed and reinterred at Arlington National Cemetery, where she lies in Section 21, known as the Nurses' Section. In 1982, she was inducted into the American Nurses Association Hall of Fame.

Katherine Burger Johnson

See also: American Red Cross; Army Nurse Corps (ANC); Kinney, Dita Hopkins (1855–1921); Nursing; Red Cross Volunteer Nurse's Aid Corps; World War I (1914–1918).

References and Further Reading

Clarke, Mary A. *Memories of Jane A. Delano.* New York: Lakeside Publishing Company, 1934.

Gladwin, Mary Elizabeth. *The Red Cross and Jane Arminda Delano.* Philadelphia: W.B. Saunders, 1931.

Sarnecky, Mary T. *A History of the U.S. Army Nurse Corps*. Philadelphia: University of Pennsylvania Press, 1999.

DIETRICH, MARLENE (1901–1992)

World-famous actress Marlene Dietrich promoted war bonds and entertained American soldiers during World War II.

Maria Magdalene Dietrich was born in Berlin, Germany, on December 27, 1901, the daughter of Wilhelmina Felsing and Louis Dietrich, a police officer who died of a heart attack in 1907. During World War I, Maria and other girls her age were required to take on extra duties in support of the German war effort, such as knitting scarves and sweaters for soldiers. Her stepfather, Eduard von Losch, was wounded in Russia and subsequently died of an infection. In addition, her uncle Max and two of her cousins were killed in battle in World War I. At about the age of 20, she joined the first and last syllables of her two names and began referring to herself as Marlene Dietrich.

Dietrich studied violin as a youth with Professor Carl Flesch but turned to the stage and married Rudolf Sieber in 1923. The couple had one daughter, Maria Elisabath Sieber, born in 1924. At about this time, she was an associate of Leni Reifenstahl, who subsequently became Adolf Hitler's documentarian. Dietrich was discovered by Josef Steinberg, who cast her as the nightclub singer Lola Lola in *The Blue Angel* (1930), which brought her international fame. Shortly thereafter she moved to the United States and became an American citizen on June 9, 1939. After

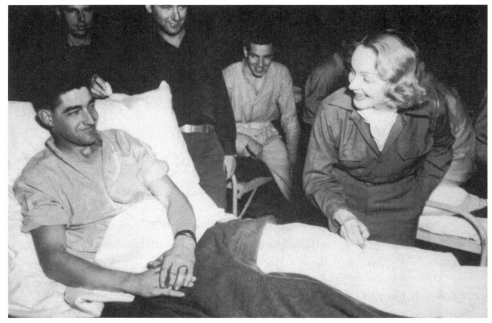

Actress Marlene Dietrich visiting soldiers in November 1944 at a hospital in Belgium where she had been entertaining the troops. (National Archives)

the outbreak of the war, she began an affair with Erich Maria Remarque, author of *All Quiet on the Western Front*, a book that had been banned by the Nazis. She soon began filming *Destry Rides Again* with Jimmy Stewart, who would later pilot an American bomber.

Dietrich was one of the first celebrities to promote war bonds for the U.S. war effort. She toured the United States in support of this effort from January 1942 through September 1943. She also undertook extended United Service Organizations (USO) tours in 1944 and 1945, appearing on the front lines in Algeria; in Italy, where she came down with pneumonia; and in France, where she contracted frostbite. She eventually entered liberated Paris with Gen. Charles DeGaulle. During these tours Dietrich lived in squalid conditions and ate canned food. Between shows, she visited wounded soliders in field hospitals. In 1944 the Office of Strategic Services (OSS) launched the Musac Project, propaganda broadcasts designed to undermine the morale of German soldiers. Dietrich recorded her hit *Lili Marlene*, originally a German song recorded by Lale Anderson, for the project. Although the song was a huge favorite of soldiers on both sides, it made Dietrich extremely unpopular in Germany. She entered Germany with Gen. George S. Patton and began an affair with Maj. James M. Gavin.

On September 19, 1945, she was reunited with her mother in Berlin. That winter, she entertained troops stationed in Berlin. In recognition of her wartime efforts, she was awarded the Presidential Medal of Freedom in 1947 and subsequently the French Légion d'Honneur.

After the war, Dietrich continued to record and perform as a cabaret artist. She returned to Germany for a tour in 1960 and received a mixed reception. Many Germans felt that she had betrayed her country. During a concert in Berlin, the audience chanted "Marlene go home." Dietrich died May 6, 1992, in Paris as a virtual recluse. She was made an honorary citizen of Berlin on May 6, 2002.

Wendell G. Johnson

See also: United Service Organizations (USO); World War I (1914–1918); World War II (1941–1945).

References and Further Reading

Riva, Maria. *Marlene Dietrich*. New York: Alfred A. Knopf, 1993.

Spoto, Donald. *Blue Angel: The Life of Marlene Dietrich*. New York: Doubleday, 1992.

DIVERS, BRIDGET
(CA. 1840–N.D.)

An Irish immigrant from a working-class background, Bridget Divers—also known as Bridget Deavers, Devens, or Devins—was likely in her early twenties when she joined the 1st Michigan Cavalry with her husband and perhaps her child. Most details of Divers's life remain a mystery, though it is clear that she served as a daughter of the regiment, part of a female support staff of the volunteer regiments. Daughters of the regiment served a variety of roles including ornamental mascot during parades and military reviews, cook, laundress, sutler, and nurse. Some of these women also undertook military roles on the battlefield.

Known to her comrades as Irish Biddy or Michigan Bridget, Divers earned a reputation for her willingness to remain with her regiment no matter what the dangers. Among the most famous moments of her military career came at the June 1862 Battle of Fair Oaks, Virginia, when Confederate forces surprised Union troops with a sudden attack. While many responded immediately, others panicked and resisted officers' attempts to rally them to fight. According to soldiers' accounts of the battle, the order to advance was all but ignored until Divers waved her cap in the air, urging them to fight to avenge her husband's death. The men rallied and drove the Confederates back.

Divers's wartime reputation also resulted from the nurturing stance she took toward the "boys" of her regiment. Several accounts detail her unwavering devotion late in the war. After a raid in which the regiment's colonel was wounded and its captain killed, Divers cared for the wounded and escorted the colonel by train to a hospital. Upon her arrival at the hospital, she discovered that the body of the captain had been left on the field. Unwilling to leave him behind, Divers reportedly rode her horse 15 miles into Confederate lines, recovered the captain's body, and brought him to the hospital. She then obtained a coffin and saw that his body was sent back home.

Divers performed another important service for the men of her regiment: coordination of their movements. She kept an unofficial directory detailing the whereabouts of the men and tracking their needs for supplies and armaments.

Regimental commanders often directed inquiries about men in the regiment to Divers. Her heroism on the field, skills as a coordinator, and concern for the men of the 1st Michigan gained her the respect not only of the regiment but also of Sanitary Commission officials and other female army nurses.

Little is known about Divers's antebellum or postwar life. However, sources agree that after the war Divers, who had become accustomed to military life, joined a regiment and traveled west for duty on the frontier.

Lisa M. Smith

See also: Camp Followers; Civil War (1861–1865); Nursing; United States Sanitary Commission (USSC); Vivandieres.

References and Further Reading

Leonard, Elizabeth. *All the Daring of the Soldier: Women of the Civil War Armies*. New York: W. W. Norton & Company, 1999.

Moore, Frank. *Women of the War: Their Heroism and Self-Sacrifice*. Chicago: R. C. Treat, 1866.

DIX, DOROTHEA LYNDE (1802–1887)

The superintendent of the U.S. Army Nurses, Dorothea Lynde Dix played many prominent roles in her lifetime. Her colorful career ranged from jobs as a teacher to acting as a psychiatric advocate in an era when it was not popular to be proactive for the needs of the mentally ill.

Born on April 4, 1802, Dorothea was the eldest of three children born to

Dorothea Dix achieved fame for her services as a Union nurse during the Civil War as well as for her work on behalf of the mentally ill. (Library of Congress)

Joseph and Mary Dix. She grew up under the stern hand of her father, a book dealer, a manufacturer, and a distributor of religious tracts, who sometimes called himself a minister though he was not ordained. The family moved often, and Dolly, as she was called, was forced to put together the booklets, stitch binding and gluing them until late at night. Her father was the dominant force in the family; her mother was weak and ineffective. Dorothea deeply resented her father's abusiveness and alcoholism, eventually running away from home at 12 to live with her paternal grandmother in Boston, Massachusetts. Her grandmother later sent Dolly to her aunt's home in Worcester for a more ladylike upbringing.

In Worcester, Dix decided to teach, opening a private school that drew many eager students. When she moved back to Boston in 1821, she opened another school, this one exclusively for young girls. Dix was one of the first educators in the nation to provide a free education for poor children, which she did at night when her paying students went home. Dix also found the time to write four books: *Conversations on Common Things* (1824), *Meditations for Private Hours* (1828), *The Garland of Flora* (1829), and *American Moral Tales for Young Persons* (1832). She was well read and well traveled and became an expert on many subjects. Rejecting her father's Methodist fire-and-brimstone approach to religion, she joined the Unitarian church and became an active advocate for the homeless and hungry.

In 1836, Dix contracted tuberculosis and had to take a break from teaching. She moved to Liverpool, England, for a year and then returned to the United States when her grandmother passed away. She continued to travel, however, and over the next four years regained the strength to return to teaching. Her first job after returning was as a teacher at East Cambridge Jail in 1841.

Appalled by the conditions in which prisoners were housed, she began a lifelong crusade against the treatment she had witnessed. She was outraged over the housing of felons and the mentally ill together, and in 1843 she wrote a memorial presented to the Massachusetts legislature by Dr. Samuel Gridley Howe, director of the Perkins School for the Blind. Although first rejected, her claims were soon proven to be true, and the legislature allocated funds for a large expansion of the State Mental Hospital at Worcester. She went on to write other memorials as well and established 13 hospitals in 11 states, including St. Elizabeth's Hospital in Washington, D.C.

Dix spent another two years in Europe in an effort to reform hospitals there. She returned to the United States in 1856, discouraged by her lack of success overseas and glad to be back in the United States.

As the Civil War began in 1861, she turned her attentions to the deplorable conditions at field hospitals set up to provide services to the soldiers. She was distressed to see the lack of concern for cleanliness and the behavior of the doctors and nurses who treated the operating room more like a bordello than a surgical theater. Drinking and flirting seemed to be more prevalent than saving lives. Dix could not stand by; at age 59, she volunteered her services to the Union and quickly thereafter was named the superintendent of the U.S. Army Nurses. Among the first items that Dix had to address were the directives to organize first aid stations, purchase supplies, set up training facilities, and recruit nurses. Performing her duties unpaid, she put together a volunteer female nursing corps that was the first in the nation and eventually included over 3,000 nurses in its ranks. Dix was criticized by the army but enthusiastically received by the civilian authorities, and she soon earned a reputation for enforcing tough, unyielding standards that some nurses and doctors resented but that were effective and long lasting.

Until Dix took over, nurses had few requirements to meet and were often untrained and unskilled. Besides requiring the nurses to have extensive training, Dix also enforced a standard of dress and appearance that many protested. She wanted the nurses to be "plain-looking" because she believed it would be more appropriate and professional to have "plain" nurses than to have attractive young women tending to the needs of the

soldiers. She also insisted that nurses wear modest clothing in black or brown and that they not wear any jewelry or hoops under their skirts. Some of the nurses started calling her Dragon Dix for her hard-nosed attitude, but her methods proved effective. The reputation of the nurses for their attentiveness and skill rose even as dissent stirred among the rest of the medical staff.

In addition, Dix made it her mission to prosecute the many doctors who operated on patients while drunk. They resented her bringing it to the public's attention. Dix clashed often with the prevailing bureaucracies but nonetheless managed to accomplish her goals of better sanitation, better treatment for soldiers, and more attention to good surgical outcomes.

After the Civil War, Dix resumed her tireless work advocating for the poor, displaced, and mentally ill. She became overwhelmed and discouraged by the lack of progress in hospitals, and in her later years she did not like to talk about her work, her life, or her career. She did not put her name on most of her publications and refused efforts to have hospitals named after her.

Dix was autonomous to the end, dying as she had lived—alone—on July 17, 1887. Dix was buried in Mt. Auburn Cemetery in Cambridge, Massachusetts.

Jay Warner

See also: Civil War (1861–1865); Nursing; United States Sanitary Commission (USSC).

References and Further Reading

Brown, Thomas J. *Dorothea Dix: New England Reformer.* Cambridge, MA: Belknap/Harvard University Press, 1997.

Dix, Dorothea L. *Asylum, Prison, and Poorhouse: The Writings and Reform Work of Dorothea Dix in Illinois,* edited by David L. Lightener. Carbondale: Southern Illinois University Press, 1999.

Dix, Dorothea L. *On Behalf of the Insane Poor: Selected Reports 1842–1862.* North Stratford, NH: Ayer Company, 1975.

Marshall, H. E. *Dorothea Dix, Forgotten Samaritan.* Chapel Hill: University of North Carolina Press, 1937.

Wilson, Dorothy C. *Stranger and Traveler.* Boston: Little, Brown and Company, 1975.

DRISCOLL, AGNES MEYER (1889–1971)

Agnes Meyer Driscoll was a U.S. cryptographer who helped crack Japanese ciphers.

Born in Geneseo, Illinois, on July 24, 1889, Agnes Meyer graduated from Ohio State University in 1911 with a triple bachelor's degree in mathematics, languages, and music. She taught math and music in Amarillo, Texas, at the Lowry Philips Military Academy from 1911 to 1917. She enlisted in the U.S. Navy as a chief yeoman, serving from July 1917 to September 1919. Meyer's fluency in German, French, and Japanese and her mathematical skills proved invaluable to the process of cryptography, and she was asked to remain in the code and signal section of the Department of Naval Communication as a civilian clerk.

From 1921 to 1922, Meyer worked at Riverham Laboratories in Chicago in the Cipher Department and probably attended training at the "Black Chamber" at New York Laboratories. She helped to invent a cipher machine in 1922 with U.S. Navy lieutenant William Gresham, for which she was later paid $15,000. During 1923 and 1924, Meyer acted as liaison to the Navy and technical adviser to the Hebern Electrical Code Company. When that company went bankrupt, she returned to the Cryptographic Research Desk (OP-20-G) under U.S. Navy lieutenant Lawrence Safford. Meyer married lawyer Michael Bernard Driscoll in 1924.

Driscoll, known as "Miss Aggie," was the instructor who trained many of the U.S. Navy's top cryptanalysts. She also excelled at breaking Japanese ciphers, in 1925 accomplishing the initial solution of the "Red Book" codes used for Japanese fleet maneuvers until 1930. In 1931, she used IBM machines to crack the "Blue Book," a breakthrough that revealed Japanese battleship speed in 1936 as well as the identities of two Pacific Fleet moles working for the Japanese, Harry Thompson and John Farnsworth.

In 1940, Driscoll's recognition that the Japanese code JN-25 was generated by a machine (M-1) gave the United States a head start in building its own decryption machine (M-3). Although briefly assigned to the Enigma codes, Driscoll concentrated on Japanese cipher traffic throughout World War II, providing crucial information in the days leading to the Battle of Midway and training most of the U.S. Navy's cryptographers.

Driscoll moved to the Armed Forces Security Agency in 1949 and to the National Security Agency in 1957, from which she retired in 1959. She died in Fairfax, Virginia, on September 16, 1971.

Margaret Sankey

See also: Espionage; World War I (1914–1918); World War II (1941–1945).

References and Further Reading

Budiansky, Stephan. *Battle of Wits*. New York: Free Press, 2000.

Layton, Edwin. *And I Was There*. New York: William Morrow, 1985.

Lujan, Susan. "Agnes Meyer Driscoll." *Cryptologia* 15 (January 1991): 47–56.

Prados, John. *Combined Fleet Decoded*. New York: Random House, 1995.

DUERK, ALENE BERTHA (1920–)

Alene Duerk was the first woman to obtain flag rank in the U.S. Navy.

Alene Bertha Duerk was born on March 29, 1920, in Defiance, Ohio. Alene's father, Albert Duerk, served in Europe during World War I, where he survived a mustard gas attack. This episode, however, left him ill after the war ended. After he returned home, nurses often came to the Duerk house to treat his illness. Alene first developed her interest in nursing witnessing professionals care for her father. Despite the nurses' efforts, her father died when Alene was four years old, leaving her mother, Emma, to care for the family.

In 1938, after finishing high school, Duerk entered the Toledo Hospital School of Nursing. She graduated in 1941. After the Japanese attack on Pearl Harbor, Duerk was recruited by the American Red Cross to join the U.S. Navy Nurse Corps, and in 1943 she was commissioned as an ensign. She served first at the Naval Hospital in Portsmouth, Virginia, before being transferred to another facility in Bethesda, Maryland.

In May 1945, Duerk was promoted to lieutenant junior grade and transferred to the hospital ship USS *Benevolence*. This vessel—stationed near the Eniwetok Atoll in the Pacific Ocean—tended to wounded men from the Third Fleet during the last months of the war. Following the surrender of Japan, the *Benevolence* was ordered to Tokyo Bay, where its crew cared for recently released Allied prisoners of war (POWs). Duerk made only one brief visit to the Japanese mainland while the *Benevolence* was anchored in the bay. Once it was fully loaded with released POWs, the *Benevolence* returned to California.

After World War II was over, Duerk returned to civilian life in June 1946. She resumed her nursing duties in her native Ohio before pursuing an advanced nursing degree at Western Reserve University. After the completion of her studies, Duerk began teaching nursing classes at Highland Park General Hospital in Detroit, Michigan. Her term as a civilian instructor proved short lived; with the coming of the Korean War, Duerk was recalled to active duty in the Navy in June of 1951.

Now holding the rank of full lieutenant, Duerk was ordered to Portsmouth, Virginia, where she became a nursing instructor. She would serve in this capacity for several years until, in 1956, she was transferred to the naval hospital in Philadelphia. Successful in her duties designing educational programs for nurses, Duerk was granted the rank of lieutenant commander. Next, Duerk found herself as a recruitment officer in Chicago, Illinois, before once again being transferred overseas. She was first tasked with being a charge nurse at a U.S. naval hospital in the Philippines before becoming the assistant chief nurse at a similar facility in Yokosuka, Japan, in 1962.

Duerk was not stationed in Japan for long, and in 1963 she was ordered to Long Beach, California, where she became senior Nurse Corps officer at the Navy's facility on Terminal Island. She served in this capacity for two years before becoming chief of the Nursing Branch at the Naval Hospital Corps School in San Diego. In 1966, as the United States' involvement in Vietnam escalated, Duerk—now a commander— was sent to Washington, D.C., to again take up recruiting duties. Two years later she was reassigned to the Great Lakes Naval Base, where she became chief nurse. Again successful in her duties, Duerk was promoted to captain.

With her new rank, Duerk became the director of the Navy Nurse Corps, once again stationed in Washington, D.C. As the highest-ranking nurse in the U.S. Navy, Duerk traveled the world inspecting naval nursing installations and ensuring that the service was as efficient as possible. She handled her duties well, and on June 1, 1972, Duerk was promoted to rear admiral. With this promotion, she became the first woman to obtain flag rank in the U.S. Navy. She continued her role as director of the Nurse Corps for three more years before retiring from the Navy in 1975.

Although her career in the armed services was over, Duerk continued to work. In addition to serving on the board of directors for a Florida insurance company, she poured herself into a number of philanthropic pursuits. Even in civilian life, Duerk remains a tireless advocate for Navy nurses.

Robert L. Glaze

See also: Korean War (1950–1953); Navy Nurse Corps; USS *Benevolence*; Vietnam War (1965–1973); World War II (1941–1945).

References and Further Reading

Godson, Susan H. *Serving Proudly: A History of Women in the U.S. Navy.* Annapolis, MD: Naval Institute Press, 2001.

McDoniel, Estelle. *Registered Nurse to Rear Admiral: A First for Navy Women.* Austin, TX: Eakin Press, 2003.

The Library of Congress. "Alene Duerk Collection." *Veterans History Project.* http://lcweb2.loc.gov/diglib/vhp/bib/28852.

DULINSKY, BARBARA J.
(N.D.–N.D.)

Master Sgt. Barbara J. Dulinsky was the first female marine to serve in a combat zone. After her request to be sent to Vietnam was granted, she served at the Military Assistance Command, Vietnam (MACV) headquarters in Saigon beginning in 1967.

In 1967, the U.S. military announced that plans were set for one officer and nine enlisted women to fill desk billets with MACV, based in Saigon. Care was taken to select mature, stable Women Marines who could be expected to adapt to strange surroundings and cope in an emergency. Interested Women Marines were asked to volunteer by notifying their commanding officer or by indicating their desire to serve in Vietnam on their fitness reports. There was no shortage of volunteers, but not all met the criteria. Other women would not volunteer for orders to a combat zone. Theoretically, all Women

Marines who served in Vietnam were volunteers in that nearly all had expressed their willingness to go and none objected. The women were sent to work in the Marine Corps Personnel Section on the staff of the commander, naval forces, and Vietnam to provide administrative support to marines assigned as far north as the Demilitarized Zone (DMZ). Between 1967 and 1973, Women Marines in Vietnam generally numbered 8 or 10 enlisted women and 1 or 2 officers at any one time for a total of about 28 enlisted women and 8 officers.

Dulinsky was the first Woman Marine to report to Vietnam for duty. She arrived at night at the airport at Bien Hoa, 30 miles north of Saigon, on March 18, 1967, after an 18-hour flight. Military regulations did not allow for travel after dark on unsecured roads, so she spent the night at the airfield. The next morning, she traveled with an armed escort by bus to the Koeppler Compound in Saigon. She, like all other arriving marines, had to attend a security briefing that covered the day-to-day security issues for life in Vietnam. The briefing that she and the other Women Marines attended focused on how to recognize booby traps and the importance of checking taxicabs for inside handles before entering. The Women Marines initially stayed at the Ambassador Hotel. Later, they moved to a hotel dormitory, nicknamed "the Plaza," that housed servicewomen from all branches as well as several hundred servicemen.

The Tet Offensive (January–February 1968) brought drastic changes to the servicewomen's lives. Because their quarters at the Plaza were under fire and bus service was disrupted, they were confined to the Plaza for extended periods of time. They were also on a 24-hour curfew. After the Tet Offensive ended, Dulinsky and the other Women Marines were quartered at the Billings Bachelor Enlisted Quarters (BEQ), which was located near the Military Assistance Command, Vietnam, Headquarters and Tan Son Nhut airbase. Most of the female officers, including Dulinsky, were quartered at Le Qui Don and primarily worked in Saigon. They were expected to work 60 hours each week, and time off was considered a luxury. In Saigon, the servicewomen often faced electrical outages. They also had to deal with the fact that there were few eating or laundry facilities available. While stationed in Saigon, the Women Marines had to return to their quarters by curfew.

Little is known about Dulinsky's life after her time in Vietnam.

Rorie M. Cartier

See also: Vietnam War (1965–1973); Women Marines.

References and Further Reading

Canwell, Diane, and Jon Sutherland. *American Women in the Vietnam War.* Milwaukee, WI: World Almanac Library, 2005.

Lacy, Linda Cates. *We Are Marines!: World War I to the Present.* Chapel Hill, NC: Tar Heel Chapter, NC-1, Women Marines Association, 2004.

Stremlow, Mary. *History of Women Marines 1946–1977.* Washington, D.C.: Government Printing Office, 1986.

Walker, Keith. *A Piece of My Heart: The Stories of 26 American Women Who Served in Vietnam.* Novato, CA: Presidio Press, 1997.

DUNWOODY, ANN E.
(1953–)

U.S. Army general Ann E. Dunwoody was the first woman to hold full general (four-star) rank and has served as the commanding general of the U.S. Army Materiel Command since July 2008.

Dunwoody was born at Fort Belvoir, Virginia, in 1953. Her family has a long record of military service extending back five generations. Her father, Harold H. Dunwoody, was a professional army officer who retired as a brigadier general. Dunwoody grew up on military installations in Germany and Belgium, where her father was stationed. She attended State University of New York College at Cortland and graduated in 1975 with a degree in physical education.

Dunwoody entered the army on graduation through the Reserve Officer Training Corps (ROTC) program as a second lieutenant. Originally planning only to honor her two-year commitment, she found the service to her liking and decided to make it a career. Dunwoody's service has been entirely with the Quartermaster Corps. She began as a platoon leader with a maintenance company at Fort Sill, Oklahoma. Subsequent assignments took her to Kaiserlautern, Germany; to Fort Bragg, North Carolina; and to Fort Drum, New York, among other places. She earned

Gen. Ann Dunwoody, the first woman to hold four-star rank, is greeted by Gen. David Petraeus after the November 14, 2008, ceremony at the Pentagon when she was given command of the U.S. Army Materiel Command. (AP Photo/Susan Walsh)

an MS degree in logistics management from the Florida Institute of Technology in 1988 and an MS degree in national resource strategy from the Industrial College of the Armed Forces in 1995.

Staff assignments include service in the office of the chief of staff of the Army; executive officer to the director, Defense Logistics Agency; and deputy chief of staff for logistics. Among notable command assignments have been that of the first woman to command a battalion in the 82nd Airborne Division. Dunwoody holds the Master Parachutist Badge. As executive officer and later division parachute officer for the 407th Supply and Transportation Battalion, 82nd Airborne Division, she deployed to Saudi Arabia during Operation Desert Shield/Desert Storm. In 2001, she commanded the I Corps Support Command in support of Operation Enduring Freedom in Afghanistan, and she had charge of establishing the Joint Logistics Command in Uzbekistan. In 2004, Dunwoody was the first woman to head the Combined Arms Support Command at Fort Lee, Virginia.

In 2005, Dunwoody became the army's top-ranking woman when she was promoted to lieutenant general and became deputy chief of staff of the Army for logistics. Nominated to serve as the commander of the U.S. Army Materiel Command, she was confirmed by the U.S. Senate on July 23, 2008. She received her fourth star on November 14, 2008. Dunwoody married Craig Brotchie in 1990; he is now a retired Air Force colonel.

Spencer C. Tucker

See also: Afghanistan; Gulf War (1991); Iraq War (2003–2011); Reserve Officer Training Corps (ROTC); Women's Army Corps (WAC).

References and Further Reading

Swarns, Rachel L. "A Step Up for Women in the U.S. Military." *International Herald Tribune*, November 22, 1908.

Swarns, Rachel L. "Commanding a Role for Women in the Military." *New York Times*, June 30, 2008.

Tyson, Ann Scott. "Army Promotes Its First Female Four-Star General." *Washington Post*, November 15, 2008.

White, Josh. "Army General's Nomination Called Historic." *Washington Post*, June 24, 2008.

Williams, Kayla, and Michael E. Staub. *Love My Rifle More than You: Young and Female in the U.S. Army.* New York: W. W. Norton, 2005.

Ziegler, Sara L., and Gregory G. Gunderson, eds. *Moving Beyond G. I. Jane: Women and the U.S. Military.* Lanham, MD: University Press of America, 2005.

DUSTON, HANNAH (1657–1730)

Hannah Duston, who was captured by Native Americans during King William's War (1689–1897), was celebrated for her killing of nine of her captors.

Born in Haverhill, Massachusetts, in December 1657, Hannah Emerson married Thomas Duston, a farmer from Dover, New Hampshire, in 1677, with whom she had eight children. The family resided in Haverhill.

When natives raided Haverhill on March 15, 1697, Duston had just given birth to her eighth surviving child. Thomas Duston and their other children were away from the house when the attack began, and they found shelter in a nearby garrison. However, Hannah and her nurse, Mary Neff, were quickly captured and the infant was killed.

The natives marched their captives to a small island settlement near the confluence of the Contoocook River and Merrimack River, just upriver from present-day Concord, New Hampshire. An extended native family of two men, three women, and seven children held Duston, Neff, and Samuel Lennardson, a young English boy captured at Worcester eight months earlier, captive.

Informed of the long march to Canada and the gauntlet they would face at its conclusion, the three captives planned to escape. Lennardson convinced one warrior to explain how to kill and scalp a person. On the night of March 30, 1697, as the natives slept, Duston and Lennardson killed and scalped 10 of their captors and returned to Haverhill. On April 21, Duston and her husband presented the scalps to the Massachusetts General Court, petitioning for the appropriate scalp bounty. Thomas Duston received £25 on behalf of his wife. Neff and Lennardson received half that amount, although Duston reportedly killed 9 of the 10 natives herself. Duston's deeds were celebrated throughout New England, most notably by Cotton Mather in his *Magnalia Christi Americana*, and she thus became a frontier legend. Duston survived her husband and died sometime in 1730.

David M. Corlett

See also: Indian Wars; North American Colonial Wars (17th–18th centuries).

References and Further Reading

Mather, Cotton. *Magnalia Christi Americana; or, The Ecclesiastical History of New-England from Its First Planting in the Year 1620, unto the Year of Our Lord, 1698: In Seven Books*. London: n.p., 1702.

Ulrich, Laurel Thatcher. *Good Wives: Image and Reality in the Lives of Women in Northern New England, 1650–1750*. New York: Knopf, 1982.

E

EARLEY, CHARITY ADAMS (1918–2002)

A member of the first class of black officer candidates in the Women's Army Auxiliary Corps (WAAC), Charity Adams Earley served as the commanding officer of the only all-black unit to serve overseas during World War II.

Earley grew up in Columbia, South Carolina, where her mother was a homemaker and retired teacher and her father was a minister. After graduating from Wilberforce University in Ohio, she returned to her hometown to teach high school mathematics and science. When the WAAC was formed in May 1942, the dean of women at Wilberforce encouraged Adams to apply for officer candidate training as a member of the first class of black officers. At the time she was attending graduate school at Ohio State University. Upon acceptance into the WAAC, Adams reported to Fort Hayes, Ohio, where she was inducted into the WAAC on July 13, 1942. On July 19, she reported for duty at the WAAC training center at Fort Des Moines, Iowa.

Adams was assigned to the 1st Training Regiment, 1st Company, 3rd Platoon. The 1st Training Regiment consisted of four companies. The 1st Company was comprised of three platoons. The 3rd Platoon was a segregated group of 39 black officer candidates. All were high school graduates, most had attended college, and some had college degrees. The 3rd Platoon lived in a segregated barrack but attended classes with 400 white officer candidates.

After completing six weeks of training, Adams was commissioned a third officer in the WAAC—comparable to second lieutenant rank in the U.S. Army. At the time, the WAAC was not part of the Regular Army but instead served under a separate command structure. Members served without Army rank, officer status, or military benefits.

Adams remained at Fort Des Moines, where she was assigned to train new recruits—or "auxiliaries"—as they arrived for duty. She served as company commander of black recruits as they processed through basic training and specialized schooling. As a training supervisor, she organized training, wrote course manuals, oversaw drills, revised operations procedures, and simplified forms. She served on the court martial board, aided in selection of recruits for officers' school, and traveled outside the fort speaking for bond drives. Her duties included inspection trips to other WAAC training centers around the country to observe black WAACs in the field.

On September 1, 1943, the WAAC ceased to exist and was incorporated into the newly formed Women's Army Corps (WAC). Members of the WAAC were given the option to leave the service or to join the WAC. Adams chose to transition to the WAC and was promoted to major.

Adams remained at Fort Des Moines until December 1944, when she left to command the only unit of black women to serve overseas during World War II. As commanding officer of the nearly 700 women of the 6888th Central Postal Directory, she and her fellow WACs were responsible for the redirection of mail to U.S. personnel in the European Theater of Operations (ETO). Known as the "Six Triple Eight," the unit directed the delivery of letters and packages to over 7 million military personnel at the front lines. Three eight-hour shifts operated seven days a week.

The 6888th operated from a post in Birmingham, England, between February and May 1945. Shortly after V-E Day they were moved to Rouen, France, to be closer to the majority of troops who were returning from the front. In October 1945, the 6888th was moved to Paris, where the unit continued to process letters and packages for the remaining U.S. military in the ETO.

In December 1945, Adams requested and was granted release from her ETO duty and returned to the United States for release from active duty. On March 26, 1946, she was relieved from active duty, but not before being promoted to lieutenant colonel, the highest rank possible in the WAC.

Adams worked for a time at the Veterans' Administration in Cleveland, Ohio. She eventually returned to the field of education as dean of student personnel services at Tennessee A&I College and Georgia State College. She married Stanley Earley Jr. in 1949 and had two children. The National Council of Negro Women honored her for her service, as did the Smithsonian's National Postal Museum. Earley died in Dayton, Ohio, on January 13, 2002.

Cheryl Mullenbach

See also: African American Women; Ten Percenters; Women's Army Auxiliary Corps (WAAC); Women's Army Corps (WAC); World War II (1941–1945).

References and Further Reading

Earley, Charity Adams. *One Woman's Army: A Black Officer Remembers the WAC*. College Station: Texas A&M University Press, 1989.

Moore, Brenda L. *To Serve My Country, to Serve My Race: The Story of the Only African American WACs Stationed Overseas during World War II*. New York: New York University Press, 1996.

Putney, Martha S. *When the Nation Was in Need: Blacks in the Women's Army Corps during World War II*. Metuchen, NJ: Scarecrow Press, 1992.

EDMONDS (SEELYE), SARAH EMMA [FRANKLIN THOMPSON] (1841–1898)

Disguised as Pvt. Franklin Thompson, Sarah Edmonds fought with the Flint Union Greys (later Company F, 2nd Michigan Infantry Regiment) during the American Civil War. She served as a male nurse with this regiment and later as a female nurse for the Union in New York.

Sarah Emma Evelyn Edmondson was born in New Brunswick, Canada, in December 1841. Her father wanted boys to help with the farming. His only son was epileptic; thus he put his five daughters to work in the fields during the day and the house at night. Sarah, the youngest girl, managed to attend grammar school, where she learned the basics; her desire for learning stayed with her throughout her life. When she was about 15, her father announced that she was to marry a much older man, and she ran away to Salisbury, Canada, where she spent two years as a dressmaker and changed her name to Edmonds. Then, for reasons still not clear, she disguised herself as a man, "Franklin Thompson," went to the United States, and became a successful Bible salesman. Her work took her to the Flint, Michigan, area in 1860, and a year later she volunteered for the Flint Union Greys, a company in the 2nd Michigan Infantry Regiment.

Edmonds enlisted on April 17 (some sources give May 17), 1861, still in her assumed identity as Franklin Thompson; no physical examination was performed. She volunteered for duty as a (male) nurse and was present at several major battles of the Civil War, including Bull Run (First and Second), the Peninsula Campaign, and the Battle of Fredericksburg. She also served stints as postmaster and as a mail carrier, a job that entailed carrying heavy loads of mail over long distances, riding unaccompanied. But after two years of service, in April 1863, Edmonds suddenly deserted the army near Lebanon, Kentucky. The reason for her desertion is not known, but it was common for women serving in male disguise to desert if they feared that someone had discovered their true identity. Edmonds herself eventually claimed that she left because she suffered from a recurring fever and her request for a leave of absence had been denied. If she had been hospitalized, her identity might have been discovered. Fellow soldiers later testified that "Thompson" had indeed taken ill with fever during the Peninsula Campaign. However, one source asserts that Edmonds's reason for desertion was to follow a lover who had left the service. Within weeks of her desertion, Edmonds was again serving the army as a nurse, this time as her true self; such work was physically demanding and would seem to belie her claim of ill health. After the war she went back to New Brunswick, where she married Linus H. Seelye, bore and lost three children, and adopted two more.

Soon after leaving the service, Edmonds composed an autobiography, published first in 1864 and reissued in 1865. *Nurse and Spy in the Union Army* was written in the first person under her true name. The book quickly became a bestseller (more than 175,000 copies sold) and gave her national prominence. Edmonds wrote about her service in the field hospitals and her adventures behind enemy lines as a spy for the Union Army but made no mention of her masquerade as Thompson or her desertion. She explained that she wrote her story after "leaving the Army because of illness." She donated a large share of her royalties to the Sanitary Commission and the Christian Commission. Edmonds gained new celebrity as her claims were publicized in the press and Congress. In interviews she disclosed more details about her past. Unfortunately, she often changed the specifics. As a result, many of Edmonds's claims have been questioned as authentic. Records confirm her service as a wartime nurse.

The most controversial claim in *Nurse and Spy*, Edmonds's alleged service as a Union spy, went unchallenged at the time and was the major reason for her subsequent popularity. Today, however, it is clear that her spying exploits were fiction. There is no corroborating evidence to support her claims and neither she nor her former colleagues made any mention of her espionage services in connection with her pension application. She wrote a sequel to her book, but it was never published and the manuscript has been lost.

If anyone questioned the story of Sarah Edmonds's service as told in *Nurse and Spy*, nothing was said until 1882, when circumstances forced her to apply for an army pension and the reality of her army life was revealed. She had been reluctant to request a pension because she knew that the Army had no record of a nurse named Sarah Edmonds. Thus she was forced to apply as Franklin Thompson, explaining that she had assumed that identity throughout her more than two years of service.

As corroboration, she obtained affidavits from her startled but cooperative former comrades of all ranks after attending a reunion and convincing them that she was the young soldier they had known as Thompson. But these developments raised new problems since Thompson's record showed that he had deserted in 1863. She countered that she had had to "leave unannounced" to get medical help that would have revealed her gender had she remained. Congress removed the charge of desertion from Franklin Thompson's record, and Edmonds was awarded the standard Army pension of $12 a month.

Edmonds moved to Texas in her last years and became the only woman elected to the George B. McClellan Post No. 9 of the Grand Army of the Republic (GAR) at Houston, Texas. When she died at age 57 on September 5, 1898, she was buried in the GAR cemetery in Houston with full military honors.

Hayden Peake

See also: Civil War (1861–1865); Espionage; Nursing; United States Sanitary Commission (USSC).

References and Further Reading

Blanton, DeAnn, and Lauren M. Cook. *They Fought Like Demons: Women Soldiers in the Civil War*. New York: Vintage, 2002.

Edmonds, Sarah Emma. *Memoirs of a Soldier, Nurse, and Spy: A Woman's Adventures in the Union Army*, edited by Elizabeth D. Leonard. DeKalb: Northern Illinois University Press, 1999.

Fishel, Edwin C. *The Secret War for the Union: The Untold Story of Military Intelligence in the Civil War*. New York: Houghton Mifflin, 1996.

Leonard, Elizabeth D. *All the Daring of the Soldier: Women of the Civil War Armies.* New York: W. W. Norton, 1999.

EDMONDSON, ISABELLA "BELLE" BUCHANAN (1840–1873)

Belle Edmondson worked as a smuggler, mail deliverer, and intelligence gatherer for Confederate forces operating in the Memphis area during the Civil War. Her diary of 1863 and 1864 provides remarkable insight into one woman's participation in the Confederate war effort and life on the homefront. She also closely followed military events, including Forrest's actions in Tennessee and Mississippi and the campaigns of the Army of Tennessee.

Isabella Buchanan Edmondson was born in 1840 in Pontotoc, Mississippi. In the late 1850s, she attended Franklin Female College in Holly Springs. She was one of eight children of Mary Ann Howard and Andrew Jackson Edmondson. In 1860, her family moved to Shelby County, Tennessee, roughly eight miles from Memphis. Early in the war, Edmondson considered becoming a teacher in New Orleans or Iuka, Mississippi, but it was not to be. Union troops seized and occupied Memphis in June 1862, and soon after, federal authorities banished Edmondson from the city for waving a rebel flag.

After her expulsion from Memphis, Edmondson began relaying supplies and information for the Confederate army. Although military documents never officially described her as a spy, she engaged in espionage on the Confederacy's behalf. Shortly before the battle of

Chickamauga, for example, she reported on William T. Sherman's movements to Capt. Thomas Henderson, who led an independent unit of Confederate scouts. Edmondson's work brought her in contact with members of the Confederate military elite, including Sterling Price, Richard Taylor, and Stephen D. Lee. In 1864, she visited Nathan Bedford Forrest's headquarters.

Federal troops arrested Edmondson in 1863 but released her when an officer learned her father was a Mason. When Union officials issued another warrant for her capture in the summer of 1864, she fled east to Waverley plantation in Clay County, Mississippi. There she was safe from the Union Army and enjoyed the upper-class lifestyle befitting the master class. In addition to being staffed with servants, Waverley had not only a pond but also a swimming pool.

Edmondson was a diehard Confederate. She hated abolitionists and Yankees generally, believing them "wicked wretches." As a citizen who supported a nation that depended on human bondage, Edmondson held racial views common among white Confederates. In 1860, her father, Andrew Jackson Edmondson, owned 18 slaves. Belle believed blacks that fled to the federal lines were "deluded," and she believed her family's slaves were loyal. She used her family's slaves to smuggle clothes and other items through Yankee lines. In addition, she did not think highly of African American Union troops. She thought black pickets more lax than white ones and refused to believe that white Confederate soldiers would ever surrender to black troops. Despite her prejudices, Edmondson recoiled in horror at the sight of seeing a dead black soldier in April 1864. While at Waverley, she noted attending a black religious service. After a slave at the plantation had a child, she asked Belle to come up with a name. Belle did—"Dixie."

In some ways, Belle was very much like other women of her time. She was religious, a reader of the Bible who often asked for God's aid in overcoming her own "wickedness" and in defeating the Yankees. As did many women of the 19th century, she took morphine to alleviate physical pain. She also suffered frequently from depression, what people then called melancholia. In addition, she continued to perform more traditional tasks on behalf of the Confederacy. She sewed for Southern soldiers and nursed nearby sick and wounded soldiers.

In other ways, Edmondson was unusual. Unlike most women of the Old South, she was well educated and enjoyed the best comforts of slaveholder society. She liked playing cards at Waverley and often stayed up late and slept until late morning. Despite three engagements and her longing for a child, she never married, nor did she have children.

She was well liked by Confederate soldiers, especially Missouri troops, for her bravery. In 1863, her fiancé, Dr. Gratz Ashe Moses, broke off their engagement, perhaps because of her role in the Southern military effort. Indeed, she flirted with federal troops as a means of distracting them from her smuggling and intelligence gathering, and at one point, she spoke of hiding contraband items under her hoopskirts.

Historians have not found any of Edmondson's writing beyond her November 1864 diary. Thus, little is known about her views on the Confederacy's

surrender, her postwar activities, or her engagement and sudden death in 1873. What is clear is that in wartime, Edmondson proved a model of independent Confederate womanhood.

Colin Woodward

See also: Civil War (1861–1865); Espionage; Nursing.

References and Further Reading

Clinton, Catherine, and Nina Silber, eds. *Divided Houses: Gender and the Civil War.* New York: Oxford University Press, 1992.

Galbraith, William, and Loretta Galbraith, eds. *A Lost Heroine of the Confederacy: The Diaries and Letters of Belle Edmondson.* Jackson: University Press of Mississippi, 1990.

ESPIONAGE

A government's systematic use of secret agents to discover hard-to-find military and political information and actions of other nations, the term *espionage* has been broadened in popular usage to indicate other intelligence activity, including analysis, research, covert political actions, and paramilitary activity. American women have played espionage-related roles in all of the nation's wars, demonstrating that women's special talents and their desire for independence from confining domesticity have significantly contributed to American intelligence activity. Exact numbers are impossible to gather because many women involved in espionage never revealed their role.

Women played integral roles in espionage and intelligence gathering from the beginning of the nation. As anti-British sentiment grew during the Revolutionary period, women began to chafe against the assumption that their proper role was as a domestic helpmate, though this view actually allowed women to move into clandestine roles. The societal assumption that women had little understanding of or interest in war or politics allowed many women to pass unnoticed through enemy lines or gather vital information. For example, Philadelphian Quaker Lydia Barrington Darragh passed key information to Gen. George Washington at Valley Forge. Anne Trotter Bailey and Emily Geiger played similar roles, and Sarah Bradlee Fulton, the "Mother of the Boston Tea Party," carried dispatches to American officers through enemy lines. Ann Bates, a Loyalist American, spied on Washington's troops for the British as "Mrs. Barnes," enumerating the strength of each American brigade, the numbers of their cannons, and even the weights of their cannonballs.

Although loyalty to country, positions on slavery, family ties, revenge for dead loved ones, and sheer boredom, as well as a desire for adventure, notoriety, power, and importance, impelled over 400 women from the Confederacy and Union to engage in espionage, few women were punished for their roles as spies or couriers. During the Civil War, societal attitudes that dismissed women as beautiful but uninterested in the male sphere of politics and war protected female spies from detection. Those attitudes also generally saved those who were captured from execution. The only female spy who was executed was Southerner Mary Surratt, who was hanged for her role in the assassination of President Abraham Lincoln. Other female spies were kept under house arrest or imprisoned.

Female spies played vital roles in the Civil War. For the Union, Elizabeth Van Lew of Richmond, Virginia, entertained Confederate officers at her home and then relayed the information that they revealed to Union officials. To do so, she created a secret code and a network of couriers, funneling information to Washington for four years. Other women took to the field of battle for the Union. Sarah Emma Edmonds disguised herself and fought as Union private "Thompson" for two years, and Union major Pauline Cushman proved to be a formidable actress-spy. Abolitionist and runaway slave Harriet Tubman recruited former slaves to scout Confederate camps and troop movements. Both a Union spy and a soldier, Tubman received a government pension as the first female African American veteran of the U.S. military.

The Confederacy also enjoyed the benefits of female spies. Southerner Belle Boyd carried letters and papers through Union lines for Gen. Stonewall Jackson, as did 20-year-old Nancy Hart, who, disguised as a peddler, shot her way out of a Yankee prison. Virginian Antonia Ford, commissioned by Gen. J. E. B. Stuart as his "honorary aide-de-camp," helped capture a Union general, 32 other Yankee soldiers, and 58 horses. Washington, D.C., society hostess Rose O'Neal Greenhow served two prison terms for passing information that helped Confederates win the Battle of Bull Run (Manassas).

After the Civil War, the traditional image of women as separate from war and politics persisted in the United States. Consequently, most of the 30,000 American women who served in World War I did so as nurses. A few worked in clerical positions for the U.S. Signal Corps, though by 1918 severe British losses had brought thousands of educated women into their Directorate of Military Intelligence and the Postal Censorship Branch. Within the United States, fear of subversion ran high, and U.S. antisedition legislation targeted women like Russian-born Rose Pastor Stokes, convicted under the Espionage Act in 1917 for writing a letter criticizing U.S. policy to a newspaper.

After the Japanese attack on Pearl Harbor on December 7, 1941, U.S. mobilization brought women into greatly expanded new roles, from riveting to espionage. The newly established Office of Strategic Services (OSS), the United States' first formal intelligence service, employed over 4,500 women, mostly as cryptographers, cartographers, propaganda experts, agent recruiters, and communication technicians. Women also worked as spies, saboteurs, and guerrilla fighters.

The U.S. intelligence community still reveres its otherwise little-known female secret agents, like their most valuable World War II field operative, Virginia Hall, "the limping lady of the OSS." Despite having lost her left leg in a prewar hunting accident, Hall became a formidable field officer, specifically targeted by the Gestapo as a dangerous operative. She gathered information disguised as an elderly milkmaid selling goat cheese to Nazi officers and coordinated sabotage and air drops for D-Day. Hall was the only civilian woman during the war to receive the U.S. Distinguished Service Cross, the second highest award

for valor in combat, and later she became one of the CIA's first female operations officers.

OSS and Women's Army Corps (WAC) agent Barbara Louwers played a vital role in Operation Sauerkraut, which attempted to undermine German morale, and "Code Name Cynthia," Betty Pack, cracked a safe in a guarded room of the Vichy French Embassy in Washington to steal French Navy code books. Culinary expert Julia Child did OSS work in China, where she headed the registry of the OSS Secretariat, one of over 900 women the OSS transferred overseas in 1944. Child also helped develop a shark repellent to safeguard anti-U-boat explosives, a recipe NASA later used to protect reentering astronauts.

Female celebrities also contributed effectively to U.S. wartime espionage. Legendary actress Marlene Dietrich, a German anti-Nazi who became a U.S. citizen in 1937, effectively lured her former countrymen with songs beamed from London to Germany, braved mud and blood to entertain U.S. troops, and earned the United States' highest civilian honor, the Medal of Freedom. American-born black exotic dancer Josephine Baker volunteered for French intelligence, stuffing notes on information she obtained on her tours into her underwear for transmission to the Allies. She received the Legion of Honor, France's highest decoration, and was the first American woman buried on French soil with military honors.

After World War II, many American women had to go back to their prewar domestic roles. In 1947, the United States disbanded the OSS and created the Central Intelligence Agency (CIA) to coordinate intelligence and the National Security Agency (NSA) to research codes and electronic communication, focusing on left-wingers and Soviet spy networks. Increasingly sophisticated technology allowed intelligence gathering to burgeon during the Cold War, from roughly 1947 to 1991, when the Soviet Union and its satellites faced off against the United States and its allies in a nuclear arms race.

The CIA had continued the OSS tradition of a male "brotherhood" that controlled assignments and promotions, keeping most of its women employees in support positions, but the Soviets had no such scruples. Even during the war the KGB had mounted massive espionage efforts to obtain nearly every American military and defense secret. In 1953, Ethel Rosenberg became the first woman to be executed in the United States for "conspiracy to commit espionage," by helping to pass nuclear secrets to the Soviet Union. Elizabeth Bentley and Judith Coplan were also convicted of un-American activities.

During the 1980s, the CIA's all-male Directorate of Operations, lacking sufficient midrange field-experienced male operatives, began to cross-train women as operations officers and to assign them overseas. The CIA then began to recruit women operations officers actively. However, although women made up 40 percent of the CIA's personnel in 1991, they held only 9 percent of Senior Intelligence Service positions. A class-action lawsuit settled by the CIA in 1995 brought women short-term benefits but few long-term changes.

After the September 11 terrorist attacks, telecommunications and computer technology, especially the Internet and the Interlink, have offered women increased career potential in military and civilian government intelligence agencies. The Interlink, completely separate from the public Internet, delivers sensitive data over the Department of Defense's classified data networks to officially cleared individuals on a need-to-know basis. Today the CIA's Directorate of Intelligence employs almost equal numbers of men and women.

The contemporary CIA, the NSA, and seven other U.S. intelligence-gathering agencies currently counter the espionage efforts of China, Russia, Islamic nations, and other entities. U.S. intelligence agencies analyze diplomatic reports, commercial statistics, technical publications, radio signal interceptions, and high-altitude photography, and all media—newspapers, periodicals, radio and television broadcasts, and Internet items—work at which well-trained, detail-oriented women can excel. Women also serve in the War on Terror in advanced computerized code making and breaking, used in both guerrilla warfare and counterinsurgency as well as in counterespionage, the defensive side of intelligence activity.

American women also play important contemporary covert antiterrorist roles, often exercising female perspectives in combating Muslim terrorism. As a CIA intelligence officer trained in institutional loyalty, secrecy, and excellence, Melissa Mahle worked on Persian Gulf issues and on counterterrorism measures against radical Palestinian groups prior to 9/11. Iraqi-born Rita Katz, author of *Terrorist Hunter* (2003), infiltrated radical Islamic groups operating in the United States with fronts as certain Muslim charities. Though not strictly a spy, Jessica Stern, a faculty member at Harvard's Kennedy School of Government, went undercover in traditional Muslim-woman garb to do research for *Terror in the Name of God* (2003). She investigated the motivations behind Muslim hatred of the West and promoted the possibility of covertly dismantling terrorist networks and sowing dissent among poverty-stricken Muslim populations.

Whether American women engage in espionage to gain power, to serve their countries, to avenge real or imagined wrongs, or simply to escape traditional domestic duties, female intelligence agents throughout the nation's history have demonstrated exceptional devotion, intellectual distinction, and valor.

Mitzi M. Brunsdale

See also: Afghanistan; African American Women; American Revolution (1775–1783); Army Signal Corps; Asian American Women; Bailey, Anne Hennis Trotter "Mad Anne" (1742–1825); Baker, E. H. (n.d.–n.d.); Baker, Josephine (1906–1975); Bates, Ann (1748–1801); Bentley, Elizabeth Terrill (1908–1963); Bowser, Mary Elizabeth (ca. 1839–n.d.); Boyd, Marie Isabelle "Belle" (1844–1900); Brion, Irene (1920–); Burgin, Elizabeth (n.d.–n.d.); Caracristi, Ann Zeilinger (1921–); Child, Julia McWilliams (1912–2004); Civil War (1861–1865); Cold War (ca. 1947–1991); Culper Spy Ring; Cushman, Pauline [Harriet Wood] (1833–1893); Darragh, Lydia Barrington (ca. 1728–ca.–1790); Davis, Ann Simpson (1764–1851); Davis, Wilma Zimmerman (1912–2001); Dietrich, Marlene (1901–1992); Driscoll, Agnes Meyer (1889–1971); Edmonds (Seelye), Sarah Emma [Franklin Thompson] (1841–1898); Edmondson, Isabella "Belle" Buchanan (1840–1873); Feinstein, Genevieve Grotjan (1912–2006); Ford (Willard), Antonia (1838–1871); Friedman, (Clara) Elizebeth Smith (1892–1980); Fulton, Sarah Bradlee (1740–1835); Greenhow, Rose O'Neal (ca. 1814–1864); Gulf War (1991); Gulovich, Maria (1921–2009); Hall (Goillot), Virginia (1906–1982);

Hart, Nancy (ca. 1843–1902); Hispanic American Women; Hitt, Genevieve Young (1885–1963); Indian Wars; Iraq War (2003–2011); Keichline, Anna Wagner (1889–1943); Kennedy, Claudia J. (1947–); Korean War (1950–1953); Latin American Military Interventions; Lauwers, Barbara (1914–2009); McIntosh, Elizabeth P. McDonald (1915–); Meyer, Marie Anne (1897–1969); "Miss Jenny" (ca. 1760–n.d.); Moody, Juanita Morris (ca. 1934–); Moon, Charlotte "Lottie" (1829–1895); Moon, Virginia "Ginnie" (1844–1925); Mountain Charley [Elsa Jane Guerin a.k.a. Charles Hatfield] (n.d.–n.d.); Native American Women; North American Colonial Wars (17th–18th centuries); Prather, Mary Louise (1913–1996); Rosenberg, Ethel Greenglass (1915–1953); Spanish-American War (1898); Strong, Anna "Nancy" Smith (1740–1812); Swantek, Elizabeth (n.d.–n.d.); Thorpe (Pack), Amy Elizabeth "Betty" (1910–1963); "355"; Tubman, Harriet [Araminta Ross] (ca. 1820–1913); Urdang, Constance (1922–1996); Van Lew, Elizabeth (1818–1900); Vietnam War (1965–1973); War of 1812 (1812–1815); War on Terror (2001–); Wilson, Ruth Willson (n.d.–n.d.); World War I (1914–1918); World War II (1941–1945).

References and Further Reading

Berkin, Carol. *Revolutionary Mothers: Women in the Struggle for America's Independence.* New York: Alfred A. Knopf, 2005.

Haynes, John Earl, and Harvey Klehr. *Early Cold War Spies: The Espionage Trials That Shaped American Politics.* New York: Cambridge University Press, 2006.

Jeffreys-Jones, Rhodri. *American Espionage.* New York: Free Press, 1977.

Mahle, Melissa Boyle. *Denial and Deception: An Insider's View of the CIA from Iran-Contra to 9/11.* New York: Nation Books, 2004.

McIntosh, Elizabeth. *Sisterhood of Spies: The Women of the OSS.* Annapolis, MD: Naval Institute Press, 1998.

Pearson, Judith. *Wolves at the Door: The True Story of America's Greatest Spy.* Guilford, CT: Lyons Press, 2005.

Proctor, Tammy M. *Female Intelligence: Women and Intelligence in the First World War.* New York: New York University Press, 2003.

Varon, Elizabeth R. *Southern Lady, Yankee Spy.* New York: Oxford University Press, 2003.

EXECUTIVE ORDER 9981 (JULY 26, 1948)

President Harry Truman signed Executive Order 9981 into law on July 26, 1948. This act stated, "It is hereby declared to be the policy of the President that there shall be equality of treatment and opportunity for all persons in the armed services without regard to race, color, religion, or national origin." This act was groundbreaking because it paved the way for the immediate desegregation of the U.S. military in the years between the end of World War II and the United States' entrance into the Korean War.

Passed during the Jim Crow era, when segregation was the law of the South and the Supreme Court ruled in *Plessy v. Ferguson* that separate was equal, Executive Order 9981 was one of the most controversial acts of Truman's presidency. Truman, a World War I veteran, knew firsthand the degree of sacrifice made by those serving in the military, and his decision was about democracy and equality. Based on information that Truman received from the Committee on Civil Rights, he knew that all branches of the military had attempted to keep African Americans from holding leadership positions. In 1946, only 1 in 70 African Americans was a commissioned officer in the Army, compared to 1 in 7 whites. The same was true in the other branches of the armed services as well, where African Americans were less represented than in the Army. Blacks made up only 4.4 percent of the total enlistment of the Navy and 4.2 percent of the Coast Guard. Truman believed that it was unfair to ask African Americans to die for their country but not afford them the same rights in the military as whites, so he felt that he needed to take action. Knowing that Congress would never pass such a controversial piece of legislation, he decreed it by executive order.

Executive Order 9981 caused an immediate firestorm throughout the United States, especially in the South. Even Gen. Omar Bradley, Truman's military chief of staff, expressed his opposition. Truman, ignoring the criticism, insisted that the military be desegregated. To ensure that this would happen, he created the President's Committee on the Equality of Treatment and Opportunity in the Armed Services, also known as the Fahy Committee, to recommend changes in military policy so that Executive Order 9981 would be carried out as quickly as possible.

This act had almost immediate results. By the early 1950s, African Americans in the military were able to serve as officers and held leadership positions over both whites and blacks. By 1953, the Army announced that over 95 percent of African American soldiers were serving in integrated units. By 1954, the last all-black units in the military were abolished. Along with Executive Order 9980, which desegregated the federal workforce, Truman had essentially guaranteed that there would be equality for all workers, regardless of color, in the federal government.

Elizabeth Ann Bryant

See also: African American Women; Korean War (1950–1953); World War I (1914–1918); World War II (1941–1945).

References and Further Reading

Gardner, Michael R. *Harry Truman and Civil Rights: Moral Courage and Political Risks.* Carbondale: Southern Illinois University Press, 2002.

Mershon, Sherie, and Steven Schlossman. *Foxholes and Color Lines: Desegregating the U.S. Armed Forces.* Baltimore, MD: John Hopkins University Press, 1998.

F

FAULKNER, SHANNON RICHEY
(1975–)

On August 12, 1995, Shannon Faulkner became the first female cadet at The Citadel.

Shannon Richey Faulkner was born in 1975 in Powdersville, South Carolina. She attended Wren High School in neighboring Easley, where she excelled as an honor student and varsity athlete. In the fall of 1993, she submitted an application for admission to The Citadel, a military college in Charleston, South Carolina. Founded in 1842, The Citadel was one of two remaining state-supported military colleges that maintained an all-male admissions policy for its Corps of Cadets student body.

Faulkner removed all evidence of her gender in her application. Believing it submitted by a male applicant, the Citadel's admissions office granted her acceptance to the college. However, the admissions office soon withdrew the

nomination upon learning the applicant was female. Asserting that she was academically qualified to attend the institution but was rejected solely because of her gender, Faulkner initiated a lawsuit against the college. Her attorneys argued that because 30 percent of the school's funding came from the state, there was no justification for an exclusionary admissions policy and, therefore, it was a violation of her constitutional rights. On March 2, 1993, Faulkner filed a lawsuit against The Citadel to that effect. Like male applicants, she desired admission to The Citadel for its prestige, 24-hour military training, alumni network, and the potential it offered for a military career.

Faulkner spent her first semester at the University of South Carolina–Spartanburg as she awaited the judgment of the legal system. On August 12, 1993, U.S. District Judge C. Weston Houck issued a preliminary injunction allowing Faulkner to take day classes at The Citadel but not to become a member of the Corps of Cadets. This decision stayed

Shannon Faulkner, the first woman admitted to the Citadel, marches with her company on August 14, 1995, her first day in the Corps of Cadets. (AP Photo/Wade Spees)

until January 12, when she was officially allowed to enroll as a civilian. At this point she was allowed to take classes while living in her lawyer's house in downtown Charleston. The case went to trial on May 16, 1994, and lasted two weeks. The district court ruled in favor of Faulkner and ordered The Citadel to admit her into the Corps of Cadets unless the school was able to employ an alternative program by August 1995. The Citadel filed an appeal. On April 13, 1995, however, the Fourth Circuit Court of Appeals confirmed the district court's decision that South Carolina and The Citadel had denied Faulkner equal

protection of the law in violation of the Fourteenth Amendment.

The Citadel continued to fight the decision, and in May 1995 it secured $10 million of state funding to create the South Carolina Women's Leadership Institute at Converse College in Spartanburg as part of the option for an alternative stipulated in the original ruling. However, Judge Houck stated on July 24 that an adequate trial on this program could not be held until November and that Faulkner would enroll as a cadet in August. The Citadel made a last-minute emergency appeal to Houck on August 2, arguing that Faulkner's physical condition (her weight and knee injuries) should disqualify her from admission. However, these appeals were overruled. On August 11, the school appealed to the U.S. Supreme Court to temporarily keep Faulkner out. However, the Court rejected the appeals, allowing Faulker to proceed with beginning the matriculation process.

Faulkner became The Citadel's first female cadet on August 12, 1995, amid worldwide military attention. However, by August 14, Faulkner suffered from symptoms of head exhaustion and was admitted to the hospital infirmary. She stayed there for the remainder of the week and missed taking the Cadet Oath with her classmates. Doctors cleared her to return to duty on August 17, but she emerged from the hospital the following day to announce that she would be leaving The Citadel. She explained that the stress of the past 2-1/2 years of legal battles and harassment had broken her physically and emotionally and made her unable to remain part of the corps. The raucous celebration of the male cadets after her announcement drew substantial negative attention for the school and sympathy for Faulkner as it created the perception that she was individually targeted and bullied out of the Corps of Cadets.

The long-term legacy of Faulkner's ordeal, however, has been mixed. She has been both praised for her courage and vilified for her failure by feminist groups and the general public. In 1996, four new female cadets enrolled in The Citadel, with its first women graduates receiving their diplomas in 1999. That same year, the Supreme Court ruled against the Virginia Military Institute's all-male admissions policy, and it

accepted its first female cadets in the fall of 1997. As of May 2010, The Citadel's Corps of Cadets included over 120 female cadets, 6 percent of the total student population. Faulkner currently works as a middle school teacher at Hughes Academy of Science and Technology in Greenville, South Carolina.

Bradford A. Wineman

See also: *United States v. Virginia* (1996).

References and Further Reading

Mace, Nancy Mace. *In the Company of Men: A Woman at The Citadel*. New York: Simon and Schuster, 2002.

Manegold, Catherine S. *In Glory's Shadow: The Citadel, Shannon Faulkner, and a Changing America*. New York: Random House, 2001.

FEINSTEIN, GENEVIEVE GROTJAN (1912–2006)

Mathematician and cryptanalyst Genevieve Feinstein (née Grotjan) helped the Signal Intelligence Service (SIS) crack some of the most important enemy codes during World War II and the Cold War, thus saving countless lives.

Born in 1912, little is known about Feinstein's early years except that, from a young age, she developed a passion and talent for mathematics. Genevieve Grotjan originally dreamed of being a math teacher, but during World War II, President Franklin Delano Roosevelt authorized women to obtain noncombatant military roles. After she passed the tests to become a professional government mathematician, William Friedman hired her as a cryptanalyst for the SIS in 1939.

Her main work during World War II centered on cracking the "Purple" code machine used by the Japanese to send secret messages. The SIS struggled with the code for 18 months analyzing and studying intercepted messages. By the summer of 1940, the SIS cryptanalysts had begun to despair they would never be able to discover the secret of the code. Finally, on September 20, 1940—the same day Japan announced it had joined with Germany and Italy to form the Tripartite Pact—a breakthrough was made in the deciphering of the "Purple" machine. While looking at the intervals between letters, Genevieve Grotjan detected a previously unnoticed correlation. From this discovery, other cryptanalysts were able to find similar links, and only a week later the first message was deciphered. From there the SIS created their own "Purple" analog machine to decode Japanese diplomatic messages and gave a copy to their allies in Britain. From 1940 onward, U.S. intelligence had knowledge of virtually all the information that passed between Tokyo and its embassies abroad. This enabled the U.S. government to make informed decisions and life-saving military maneuvers. To this day, Feinstein's breakthrough is considered one of the greatest achievements in the history of U.S. codebreaking, for which she was awarded the Exceptional Civilian Service Award in 1946.

While working for the SIS, Genevieve met and married Hyman Feinstein, a chemist at the National Bureau of Standards in 1943. The couple then had a son, Ellis. Following World War II, Genevieve Feinstein continued her cryptanalytic research, this time aiming her skills at the Soviet cipher system. In a top-secret project called VENONA the SIS set out to crack encrypted Soviet cables sent by agents of the KGB and the GRU, the Soviet military intelligence agency.

The Soviets saw, through the cracking of the Japanese "Purple" code machine as well as the German code machine Enigma during World War II that, although much simpler to use, machines were vulnerable to enemy deciphering. Therefore they used the much more labor-intensive method of a one-time pad. The Soviet intelligence officer would write out his or her message and hand it to a cipher clerk to convert the text into four-digit numerical codes. From there the cipher clerk would use the one-time pad to determine what unique numerical value to add to the previously determined code and then convert the final numbers into Latin letters. Because each message in this one-pad system had a unique cipher, there was no way for a cryptanalyst to decipher the message.

The downfall of the Soviet code came as a result of the enormous number of messages that had to be sent. This required cryptographers to create thousands of unique one-time-use pages. The strain was so great that the one-time pads came to be used more than once. The duplicated pages were mixed into one-time pads sent all over the world, but the global reach of the U.S. National Security Agency (NSA) was so great it was still able to collect enough of the duplicated codes to give its cryptanalysts an opportunity to break them.

Once again, Feinstein made one of the most important discoveries of the entire project, this time devising a process for recognizing the reuse of the supposedly unique numerical values. From here, entire Soviet KGB messages could be read.

On May 4, 1947, Feinstein resigned from the government and briefly became a professor of mathematics at George Mason University. Her husband, Hyman, also became a professor of chemistry there until his death in 1995 at age 84. Genevieve survived him by 11 years, dying in 2006 at age 93. The Feinsteins' legacy continues at George Mason University as Hyman established an award in cryptology to honor his wife, and there is a yearly award given by the Department of Chemistry and Biochemistry in his honor. Genevieve's estate established a $1 million bequest used to establish the Ellis F. Feinstein Scholarship Endowment in memory of the couple's son.

In early 2011, the NSA inducted Feinstein into the NSA's Hall of Honor, which honors those who have given distinguished service to American cryptology.

Megan Findling

See also: Cold War (ca. 1947–1991); Espionage; World War II (1941–1945).

References and Further Reading

Bauer, Friedrich Ludwig. *Decrypted Secrets: Methods and Maxims of Cryptology.* Berlin: Springer-Verlag, 2007.

De Leeuw, Karl, and Jan Bergstra. *The History of Information Security: A Comprehensive Handbook.* Amsterdam: Elsevier, 2007.

Haynes, John Earl, and Harvey Klehr. *Venona: Decoding Soviet Espionage in America.* New Haven, CT: Yale University Press, 1999.

FIELDS, EVELYN JUANITA (1949–)

Rear admiral Evelyn Juanita Fields was the first African American and the first woman to be director of the National Oceanographic and Atmospheric Administration (NOAA).

Born in Norfolk, Virginia, on January 29, 1949, Fields was the first of five children in her family. She was educated in Norfolk's segregated schools during the era of resistance to desegregation and graduated from Booker T. Washington High School, one of the most famous African American schools in Virginia. She attended Norfolk State College and graduated in 1971 with a BS in mathematics. Fields began her career as a civilian cartographer working for NOAA in 1972 at its Norfolk station. In 1973, she was commissioned as an ensign in the NOAA Commissioned Corps shortly after it was opened to women, making her the first African American woman to be allowed to join the corps. The NOAA Commissioned Corps is one of the seven uniformed services of the United States, and its members are considered part of the U.S. military.

Over the rest of her career, Fields was often a trailblazer for women in the NOAA Commissioned Corps. Initially, she served as a hydrographer, a skill that influenced the rest of her career. Because of her expertise in hydrography— mapping bodies of water—most of her assignments revolved around making oceanographic charts or finding more efficient ways for others to make charts. Field's hydrographic skill led her to play an important role in preparing charts for the U.S. Navy's use during the 1991 Gulf War. After serving as an operations officer on several ships and executive officer of the NOAAS *Rainier* (S221), Fields was appointed commanding officer of the NOAAS *McArthur* (S330) in January 1989. The appointment made her the first woman to command a NOAA vessel and the first African America woman to command a commissioned vessel of a U.S. uniformed service for a substantial amount of time. She commanded NOAAS *McArthur* for 18 months, during which time it was stationed on the Pacific Coast of the United States.

After relinquishing command of NOAAS *McArthur*, Fields continued to flourish. She held several positions outside of NOAA, including serving as an administrative officer of the National Geodetic Survey and participating in the Commerce Department's Science and Technology Fellowship Program. After returning to NOAA, she was appointed chief of hydrographic surveys and later served as director of the Commissioned Personnel Center. She was subsequently selected to be acting deputy administrator of the National Ocean Service. Fields proved to be a highly competent administrator and introduced much-needed reforms to the service in the midst of substantial budget cuts in the 1990s. Under her leadership, NOAA vastly improved and streamlined its chart-making capabilities. Her reforms, which included bring in new technology, doubled the rate of chart production and cut the time it took to update a chart from 47 weeks to 4.

These reforms proved vital because in 1995 the Clinton administration had decided to eliminate the NOAA Commissioned Corps and replace it with civilian workers. A 1995 hiring freeze began the process of attrition, which saw the 400-person corps contract by nearly 50 percent by the end of the decade. In 1998, Congress voted to keep the corps after new studies showed that NOAA's productivity was such that it would produce only a marginal cost savings to civilianize the service.

In 1999, President Bill Clinton nominated Fields to be the director of the NOAA Commissioned Corps and NOAA Corps Operations. Despite tensions between the Democratic president and the Republican-controlled Senate, which stalled some appointees, Fields was easily confirmed in only four months. As part of her promotion, Capt. Fields was promoted directly to rear admiral of the NOAA Commissioned Corps.

Upon taking office, she became responsible for a force of 15 research vessels, 14 aircraft, and a staff of over 700 commissioned officers and civilians. In 1999, the Congressional Black Caucus Foundation awarded Fields the Ralph M. Metcalfe Health, Education, and Science Award, and in 2000 she was decorated with the Department of Commerce's highest award, the Gold Medal, in recognition of her exceptional contributions to NOAA's mission. She served under Clinton and continued under George W. Bush until her retirement in 2002.

Andrew Orr

See also: African American Women; Gulf War (1991).

References and Further Reading

Henderson, Ashyia N., ed. *Contemporary Black Biography*. Vol 27. Detroit, MI: Gale Group, 2001.

Polimar, Norman. *The Naval Institute Guide to Ships and Aircraft of the U.S. Fleet*, 18th ed. Annapolis, MD: U.S. Naval Institute, 2005.

Reef, Catherine, ed. *African Americans in the Military, Revised Edition*. New York: Facts on File, 2010.

FINCH, FLORENCE EBERSOLE SMITH (1915–)

Florence Ebersole Smith Finch is the recipient of the Presidential Medal of Freedom, the highest civilian honor in the United States, for her participation in the Philippines resistance movement after the Japanese invasion in late 1941. After spending six months in Japanese prison camps, Finch (then Smith) sailed for the United States and enlisted with the U.S. Coast Guard Women's Reserve (SPARs) in July 1945. Seaman First Class Smith was the first SPAR awarded the Asiatic-Pacific campaign ribbon for her clandestine service in the Philippines.

Daughter of a Filipino mother and an American father, Ebersole was born in Santiago, Isabela Province, Philippines, on October 15, 1915. Her father, Charles G. Ebersole, fought with the U.S. Army in the Philippines during the Spanish-American War and later settled there.

Although she had no intelligence training, Florence began working for U.S. Army Intelligence after graduating from high school. Reporting to Fort Santiago outside of Manila, she served under the direct command of Maj. E. Carl Engelhart, who worked in the office of the assistant chief of staff of U.S. Army Intelligence (G-2). Her employment also introduced her to her soon-to-be husband, chief electrician's mate Charles Edward ("Smitty") Smith of the U.S. Navy. The couple married on August 19, 1941.

After the Japanese bombed key military targets in Manila on December 9, 1941, all military personnel, including Engelhart and Smith, evacuated on Christmas Eve to relocate to Corregidor. Claiming Filipino citizenship, Florence Smith remained in Manila and avoided internment with other Americans following Japanese occupation. In fact, her neat penmanship won her a job with the Japanese-controlled Philippine Liquid Fuel Distributing Union, where she wrote vouchers for fuel distribution. Shortly thereafter, two Japanese officers brought her a note from Engelhart, informing her that her husband had been killed in action on February 8, 1942.

Her husband's death further inspired her to join other Filipino citizens in sabotaging Japanese military operations and funneling fuel supplies to guerillas working with the Philippine Underground. She also smuggled food and medicine to American detainees after Engelhart, recently captured, quietly alerted her to the deplorable conditions in Japanese prison camps. She even laundered the clothes of American internees at Santo Tomas until October 1944, when the Japanese closed the front gates following the U.S. victory at the Battle of Leyte Gulf.

After the Japanese commandeered her home in Manila, Smith left her fuel-distributing post and moved to Tondo. There she was arrested for her participation in the Philippine Underground and sentenced to three years hard labor after being transferred to Bilibid prison. She endured electric shock treatments and beatings during interrogations, but she never revealed any information to the Japanese. The Japanese transferred her to Mandaluyong women's prison to serve her sentence, but the United States liberated the prison five months later.

Along with about 2,000 U.S. citizens, Smith left the Philippines aboard the USS *Admiral E. W. Eberle* on April 10, 1945. On May 2, she arrived in San Pedro, California, and joined her aunt, Maybelle H. Lewis, in Buffalo shortly thereafter. To avenge her husband's death, Smith joined SPAR and reported to Manhattan Beach Training Station in July 1945. Hearing of her courageous service in the Philippines, her superiors awarded her the Asiatic-Pacific campaign ribbon, the first of its kind given to a servicewoman. Smith was then assigned to the Coast Guard League Office in Washington, D.C. However, the SPARs were the first service branch disbanded following World War II, and Seaman Second Class Smith was discharged in May 1946.

She later married Robert T. Finch. She was shocked to hear she would be awarded the Presidential Medal of Freedom in November 1947. Engelhart's testimony brought her "meritorious service" in the Philippines to the attention of public officials. The woman who formerly claimed her service in the Philippines was "of no importance" found herself praised for her "outstanding courage and resourcefulness in providing vitally needed food, medicine, and supplies" for American POWs and internees.

Finch and her husband settled in Ithaca, New York, where they raised two children, Betty Finch Murphy and Robert T. Finch Jr. In 1995, the U.S. Coast Guard honored Finch by naming an administration building on base on Sand Island, Hawaii, after her. In March 2011, at 95, Finch received four medals from the country of her birth: the Philippine Defense Medal, the World War II Defense Medal, the Asiatic Campaign Medal, and the Philippine Presidential Unit Citation Badge.

Ilouise S. Bradford

See also: Asian American Women; Espionage; Prisoners of War; Spanish-American War (1898); United States Coast Guard Women's Reserve (SPAR); World War II (1941–1945).

References and Further Reading

Finch, Florence E. S. Oral history interview by William Thiesen. United States Coast Guard, January 28, 2008.

Medina, Jun. "Florence Ebersole Finch, a Living Fil-Am WWII Hero." *Philippine Mabuhay News*, March 11–17, 2011.

Poulos, Paula Nassen, ed. *A Woman's War, Too: U.S. Women in the Military in World War II.* Washington, D.C.: National Archives and Records Administration, 1996.

U.S. Coast Guard Historian's Office. "Florence Ebersole Smith Finch, USCGR (W): Coast Guard SPAR Decorated for Combat Operations during World War II." United States Coast Guard, January 26, 2012.

FLEMING, MARGARET ZANE (1917–1997)

Margaret Zane Fleming's military nursing career spanned the battlefronts of World War II and the Korean War. During both wars she served in hospitals set up near combat areas close to the fighting. Fleming was part of this new method of providing critical medical care to wounded soldiers who might otherwise have died due to shock and blood loss. These medical units helped to save countless lives and significantly decreased the number of battlefield deaths.

Born November 22, 1917, to Matthew and Rose Zane, Margaret was the 7th of 10 children, 4 boys and 6 girls. She graduated from Utica Free Academy in June 1935 and then went on to St. Luke's Hospital Training School for Nurses. After graduating, she started a distinguished nursing career in the New York area. She spent three months at Children's Hospital in Buffalo, and then she moved to New York City, where she worked at St. Luke's, Bellevue, New Rochelle, and Lenox Hill Hospitals.

At Lenox Hill, she worked with Dr. Otto Pickhardt. After the Japanese attack on Pearl Harbor in December 1941, Pickhardt organized an evacuation hospital unit modeled on the system the U.S. Army experimented with during World War I and which enjoyed some success during the Meuse-Argonne campaign. In addition, Dr. Paul C. Morton, the attending surgeon at St. Luke's in New York City, was also instrumental in reinstituting these special evacuation hospital units.

Zane's contact with both Pickhardt and Morton and the Army's need for skilled nurses motivated Zane to take a four-week training course on military systems and protocol. At the completion of the course, she was sworn into the Army Nursing Corps as a second lieutenant. She served as a member of the staff of one of the first American military hospitals in Europe, set up under tents in October 1943. These hospitals were affectionately called "guinea pig" hospitals. Stationed in Wales and then in France and Belgium, Zane distinguished herself throughout the war. For her exemplary service she was awarded four battle stars and five campaign ribbons at the end of World War II.

Promoted to first lieutenant after the war, she was assigned to the Walter Reed Hospital Nursing Corps as assistant operation room supervisor from 1946 to 1950. When war with North Korea broke out in 1950, Zane was assigned to the Army's 1st Mobile Army Surgical Hospital (MASH) unit. Later, the army would designate this unit as the 8209th and then the 46th MASH. Zane was with a group of 12 other army nurses who landed with X Corps at Inchon on September 15, 1950. They immediately took over the operation of an improvised children's hospital. The 1st MASH then moved forward to Pusan with the Seventh Infantry Division. On October 9, 1950, they were part of a column approximately 1,000 yards long that was ambushed by a battalion of North Koreans. After surviving this attack, the nurses started calling themselves "The Lucky 13."

The 1st MASH moved farther north than any other MASH unit, but a North

Korean counterattack forced the Americans to retreat southeast to Hungnam Beach on the east coast, where on December 13, 1950, they were evacuated to Pusan Harbor. On December 27, the nurses debarked again at Pusan and were part of the front-line medical support units in the UN counteroffensive against the Chinese and North Koreans. The 1st MASH went from Suwon to Chechon in February 1951 and received, treated, and evacuated significant casualties from both the Battle of Twin Tunnels and the Battle of Chipyongni. Finally, in mid-April at Chunchon, they were enveloped by the Chinese army and forced to return to Wonju.

Zane remained with the 1st MASH throughout the remainder of the war and then resigned from the Army Nurses Corps as a captain. In 1954, she married Ray Edward Fleming. Her husband served two tours of duty in Korea, and the couple moved to Albuquerque, New Mexico, in 1958. They were married 43 years when she died on January 21, 1997. She is buried in Santa Fe, New Mexico.

Zane's notebook and a collection of newspaper clippings she saved are at the Women in Military Service for American Memorial Foundation, Inc. archives in Arlington, Virginia.

Thomas Francis Army, Jr.

See also: Army Nurse Corps (ANC); Korean War (1950–1953); Mobile Army Surgical Hospital (MASH); Nursing; World War II (1941–1945).

References and Further Reading

Cob, Edna. "She Won't Leave G.I.s: Utica Nurse Brings Healing Hand—and Heart— to Pain-Wracked Korean Front." *Utica Observer-Dispatch*, April 29, 1951.

Witt, Linda, Judith Bellafaire, Britta Granrud, and Mary Jo Binker. *"A Defense Weapon Known to Be of Value": Servicewomen of the Korean War Era.* Lebanon, NH: University Press of New England, 2005.

Women in Military Service for America Memorial Foundation, Inc. "Margaret Zane Fleming." http://www.womensmemorial.org/H&C/Collections/collectionsarkorea.html.

FLINN, KELLY
(1970–)

Kelly Flinn became the first female officer certified to fly the B-52. Her military accomplishments, however, have been overshadowed by her dismissal from the Air Force for her relationship with the civilian husband of a married colleague.

Flinn was born on December 23, 1970, in St. Louis, Missouri, to Mary and Donald Flinn. As a child, she attended Space Camp in Huntsville, Alabama, where she was chosen as an "Outstanding Camper."

She attended the Air Force Academy near Colorado Springs, Colorado. She graduated in 1995 and received a commission as a second lieutenant. After graduation, Flinn went on to pilot school, where she achieved distinction for being the first female officer certified to fly the B-52, a strategic bomber first introduced in the 1950s and a key bulwark of the Air Force's nuclear weapons delivery systems. By many accounts, Flinn proved an excellent pilot, earning a "most distinguished" award at the B-52 training school.

By 1997, Flinn had risen to the rank of first lieutenant. As a 26-year-old pilot, she was assigned to the 5th Bomb Wing, based at Minot Air Force Base in North Dakota. During the course of an investigation into sexual misconduct by another officer on the base, allegations arose that Flinn had had an affair with Marco Zigo, the husband of an Air Force enlisted woman, Airman Gayla A. Zigo. While military regulations strictly forbade fraternization between officers and enlisted personnel, the rules and policies regarding adulterous affairs with civilians, in this case a civilian married to enlisted personnel, proved a source of controversy.

According to the Air Force, Flinn lied when she signed a statement that her relationship with Marco Ziglo was platonic, and she disobeyed an order from her superior to not see Ziglo again. The public scrutiny of the Air Force's handling of the case was a staple of the daily news during the spring of 1997. During the early 1990s, the U.S. military not only faced major cutbacks in its budget due to the end of the Cold War but also faced several sex scandals such as the Tailhook affair in 1991. When the Flinn story broke, Air Force general Joseph Ralston was under consideration to succeed Gen. John Shalikashvilli as chairman of the Joint Chiefs of Staff; dogged by allegations of adultery, Ralston was ultimately forced to withdraw his candidacy in the midst of the public storm that erupted over the Flinn controversy. *Newsweek* magazine even put the story on its front cover.

Public opinion favored Flinn, and lawmakers publicly showed their support for the embattled pilot. Senator Trent Lott of Mississippi, the Republican majority leader, went so far as to criticize the Air Force for its treatment of Flinn

and for what he perceived as an unrealistic approach to dealing with such infractions. In general, Flinn's defenders argued that she, as a woman, was being unfairly treated by the Air Force, which they said had a double standard for dealing with adultery and other instances of sexual misconduct within its ranks.

Critics, on the other hand, pointed out that Flinn had lied under oath, disobeyed direct orders, and fraternized in a manner unbecoming an officer. Air Force chief of staff Gen. Ronald Fogleman, appearing before a Senate committee, defended the Air Force's decision to pursue a criminal prosecution of the case, claiming that it was not about adultery but rather about the trustworthiness of an officer. Air Force secretary Sheila Widnall clarified that the Air Force would not give Flinn an honorable discharge because of Flinn's "lack of integrity and disobedience to order."

On May 22, 1997, Flinn accepted a general discharge, which allowed both her and the Air Force to avoid the public scrutiny of a full court-martial proceeding. If found guilty of the charges through a court-martial, Flinn would have faced up to as much as nine years' imprisonment. Though Flinn had expressed interest in flying for the Air National Guard, the conditions of her discharge disqualified her from doing so.

The controversy did not end with Flinn's discharge. The settlement worked out between Flinn and the Air Force generated further public discourse, both in the media and in Congress, over the military's treatment of its female members. Many publicly stated that Flinn's case highlighted both the male-dominated culture of the U.S. military and the outdated policies the military had in place for dealing with sexual misconduct among its members.

After she left the service, Flinn wrote a memoir about her time in the Air Force and the subsequent scandal that forced her out. *Proud to Be: My Life, The Air Force, The Controversy* was published in late 1998.

L. Bao Bui

See also: Widnall, Sheila Evans (1938–).

References and Further Reading

Beck, Joan. "She's Gone, but the Issue Hangs in the Air." *Chicago Tribune*, May 25, 1997.

Flinn, Kelly. *Proud to Be: My Life, The Air Force, The Controversy.* New York: Random House, 1998.

Kilian, Michael. "Air Force, Lt. Flinn Put End to Ordeal, General Discharge Averts Court-Martial, Ends Military Career." *Chicago Tribune*, May 23, 1997.

Sciolino, Elaine, and Shenon, Philip. "Much Anguish on Both Sides in Pilot's Case." *New York Times*, May 25, 1997.

Vistica, Gregory L. "Sex and Lies." *Newsweek*, June 2, 1997.

FONDA, JANE [LADY JAYNE SEYMOUR FONDA] (1937–)

Jane Fonda is a well-known actress and antiwar activist who rose to fame in the 1960s. Known in the 1980s for her exercise videos, she is now perceived as a heroic antiwar icon by some and a traitor by others. Conflicting views of her antiwar activism stem mainly from her long-standing and very vocal opposition to the Vietnam War.

Born December 21, 1937, in New York City to Frances Ford Seymour and Henry Fonda, Lady Jayne Seymour Fonda attended the Emma Willard School and Vassar College. She dropped out of college to become a model and then moved into an acting career.

Fonda quickly became a well-known opponent of the Vietnam War in the early 1970s, objecting especially to the government's reliance on civilian bombing during the war. From 1970 to 1975, she used her celebrity status to raise money for various antiwar groups. She traveled across the United States in 1970 visiting GI coffeehouses run by veterans and civilians. Her reputation for strong antiwar speeches and generosity in funding antiwar causes soon resulted in large crowds at her public appearances.

During this time, Fonda made significant contributions to the U.S. Serviceman's Fund and, in 1970, formed the Free the Army Tour with Fred Gardner and Donald Sutherland. The Free the Army road show toured through 1972 and was then made into a film titled *F.T.A.* In addition, Fonda played a major role in the Winter Soldier Investigation into war crimes, raised funds for Vietnam Veterans Against the War (VVAW), and helped to establish the Indochina Peace Campaign, an antiwar education organization. She also founded the GI Office in Washington, D.C., which provided legal aid for draftees.

Praised by some with helping connect the Vietnam antiwar movement to the cultural mainstream, Fonda was vilified and attacked by others for her antiwar activities. A large part of the attacks stemmed from Fonda's 1972 trip to Hanoi, a pivotal moment in her antiwar activism. While in Vietnam, she spoke

American actress and anti–Vietnam War activist Jane Fonda seated at a North Vietnamese antiaircraft gun during a visit to Hanoi in July 1972. Propaganda broadcasts of Fonda's trip were a coup for the North Vietnamese and an affront to many Americans. Years later, Fonda apologized for this photo. (AP/Wide World Photos)

out against the war, highlighting the mistreatment of civilians, calling the war a lost cause, and condemning both the Johnson and Nixon administrations. She argued that the war was for the benefit of U.S. businessmen and not in the interests of American citizens generally. Her speeches emphasized the tolls of war on individual families, on children, and on poor or underprivileged communities both in Vietnam and in the United States.

Fonda is often credited with publicly exposing the strategy of bombing the dikes in Vietnam through images she captured during her July 1972 visit of craters and bomb damage. While in Vietnam, Fonda also visited American prisoners of war and publically asserted that the POWs assured her they had not been tortured. These public statements

resulted in much animosity towards Fonda by both American citizens and the State Department. In the years following Fonda's Hanoi visit, people circulated accusations that she caused POWs suffering and torture.

A now infamous photo of her seated on an antiaircraft battery used against American pilots further fueled the negative characterization of her as "Hanoi Jane." Fonda apologized for this photo 16 years later in an interview with Barbara Walters. Directing her comments to the soldiers who served in Vietnam, Fonda carefully crafted her apology so as to only include the photo incident and not the rest of her antiwar activism. In a *60 Minutes* interview on March 31, 2005, Fonda reiterated she did not regret her trip to North Vietnam in 1972 but that she did regret her pose in that particular photo.

Named in 1999 by ABC News as one of the 100 most important women of the 20th century, Fonda continues her work as a peace activist. She has continued to place particular emphasis on war's impact on women, often reiterating that war is rooted in patriarchy and acts as one of the greatest threats to democracy. In 2002, she visited Israel and demonstrated with the Women in Black against the Israeli occupation of the West Bank and Gaza Strip. More recently, Fonda has argued that the so-called War on Terror will result in more terrorist attacks and an increased global hatred of Americans. Fonda and George Galloway organized an antiwar bus tour for 2005 but postponed the tour to focus on to the relief operations in the Gulf Coast necessitated by Hurricane Katrina. In 2007, Fonda participated in an antiwar rally in Washington, D.C. Currently, Fonda remains active in feminist and peace activist movements, focusing in recent years on war in the Congo and violence against women.

Natalie Wilson

See also: Prisoners of War; Vietnam War (1965–1973); War on Terror (2001–).

References and Further Reading

Andersen, Timothy P. *Citizen Jane: The Turbulent Life of Jane Fonda*. New York: Henry Holt, 1990.

Burke, Carol. *Camp All-American, Hanoi Jane, and the High-and-Tight*. Boston: Beacon, 2004.

Hershberger, Mary. *Jane Fonda's War: A Political Biography of an Antiwar Icon*. New York: New Press, 2005.

Hershberger, Mary. *Jane Fonda's Words of Politics and Passion*. New York: New Press, 2006.

FOOTE, EVELYN PATRICIA "PAT" (1930–)

"Pat" Foote became the second woman, after Gen. Mary Clarke, to command a U.S. Army post. She has been a strong supporter of opening all military roles to women, including combat roles, and has spoken out on issues ranging from supporting the deployment of mothers during the Gulf War to educating the public about the important role of servicewomen. She served during a time of great change for American military women. When Foote was commissioned in 1960, the highest rank women could attain was lieutenant colonel. She retired as an army brigadier general.

Born May 19, 1930, in Durham, North Carolina, Foote earned a BA in 1953 from Wake Forest University and an MS degree in government and public affairs from Shippensburg State University in 1977. She entered the Army in 1960, advancing through the ranks to brigadier general in 1986. Foote served in a variety of positions throughout her army career, including platoon officer, Women's Army Corps (WAC), at Fort McClellan, Alabama; public affairs officer during a tour of Vietnam in 1967; personnel management officer; faculty member at the U.S. Army War College; and from 1983 to 1985, commander of the 42nd Military Police Group in Mannheim, Germany.

In October 1988, she became the commanding general of Fort Belvoir,

Virginia, the first woman to command that army post. At Fort Belvoir, Foote supervised the transition of the post from the Army Engineering School to a Military District of Washington post. When she retired from the Army on September 1, 1989, she was the only woman in command of an army post. Foote was recalled to active duty in November 1996 to serve as the second-ranking member of a panel convened by Army secretary Togo D. West Jr. to review policies on sexual harassment and make recommendations for ending it in the Army. She retired again in October 1997. She spoke to the House National Security Military Personnel Subcommittee, making a strong statement in support of gender-integrated training. She did not believe in separate platoons or separate barracks for male and female recruits.

In March 1998, Foote spoke at the Pentagon during the Department of the Army's observance of Women's History Month. Foote's awards include the Distinguished Service Medal, Legion of Merit with an Oak Leaf Cluster, and the Bronze Star.

Vicki L. Friedl

See also: Clarke, Mary E. (1924–); Vietnam War (1965–1973); Women's Army Corps (WAC).

References and Further Reading

Foote, Evelyn P. "War Is No Time to Make Changes." *Washington Post*, February 19, 1991, 17A.

Holm, Jeanne. *Women in the Military: An Unfinished Revolution.* Novato, CA: Presidio Press, 1993.

FORD (WILLARD), ANTONIA (1838–1871)

Instrumental in the capture of a number of Union soldiers, Confederate spy Antonia Ford was made an honorary aide-de-camp by Confederate general J. E. B. Stuart. After her capture in May 1863 and imprisonment in Washington's Old Capitol Prison, she married the Union colonel who had arrested her.

Ford was born in 1838 in Fairfax Court House, Virginia, to a prosperous merchant and slaveholding family. After receiving a degree in English literature from the Buckingham Female Collegiate Institute in 1857, she returned to her family home. There she assisted her father in hosting a variety of guests, who ranged from businessmen to attorneys, as he promoted his business.

During the Civil War, the town frequently changed hands between the North and the South. In periods of Union occupation, Ford's father readily welcomed Union officers into his parlor, where he sought the opportunity both to continue his trade as well as to secretly gather intelligence that he would pass to the Confederate army. Antonia, using the enormous arsenal of skills she possessed, which included both her high intellect as well as her legendary charms, also worked to obtain vital information from these enemy officers. She purportedly feigned no understanding or interest in the war or the details of military strategy as she assumed the guise of a beautiful yet naïve young lady. As a result, many of her father's guests spoke freely in her presence. Often, they boasted of their experiences as well as their plans for battle in the hope of impressing Antonia. She collected this valuable information and then passed it on to Confederate officials, including Maj. Gen. Stuart, a friend of her family and the commander of the Cavalry Corps of the Army of Northern Virginia. Other members of Rose O'Neal Greenhow's spy ring, a group in which Ford also served at various times during the war, often delivered Ford's information to officials. In recognition of her efforts, on October 7, 1861, Stuart commissioned Ford as an honorary aide-de-camp.

Although many of Ford's exploits are lost to history, as is the case in most espionage, documentation of some of her successful endeavors exists. In August 1862, she provided intelligence to Stuart prior to the Second Battle of Manassas (Bull Run). Ford learned that the Union troops were planning to display Confederate flags in order to move their forces into a position of advantage. Ford traveled 20 miles by horse and carriage, in part through enemy territory, to reach Stuart. Ford's report was a significant factor in the Confederate victory that would mark the end of this battle.

Ford also played an important role in the capture of Union brigadier general Edwin H. Stoughton. In early 1863, Union troops were again occupying the town of Fairfax Court House. The Ford home was compelled to host the mother and sister of the general, who himself established his local headquarters at a nearby residence. On March 9, 1863, on the intelligence provided by Ford to Col. John S. Mosby, one of Stuart's officers, Confederates captured Stoughton while he was sleeping after a party in the Ford home in honor of his family. In

this raid, Mosby's Rangers also captured dozens of Union soldiers, horses, and weapons.

The high profile of the raid attracted the attention of the federal government, which was convinced that a spy ring operated in Fairfax Court House. On the orders of Secretary of War Edwin M. Stanton, the government launched a counterintelligence effort and dispatched a female Union agent to the locale. Pretending to be a displaced society woman from New Orleans seeking a safe haven from Union troops, the agent endeared herself to Antonia Ford. She gained Ford's confidence and gathered enough evidence, including the commission granted by Stuart, to have her arrested. Consequently, Ford was incarcerated in the Old Capitol Prison in Washington, D.C.

Ford's jailer was Maj. Joseph C. Willard, a Union officer, former provost marshal in Fairfax Court House, as well as the co-owner of the Willard Hotel in the U.S. capital. Willard knew Ford prior to her arrest, having previously courted her unsuccessfully. During Ford's initial imprisonment, Willard tried tirelessly to convince Ford to take an oath of loyalty to the Union in order to hasten her own release. He also convinced her to marry him. Ford negotiated with her jailer and admirer, demanding that if she agreed to his requests, he resign his commission from the military; she vowed that she would never genuinely renounce her support for the Confederacy. On March 10, 1864, the couple married in a grand occasion in Washington, D.C., and honeymooned in Philadelphia and New York City before establishing their home in the U.S. capital.

Antonia Ford Willard died in February 1871 as the result of complications from childbirth.

Leonard H. Lubitz

See also: Civil War (1861–1865); Espionage; Greenhow, Rose O'Neal (ca. 1814–1864).

References and Further Reading

Furguson, Ernest B. *Freedom Rising: Washington in the Civil War*. New York: Alfred A. Knopf, 2004.

Leonard, Elizabeth D. *All the Daring of the Soldier: Women of the Civil War Armies*. New York: W. W. Norton & Company, 1999.

Taylor, Amy Murrell. *The Divided Family in Civil War America*. Chapel Hill: University of North Carolina Press, 2005.

FOX, ANNIE G. (1893–1987)

First Lieutenant Annie G. Fox, Army Nurse Corps, was the first woman awarded a Purple Heart. She earned it for her actions during the Japanese attack on Pearl Harbor on December 7, 1941.

Born on August 4, 1893, Fox was the head nurse at the Station Hospital at Hawaii's Hickam Field, which was opened in early 1941. The nurses under her command liked and respected her. During the bombardment of Pearl Harbor and Hickam Field, Fox performed in an exemplary manner. Despite the chaos of the attack, she continued running the hospital and administering anesthesia to patients even in the heaviest moments of the bombardment. Furthermore, according to witnesses,

Fox retained her sense of calm and professionalism throughout the attack. She not only cared for patients but also taught civilian volunteers how to roll and apply dressings.

On September 23, 1942, Brig. Gen. W. E. Farthing recommended Fox be awarded a Purple Heart for her bravery and service. On October 26, 1942, the post commander of Hickam Field awarded the medal to Fox, making her the first woman to receive the Purple Heart.

The Purple Heart was originally issued by George Washington in 1796 and is generally awarded to soldiers injured in combat. However, when the medal was reissued in 1932 to commemorate Washington's 200th birthday, the award was extended to include "singularly meritorious act[s] of extraordinary fidelity or essential service," and it was under this rubric that Fox and others were awarded Purple Hearts between 1941 and 1943. President Franklin Roosevelt, in Executive Order 9277 (December 3, 1942), extended the medal to all branches of the military but restricted it to servicemen who had been injured by enemy fire. As a result of this order, the Purple Hearts were withdrawn from individuals, like Fox, who had earned them through meritorious acts. Other medals were given in replacement.

On October 6, 1944, Fox was awarded the Bronze Star. The text of her Bronze Star citation is fundamentally the same as that of her Purple Heart, and it made it clear that the Bronze Star was awarded in lieu of the Purple Heart on the grounds she had not been injured in battle.

It is significant that Fox was awarded a Purple Heart because the medal is one given to soldiers for doing their job well.

It was through her military service that Fox, like other women and minorities, was able to demonstrate her commitment to her nation and her value to the military. Early in the process of translating military service into acceptance into society, medals like the Distinguished Service Cross or the Medal of Honor (medals which women had earned during the Civil War and World War I) demonstrated that all people, regardless of sex or race, were capable of significant and outstanding service. Later in the process of military service, awards like the Purple Heart (which requires relatively little above and beyond the regular call of duty) show that a more general cross section of minorities is worthy of respect. World War II was the first war in which enough women were serving to receive such ordinary medals.

Even so, Fox and other women in uniform continued to struggle against societal assumptions. The final paragraph of Fox's Bronze Star commendation is particularly telling. It begins, "The Bronze Star is awarded in lieu of the Purple Heart awarded him" (*sic*). This error highlights the overriding assumptions about to whom medals were awarded in times of war. These male-centered assumptions continue to persist—many reports about Fox's accomplishment falsely report that she was injured or even killed in the attack on Pearl Harbor, highlighting the idea that Fox's heroism represented service above and beyond her duties. Instead, Fox was a hero because she did her job well under trying circumstances. She, and other women in uniform during World War II, proved that any woman could soldier as well as any man.

After the war, Fox returned to private life. She never married and died in San Mateo County, California, on January 20, 1987. She is buried in San Francisco. Today, there is a room dedicated to Fox at Hickam Airfield in Hawaii, which is maintained by the medical group of the 15th Airlift Wing.

Mike Timonin

See also: Army Nurse Corps (ANC); Nursing; World War II (1941–1945).

References and Further Reading

Bellafaire, Judith A. *The Army Nurse Corps: A Commemoration of World War II Service.* Washington, D.C.: U.S. Army Center for Military History, 2001.

Sarnecky, Mary T. *A History of the U.S. Army Nurse Corps.* Philadelphia: University of Pennsylvania Press, 1999.

FRIEDMAN, (CLARA) ELIZEBETH SMITH (1892–1980)

Clara Elizebeth Friedman was a writer, cryptanalyst, and pioneer in U.S. cryptology who deciphered codes of enemies of the United States during World War I and World War II.

Born in Huntington, Indiana, on August 26, 1892, Clara Elizebeth was John Smith and Sopha Strock Smith's ninth child. The Smiths were Quakers, and although her father was a banker and politician, the occupation he gave to census workers for official records was farmer. Smith finished high school at Huntington and briefly attended the

College of Wooster in Ohio before matriculating from Hillsdale College at Michigan in 1915. Although she studied German, Greek, and Latin and dabbled in a number of other subjects, she earned an English degree.

She briefly worked at the Newbery Library in Chicago, Illinois, in 1916 before one of the librarians introduced her to Col. George Fabyan. Fabyan was a millionaire who turned his 500-acre estate, Riverbank, at Geneva, Illinois, into Riverbank Laboratories, the first privately owned research facility in the United States, which is now recognized as the birthplace of cryptology. What interested Elizebeth in joining Fabyan's coterie of scientists was his desire to prove Sir Francis Bacon's authorship of Shakespeare's plays using Bacon's own ciphers.

Although Elizebeth worked closely with Elizabeth Wells Gallup and her sister to support the Baconian thesis, her work collating the work of other staff members eventually brought her into contact with William Frederick Friedman—originally born Wolfe Friedman on September 24, 1891, in Kishinev, Russia. Elizebeth and William married on May 21, 1917, and worked together at Riverbank for the next four years. The United States entered World War I a month prior to their wedding. Riverbank received an influx of cryptograms from a variety of government agencies.

William Friedman taught cryptology to a class of U.S. Army officers. An offshoot of this course was Riverbank's publishing of a series of instructional pamphlets in cryptology on which the Friedmans collaborated. The Friedmans also taught a cryptology course for the

U.S. Army when the United States created its Cipher Bureau in 1917. Working alone, William was sometimes stymied, but when he turned to his new wife and asked her for a cipher key, she regularly delivered exactly what was desired. This collaboration helped when the U.S. military passed Pletts crytographs on to William in 1918 to see if he could break the cipher machine that the British Army was manufacturing near the end of World War I.

At the end of 1920, the Friedmans left Riverbanks. As the most famous couple in cryptology, their work in cryptology took them east to the District of Columbia to the War Department. On January 1, 1921, William began a six-month contract with the Signal Corps to create cryptosystems, and after that term of employment he would take a civil service appointment with the War Department for $4,500 a year. Elizebeth Friedman worked for the U.S. Navy in 1923 as a cryptanalyst, which led to positions with the U.S. Treasury Department's Bureau of Prohibition and Bureau of Customs. During Prohibition, she solved the codes of rum runners, and while working for the Bureau of Customs in the 1930s, she decoded messages to counteract international smuggling, especially in the area of narcotics trafficking. Messages among drug traffickers were sent by radio, and Friedman intercepted and decoded transmissions. Between World War I and World War II, Friedman gave birth to a daughter, Barbara (1924), and a son, John Ramsay (1927).

During World War II, Velvalee Dickinson, known as the "Doll Woman," was convicted of espionage against the United States on behalf of Japan because her correspondence was read and analyzed by Friedman. Dickinson had used her doll shop as a cover for her espionage activities—the information she provided included noteworthy naval vessel movement in Pearl Harbor. Friedman also developed a code system for the Office of Strategic Services and deciphered messaged intercepted from German spies during World War II.

After the Friedmans retired, they returned to the work that drew them together: revealing that Francis Bacon was the actual author of Shakespeare's work. Their findings were published in *The Shakespearean Ciphers Examined: An Analysis of Cryptographic Systems Used as Evidence That Some Author Other Than William Shakespeare Wrote the Plays Commonly Attributed to Him* (1957).

Friedman died October 31, 1980, of arteriosclerosis at Abbott Manor in Plainfield, New Jersey. She is buried at Arlington National Cemetery.

Rebecca Tolley-Stokes

See also: Army Signal Corps; Espionage; World War I (1914–1918); World War II (1941–1945).

References and Further Reading

Chiles, James R. "Breaking Codes Was This Couple's Lifetime Career." *Smithsonian* 18, no. 3 (June 1987): 128–44.

"Elizebeth Friedman." *Contemporary Authors*, Vol. 102 (Detroit, MI: Gale Research Company, 1981), 202.

"Elizebeth S. Friedman (1892–1980) 1999 Inductee." National Security Agency Central Security Service Hall of Honor, January 15, 2009. http://www.nsa.gov/about/cryptologic_heritage/hall_of_honor/1999/friedman_e.shtml.

Kahn, David. *The Codebreakers: The Story of Secret Writing.* New York: Macmillan, 1967.

FRONTIERO v. RICHARDSON (1973)

The 1973 U.S. Supreme Court decision in *Frontiero v. Richardson* (411 US 677) affirmed married servicewomen's rights to equal dependent benefits. Prior to this landmark case, military policy and congressional law (Public Law 80-625) asserted that married servicewomen could only obtain such benefits by demonstrating that a male spouse was dependent upon the servicewoman for at least 50 percent of his support. Consequently, servicewomen had to demonstrate need in order for them to secure such benefits for their husbands. However, servicemen only had to show proof of marriage to obtain dependent benefits for their wives, such as housing allowance and medical and dental insurance.

Plaintiff Sharron Frontiero was an Air Force lieutenant who had served as a physical therapist since 1968. She married Joseph Frontiero in 1969 and applied for dependent benefits. Without those benefits, the military continued to classify Frontiero as a single officer without dependents, which meant she was not entitled to live in on-base family housing at Maxwell Air Force Base where she was stationed, nor could she receive basic allowance for quarters (BAQ). Instead, the Frontieros had to obtain their own off-base housing at their own expense. In addition, because the military did not automatically recognize

Sharron Frontiero sits with her husband in 1971. Frontiero, an Air Force officer, filed suit after the Air Force refused to consider her civilian husband a dependent entitled to military benefits. In Frontiero v. Richardson *(1973), the Supreme Court established that it was unconstitutional for the Air Force to distinguish between married men and married women in the military. (UPI-Bettmann/Corbis)*

Joseph as the dependent of a servicewoman, he could not access medical facilities normally provided for dependents.

Frontiero applied for dependent benefits partially on the basis that her husband was currently attending college full time and was thus dependent on her for some of his support. However, because she could not demonstrate that her husband relied on her for at least one-half of his financial support, the Air Force denied her application. Frontiero responded by filing a class-action suit in the U.S. District Court in 1970 and named Secretary of Defense Elliot Richardson as the subject of her suit.

In this case, Frontiero argued that the military's policy on dependent benefits for servicewomen's spouses violated her constitutional rights on the basis of her sex. Two of the three judges rejected Frontiero's claim, leading her to appeal to the U.S. Supreme Court with the support of the American Civil Liberties Union (ACLU). The case became the first that future justice Ruth Bader Ginsberg argued in front of the Supreme Court. The justices hearing the case included William H. Rehnquist, Harry A. Blackmun, William J. Brennan Jr., Warren E. Burger, William O. Douglas, Thurgood Marshall, Lewis F. Powell Jr., Potter Stewart, and Byron R. White.

In the Supreme Court hearing, the Frontieros claimed that granting dependent benefits automatically to female spouses but not to male spouses violated the Constitution's Fifth Amendment due process clause. Historically, this clause had been interpreted to provide for equal protection under the law. Further, the Frontieros argued that classifications based on sex were as suspect as classifications based on race or national origin.

The federal government argued that the dependent policy regulations existed because it was cheaper for the government to restrict women's dependent benefits. Moreover, it was uncommon for women to need such benefits for spouses. Thus, the military saved money by requiring that servicewomen demonstrate their spouses' financial need.

The court ruled eight to one that the law was unconstitutional because it discriminated against women. The majority decision, however, split along two justifications. Justices Brennan, Douglas, White, and Marshall ruled the statute unconstitutional because discrimination on the basis of sex was suspect, just as racially discriminatory laws were.

Justice Powell and two others accepted the statute as unconstitutional because it was irrational. These justices rejected the suspect class designation of the statute as ruled by Brennan, Douglas, White, and Marshall. Powell's opinion argued that recognizing the dependent statute as a suspect class would cause problems for gender-based laws. In particular, this opinion emerged because of fears about the Equal Rights Amendment, which was then being ratified by the states.

Because the majority of the Supreme Court interpreted the statute as unconstitutional, Frontiero's case was successful. Only Justice Rehnquist agreed with the lower court's affirmation that it was not discriminatory to hold servicemen and servicewomen to different standards for dependent benefits.

The military changed its policies quickly. By September 1973, the Department of Defense ruled that women could receive dependent benefits without proving need, backdating the change to the date of the Supreme Court's decision on May 14. The Department of Defense now allowed male or female servicemembers to receive dependent benefits simply by showing proof of marriage.

Tanya L. Roth

See also: Women in the Air Force (WAF); Women's Armed Services Integration Act of 1948 (Public Law 80-625).

References and Further Reading

Basic, Christine. "Strict Scrutiny and the Sexual Revolution: *Frontiero v. Richardson*." *Journal of Contemporary Legal Issues* 14 (2004): 117.

Holm, Jeanne. *Women in the Military: An Unending Revolution (Revised Edition)*. Novato, CA: Presidio Press, 1993.

Kerber, Linda. *No Constitutional Right to be Ladies: Women and Obligations of Citizenship*. New York: Hill and Wang, 1998.

FULTON, SARAH BRADLEE (1740–1835)

Sarah Bradlee Fulton secretly helped organize the Boston Tea Party, nursed wounded men from the battlefront during the American Revolution, and carried dispatches to Gen. George Washington. She became known as the "Mother of the Revolution."

Sarah Bradlee was born on Christmas Eve in 1740 in Boston, Massachusetts, to Samuel and Mary Bradlee. She was the fourth daughter of 12 children. In 1762, at a time when the colonies were beginning to take a stand against the imposed British taxes, Sarah married John Fulton. Throughout their marriage, Sarah and John would both partake in patriotic events that surrounded the city of Boston. In 1772, the couple moved not far from Boston, to Medford, Massachusetts, and lived on Main Street in the small town.

John Fulton carpenter's shop and the kitchen within the Fultons' home were both notorious meeting places on Saturday nights for patriotic men, commonly known as the Sons of Liberty, residing in Massachusetts. On one fateful evening in December 1773, not long after British Parliament had passed the

Tea Act, John and other Sons of Liberty initiated the Boston Tea Party.

In the Fultons' kitchen, Sarah, with the help of her brother's wife, helped disguise their husbands and other Sons of Liberty as Mohawk Indians to participate in the Boston Tea Party. The women later cleaned up the men and destroyed the evidence. Participants were protesting the Tea Act and tossed approximately 342 crates of tea into the water from a ship docked at the Boston Harbor. Sarah's brother, Nathaniel Bradlee, was a well-known patriot in Boston. On the same evening as the Boston Tea Party, a spy had looked through a window in the kitchen but only saw two women busily doing housework. He was unaware that Sarah and her sister-in-law were patriots in action at that very moment.

Sarah Fulton took part in another important event during the American Revolution a little over a year later. In 1775, Paul Revere traveled through Medford during his now famous ride, alerting patriotic men and women days before the battles of Lexington and Concord took place. Not long after the battles ended, the town of Medford became the headquarters for the New Hampshire regiment of Gen. Stark. Not far from the Fultons' small house in Medford, the Battle of Bunker Hill took place. The wounded were brought into town where doctors would tend to their injuries. Sarah, along with many other women, served as nurses. They helped remove bullets and tend to other battlefield injuries.

Sarah was also known to stand up against the British during the siege of Boston from 1775 to 1776. The British soldiers looted any goods they wanted, and among them was wood for fire.

Sarah got word from others that the British were planning to take wood from her area, so she began to hide the wood. As her husband was on his way to stash the wood, British regulars stopped him. Sarah found out what happened and headed out to where the dispute was taking place. According to legend, Sarah took the reigns of the oxen carting the wood and steered them away from the British. The regulars said they would shoot her, but Sarah shouted, "Shoot away!" and continued on with the oxen and her wood. The British soldiers were in such shock they did not shoot at Sarah.

Fulton also carried dispatches to Gen. Washington. Maj. Brooks, stationed in Massachusetts and later to become the governor of the state, asked John Fulton if he could deliver the dispatches to Washington, but he was unable to do so. Instead, Sarah volunteered for the mission. She walked to Charlestown, a small neighborhood in Boston on the Charles River. At Charlestown, she got into a boat and rowed to the other side. She walked to where Washington's headquarters were, handed in the dispatches, and left for home, completing her mission within one day.

Some time later, Washington visited the Fultons at their home in Massachusetts. Later in life, Sarah moved into a home on the road that led to the small town of Stoneham. In November 1835, at the age of 94, Fulton died peacefully in her sleep from old age. She is buried in the Salem Street Cemetery in Medford.

Rebecca E. Price

See also: American Revolution (1775–1783); Espionage; Nursing.

References and Further Reading

Gunderson, Joan R. *To Be Useful to the World: Women in Revolutionary America, 1740–1790.* New York: Twayne Press, 1996.

Kerr, Barbara. *Glimpses of Medford: Selections from the Historical Register.* Charleston, SC: History, 2007.

Young, Alfred F. *The Shoemaker and the Tea Party.* Boston: Beacon Press, 1999.

G

GALLOWAY, IRENE O.
(1908–1963)

Colonel Irene Galloway served in the U.S. military from 1942 until her retirement in the early 1960s. She was the fourth director of the Women's Army Corps (WAC) from 1953 to 1957 and held assignments in both Europe and the United States, including a role at the Pentagon, during the course of her career.

Galloway grew up in Templeton, Iowa, where she was born on September 1, 1908. She was the only daughter of five children born to Franklin and Rosa Anna Galloway. Before joining the military, she attended Boyles Business College in Omaha, Nebraska, and went on to work in the home loan industry at companies in Washington, D.C., and New York. In 1942, just before her 34th birthday, Galloway enlisted in the newly formed Women's Army Auxiliary Corps (WAAC, later the WAC) to support World War II. The following month, she became part of the second WAAC

officer candidate class. Upon completion of officer training, Galloway became a third officer, the equivalent of a second lieutenant in the male ranks at that time. She received a promotion to captain a year later after the WAAC received full military status as the WAC.

During World War II, Galloway worked in the Office of the Director of the WAAC as chief of officer assignments. Her other roles during the war were also personnel related, including positions with the Army Service Forces and the Army's Office of the Assistant Chief of Staff for Personnel.

In 1948, the Women's Armed Services Integration Act made the WAC a permanent part of the U.S. military. As one of the servicewomen who elected to remain with the military in the postwar era, Galloway spent the next four years as WAC staff adviser for the European Command. During her time in Germany, she continued her education with courses through the University of Maryland. Upon her return to the United States, Galloway worked briefly as a commanding officer of the WAC Training Center in Fort Lee, Virginia.

Galloway received a temporary promotion to colonel when she became the fourth director of WAC in January 1953. As director, Galloway focused on increasing the job opportunities for women in the WAC, believing that women were in the military to assume any and all noncombat roles. She believed that military service was a natural role for women citizens and felt that the nation's growing military system in the Cold War would depend on all of the country's population to be most effective.

The new WAC Center for training Army servicewomen opened in 1954 in Fort McClellan, Alabama, while Galloway was serving as director of WAC. Also that year, the WAC created an Officer Advanced Course for the first time, which provided WAC officers with additional professional training. Galloway improved recruiters' clothing allowances and authorized a new WAC uniform, two movements designed to help make the WAC more attractive to the public and to potential recruits. For the first time, WAC officers attended the Fort Leavenworth, Kansas, Command and General Staff College in 1945. Perhaps most significantly, during Galloway's leadership Congress passed a bill that granted veteran's benefits to any WAAC members who served more than 90 days before the end of September 1943. This bill recognized WAAC members' service before the organization had secured full military status.

Because of stipulations written into the 1948 Women's Armed Services Integration Act, Galloway lost her rank as colonel when she left the director of WAC position in 1957. She reassumed her rank as lieutenant colonel and continued to serve in the WAC for several more years. Between 1957 and 1960, Galloway worked at Headquarters U.S. Continental Army Command as a member of the liaison office in the Pentagon. In early 1960, she took on a new role as a special assistant to the secretary of defense for legislative affairs.

Although she retired on temporary disability in 1961, in February 1962 Galloway was recalled to active duty as a colonel to serve on President Kennedy's President's Commission on the Status of Women. She spent nine months as a staff administrator to this commission, and then retired permanently in November 1962.

Over the course of her 20-year career, Galloway earned a number of honors, including the Legion of Merit, the Army Commendation Medal, and the WAC Service Medal. She also received the American Campaign Medal, the European-African-Middle Eastern Campaign Medal, the World War II Victory Medal, the Army of Occupation Medal with Germany Clasp, and the National Defense Service Medal with one Oak Leaf Cluster.

Galloway died of cancer on January 6, 1963, in Washington, D.C., and was buried in Manning, Iowa, a few days later. In May of that year, the military honored her service by dedicating the gate to Fort McClellan to her honor and renamed the road through the troop area as Galloway Gate Road.

Tanya L. Roth

See also: Bailey, Mildred "Inez" Caroon (1919–2009); Clarke, Mary E. (1924–); Cold

War (ca. 1947–1991); Hallaren, Mary (1907–
2005); Hoisington, Elizabeth P. (1918–2007);
Milligan (Rasmuson), Mary Louise (1911–);
Women's Armed Services Integration Act of
1948 (Public Law 80-625); Women's Army
Auxiliary Corps (WAAC); Women's Army
Corps (WAC); Women's Army Corps Training
Center (1948–1954); World War II (1941–
1945).

References and Further Reading

Holm, Jeanne. *In Defense of a Nation: Servicewomen in World War II*. St. Petersburg, FL: Vandamere Press, 1998.

Holm, Jeanne. *Women in the Military: An Unfinished Revolution (Revised Edition)*. Novato, CA: Presidio Press, 1993.

Monahan, Evelyn, and Rosemary Neidel-Greenlee. *A Few Good Women: America's Military Women from World War I to the War in Iraq and Afghanistan*. New York: Alfred A. Knopf, 2010.

Morden, Bettie J. *The Women's Army Corps, 1945–1978*. Washington, D.C.: Center of Military History, 1989.

Witt, Linda, Judith Bellafaire, Britta Granrud, and Mary Jo Binker. *"A Defense Weapon Known to Be of Value": Servicewomen of the Korean War Era*. Hanover, NH: University Press of New England, 2005.

GANG, JEANNE HAMBY (1921–2006)

Jeanne Hamby Gang worked with the American Red Cross during World War II and became a recreation worker for Army Special Services in Germany during the Korean War. For the first 15 years after she returned to the United States, she held several positions related to her work with the Red Cross.

Jeanne Yvonne Hamby was born in Piedmont, California, on May 9, 1921, to Walter P. and Nina L. Hamby. She attended Piedmont High School and later the University of California at Berkeley. While at Berkeley, she became involved in a number of on-campus organizations. She was in Treble Clef and served as head of entertainment under War Council, as president of the Students of the Graduate School of Social Welfare, and as senior representative for Alpha Chi Omega. She received her bachelor's degree in political science.

During World War II, Hamby wanted to join the Navy women's reserve (WAVES). The WAVES would not admit her because of her poor vision. As a result, Hamby joined the American Red Cross in December 1941. Deemed too young to go overseas, she worked in California as a recreational and social staff aid in Army and Navy hospitals. After the war, Hamby worked in the Bay Area of California as a member of the National Conference of Social Work. She continued her assistance in public service, working for the San Francisco Council for Civic Unity and the San Francisco Municipal Theater. She also became involved in equestrian ventures, serving with the Horsemen's Association and performing in numerous horse shows and rodeos.

At the beginning of the Korean War, Hamby volunteered for the Army Special Services. She was assigned the job of recreation worker and was sent to Germany from 1950 until 1953, where she served at the 7th Army Headquarters' Pyramid Service Club. She then assisted in the opening of the service club at Wharton Barracks in Heilbronn.

Hamby met Howard Gang while serving in Heilbronn, and they married while stationed there. On their return to the United States, the couple moved to Oregon, and for the next 15 years, Hamby (now Gang) held several positions confluent to her work with the Red Cross. She worked as a Red Cross executive for Home Service, as a Camp Fire executive for Rogue Valley, and as a caseworker for the Public Welfare Department. In the late 1960s, Gang decided to change careers and go into education. She received her secondary and five-year certificates from Southern Oregon College and spent the next 17 years teaching social studies.

Gang retired in 1987 but continued teaching English as a second language, home tutoring, and substituting. She also continued her civic activities, serving on the board of the League of Women Voters and as president of the American Association of University Women. She was also a member of the National Education Association and the Oregon Education Association, the Retired Teachers Association, the Southern Oregon Traditional Jazz Society, the Oregon Aerospace Association, and the Southern Oregon College Alumni Association. She published the book *A Coming Together: A Short History of Two Families, a Legacy.* Gang died in April 2006.

Emily Meyer

See also: American Red Cross; Korean War (1950–1953); Women Accepted for Volunteer Emergency Service (WAVES); World War II (1941–1945).

Reference and Further Reading

Witt, Linda, Judith Bellafaire, Britta Granrud, and Mary Jo Binker. *"A Defense Weapon Known to Be of Value": Servicewomen of the Korean War Era.* Hanover, NH: University Press of New England, 2005.

GAY, SAMUEL [ANN BAILEY] (N.D.–N.D.)

Samuel Gay was the alias of Ann (Nancy) Bailey during the American Revolution. Bailey was charged with and convicted for fraud and desertion, specifically for dressing in a man's clothes and enlisting as a man in the Continental Army and subsequently deserting weeks after receiving an enlistment bounty. Bailey remains the highest-ranking known female soldier of the American Revolution and one of the few known women caught disguised as a male soldier.

Ann (or Nancy) Bailey's birth date is unknown. At the time of the Revolution, she was living in Boston, Massachusetts. During the early years of the conflict, Boston suffered at the hands of the British. American boycotts of British goods, the closure of the Boston harbor by British ships, the occupation of Boston by British troops, and the siege of Boston from April 1775 to March 1776 all took their toll on the citizens of the city. It was in this climate that Bailey attempted to enlist.

Bailey enlisted on February 14, 1777, into Capt. Hunt's company in the 1st Massachusetts Regiment under Col. Joseph Vose, with Col. John Patterson as commanding officer. Disguised as a man, Bailey gave her name as "Samuel Gay." Muster master for Suffolk County Nathaniel Barber's enlistment of Gay/Bailey raised no suspicion. During the

Revolution, no physical examination existed; if the recruit appeared fit enough, had three teeth (two upper, one lower) for biting open a musket cartridge, and a trigger finger, the recruit was accepted. However, if there was some question as to the sex of the recruit, the commission that the muster master received for each recruit may have induced him to look the other way. In any case, Gay/Bailey joined the Continental Army with comparative ease and received fifteen pounds, ten shillings as a bonus for enlisting.

For three weeks, Gay/Bailey's true identity went undiscovered. Hygiene standards of the day aided this effort; soldiers typically slept in their clothes, very rarely bathed, and frequently disregarded the order to use the necessaries, or privies, choosing to relieve themselves in other locations. These conditions would have helped to hide Gay/Bailey from the scrutiny of the other soldiers. During these three weeks, Gay/Bailey distinguished herself as an outstanding recruit and was promoted to corporal. Given this fact, it is unlikely that she enlisted for purely financial motives.

After three weeks, however, Gay/Bailey disappeared. Hunt discovered that his outstanding recruit was actually a woman on Monday, March 3, 1777. Sometime around this date, Gay disappeared, and the captain swore out a warrant for her arrest on March 10, 1777, for a "Nancy Bailey," mistaking her first name. Bailey was eventually caught and arraigned for trial before the Superior Court of Judicature, now known as the Massachusetts Judicial Court. On August 26, 1777, Bailey was found guilty of dressing in men's clothing and fraudulently enlisting in the Continental Army. Bailey was sentenced to two month in prison and a fine of £16 in addition to court fees.

After sentencing, Bailey disappeared from all record. It is believed that she served her time and paid the fines. The lack of complete records has also led to misconceptions. Some sources claim her highest rank at sergeant, while others state that Bailey served two years in prison. However, the rank of corporal and the prison sentence of two months are generally accepted as accurate.

Bailey is one of the few known women who served disguised as a male soldier. Unlike other female soldiers such as Deborah Sampson and Anna Maria Lane who are remembered as heroines, Bailey's exploits resulted in punishment. The story of Samuel Gay remains one of the more shadowy accounts from the American Revolution. The lack of information and conflicting accounts highlight the struggle that historians face in researching women in combat during this era.

Ashley L. Shimer

See also: American Revolution (1775–1783); Lane, Anna Maria (n.d.–1810); Samson [Sampson] (Gannett), Deborah [Robert Shurtliff] (1760–1827).

References and Further Reading

Burgan, Michael. *Great Women of the American Revolution.* Mankato, MN: Compass Point Books, 2005.

The History Project. *Improper Bostonians: Lesbian and Gay History from the Puritans to Playland.* Boston: Beacon Press, 1998.

Leonard, Patrick J. "Ann Bailey: Mystery Woman Warrior of 1777." *Minerva* 11, no. 3 (1993): 1.

GELLHORN, MARTHA (1908–1998)

War correspondent, novelist, journalist, and travel writer Martha Gellhorn was a witness to the major conflicts of the 20th century. She produced firsthand accounts of wars from Spain in the 1930s to Panama in the 1980s.

Gellhorn was born in St. Louis, Missouri, to suffragette and social reformer Edna Fischel and medical doctor George Gellhorn. She had two older brothers, George and Walter, and one younger brother, Alfred, with whom she was particularly close. She attended the

War correspondent Martha Gellhorn gave readers firsthand accounts of wars around the globe from the 1930s to the 1980s. (Hulton Archive/Getty Images)

John Burroughs School and then Bryn Mawr College from 1927 until 1930.

After spending the early 1930s in Paris, Gellhorn returned to the United States and worked for the Federal Emergency Relief Administration (FERA), a New Deal program under the administration of President Franklin Delano Roosevelt. She reported on the plight of the unemployed in North Carolina and South Carolina, where she became known for her excellent listening and reporting skills. First Lady Eleanor Roosevelt, who was a college friend of Gellhorn's mother, invited her to stay at the White House, and the two became life-long friends. In 1936, Gellhorn wrote the well-received *The Trouble I Have Seen*, a fictionalized account of her FERA experiences.

On Christmas Day 1936, Gellhorn met Ernest Hemingway in Sloppy Joe's, a bar and one of Hemingway's favorite haunts in Key West, Florida. From 1937 to 1939, she thrived in her career as a war correspondent covering the Spanish Civil War with Hemingway. She was especially apt at reporting on the toll of the war on civilians. In 1940, the couple married. From 1942 to 1943, they lived together in Cuba, where Gellhorn wrote *Liana*, a collection of short stories. At first, Gellhorn enjoyed sharing her life and writing schedule with Hemingway. She eventually found life with Hemingway in Cuba suffocating, however. She became restless and yearned to return to war reporting. Their marriage would end in December 1945.

She returned to life as a war correspondent, covering the Nazi Blitz on Britain, the landing at Normandy, and other wartime events. In December 1944, Gellhorn reported on the Battle of the Bulge. Her story captured Adolf Hitler's desperate attempt to wage an offensive on the Western Front and is considered by journalists and historians to be one of the greatest war dispatches ever written. In May 1945, shortly after American soldiers liberated Dachau, she reported from the Nazi concentration camp.

After World War II, Gellhorn lived in Washington, D.C., Mexico, and Israel. In Israel, she covered Adolf Eichmann's trial. In November 1949, she adopted her son, Sandy, from an Italian orphanage. They lived in New Mexico, then Rome, and then London, where she married Time, Inc., editor T. S. Matthews in February 1954. Matthews also had a son named Sandy, with whom Gellhorn forged a close relationship. Her marriage to Matthews, however, did not last long, and the couple divorced in 1963, with Gellhorn once again returning to work as a war correspondent.

In the mid-1960s, Gellhorn traveled to Vietnam, where she worked for the *Guardian* of London. Unlike other war correspondents who reported on the political nature of the war, Gellhorn focused her stories on the war's profound effects on women and children. Her stories were shocking, filled with outrage, and highly critical of the United States.

In 1970, in her early sixties, Gellhorn bought a flat in the fashionable Cadogan Square in London, where she lived for the last three decades of her life as a cosmopolitan expatriate. Despite her reputation as a mentor to male journalists exclusively, whom she referred to as her "chaps," Gellhorn also reached out to aspiring female journalists by sending them congratulatory notes on their work and words of encouragement to continue to produce good stories.

Publicly, Gellhorn was a courageous and candid war correspondent. However, in letters to her friends and family she struggled with feelings of self-doubt and a profound sense of failure. Despite her public persona as a writer in general and as a war correspondent in particular, she was a deeply private person, and she pushed away biographers' attempts to understand her life fully. Her memoir *Travels with Myself and Another* (1978) is the closest of her writings to an autobiography. In 1988, the Atlantic Monthly Press published over 30 of her most significant stories in the brilliant antiwar book *The Face of War*. In 1998, at the age of 89, suffering from cancer of the ovaries and liver, she killed herself. She was cremated, and her stepson Sandy Matthews threw her remains off the Thames Tower Bridge.

Over the course of her productive and prolific career, Gellhorn wrote 12 works of fiction and 3 works of nonfiction. Her stories appeared regularly in the *Spectator, Collier's*, the *New Republic*, the *Saturday Evening Post*, the *Atlantic Monthly, Ladies' Home Journal, Harper's*, the *New York Times, New York Magazine, Observer Magazine, Granta*, and the *Guardian*.

Theresa C. Lynch

See also: Vietnam War (1965–1973); World War II (1941–1945).

References and Further Reading

Gellhorn, Martha. *The Face of War*. New York: Atlantic Monthly Press, 1988. Originally published 1959.

Gellhorn, Martha. *Point of No Return*. Lincoln: University of Nebraska Press, 1989. Originally published 1948.

Gellhorn, Martha. *Selected Letters of Martha Gellhorn*. Edited by Caroline Moorhead. New York: Henry Holt and Company, 2006.

Gellhorn, Martha. *Travels with Myself and Another*. New York: Jeremy P. Tacher/ Putnam, 1978.

Gellhorn, Martha. *The View from the Ground*. New York: Atlantic Monthly Press, 1988.

Moorhead, Caroline. *Gellhorn: A Twentieth-Century Life*. New York: Henry Holt and Company, 2003.

Rollyson, Carl. *Beautiful Exile: The Life of Martha Gellhorn*. Lincoln, NE: iUniverse, 2001.

GLASPIE, APRIL CATHERINE (1942–)

April Glaspie was the first woman appointed as a U.S. ambassador to an Arab state. From 1989 to 1990, she served as ambassador to Iraq, appointed to that post by President George H. W. Bush.

Born on April 26, 1942, in Vancouver, Canada, Glaspie graduated from Mills College in 1963 with a BA and from the Johns Hopkins University Paul H. Nitze School of Advanced International Relations in 1965 with an MA. She entered the U.S. diplomatic corps in 1966 and held a variety of posts, mainly in the Middle East.

Fluent in Arabic, Glaspie is best remembered for a meeting with Iraqi president Saddam Hussein on July 25, 1990, eight days before the Iraqi invasion of Kuwait. Two transcripts exist of this meeting: excerpts provided by the government of Iraq to the *New York Times* and published on September 23, 1990, and a U.S. version from a cable, sent by the U.S. Embassy in Baghdad, summarizing the meeting.

Based on both transcripts but particularly on the Iraqi version, some have alleged that Glaspie's statements to Hussein encouraged him to invade Kuwait by giving him the impression that the United States was disinterested in Iraq's feud with Kuwait, including its military buildup along the Kuwaiti border. According to the Iraqi transcript, Glaspie allegedly gave Hussein a "green light" to invade Kuwait by telling him that "we have no opinion on the Arab-Arab conflicts, like your border disagreement with Kuwait[,] . . . and [Secretary of State] James Baker has directed our official spokesmen to emphasize this instruction." The U.S. transcript, however, has Glaspie first asking Hussein about his intentions, based on his declaration that recent Kuwaiti actions were the equivalent of military aggression and his deployment of troops along Kuwait's border. Only then did she say that "we take no position on these Arab affairs," without specifically mentioning the border dispute between Iraq and Kuwait. According to the U.S. cable, however, the ambassador made clear that the United States could "never excuse settlements of dispute by other than peaceful means."

Because Iraq's invasion of Kuwait was unexpected in Washington, Glaspie's words were seen by some as encouraging Hussein to invade Kuwait. Although she clearly did not take a position regarding Iraq's border dispute with Kuwait, this was not the same thing as saying that she invited or endorsed an Iraqi invasion.

Also, neither the United States, Kuwait, the rest of the Arab world, nor even Egyptian president Hosni Mubarak, who was mediating the dispute and had brokered a series of upcoming meetings between Iraq and Kuwait, expected an invasion. Instead, Hussein was believed to be merely bluffing to intimidate Kuwait into forgiving Iraq's large debts to Kuwait amassed during its eight-year war with Iran (1980–1988) and to lower its oil production to raise the price of oil and thus enhance Iraqi revenues.

Even if Hussein had indeed asked to meet with Glaspie to gauge her response on the United States' position regarding Iraq's dispute with Kuwait, she cannot be blamed for saying something that she was neither authorized nor expected to communicate. Also, it is highly unlikely that Hussein would have been deterred from invading Kuwait by mere words alone, particularly given the fact that the United States had scant military resources to back up any such warnings. On the other hand, the meeting between Hussein and Glaspie raises a cautionary note from which all diplomats can learn, that is, what one does not say can be just as telling as what one actually utters.

After leaving Iraq following the Iraqi invasion of Kuwait, Glaspie was posted to the U.S. Diplomatic Mission to the United Nations. She concluded her diplomatic career as consul general in Cape Town in South Africa in 2002, when she retired.

Stefan Brooks

See also: Cold War (ca. 1947–1991); Gulf War (1991).

References and Further Reading

Bush, George, and Brent Scowcroft. *A World Transformed.* New York: Knopf, 1998.

Freedman, Lawrence, and Efraim Karsh. *The Gulf Conflict, 1990–1991: Diplomacy and War in the New World Order.* Princeton, NJ: Princeton University Press, 1993.

Sifry, Micah, and Christopher Cerf, eds. *The Gulf War Reader.* New York: Three Rivers Press, 1991.

GOLD STAR MOTHERS' PILGRIMAGES (1930s)

Between 1930 and 1933, the U.S. government underwrote and organized a series of trips to Europe to allow mothers and widows of servicemen killed in World War I to visit the graves of their loved ones. More than 6,600 women—the vast majority of them mothers—participated in what were commonly called the "gold star mothers' pilgrimages." The campaign for the legislation, as well as the government's conduct of the pilgrimages, reveal the potency of a highly sentimental, nationalistic, and racialized conception of motherhood during the interwar period.

Enacted in March 1929, the pilgrimage legislation stands out as a striking departure in an era noted for its fiscal conservatism and limited conception of government. Although private organizations in the United States and other combatant nations had arranged for pilgrimages to World War I battlefields and cemeteries during the 1920s, in no other instance did a government assume responsibility for funding and conducting such a program. The legislation owed its success to the efforts of newly founded war mothers' organizations that tirelessly promoted the pilgrims during the 1920s. Advocates portrayed the pilgrimages as providing a social service designed to meet the special needs of a uniquely deserving group of citizens: only by actually witnessing their sons' gravesites, they argued, would the nation's grieving mothers be able to reconcile themselves to their enormous sacrifice. The term *gold star mother* referred to the tradition, first established during the war, of using service flags with blue stars to signal a family member serving the military; if a serviceman died, a gold star would be superimposed over the blue star.

Largely forgotten today, the pilgrimages made front-page news in the 1930s. The program even inspired a Hollywood movie, John Ford's *The Pilgrimage*, released in 1933. Although some congresspeople had argued that the Red Cross should conduct the pilgrimages as peace missions, responsibility for the program instead fell to the Quartermaster Corps of the U.S. Army, which ran the pilgrimages as quasi-military ventures steeped in patriotic ritual. Small towns often held ceremonies to mark the departure of their local heroines, who first traveled to New York to board liners that carried them across the Atlantic. The women spent a total of two weeks in Europe (mostly in France), shepherded though detailed itineraries that included not only trips to the newly completed U.S. military cemeteries but also sightseeing and shopping excursions. An article in the Quartermaster Corps' official publication captured the tone of the venture when it promised that each pilgrim would feel "as though some 'influential' friend, with 'means,' had invited her to take a trip to Europe, which is exactly the case." Letters from many grateful pilgrims bear out this prediction. For instance, one woman who fell ill during her pilgrimage later wrote to President Herbert Hoover that she had been treated like a queen.

One group of women, however, did not receive first-class treatment—at least not while they remained in the United States. Whereas the War Department grouped all the other pilgrims according their home states, African American gold star mothers and wives were required to sail in separate, segregated groups. Moreover, they stayed in facilities like the Harlem Young Womens' Christian Association (YWCA) in New York and traveled on second-tier passenger ships, whereas the larger white parties stayed in first-class hotels and sailed on luxury liners. African Americans vehemently protested this discriminatory treatment, pressuring the Hoover Administration to reverse its Jim Crow policy. When their efforts failed, the NAACP, along with leading black newspapers like the *Chicago Defender* and the *Pittsburgh Courier*, urged all eligible women to boycott the pilgrimages. Though dozens of women upheld the boycott, roughly 280 black gold star mothers and wives ultimately took part in the pilgrimages, traveling in separate groups overseen by Lt. Col. Benjamin O. Davis, then the highest-ranking African American in the U.S. Army. The parties received a warm welcome in Paris, where famous African American expatriates like Noble Sissle and "Bricktop" Smith feted them.

Although many individual pilgrims expressed satisfaction with their experiences, the government's discriminatory treatment of the black gold star pilgrims remained a potent political issue well into the 1930s. Indeed, rumors that the pilgrims had been sent to Europe on "cattle boats" circulated widely in black communities, helping to fuel African Americans' abandonment of the Republican Party.

Although the pilgrimage legislation enjoyed broad, bipartisan support, the war mothers' success reflected a rightward political shift and a growing polarization within the ranks of organized womanhood. As patriotic women's groups gained strength and visibility in the 1920s, progressive women who had long lobbied for social welfare legislation increasingly found their proposals denounced as "Bolshevist." Only a few months after enacting the pilgrimage bill, Congress refused to renew funding for progressive women's most critical achievement—the Sheppard-Towner Act, a federally funded program designed to improve the health of mothers and children. Thus, even as Congress enacted an expensive measure designed to honor bereaved war mothers, it withdrew support for the more material needs of "practicing" mothers.

Rebecca Jo Plant

See also: African American Women; World War I (1914–1918).

References and Further Reading

Budreau, Lisa. *Bodies of War: World War I and the Politics of Commemoration in America,* *1919–1933.* New York: New York University Press, 2009.

Graham, John. *The Gold Star Mother Pilgrimages of the 1930s.* Jefferson, NC: McFarland, 2005.

Piehler, G. Kurt. "The War Dead and the Gold Star: American Commemoration of the First World War." In *Commemorations: The Politics of National Identity,* edited by John R. Gillis, 168–85. Princeton, NJ: Princeton University Press, 1994.

Plant, Rebecca Jo. *Mom: The Transformation of Motherhood in Modern America.* Chicago: University of Chicago Press, 2010.

GOODRICH, ANNIE WARBURTON (1866–1954)

Annie Warburton Goodrich was the first dean of the U.S. Army School of Nursing (1918–1919).

Goodrich was born on February 6, 1866, in New Jersey to Samuel Griswold and Annie Butler Goodrich. One of seven children, her parents both came from prominent New England families. Her grandfather, John S. Butler, MD, was a psychiatrist who ran the Hartford Retreat for 30 years. Her early education came from governesses and private schools in the United States as well as in France and England, where her father's business took the family. When her father became ill, they returned and settled in Hartford, Connecticut, and the Butler grandparents came to live with them. Upon the death of both of her grandparents and understanding that the illness of her father required her to be self-supporting, she looked into the limited career options open to young women. Goodrich overcame her distaste for dealing with illness and applied to the New York Hospital's Nurses' Training School. She was accepted at age 24 and six months, when the minimum age for acceptance into the program was normally 25.

In addition to having a good bedside manner, Goodrich was found to be responsible, disciplined, and able to face emergencies with poise. She earned her RN in 1892. Out of school for just over a year, she was offered the position of superintendent of nurses at New York Post-Graduate Medical School and Hospital. Founded in 1885, it was the third training school for nurses in New York City after Bellevue and her alma mater. It was while she was in this position that Goodrich became aware of many of the difficulties in the methodology of nursing education. Her talent for administration was brought out as Goodrich worked to establish professional standards for nursing at New York Post-Grad for seven years. From there she went on to be director of training school at three other New York schools: first at St. Luke's, followed by New York Hospital, and then at Bellevue.

After 17 years of experience she became inspector of nurses' training schools for the state of New York, a position she held until 1914. Goodrich observed that the trend since her training years had been to take younger and younger women into training, so that many of the incoming nursing students were only 17 or 18 years old, and some had only a grade school education. New York soon passed a new law that required one year of high school on applications, while all four schools where she worked continued to require a high school diploma for admission.

In 1914, Goodrich became an assistant professor at Teachers College, and in 1917 added director of Henry Street Visiting Nurses' Service to her responsibilities. World War I interrupted her life and career, as it did that of most Americans. In February 1918, she was named chief inspecting nurse of all U.S. Army hospitals to which nurses were assigned. She saw a need for more trained nurses and immediately developed a plan for a school of nursing to meet the needs of the Army. By May, the secretary of war approved her plan, and she was named dean of the new Army School of Nursing. When the armistice came six months later, it was shown that the plan would be effective in peacetime as well, so the school operated until 1931. Meanwhile, Goodrich returned to civilian life in 1919. In 1923, she worked with a committee to establish the Yale University School of Nursing and was named its first dean and professor of nursing education. Eleven years later, she helped establish the Yale Graduate School of Nursing.

Goodrich retired at the age of 68 and returned to Hartford but did not completely settle down. She served as a consultant to the Hartford Retreat, by then renamed the Institute for Living. She celebrated her 80th birthday at the Waldorf Astoria in New York City, a party attended by hundreds of nursing leaders and educators from around the country. The president of the United States sent birthday greetings, and actress Helen Hayes delivered birthday wishes in person. Other honors she received include the Distinguished Service Medal (1923), an honorary degree of doctor of science (ScD) from Mount Holyoke College (1921), an honorary degree of master of arts (MA) from Yale University (1923), and the honorary degree of doctor of laws (LLD) from Russell Sage College (1936).

Goodrich died on December 31, 1954, leaving a legacy for military and civilian nurses alike.

Katherine Burger Johnson

See also: Nursing; World War I (1914–1918).

References and Further Reading

Goodrich, Annie Warburton. *The Social and Ethical Significance of Nursing: A Series of Addresses*. Reprint, New Haven, CT: Yale University School of Nursing, 1973.

Koch, Harriet Berger. *Militant Angel*. New York: Macmillan, 1951.

Sicherman, Barbara, and Carol Hurd Green. *Notable American Women: The Modern Period: A Biographical Dictionary, Volume 4*. Cambridge, UK: Radcliffe College, 1980.

GOVERNMENT GIRLS

The term *government girls* was initially used to identify young women who came to work for the expanding federal government during the Civil War, many as clerks in the Treasury and War departments. The term was again employed during World War II to describe women working in war-related jobs.

During the Civil War, women took on the tasks left empty by the men who had left for the battlefield. In the Treasury Department, they trimmed and counted currency and worked as copyists. Their $600 annual pay was half that of men doing the same work. Some men in Washington found government girls'

standing as independent women dangerous. In one instance in 1864, critics, including congressmen, instigated an investigation that involved breaking into government girls' rooms and confiscating their diaries and letters. In addition, they forced some women to sign confessions admitting to their supposedly immoral behavior. This reputation proved difficult to shake, in spite of the women's devotion to the war effort.

The term reappeared during World War II, with a massive increase in government. Government girls, also known as GGs, converged in the thousands on Washington, D.C., to take war-related jobs. At its peak, the federal government employed 3,750,000 civilian employees during World War II. Over 2 million women across the nation took office jobs, and women's clerical jobs increased twofold during the war. *Government girls* also became an appellation for women who took government jobs in other cities and overseas. The New York City Defense Recreation Committee, for example, advertised dances for local "Government Girls."

Like "gunpowder girls," also known as Rosie the Riveter or Wanda the Welder, in war-related industries, government girls came from across the country, even if the press and public deemed clerical work less dramatic than the construction of airplanes or ships. Calls for women to help with war work cast a wide net. Propaganda included government-produced posters, films, and newsreels. In addition, a film by the War Production Board, *The Glamour Girls of 1943*, urged women with high school diplomas and college degrees to come to Washington. Agencies including the Office of Price Administration, War

Department, Civil Service Commission, and War Production Board sent recruiters across the country.

When the arrival of women workers in the nation's capital increased in early 1942, news stories extolled women's eagerness to join the war effort and highlighted the new tasks and difficulties facing these workers. These reports often focused on the assumed superficial aspects of government girls, labeling these women the "lipstick brigade" or the "Secretaries of War." In reality, government girls fulfilled many necessary tasks. Although much of the work was clerical and included typing military requisition forms and checking counterfeit ration stamps, others involved cryptology or manual work in the Bureau of Engraving or in the Washington Navy Yard. Some women took civilian jobs in the military branches; others joined the Office of Strategic Services, where they ended up in service overseas in morale- and espionage-related activities.

Pay for World War II government girls started at $1,440 a year. In December 1942, Congress passed the Federal Overtime Pay Bill, which raised salaries for those who worked overtime and raised morale as well. Those not permitted overtime pay received a salary increase. The highest wages reached about $3,000 a year.

The government struggled to organize quickly the immense task of running a war effort. Not enough structures existed to hold wartime employees, so temporary buildings were placed on the National Mall. In the temporary buildings thrown up on the Mall, sultry summers made the interiors so hot that salt tablets were placed near water fountains. Workers could be dismissed on days when the temperature hit 90 degrees. Although many women worked long hours, others objected to not having enough to do.

Seeking more space for its ever-expanding needs, the federal government requisitioned private buildings, transforming kitchens and bathrooms into workspaces. Facing a shortage of typewriters, government agencies advertised for donations from across the country, reminding citizens that it took 25 girls behind typewriters to put one man behind the trigger. Dozens of women were needed to calculate figures that might, in the computer age, take one person a few minutes. Thousands of other women came to the capital to work in war-related jobs, from domestic work to jobs in retail or private industry.

Much of wartime life was impromptu and at times uncomfortable. In addition to dealing with the rationing of food and other goods, this new workforce faced a critical housing shortage. Tripling up in one room was common, although some women found single rooms in government-sponsored housing. The Arlington Farms Residence Hall, across the Potomac near the newly constructed Pentagon, was one of 10 residences that housed 5,000 single female government workers. The enlightened efforts at Arlington Farms, with the backing of First Lady Eleanor Roosevelt, had a beauty parlor, a cafeteria, a small department store, an infirmary, and Works Progress Administration (WPA) art in public areas.

For some women, the adjustment to life as a government girl proved difficult in other ways. The War Department initiated budget-training classes to help women manage their slim salaries.

In addition, the government made mental health workers available for its employees. A film inspired in part by these changes, *Government Girl* starring Sunny Tufts and Olivia de Havilland, opened in January 1944.

One issue deemed potentially troubling to officials was the greater number of women than men in government workplaces. This concern fed the national anxiety about young women's independence, which included new sexual opportunities. Many women reveled in this freedom. Some became hostesses at United Service Organizations (USO) canteens. Others enjoyed the bustling city's nightlife and mingled with soldiers who came through on weekends. Some personnel branches organized buses for women to get to nearby Fort Meade for dances.

Racial segregation remained the rule in wartime Washington, as it did in the U.S. armed forces, but there were challenges in the capital. In 1938, 90 percent of black workers in the federal government toiled in custodial work. Although thousands of African American women received telegrams inviting them to come to the District, they were initially limited to menial jobs. As students from Howard University protested segregated restaurants, the National Council of Negro Women and its director, Mary McLeod Bethune, protested the employment restrictions. In response, the federal government told the heads of its major agencies to promote black women to higher employment grades. By 1942, 48 percent of black women were in clerical, administrative, and professional jobs in the federal government, advances that helped fuel the civil rights movement. Even as

D.C. remained a Jim Crow town, blacks and whites mingled in the U Street Corridor, not far from the White House.

Women workers were not without their faults or critics. As the war wound down, some congressional critics objected to some women's low productivity and long coffee breaks as well as to women coming to work drunk. Congressman Earl Wilson of Indiana proposed, unsuccessfully, a 10:00 p.m. curfew for government girls to curtail their evening outings. By August 1945, the government promised to pay fares for women who were returning home. Although often controversial, government girls proved invaluable to the United States' war effort.

Page Dougherty Delano

See also: African American Women; Bethune, Mary McLeod (1875–1955); Civil War (1861–1865); Rosie the Riveter; United Service Organizations (USO); World War II (1941–1945).

References and Further Reading

Brinkley, David. *Washington Goes to War.* New York: Knopf, 1988.

Campbell, D'Ann. *Women at War with America: Private Lives in a Patriotic Era.* Cambridge, MA: Harvard University Press, 1984.

Chafe, William. *The American Woman: Her Changing Social, Economic and Political Roles, 1920–1970.* New York: Oxford University Press, 1972.

Davol, Leslie T. "Shifting Mores: Esther Bubley's World War II Boarding House Photos." *Washington History* 10, no. 2 (1998–1999): 44–62.

Massey, Mary Elizabeth. *Women in the Civil War.* Lincoln: University of Nebraska Press, 1994.

Murray, Pauli. *Song in a Weary Throat: An American Pilgrimage.* New York: Harper and Row, 1987.

Sewell, Leslie, dir. *The Government Girls of World War II.* Documentary film. 2004.

Silber, Nina. *Daughters of the Union: Northern Women Fight the Civil War.* Cambridge, MA: Harvard University Press, 2005.

WETA TV. *Homefront: World War II in Washington.* Documentary film. 2007.

Zeinert, Karen. *Those Courageous Women of the Civil War.* Millbrook, CT: Millbrook Press, 1998.

GRAY LADY CORPS

The Gray Lady Corps is the unofficial name for the Hostess and Hospital Service and Recreation Corps, a volunteer branch of the American Red Cross. It was founded in 1918 at the Walter Reed Army Hospital in Washington, D.C., by the head of the Red Cross, Mabel Boardman. The organization was dissolved in the mid-1960s. The Gray Lady Corps peaked in membership during World War II, with almost 50,000 members.

The Gray Ladies got their name from their uniforms of gray dresses and white veils. From the beginning, the Gray Ladies were associated with services provided by the American Red Cross to soldiers and veterans. The primary purpose of the Ladies was to provide non-medical care to patients, such as reading books to them, writing letters for them, tutoring patients, driving cars to provide soldiers' outings, and shopping for patients who were bedridden. Often, the Gray Ladies became the primary caregivers for the soldiers; nurses and doctors provided all of the medical care, but it was the Gray Ladies as an organization that saw to the soldiers' needs on a daily basis. Ladies usually served only one day a week, so soldiers who saw a Gray Lady regularly rarely saw the same woman from one day to the next. This practice led to the Gray Ladies' nickname—soldiers referred to the constantly changing women as "my Monday Gray Lady, my Tuesday Gray Lady. . . ."

In addition to providing care to invalid soldiers, the Gray Ladies also provided basic services within Walter Reed Army Hospital, serving as guides and hostesses and working at information desks. As a result, not only were Gray Ladies the figures that soldiers were most likely to encounter in the hospital, they also served as the hospital's public face.

During the 1930s, the role of the Gray Ladies changed in a number of ways. In an effort to combat unemployment during the Great Depression, President Franklin D. Roosevelt created the Veterans Administration, which took over the professional staffing of veteran hospitals like Walter Reed. As a result, in 1931 the Red Cross began to pull its professional staff out of newly created Veterans Administration hospitals. This withdrawal left a need for the sort of direct care that the Gray Ladies were known for, and so the Ladies stepped in to fill the void and began to spread to other hospitals, both military and civilian, all over the United States.

At the same time, Roosevelt began a process of replacing volunteers by hiring unemployed people directly onto the federal payroll. Although this type of hiring had a negative effect upon volunteer organizations in general, the Red Cross prospered during this period.

In particular, a growing demand for first aid training resulted in a need for more trained volunteers to teach first aid classes. The expansion of the mission of the Gray Ladies, combined with the general expansion of the American Red Cross, resulted in a significant increase of membership in the Gray Ladies. This expansion, combined with a sense that the work being done by the group was necessary and a belief that the training provided to the Ladies was authentic and valuable, made the Corps significant in ways unrelated to their role within the Red Cross. In 1934, the name of the branch was shortened to Hospital and Recreation Corps.

During the 1930s, the use of uniforms in the Gray Lady Corps helped to combat a strong belief that the Red Cross was particularly interested in upper-class volunteers. Seeing that uniforms served to blur the distinctions between social classes, Boardman introduced elements of the uniform, such as service pins and chevrons for hours served, to the other volunteer branches. By 1938, full uniforms, an idea that had started with the Gray Ladies, were common throughout the American Red Cross.

During World War II, the Hospital and Recreation Corps recruited extensively in the United States, especially in cities that were home to military bases and military hospitals. As of 1944, the Corps consisted of 49,882 qualified volunteers, serving in over 1,000 military and veterans' hospitals across the United States. The Gray Ladies continued to provide an important service to recovering soldiers, acting as the primary caregivers. Many of the women who volunteered for service as Gray Ladies on the homefront stated that they were providing for soldiers the same services that other members of the American Red Cross were providing for their husbands and sons overseas. As a result, the Gray Lady Corps was an important way for women to see themselves as connected to the war effort.

After the war, the American Red Cross acknowledged the common nickname for the Hospital and Recreation Service and, in 1947, renamed the group the Gray Lady Service. The service was also expanded again, with some members of the Gray Ladies beginning to serve in military hospitals overseas. During the Korean War, wounded servicemen might have encountered members of the Gray Lady Service in hospitals in Japan as well as upon their return to the United States. One of the new services that the Gray Ladies provided overseas was a free "first call home" service for wounded soldiers; the Gray Ladies often brought phones directly to the beds of soldiers so they could make the call.

Membership in the Gray Lady Service peaked during World War II. As women found new ways to gain skills and work outside the home, interest in the Service declined. In the mid-1960s, the American Red Cross decided to consolidate all of its volunteer branches into a single Red Cross Volunteer branch, and the Gray Lady Service ended. Despite that, the lingering memory of the Service has kept the name in circulation, and many chapters of the Red Cross still refer to volunteers providing hospitality and recreation services as Gray Ladies or Gray Lads.

Mike Timonin

See also: American Red Cross; Korean War (1950–1953); Roosevelt, Eleanor (1884–1962); World War II (1941–1945).

References and Further Reading

Gilbo, Patrick F. *The American Red Cross: The First Century.* New York: Harper and Row, 1981.

Hurd, Charles. *The Compact History of the American Red Cross.* New York: Hawthorn Press, 1959.

Smith, Jill Halcomb. *Dressed for Duty: America's Women in Uniform 1898–1973, Vol I.* San Jose, CA: R.J. Bender Publishing, 2001.

Confederate spy Rose O'Neal Greenhow continued her espionage activities while under house arrest with her youngest daughter. (Library of Congress)

GREENHOW, ROSE O'NEAL (CA. 1814–1864)

A Confederate spy during the American Civil War, Rose O'Neal Greenhow published her wartime diary in 1863.

Confusion exists as to the exact year of the birth of Maria Rosatta O'Neale, popularly known as Rose O'Neal Greenhow. Many sources state the year as 1817, while others confidently place it three years earlier in 1814. In any case, she was born on her family's plantation in Montgomery County, Maryland, to Eliza Henrettia Hamilton and John O'Neale. She was the third of five daughters.

The untimely death of her father left the family in financial difficulties, which prompted Rose and her sister Eleanor to relocate with an aunt and uncle in Washington, D.C. These relatives operated the Congressional Boarding House close to the Capitol. In this setting, Rose mingled with numerous politicians of the day, developing a close relationship with many of them, including two-time vice president and senator John C. Calhoun. She also became a noted fixture at social gatherings of the rich and powerful.

Rose wed Dr. Robert Greenhow, a U.S. State Department employee, in 1835. The couple had seven children during their marriage, only three of whom lived to adulthood. The Greenhows left behind their socialite lives in 1850 to move to San Francisco, where Robert opened a law firm. In March 1864, while Rose was visiting family in D.C., her husband died from complications of injuries he sustained from a fall. She returned to California, where she successfully sued the city for his injuries. She won a $10,000 settlement and returned to the capital to resume her old life. During this period, she became one of Washington's most influential people. She maintained friendships with President James Buchanan as well as with a stable of government employees and statesmen.

The political climate of D.C. changed in 1860 with the election of Abraham Lincoln. Tensions increased with the secession of South Carolina in December, followed by that of other slaveholding states in early 1861, and the Confederate capture of Fort Sumter that April. Greenhow's connections and pro-South loyalties marked her as a valuable asset in the world of espionage. Thomas Jordan, a U.S. captain with Confederate ties, put together one of the earliest Confederate spy rings. Jordan approached Greenhow to join this fledgling operation, and after training and organizing it he placed Greenhow in charge of the spy ring.

After remaining with Union general Winfield Scott's staff for a month to gather information, Jordan departed to join the Confederate ranks. He left a cipher key for members of the spy ring to use. Greenhow mastered this cipher and expanded the number of spies. She continued to exploit her own relationships with those in power who backed the Northern war effort.

Through these systems, Greenhow obtained vital information regarding federal troop movements and strength in July 1861. She ably placed this information in the headquarters of Confederate general P. G. T. Beauregard. Forewarned, the Confederates used the information to improve their situation at the resulting Battle of Manassas (Bull Run). Greenhow received thanks for her services from President Jefferson Davis and a solicitation for more intelligence in a note from Jordan.

The federals were aware that there were holes in their security and appointed Allan Pinkerton, head of Lincoln's Secret Service, to root out the Confederate spies in D.C. On August 23, 1861, Greenhow was arrested and put under house arrest with her youngest daughter. Despite the presence of federal guards around her home, Greenhow continued to collect and transmit information. Greenhow and her daughter were transferred to harsher quarters in the Old Capitol Prison in January 1862. Five months later the two were released, officially banished from Northern territory.

The Greenhows made their way to Richmond, where President Davis met with them and praised Rose for her help at Bull Run. That summer, she boarded a blockade runner to Europe, tasked with drumming up support for the Confederacy overseas. Immersed in this new social scene, which included royalty, Greenhow found time to write her memoir of service, *My Imprisonment and the First Year of Abolitionist Rule* (1863). She decided to return to the Confederacy in 1864, once again chancing a blockade runner.

Her return ship, the *Condor*, ran aground outside the heavily guarded port of Wilmington, North Carolina. Anxious to avoid imprisonment, Greenhow and two other passengers disregarded the advice of the captain. They boarded a rowboat and tried to land ahead of the advancing federal warship. Heavy waves flipped their rowboat over. Greenhow, carrying a large cache of gold on her person, drowned. The next day a Confederate sentry found her body washed up on the beach. He looted the body before pushing it back out to sea. Hours later her body was rediscovered by

Confederates. Upon learning Greenhow's identity, the soldier who had taken the gold returned it.

Greenhow's body lay in state, shrouded with a Confederate flag, the night before her burial. On October 1, 1864, a processional of local Confederates placed Greenhow to rest in Oakdale Cemetery in Wilmington beneath a monument inscribed with her name and the legend "A Bearer of Dispatches to the Confederate Government."

Michael D. Coker

See also: Civil War (1861–1865); Espionage.

References and Further Reading

Axelrod, Alan. *The War between the Spies: A History of Espionage during the American Civil War.* New York: Atlantic Monthly Press, 1992.

Bakeless, John. *Spies of the Confederacy.* Mineola, NY: Dover Publications, 1970.

Blackman, Ann. *Wild Rose: The True Story a Civil War Spy.* New York: Random House, 2006.

Greenhow, Rose O'Neal. *My Imprisonment and the First Year of Abolition Rule at Washington.* London: Richard Bentley, 1863.

Markle, Donald E. *Spies and Spymasters of the Civil War.* New York: Barnes and Noble Publishing, 1994.

GREENWOOD, EDITH ELLEN (1920–)

Lieutenant Edith Ellen Greenwood served with the Army Nurse Corps (ANC) during World War II and was the first female recipient of the Soldier's Medal.

Born in 1920 in North Dartmouth, Bristol, Massachusetts, to Ellen E. (Pearson) and Frederick James Greenwood, she graduated from St. Luke's Hospital School of Nursing in New Bedford, Massachusetts.

Greenwood began serving with the ANC on September 16, 1942. She was assigned to the 37th Station Hospital near Yuma, Arizona, part of the Army's Desert Training Center, California-Arizona Maneuver Area (CAMA). CAMA was a new center established by Maj. Gen. George S. Patton and designed to provide military personnel with the special desert training needed for the war in North Africa. It consisted of 11 camps and was the largest military training ground in the history of military maneuvers, stretching from west of Pomona, California, to near Phoenix, Arizona, and from Yuma, Arizona, to Searchlight, Nevada. By January 1943, the center was ordered to function like a simulated theater of operations in a combat setting in order to establish a more realistic training environment. Due to this change, the Army Ground Forces decided that CAMA required the same type of hospitalization found in an actual theater of war. Nurses like Greenwood who served with the hospital units at CAMA received practical and invaluable training and experience.

At 6:30 a.m., on April 17, 1943, a stove exploded in the 37th Station Hospital's diet kitchen, setting fire to the nearby ward where Greenwood was responsible for overseeing the care of 15 patients. Greenwood sounded the alarm and attempted to extinguish the blaze, but the fire quickly spread, with reports indicating that the ward burned down within five minutes. Greenwood safely evacuated all of her patients with the assistance of a young ward attendant, Pvt. James F. Ford. By direction of President Franklin Delano Roosevelt, both Greenwood and Ford were awarded the Soldier's Medal on June 10, 1943, a medal given to a person in the armed forces for heroic conduct not involving conflict with the enemy. The medals were presented by Brig. Gen. Joseph Burton Sweet in a ceremony at CAMA. The War Department announced the conveying of the award on July 15, 1943.

Greenwood's efforts highlight the work of thousands of women with the ANC who remained in the continental United States during the war. These nurses worked at veterans' hospitals, military bases, hospital trains, and debarkation stations and saw to the care of military personnel in training or returned home. Though they were not exposed to the front-line conditions of their nursing sisters, ANC nurses on the homefront exhibited extraordinary heroism and sacrifice in service to their country.

Anne M. E. Millar

See also: Army Nurse Corps (ANC); Nursing; World War II (1941–1945).

References and Further Reading

"Army Nurses Receive Medals for Heroism." *New York Times*, July 16, 1943, 4.

Beall, C. C. "The Heroine on the Cover." *Collier's Illustrated Weekly* 113, no. 6 (April 15, 1944): 65.

Howard, George. "The Desert Training Center/California-Arizona Maneuver Area."
Journal of Arizona History 26, no. 3 (Fall 1985): 273–94.

Jackson, Kathi. *They Called Them Angels: American Military Nurses of World War II*. Lincoln: University of Nebraska Press, 2000.

Sadler, Christine. "Nurses' Morale Bubbling Over." *Washington Post*, August 15, 1943, B4.

Tomblin, Barbara Brooks. *G.I. Nightingales: The Army Nurse Corps in World War II*. Lexington: University Press of Kentucky, 1996.

GULF WAR (1991)

The Persian Gulf War, also known as Operation Desert Storm or the first Gulf War, began in response to Saddam Hussein's August 2, 1990, invasion of Kuwait. A coalition force of 34 countries joined in opposition to Saddam's invasion with the hope of driving Iraqi forces out of Kuwait. U.S. president George H. W. Bush deployed American forces to the Gulf, with Saudi Arabia, the United Kingdom, and Egypt also sending significant numbers of military personnel. The initial conflict began on January 17, 1991, with an aerial assault, followed by 100 hours of ground war beginning on February 23, 1991. A cease-fire was officially declared on February 28, 1991.

The Gulf War was the first major military deployment since Vietnam and involved a record number of American military women. It was also the first time that men and women served in integrated units in a war zone.

At the time, women constituted 8 percent of the armed forces, which was double the 4 percent they represented in 1989. In July 1991, the Pentagon reported that approximately 40,782 women had served in the Gulf, representing approximately 7.2 percent of the U.S. forces deployed. The majority of servicewomen came from the Army (approximately 26,000), with the Air Force, Navy, and Marines each also contributing significant numbers. Members of the National Guard were also deployed, as were 13 women from the Coast Guard.

Women served in a variety of roles in the Gulf War, some of which they had filled in previous wars. These included clerical, administrative, communications, and medical positions, in addition to positions on support and repair ships and as pilots of jets and helicopters. In the Gulf War, unlike in previous wars, women also operated prisoner of war (POW) camps and, for the first time, directed artillery fire and served with Patriot missile crews.

The experiences of servicewomen in the Gulf War demonstrated that the line between combat and support was not very distinct. Although women were excluded from the major U.S. fighting forces at the time, as well as any combat or service support units serving near the front lines that would expose them to direct combat, hostile fire, or capture, the war highlighted the difficulty of differentiating between combat and support roles.

In *Women in Combat: The U.S. Military and the Impact of the Persian Gulf War*, Georgia Clark Sadler gives some examples of how the line between combat and support was blurry in the Gulf War. For example, one Army military police unit with women assigned to it was airlifted to take charge of enemy prisoners and ended up ahead of two combat units (and behind only one). In

addition, although Air Force women were not allowed to fly fighter planes, they flew the tankers that refueled the fighters over Iraq.

As a result of this discrepancy, debate increased over the roles women could and should play in the military. In 1991, a Commission on the Assignment of Women in the Armed Forces was formed under Bush and on recommendation from Congress. The report considered the roles women should have in combat as well as the impact any changes would have on the military, particularly in terms of combat readiness.

After the war, proponents of expanding opportunities for women in the U.S. military used the discrepancy between what the laws and policies allowed for and the reality of women's experience in the war as evidence that the restrictive laws and policies should be removed. They also used the generally positive evaluations U.S. female military personnel received for their participation in the Gulf War. The Department of Defense (DoD) report to Congress on the war indicated that women had played an integral role in the operation, and General Accounting Office (GAO) interviews with deployed men and women showed that attitudes about women's performance were very positive. In addition, 14 Gulf War servicewomen received combat awards for crossing minefields during the ground war or for receiving and returning enemy fire.

A Roper Organization poll taken after the Gulf War showed growing acceptance of women in combat roles. Seventy-six percent of the public thought U.S. national security was best served by assigning the most qualified person to direct combat, regardless of sex, if that person met the qualifications. When asked about specific assignments, over 50 percent of the interviewees responded positively. Public response showed reluctance about putting women into combat only in the cases of being a marine landing on shore to attack the enemy or an infantry soldier fighting in hand-to-hand combat.

Growing public acceptance of women in combat roles was reflected in legal changes made shortly after the Gulf War. On May 22, 1991, as part of the Defense Authorization Act for fiscal years 1992 and 1993, the House removed all restrictions against Air Force, Navy, and Marine Corps women flying in combat aviation. Then, in November 1993, Congress reversed the combat ship exclusion as part of the National Defense Authorization Act for fiscal year 1994.

The debate over the role of women in the military has not changed much since the 1970s. Those opposed to women's inclusion claim various reasons. First, they argue that women are physically unfit for war. However, experience has shown that women's strength has been sufficient in many combat situations. Moreover, the increasingly important role of technology over hand-to-hand combat in warfare has made strength less important and women's physical abilities, such as speed and agility at fine motor skills, more relevant. However, the gender ratio of combat forces has only changed marginally compared to the widespread introduction of technology.

Second, those opposed to women in the military claim that women would negatively affect the cohesion and effectiveness of military units. This notion of "male bonding" underlies the U.S. military's policies excluding women from combat. Third, cultural expectations regarding gender roles have also been used to argue against the inclusion of women in the military. The argument suggests that women's alleged lower levels of aggression and greater nurturing tendencies prevent them from fighting successfully, although historically that has not been the case.

On the other hand, proponents of expanded roles for military women stress equality and its relationship to military service. They reject the idea that women are naturally unsuitable for military service and argue that women have the right to participate in all social and political roles in society without discrimination.

The increased presence of military women during the Gulf War brought the issue of pregnancy to the forefront of public discussion. The debate reflected the more general argument against the inclusion of women in the military, which held that women were physically unfit, and impractical, for military service.

At the time of the Gulf War, military policy granted women who had given birth maternity leave, after which they could return to duty. A February 1991 Associated Press poll demonstrated that Americans opposed the policy of sending mothers to the Gulf War by a 2-to-1 ratio; however some Americans expressed the opinion that mothers should not receive special treatment over military fathers.

The media often focused on military mothers, even referring to the operation as the "Mommy War" despite the fact that it was mostly servicemen who were deployed. This role reversal, which saw women becoming soldiers and men remaining at home to be the sole caregivers, captured the media's attention.

Public concern for families separated by war, particularly for children in a parentless home, increased. The House Subcommittee on Military Personnel and Compensation held hearings in February 1991 to evaluate the impact of Desert Storm deployments on service families headed by single parents and military couples. Although legislation was introduced to prohibit the combat deployment of sole parents and both members of a dual military couple, this legislation was opposed by the armed services and by military women's advocates, and it died. Some viewed the political debate as an attempt to undermine women's acceptance as military professionals, and military women insisted that they, rather than the government, had the right to make decisions for themselves concerning the care of their children.

The presence of women in the military also brought up the issue of sexual harassment in the military. During this period, the Tailhook scandal brought the problem of sexual harassment within the military to the public's attention. At the 35th Annual Tailhook Convention in Las Vegas, Nevada, on September 8–12, 1991, 83 female military personnel and 7 men reported being sexually harassed or assaulted.

When the incident was reported to Navy command, it blamed the women who had complained, and ignored the allegations. The DoD inspector general's office took over the investigations in June 1992, and after the Pentagon's initial report on September 24, 1992, the three Navy personnel responsible for the Tailhook investigation were removed

from their jobs. The final report, released on April 28, 1993, implicated 117 officers in indecent acts or failed acts of leadership. Altogether, approximately 50 people were disciplined, with most receiving letters of censure. As a result of the scandal, the Navy reinforced the Pentagon's 1988 "zero tolerance" policy on sexual harassment. Some scholars debate the merits of the "zero tolerance" policy, instead arguing that the change in policy barely affected the practice of sexual harassment in the U.S. military.

Despite the difficulties, many women rose to prominence during the Gulf War. Although her exact assignment has remained a secret, Sgt. Theresa Lynn Treloar, dubbed the "Ice Lady" by her colleagues, was the closest woman to the battlefront in the Gulf. She served with a squad affiliated with the Army's 2nd Armored Cavalry Regiment. Other women similarly played vital roles in the U.S. involvement.

Maj. Rhonda Cornum, an Army flight surgeon, served in the Gulf with the 101st Airborne Division. She became a POW after her Black Hawk helicopter was shot down on February 27, 1991, as she attempted to rescue a downed F-16 fighter pilot. Five of the eight people aboard were killed, and Cornum and two others were taken prisoner. She spent eight days as a POW before her release.

Other women faced difficult situations as well. Specialist Melissa Rathbun-Nealy was the first American female to be listed as missing in action (MIA), when Iraqi soldiers captured her in January 1991 after her truck became stuck in the sand. She was held for 34 days as a POW before her release.

Thirteen military women were among the 375 U.S. servicemembers killed in the Gulf War, five of them in action. Twenty-one were wounded in action. The first Americans to die in a war since Vietnam, and the first enlisted women ever to be killed in action, perished with 25 of their male colleagues on the night of February 25, 1991, when a Scud missile slammed into the military barracks near Dhahran. These women were Specialist Beverly Clark, Specialist Christine Mayes, and Specialist Adrienne L. Mitchell.

Some of the other 13 women to lose their lives in the war included Maj. Marie T. Rossi, Sgt. Cheryl LaBeau-O'Brien, Specialist Cindy Marie Beaudoin, Pvt. 1st Class Pamela Yvette Gay, Capt. Terry VandenDolder, Lt. Lorraine Kerstin Lawton, Sgt. Tracey Darlene Brogdon, and Pvt. Candace Moriah Daniel.

Alena Papayanis

See also: African American Women; Asian American Women; Cornum, Rhonda (1954–); Hispanic American Women; Holm, Jeanne M. (1921–2010); Howard, Michelle (1960–); Native American Women; Prisoners of War; Rathbun-Nealy (Coleman), Melissa (1970–); Rossi, Marie Therese (1959–1991).

References and Further Reading

Cornum, Rhonda. *She Went to War: The Rhonda Cornum Story.* Novato, CA: Presidio Press, 1992.

D'Amico, Francine. "Tailhook: Deinstitutionalizing the Military's 'Women Problem.' " In *Wives and Warriors: Women in the Military in the United States and Canada*, edited by Laurie Weinstein and Christie C. White, 235–43. Westport, CT: Bergin and Garvey, 1997.

Goldstein, Joshua S. *War and Gender.* New York: Cambridge University Press, 2001.

Holm, Jeanne. *Women in the Military: An Unfinished Revolution*, rev. ed. Novato, CA: Presidio Press, 1992.

Sadler, Georgia Clark. "Women in Combat: The U.S. Military and the Impact of the Persian Gulf War." In *Wives and Warriors: Women in the Military in the United States and Canada*, edited by Laurie Weinstein and Christie C. White, 79–97. Westport, CT: Bergin and Garvey, 1997.

U.S. General Accounting Office. *Women in the Military: Deployment in the Persian Gulf War.* NSIAD-93-93. Washington, D.C.: General Accounting Office, July 1993.

Zimmerman, Jean. *Tailspin: Women at War in the Wake of Tailhook.* New York: Doubleday, 1995.

GULOVICH, MARIA (1921–2009)

Maria Gulovich was a schoolteacher-turned-resistance-fighter during World War II who became highly involved in American spy networks and was subsequently nicknamed the "Sweetheart of the OSS" for her work with the Office of Strategic Services (OSS).

Born in Jakubany, Czechoslovakia, on October 19, 1921, to a Greek Orthodox Catholic priest and a teacher, she was the eldest of five daughters. Wishing to nurture her desire to learn and inform, she enrolled in a faith-based institution in Prešov. Through extensive schooling, she became fluent in German, Hungarian, Russian, and English. By 1940, she attained an educational job, but her vocation was overshadowed by the Nazi occupation of her homeland beginning in March 1939. For the first five years of the Third Reich's domination of the Czech people, Gulovich remained frustrated but largely secure in her position of instructor in the town of Hriňová.

Her initiation into covert activities began unintentionally. In 1944, her sister, Maria, persuaded Gulovich to safeguard two displaced Jews who had been hiding in a nearby mill. Within a month, Slovak Army captain Milan Polak learned about Gulovich's exploits and confronted her with a surprising proposal: collaborate with the underground and allow him to find shelter for her fugitives, or he would report her to the Gestapo for harboring wanted persons. The best option to the captain's blackmail was obvious. She became a courier with the Slovakian underground resistance.

Relocating to Banská Bystrica, the nest of the ultimately unsuccessful Slovakian Uprising, she was forced to leave her teaching position, serve as an interpreter, and become involved in an enigmatic lifestyle. She quickly learned some Slovak partisans and Soviet liaisons could be as ruthless as the Germans themselves. Her adept linguistic abilities rescued her from more than one dangerous situation. Her first covert task was to sneak a radio transmitter through German checkpoints in a suitcase. While on a passenger train, the mission was nearly discovered when Nazi police began rummaging through luggage. However, given her skill in speaking German, she flirted with Wermacht officers to evade capture.

While based in Banská Bystrica, she came into contact with American operatives of the OSS who were known as the Dawes team. Established in 1944, the band's goal was to rescue, shelter, and remove Allied pilots while supplying intelligence to combatants and informants in the Czeck Slovak Forces of the Interior. An ulterior motive of the Dawes team was to gather information regarding the Soviet Union's intentions of seizing Czechoslovakia once the Germans were pushed out. Accustomed to the brutality of some partisans, Gulovich quickly became enamored with the American agents. She herself eventually became a member of their task force and led downed airmen through the passes of the frequently treacherous Tatra Mountains to safe houses and routes of escape.

Infuriated by enemy activities taking place under their noses, squads of SS troops frequently roamed the hills and surrounding communities, killing locals who were uncooperative or suspected of harboring Allied troops. Gulovich barely evaded capture that December when Germans seized a lodge used to conceal fugitives and supplies. Her foraging mission that day prevented her from being taken prisoner, but many of the American airmen seeking shelter there were captured and later executed. She and fellow survivors made a harrowing journey through the snow-covered mountains in their attempt to reach the Soviet lines. Gulovich sustained a bad case of frostbite on her foot but nevertheless showed the perseverance to endure their tumultuous travels to a Soviet sector. Unfortunately for the weary party, the Soviets were nearly as hostile in their temperament, accusing Gulovich and her comrades of being spies. In the process of being transferred by train to Odessa, the team was able to lure the help of American GIs stationed in Bucharest, Romania. The prisoners were freed in what almost amounted to a desperate showdown between two small detachments of U.S. and Soviet troops.

Soon after she transferred to Italy and then back to Czechoslovakia, she became fully adopted into the OSS and collaborated with celebrated intelligence officers "Wild Bill" Donovan and Allen Dulles. In 1946, Gulovich was awarded the Bronze Star by Gen. Donovan at West Point, became a U.S. citizen in 1952, and married twice. In subsequent decades, she received formal recognitions for her actions but spent much of her time enjoying a successful career in real estate in California. Maria Gulovich passed away on September 25, 2009.

Jared Frederick

See also: Espionage; World War II (1941–1945).

References and Further Reading

Atwood, Kathryn J. *Women Heroes of World War II: 26 Stories of Espionage, Sabotage, Resistance, and Rescue.* Chicago: Chicago Review, 2001.

Central Intelligence Agency. *A Look Back … Maria Gulovich: Sweetheart of the OSS.* Langley, VA: CIA, 2010.

Jason, Sonya. *Maria Gulovich, OSS Heroine of World War II: The Schoolteacher Who Saved American Lives in Slovakia.* Jefferson, NC: McFarland, 2009.

McIntosh, Elizabeth P. *Sisterhood of Spies: The Women of the OSS.* Annapolis, MD: Naval Institute, 1998.

O'Donnell, Patrick K. *Operatives, Spies, and Saboteurs: The Unknown Story of the Men and Women of World War II's OSS.* New York: Free Press, 2004.

H

HALL (GOILLOT), VIRGINIA (1906–1982)

As one of the most daring under-cover Allied agents operating in Nazi-occupied France during World War II, Virginia Hall pioneered an active role for women in the intelligence services. Her long, extraordinary career in the male-dominated world of diplomacy and intelligence-gathering included stints with the U.S. Department of State, the British Special Operations Executive (SOE), the Office of Strategic Services (OSS), and the Central Intelligence Agency (CIA).

Hall was born on April 6, 1906, in Baltimore, Maryland, where her father owned a cinema and was a well-known figure in the business community. An excellent student, she attended Radcliffe and Barnard Colleges on the East Coast and the Sorbonne in Paris.

Having excelled at foreign languages (French, German, and Italian), she worked at several U.S. consulates and embassies in Poland, Estonia, Austria, Italy, and Turkey. In 1933, while in Turkey, she suffered a hunting accident that resulted in the loss of her left leg below the knee; she would walk with a limp for the rest of her life. Hall named her wooden prosthesis "Cuthbert," which would be the codename used by the SOE to refer to her wooden leg during World War II. The injury, combined with the State Department's resistance to promoting women to its upper ranks, led to Hall leaving the State Department in 1939.

Undaunted by her injury, she continued to live and work as a journalist in Europe. When France fell in June 1940, she was serving in an ambulance unit for the French army. Because the United States was still a neutral country, Hall's passport allowed her to cross the Channel to England, where her language skills brought her to the attention of the SOE. The SOE trained her in the major aspects of clandestine field operations; only parachuting was left out of Hall's training due to her wooden leg.

Sent back to France as a secret operative, she posed as Marie, a reporter for the *New York Post*. She conducted various clandestine and intelligence-gathering operations in Lyons, which lay in the southern, unoccupied party of Vichy France. Besides being a key figure (codenamed "Heckler") in the SOE operations in the area, she was active in the resistance networks and participated in the rescue of Allied pilots who had been shot down over France.

When the British and U.S. troops landed in North Africa in November 1942, the Germans immediately occupied the rest of Vichy France, forcing Hall to flee—on foot in the midst of the winter—for safety in Spain before returning to London. The SOE sent her to Madrid, but Hall found the work uninspiring and asked for reassignment.

In spring of 1944, as an agent of the OSS she returned to France under the codename "Diane." A British motorized torpedo boat landed her in Brittany on France's northern coast. Her mission in the Haute-Loire region of central France did not go unnoticed by the Gestapo, who were on the lookout for an agent they nicknamed "Artemis." The Gestapo posted fliers that notified the public to be on the lookout for a woman who had a noticeable limp. Disguised as a milkmaid, she outwitted the Germans by walking with a slow, swinging gait. Her second mission in France brought her into contact with Paul Goillot, a fellow OSS operative. Born in Paris, Goillot immigrated to the United States in 1928 and lived in New York before the war. In 1950, she and Goillot were married.

A year later, she joined the CIA, the successor to the OSS, after the war but kept a low profile, even though she had risen to the rank of GS-14. In 1966, at age 60, she retired from a distinguished career in the clandestine services and retired to a quiet life on a farm in Maryland, not far from her native roots.

Her decorations included the Order of the British Empire and the Distinguished Service Cross (DSC). The citation for the latter award noted her "for extraordinary heroism in connection with military operations against the enemy." President Harry Truman wanted a public ceremony to give Hall the DSC. However, fearing that such publicity would jeopardize her qualifications for future clandestine work, she refused the honor. In a private ceremony, the DSC was pinned on her personally by Gen. Bill Donovan, the head of the OSS in 1945. Hall was the first woman recipient to receive the DSC, and the only woman, civilian or military, to receive that medal during World War II.

Virginia Hall Goillot died at Shady Grove Adventist Hospital in Washington, D.C., on July 14, 1982. In 2006, the British and French governments honored Hall's memory with a reception and award ceremony at the residence of the French ambassador in Washington. Hall's only surviving relative, her niece Lorna Catling, accepted the awards on behalf of her deceased aunt.

L. Bao Bui

See also: Espionage; World War II (1941–1945).

References and Further Reading

Nouzille, Vincent. *L'espionne: Virginia Hall, une Americaine dans la guerre*. Paris, France: Fayard, 2007.

Pearson, Judith L. *The Wolves at the Door: The True Story of America's Greatest Female Spy.* Guilford, CT: Lyons Press, 2005.

"Virginia Goillot, of French Resistance, Dies." *Baltimore Sun*, July 13, 1982.

"We Must Find and Destroy Her." *US News and World Report*, January 27, 2003.

HALL, FLORENCE LOUISE (1888–1983)

Florence Louise Hall was the director of the Women's Land Army (WLA) during World War II after 20 years as a home economist with the U.S. Department of Agriculture (USDA). Under her leadership, the federal WLA supported local and state organizations with conferences, informational programs, letters, and a national propaganda campaign.

Daughter of Jessie Emery and James Henry Hall, Florence was born in 1888 and grew up in Port Austin, Michigan. Her father, a lawyer and banker, raised blooded stock on a farm near the family home, but Hall was not raised a "farm girl" despite her capacity to milk a cow and ride horses. Along with schoolwork, Hall balanced childhood jobs, once selling milk and working in a canning factory to earn extra spending money. She later earned a BS in home economics from Michigan State Agricultural College (now Michigan State University). After graduation, Hall took a job in nutrition at Teachers College, Columbia University, and briefly taught high school mathematics in Lansing, Michigan.

In 1917, Hall began her long career in public service as a home demonstration agricultural agent for Alleghany County, Pennsylvania. Her educational background and experiences during World War I helped her educate women about food, recipes, and clothing conservation. Taking her expertise to the federal level, Hall moved to Washington, D.C., in 1922 to assist Florence Ward in organizing the Milk for Health campaign of the USDA's Bureau of Dairy Industry. The national campaign put Hall in personal contact with farm families throughout 32 states and introduced her to what would become her life's work.

Six years later, Hall became an Extension Service field agent for 12 Northeastern states, a position that required close contact with farm organizations, women's clubs, and consumer groups to coordinate home demonstration work. In light of her significant contributions in rural communities, her alma mater awarded her an honorary MA in home economics in 1933. In 1937, she toured 10 European countries to observe foreign farm schools and cooperatives for the USDA. But her position with the Extension Service became vitally important when the United States entered World War II, as she helped implement wartime programs, such as nutrition, home food supply, and conservation programs. The decentralized New Deal programs of the Depression era would serve as the primary models for the USDA's response to wartime labor shortages.

On April 12, 1943, the USDA's War Food Administration appointed Hall national director of the WLA, formed to employ 60,000 women—10,000 as year-round farm employees and 50,000 as seasonal laborers—to combat the severe labor shortages on U.S. farms. As part of the Emergency Farm Labor Program, Hall's "farmerettes" would join convicts, high school students, imported workers from Mexico and the Caribbean, and prisoners of war to replace 2 million farmhands who had joined the military or taken industrial jobs between April 1940 and July 1942. One of Hall's primary duties was to convince skeptical farmers that even "city girls" could tackle the physical demands of farm labor. She also coordinated the recruiting and training efforts of WLA representatives in each state. On May 10, 1943, Hall described the program at a press conference with Eleanor Roosevelt and displayed the uniforms available for purchase by WLA workers.

Hall's hard work paid off. By the end of 1943, the WLA's "farmerettes" made up 600,000 of the 3.5 million emergency farm workers. With the help of local placement offices, county extension agents placed 250,000 of the women on farms—picking beans in Maryland, fruit in Maine, peaches in Ohio, and strawberries in Connecticut by midsummer 1943. Hall's ranks also pitched hay in South Dakota, detassled corn in Illinois, and cultivated onions and picked strawberries in Michigan. Given the success of the program, the WLA planned to recruit 800,000 to address rising labor shortages in 1944. In 1945, 2 million women were employed on U.S. farms, even in Midwestern states, where farmers had been most skeptical about the reliability of nonfarm women in the fields.

After the war, Hall returned to her prewar post with the USDA Extension Service. In September 1947, Hall attended the triennial Associated Country Women of the World conference in Amsterdam, which stressed peaceful resolutions to world conflict and encouraged farmwomen to support UN activities. Hall retired from public service in 1952. In 1954, the National Extension Association of Family and Consumer Services established the Florence Hall Award to recognize outstanding programs addressing new concerns and interests of American families.

On February 16, 1983, at the age of 94, Hall died of cardiac arrest at Bethesda Retirement and Nursing Center.

Ilouise S. Bradford

See also: Prisoners of War; Roosevelt, Eleanor (1884–1962); Women's Land Army; World War I (1914–1918); World War II (1941–1945).

References and Further Reading

Carpenter, Stephanie A. " 'Regular Farm Girl': The Women's Land Army in World War II." *Agricultural History* 71, no. 2 (Spring 1997): 162–185.

Gregory, Chester W. *Women in Defense Work during World War II: An Analysis of the Labor Problem and Women's Rights*. New York: Exposition Press, 1974.

"Land Army Described: Head of Women's Program Also Shows Model of Uniform." *The New York Times*, May 11, 1943, 18.

"Will Head Women in New Crop Corps: Miss Florence Hall, Senior Home Economist in Agricultural Extension Service, Is Named." *Washington Post*, April 13, 1943, 22.

HALLAREN, MARY (1907–2005)

Col. Mary Hallaren, who led the Women's Army Corps (WAC) during its transition to permanent military status beginning in 1948, served in the military from 1942 to 1960. Often referred to as the "Little Colonel" because of her short height (barely 5 feet tall), Hallaren was one of the most vocal advocates for women's permanent military service in the years following World War II. As the third director of WAC, she testified before Congress along with military leaders such as Dwight Eisenhower to help secure women's place in national defense. Following the passage of the Women's Armed Services Integration Act in 1948, Hallaren became the first woman sworn into the regular WAC.

Hallaren was born in Lowell, Massachusetts, in 1907. She studied at Lowell State Teachers College and Boston University and then became a teacher with a fondness for traveling in her summer vacations. When World War II began, Hallaren became one of the first women to attend Officer Candidate School for the Women's Army Auxiliary Corps (WAAC). In late 1942, Hallaren became executive officer and then commanding officer over the 1st WAAC Separate Battalion. Within a year, Hallaren and her battalion of 555 enlisted women and 19 officers became the first WAACs to serve in the European theater of the war, initially stationed in London. In 1943, the WAAC achieved full military status and became the WAC, and Hallaren continued in her position after this change. Hallaren served as WAC staff adviser for the battalion and WAC staff adviser for all WACs in the European theater from 1945 to 1946. After completing her European tour of duty, Hallaren became deputy director of the WAC under then-director Westray Battle Boyce. In 1947, Boyce retired for medical reasons and Hallaren became third director of WAC and assumed responsibilities for helping

promote legislation then in Congress to make the women's military services permanent.

As director of WAC, Hallaren worked tirelessly to gain support for the Women's Armed Services Integration Act, which passed successfully in mid-1948. In particular, Hallaren testified before Congress about the importance of including women in national defense to ensure the nation would be prepared in the event of a future war. She argued that in the future, the nation would again need all of its citizens to protect the country.

After securing women's roles in national defense, Hallaren supervised the first WAC training programs at Fort Lee, Virginia, as well as women's integration into the Army and Army Reserve. During the Korean War, Hallaren led efforts to expand the number of WACs, beginning in 1950. In two years, she helped grow the WAC from just over 7,000 members to nearly 12,000 members.

Her other notable accomplishments as director of WAC included a new direct commissioning program for WAC officers, uniform development, and gaining congressional approval for funds to create a new WAC training facility and base at Fort McClellan, Alabama.

In early 1953, Col. Hallaren stepped down from the director position and reverted to the rank of lieutenant colonel as required by law at that time. For the next four years, she served in personnel in the Headquarters of the U.S. European Command, Frankfurt, Germany. During the last three years of her military service (1957–1960), she worked as an operations officer in the Office of the Assistant Secretary of

Defense of Personnel and Reserve Affairs. When she retired on June 30, 1960, she received a third Legion of Merit award for her dedicated military service. Additional military awards included the Bronze Star with one Cluster, the French Croix de Guerre avec Vermeil, the Army Commendation Medal with Oak Leaf Cluster, the Legion d'Honneur, the WAAC Service Medal, the American Campaign Medal, the European Theater of Operations Campaign Medal with battle star for Northern France, the World War II Victory Medal, the Army of Occupation Medal (Germany), the National Defense Medal, and the General Staff Identification Badge.

After leaving military service, Hallaren completed an additional bachelor's degree through George Washington University and became executive director of Women in Community Service (WICS), part of the U.S. Department of Labor, a position she held for more than 13 years. She then became a consultant for the organization, served on the WAC Foundation Board of Directors, and participated in a number of local activities. During the 1990s, she became an advocate for the Women in Military Service for America Memorial. The National Women's Hall of Fame (Seneca, New York) selected her for inclusion in their organization in 1996. Throughout her retirement years, Hallaren spoke frequently in public venues on the topic of women's contribution to national defense and other matters. She also traveled extensively: at age 92 she accompanied WICS on a trip to China. Journalist Tom Brokaw included Hallaren in his book *The Greatest Generation*.

Hallaren passed away on February 13, 2005, from stroke-related complications.

At the time of her death, she was 97 years old and living in an assisted living facility.

Tanya L. Roth

See also: Bailey, Mildred "Inez" Caroon (1919–2009); Clarke, Mary E. (1924–); Galloway, Irene O. (1908–1963); Hoisington, Elizabeth P. (1918–2007); Korean War (1950–1953); Milligan (Rasmuson), Mary Louise (1911–); Women in Military Service for America Memorial; Women's Armed Services Integration Act of 1948 (Public Law 80-625); Women's Army Auxiliary Corps (WAAC); Women's Army Corps (WAC); World War II (1941–1945).

References and Further Reading

Brokaw, Tom. *The Greatest Generation*. New York: Random House, 1998.

Holm, Jeanne. *In Defense of a Nation: Servicewomen in World War II*. St. Petersburg, FL: Vandamere Press, 1998.

Holm, Jeanne. *Women in the Military: An Unfinished Revolution (Revised Edition)*. Novato, CA: Presidio Press, 1993.

Monahan, Evelyn, and Rosemary Neidel-Greenlee. *A Few Good Women: America's Military Women from World War I to the War in Iraq and Afghanistan*. New York: Alfred A. Knopf, 2010.

Morden, Bettie J. *The Women's Army Corps, 1945–1978*. Washington, D.C.: Center of Military History, 1989.

Witt, Linda, Judith Bellafaire, Britta Granrud, and Mary Jo Binker. *"A Defense Weapon Known to Be of Value": Servicewomen of the Korean War Era*. Hanover, NH: University Press of New England, 2005.

HANCOCK, JOY BRIGHT (1898–1986)

A captain in the U.S. Navy, Joy Bright Hancock served during both world wars and continually worked for women's rights in the Navy.

Born in New Jersey in 1898, Hancock first enlisted as a naval yeoman (F) in the Women's Naval Reserve during World War I. After the war, she served as a civilian employee in the Bureau of Aeronautics, Department of the Navy. Hancock was a pilot herself and was twice married to (and widowed by) naval aviators. She wrote her first book, *Airplanes in Action*, in 1938.

At the outbreak of World War II, she successfully lobbied for the reestablishment of the Women's Naval Reserve. She was commissioned as a lieutenant, U.S. Navy Reserve, in October 1942. The highest-ranking woman at the Bureau of Aeronautics, she was the Women Accepted for Volunteer Emergency Service (WAVES) representative to both that bureau and to the deputy chief of naval operations (air), as well as the liaison between the bureau and Lt. Cmdr. Mildred McAfee, the Women's Reserve director. McAfee and her advisors at the Bureau of Personnel had come from the educational and professional worlds; Hancock's naval expertise proved invaluable to them. Hancock has been described as "the only WAVE leader with a clear idea of how the navy operated." Hancock advocated gender-integrated specialist training at aviation schools for WAVES members and the opening of jobs in aviation mechanics to women. The decision that permitted 3,000 women to serve as aviation machinist's mates was a major breakthrough for women in the armed services. She was also instrumental in opening up overseas service to WAVES members.

After World War II, Hancock remained on active duty, taking over as director of the Women's Reserve in 1947 and leading the effort to maintain the Women's Reserve as a peacetime organization. The Women's Armed Services Integration Act, passed on June 12, 1948, codified the Women's Naval Reserve in law. Hancock left active duty in May 1953 upon reaching the statutory retirement age.

In 1971, Hancock moved to a U.S. Navy retirement home in McLean, Virginia. She maintained an active interest in women in the Navy until her death in 1986. She continually advocated integrated training and service for Navy women. Hancock's memoirs, published by the Naval Institute Press in 1972, are one of the most useful sources to date on the history of the WAVES.

Patrick J. O'Connor

See also: McAfee (Horton), Mildred Helen (1900–1994); Women Accepted for Volunteer Emergency Service (WAVES); Women's Armed Services Integration Act of 1948 (Public Law 80-625); World War I (1914–1918); World War II (1941–1945); Yeoman (F).

References and Further Reading

Alsmeyer, Marie Bennett. *The Way of the WAVES: Women in the Navy*. Conway, AR: HAMBA Books, 1981.

Hancock, Joy Bright. *Lady in the Navy: A Personal Reminiscence*. Annapolis, MD: Naval Institute Press, 2002. Originally published 1972.

Weatherford, Doris. *American Women and World War II*. New York: Facts on File, 1990.

HARRIS, MARCELITE JORDAN
(1943–)

The first female aircraft maintenance officer in the U.S. Air Force, Marcelite Jordan Harris also became the first African American female general in the Air Force. She also became the first woman to head an air base and one of the first two women air officers commanding at the U.S. Air Force Academy. At the time of her 1997 retirement, Harris was the highest-ranking female officer in the Air Force.

Marcelite Jordan was born January 16, 1943, in Houston, Texas, to a former postal worker, Cecil O'Neal Jordan, and a high school librarian, Marcelite Terrell Jordan. Her parents insisted that their three children get good educations. Marcelite excelled through high school and entered Spellman College with the hopes of becoming an actress. Spurred by her parents, who taught her to set her sights high in whatever she aspired to do, Marcelite graduated from Spellman with a degree in speech and drama in 1964. During college, she traveled to Germany and France in a United Service Organizations (USO) tour. After her graduation, she realized there were few jobs available for actors. After struggling with the difficulties of finding acting work, she made it a priority to find steady employment.

After a stint with a Young Men's Christian Association's Headstart program and the added multitasking duty of attending law school at night, Jordan reevaluated her goals into two priorities: getting a steady job and seeing the world.

Jordan realized that the military held healthy long-term opportunities for her.

Jordan entered Air Force Officer Training School in Lackland, Texas, in 1965, driven with determination to succeed. On December 21, 1965, she was commissioned as a second lieutenant. After working as assistant director for administration at Travis Air Force Base in Texas, she earned a promotion to first lieutenant. The Air Force then deployed her to West Germany as administrative officer for the 71st Tactical Missile Squadron at Bitburg Air Force Base. In West Germany, Jordan decided to switch from administration to aircraft maintenance. As a result, in May 1969 she became the first female officer in the aircraft maintenance department, a male-dominated job and field. However, she still had to fight to get what she wanted. She received little respect from her male colleagues and faced repeated rejections in her efforts to enter the Aircraft Maintenance Officer School.

Jordan finally gained entry to the Aircraft Maintenance Officer School and graduated from it in May 1971. She was first stationed at Korat Air Base in Thailand for the 469th Tactical Fighter Squadron. Her next assignment was as control officer for the 916th Air Refueling Squadron at Travis Air Force Base in California. She became the unit's field maintenance officer in September 1973. Jordan also served as a personnel staff officer at Air Force Headquarters (1975–1978) and as social aide to President Gerald Ford and President Jimmy Carter. She commanded Cadet Squadron 39 at Colorado Springs' Air Force Academy from 1978 to 1980. She served as a maintenance control officer for the 384th Refueling Wing at McConnell Air Force Base in Kansas. She became the first female maintenance squadron commander in the Strategic Air Command in 1981 and returned to Asia in November 1982 as part of the Pacific Air Forces Logistic Support Center in Japan.

Jordan married Air Force officer Maurice Anthony Harris on November 29, 1980. They had a son and two daughters. She earned a bachelor of science in business management in 1986.

Harris continued to rise through the ranks. She earned promotion to colonel on September 1, 1986. She took command of the 3300th Technical Training Wing at Keesler Air Force Base in Mississippi in December 1988. She became the first African American female general in the Air Force on September 8, 1990, when she was promoted to brigadier general. She earned promotion to major general on May 25, 1995. This promotion made her the highest-ranking woman in the Air Force. It also made her the highest-ranking African American woman in the Department of Defense. She was stationed at the Pentagon as director of maintenance and deputy chief of staff.

Harris's Air Force career was a testament to her ability to build relationships, show a flawless work ethic, demonstrate leadership skills, and advocate the fair treatment of women in the military. Before her 1997 retirement, Harris worked on establishing an office for the Committee on Women in NATO. For her military service, she received many awards, including the Legion of Merit with Oak Leaf Cluster, Bronze Star, Meritorious Service Medal with three Oak Leaf Clusters, Air Force Commendation Medal with one Oak Leaf Cluster, Presidential Unit Citation, Air Force Outstanding Unit Award with "V" device and eight Oak Leaf Clusters, and the Republic of Vietnam Campaign Medal. She has also received many civilian honors.

Harris is the treasurer of the National Association for the Advancement of Colored People's Atlanta Branch. She also is on the Board of Directors of the Peachtree Hope Charter School. On September 15, 2010, President Barack Obama appointed her as a member of the Board of Visitors for the U.S. Air Force Academy.

Aineshia Carline Washington

See also: African American Women; United Service Organizations (USO); Vietnam War (1965–1973); Young Men's Christian Association (YMCA).

References and Further Reading

"Brig. Gen. Marcelite J. Harris: The Air Force's First Black Female General." *Ebony Magazine*, December 1992, 62–66.

Hawkins, Walter L. *African American Generals and Flag Officers: Biographies of Over 120 Blacks in the United States Military.* Jefferson, NC: McFarland & Company, 1992.

HART, NANCY
(CA. 1843–1902)

Nancy Hart, a young and beautiful Confederate spy, served as a scout, guide, and cavalry trooper for the

Southern cause before experiencing a dramatic capture and escape from Northern soldiers.

Not to be confused with the Nancy Hart of Revolutionary War fame, Hart was born in the early 1840s. As an infant, she moved from Raleigh, North Carolina, to Tazewell, Virginia (later West Virginia). Hart became an expert horsewoman and cultivated a familiarity with the Virginia outdoors. Although she never learned to read or write, she explored the wilderness and became a deadeye riflewoman.

In 1861, Hart visited the home of her sister and brother-in-law, William Price, just as Union soldiers arrived to escort Price to the nearby town of Spencer to speak in favor of the Union. Price never arrived in Spencer; he was found on the road shot in the back, sparking in Hart a hatred for Union soldiers. Soon after, at a party celebrating the departure of her neighbor's sons for the Confederate Army, Union soldiers rode by during the affair and fired a rifle several times at the home. Three days later, Hart rode off to join the Confederate cause.

Hart joined the Moccasin Rangers, a pro-Southern guerrilla unit. She served as a scout, guide, and spy, carrying messages while traveling alone between Southern armies by night. Hart peddled eggs and vegetables to Northern troops to gain access to information. She also visited Northern outposts in the mountains to learn and report of their strength, population, and vulnerability.

In July 1862, Union forces offered a large reward for Hart's capture. Union soldiers under the command of Lt. Col. William C. Starr of the 9th West Virginia arrested Hart at a log cabin where she was crushing corn with a young female friend. Hart was jailed in the upper portion of a dilapidated house-turned-makeshift-jail in the nearby town of Sommersville, in western Virginia, guarded by a sentry at the door, quartered soldiers downstairs, and troops on patrol around the building. A young woman of striking beauty, Hart beguiled a young soldier, who allowed her to examine his weapon, upon which she promptly shot him in the head. Hart jumped out a second-story window, stole Starr's horse, and rode off for Confederate territory. On July 25, 1862, she returned, still riding Starr's horse, along with approximately 200 of Gen. Stonewall Jackson's cavalrymen. During the raid of Sommersville, Southern soldiers took mules, horses, and several prisoners (including Starr), and they burned much of the town to the ground.

During the war, Hart met Joshua Douglas, also a former Ranger, and nursed him back to health following his near-fatal wounds. He left and joined the Confederate Army, but after the war he returned to the area, found Hart, and married her. They settled in Greenbriar County, where they lived until her death in 1902. Hart is buried in Mannings Knob, Greenbriar Country, West Virginia.

Eloise Scroggins

See also: Civil War (1861–1865); Espionage.

Reference and Further Reading

Broadwater, Robert P. *Daughters of the Cause: Women in the "Civil War."* Santa Clarita, CA: Daisy Publishing Company, 1993.

HART, NANCY MORGAN (CA. 1735–1830)

Revolutionary War Patriot Nancy Hart dressed as a man to fight against the British and Loyalists.

The details of Nancy Ann Morgan's birth are somewhat sketchy. It is believed that she was born in North Carolina in 1735, though some think that she was born in Pennsylvania at a later date. Nancy married Benjamin Hart of Virginia and after 1755 moved to Georgia, settling in the Broad River section of the state.

According to contemporary descriptions, Nancy Hart was over 6 feet tall, muscular and clumsy, with red hair and a complexion scarred by smallpox. She was cross-eyed, rude of manner, and was said to take frequent fits of uncontrollable temper. She was also acknowledged as being a sharpshooter and as fine a marksman as any man in the region.

The Broad River area was the scene of much fighting during the Revolution, as British forces sought to wrest it away from Patriot control. So much fighting occurred here that participants on both sides referred to it as the "Hornet's Nest." In this atmosphere, Hart had opportunity for numerous encounters with bands of British troops and many chances to prove her loyalty to the Patriot cause.

Hart is credited with capturing many Loyalists in the area, including some whom she took from their own homes. In one instance, when a Loyalist spied on Hart when she was making soap outside, she threw a vat of hot lye in his face, blinding him and allowing her to take him prisoner. In another instance, she captured three mounted Loyalists singlehandedly.

An illustration of Patriot Nancy Hart's capture of Loyalist soldiers at her cabin during the American Revolution. (North Wind Picture Archives)

Hart frequently gathered information for the Patriots by dressing in men's clothing and sneaking behind enemy lines. On one such mission to Augusta, she obtained intelligence concerning a planned British offensive that greatly benefited the Patriot forces. Another time, she made a raft from logs and vines and drifted across the Savannah River, gathering information important to the Patriot forces in South Carolina.

Hart's best-known exploit occurred when five Loyalists stopped by her cabin on the way from murdering a local militia officer to inquire as to the whereabouts of other rebels. When one of the Loyalists questioned Hart about rumors that she had helped a rebel escape capture by the King's soldiers, she openly admitted to the deed and even gave particulars about how she accomplished it. The bold way she confessed to her actions won the grudging respect of the Loyalists, who ordered her to prepare food for them instead of taking her prisoner for her treason. Hart refused. She asserted that she would not feed traitors to her country and that even if she was so inclined, the only meat on the premises was a turkey foraging near the house. One of the Loyalists spotted the turkey and shot it. Bringing it inside, he demanded Hart clean and cook it for them. She eventually consented and brought a jug of liquor to the Loyalists to entertain them as she plucked the bird's feathers. Her daughter, Sulkey, who had been in the house with her, was instructed to go outside to a spring to bring some water. Hart secretly gave the girl a message for her father, who was working in nearby fields, to gather a band of Patriots and rush the house when Nancy gave them a signal.

The Loyalists enjoyed the jug of liquor, whose effects helped dispel their suspicions about Hart. As Hart plucked and cut the turkey, she also used her knife to chip away the chinking between two logs in the cabin. The Loyalists' muskets were stacked against the wall, close to Hart. Once she had chiseled away a hole between the logs, Hart began secretly passing the muskets through to the outside. She had disposed of two and was getting rid of a third when the enemy discovered her actions. The Loyalists sprang to their feet, and Hart raised the musket to her shoulder, announcing she would shoot the first man to move. After a short pause, one of the men tested her, and Hart shot him dead. Grabbing another musket, she held them at bay, until Sulkey returned to announce that Mr. Hart and his friends would soon arrive. The Loyalists did not relish the idea of being captured and decided to rush Hart, as she could only shoot one of them before they would be on her. However, because she was cross-eyed, each of the four soldiers was sure that Hart was looking directly at him, and none of them made a move on her. When her husband and the other men arrived, they took the Loyalists into custody. Hart suggested they be hung immediately for the murder of the militia officer. According to her wishes, they were hung from a tree in the Hart yard.

The Harts continued to live in Broad River after the Revolution, moving to Brunswick in the late 1780s. When her husband died, Hart returned to Broad River and discovered that her cabin had been swept away in a flood. She went to live with her son, John, along the Oconee River near Athens. When John moved his family to Henderson County,

Kentucky, around 1803, she went with them. Hart died in 1830 in Henderson County Kentucky. She was buried in the Hart Graveyard, which is called the Book Cemetery today.

Robert P. Broadwater

See also: American Revolution (1775–1783).

References and Further Reading

Broadwater, Robert P. *Liberty Belles: Women of the American Revolution*. Bellwood, PA: Dixie Dreams Press, 2004.

Cannon, Jill. *Heroines of the American Revolution*. Santa Barbara, CA: Bellerophon Books, 1995.

Kierner, Cynthia A. *Southern Women in the Revolution, 1776–1800: Personal and Political Narratives*. Columbia: University of South Carolina Press, 1998.

HASSON, ESTHER VOORHEES (1867–1942)

Nurse Esther Voorhees Hasson served on a hospital ship during the Spanish-American War. She became the first superintendent of the Navy Nurse Corps. She also served in World War I through the Army Reserves Nursing Corps.

Hasson was born in Baltimore, Maryland, on September 20, 1867. Her father was an Army surgeon. She attended Connecticut Training School for Nurses in New Haven in 1897.

In June 1898, Hasson became a nurse with the U.S. Army during the Spanish-American War. Hasson eventually served on the hospital ship *Relief*, a passenger liner used to evacuate casualties from Cuba. Hasson learned a great deal about using minimal resources to maximum advantage aboard the *Relief*, as she was one of six nurses charged with caring for 1,485 sick and wounded men. After the war, Hasson served as chief nurse at the Brigade Hospital at Vigan in the Philippine Islands. After she received an honorable discharge from the Army in August 1901, Hasson returned to the United States. When the Navy Nurse Corps bill came up for congressional action in 1903, Hasson applied for the job of superintendent. The bill failed, but Hasson went on to serve as a nurse in the Panamanian Isthmus, also called the Canal Zone, from 1905 until 1907.

In 1908, when the Navy Nurse Corps was finally established, Hasson became its first superintendent. Before she took office on August 18, 1908, a three-member board subjected Hasson to a test regarding her knowledge of nursing, first aid, and other central issues. The board also required her to pen an essay concerning military nursing and the administration of the Navy Nurse Corps. Satisfying the board of her competence and edging out several other women for the job, Hasson assumed her new position. From the beginning of her tenure, she predicted the future of the Corps as a dignified and respectable institution.

At her new job, Hasson created and implemented an instructional course for all incoming nurses. Hasson also conducted inspections, fielded public relations questions, and managed complaints and reports of incompetence, misconduct, and illness. Despite not being in charge of hiring, Hasson had specific ideas about what kind of people should be nurses. She only wanted those who exhibited good moral character, such as self-control, quiet dignity, and cheerfulness. When one nurse began clandestinely meeting a man on Saturday nights, Hasson employed detectives to follow her, eventually discharging the woman under the premise of ill health. Hasson also designed a uniform for the nurses, a modest outfit with clerical collars and long sleeves.

Within her first year, Hasson had trained 19 nurses who, together with Hasson, became known as the "Sacred Twenty." Throughout her tenure as superintendent, Hasson remained in close contact with the nurses, and she maintained a friendly correspondence with many of them. After the initial hiring of qualified candidates, Hasson recognized in 1910 that the number of good candidates applying to the Corps had fallen, and she championed greater pay for nurses in order to attract more individuals to the field.

To expedite the hiring process, she received approval from the surgeon general for applicants to apply to positions by submitting an essay rather than undergoing an in-person examination. As such, candidates were spared the economic hardship of traveling to Washington, D.C., without the guarantee of a job. Once the essay was approved, nurses could submit to an examination by a medical officer who lived near them.

During her service as superintendent, Hasson published several articles in the *American Journal of Nursing*. Some of her articles educated the public about the Corps, detailing the uniforms she had designed and the living conditions of the nurses. Hasson also published several articles of a more practical nature, such as instructions on how to become a trained nurse and an explanation of hookworm disease.

Hasson encountered personal difficulty when Rear Adm. Charles F. Stokes became the new surgeon general under President William Howard Taft. Stokes began questioning Hasson's leadership, and rather than let her continue managing day-to-day operations, he implemented discipline and excessive leave without pay to the nurses. Hasson resented these trespasses on her leadership. She tried to quit her post a number of times, first offering her resignation in the summer of 1910 and eventually tendering it on January 14, 1911. She left the Corps because she believed that Stokes had failed to provide the necessary support and confidence for her to do her job, and she appended her resignation with a litany of complaints. Stokes replied that he believed Hasson had a temperament unsuited for leading the Navy Nurse Corps. At the time of her resignation, the Corps had grown to 85 trained nurses. Lenah Surcliff Higbie succeeded Hasson as superintendent.

After her resignation, Hasson joined the U.S. Army Reserve Nursing Corps and was called to active duty in 1917 to aid in Europe during World War I. That year, she petitioned the United States War Department for longevity pay. Hasson argued that despite having served intermittently, her combined service in the Army and the Navy warranted the additional pay. The Justice Advocate General agreed, ruling in her favor. During her service in Europe, which lasted until 1919, Hasson worked as the chief nurse of two Army base hospitals, later remembering the experience as great and adventurous despite the many hardships she faced there.

Hasson died on March 8, 1942, in Washington, D.C.

Emily Meyer

See also: Navy Nurse Corps; Nursing; Spanish-American War (1898); USS *Relief*; World War I (1914–1918).

References and Further Reading

Gavin, Lettie. *American Women in World War I: They Also Served*. Niwot: University Press of Colorado, 1997.

Godson, Susan H. *Serving Proudly: A History of Women in the U.S. Navy*. Annapolis, MD: Naval Institute Press, 2001.

Sarnecky, Mary. *A History of the U.S. Army Nurse Corps*. Philadelphia: University of Pennsylvania Press, 1999.

HAYS, ANNA MAE McCABE (1920–)

The first woman to become a brigadier general, Anna Hays was in the Army Nurse Corps (ANC) from 1942 to 1971. She served in Korea and Vietnam; held senior positions at Walter Reed Hospital in research, administration, and praxis; and acted as Eisenhower's personal nurse for a short time in the mid-1950s. Hays played a pivotal role in developing the Walter Reed Army Institute of Nursing (WRAIN) and saw the ANC through the turbulence of the Vietnam War.

Anna Mae Hays was born Anna Mae V. McCabe on February 16, 1920, in New York, the middle child with two siblings. Her family moved from New York to Pennsylvania when she was 12. Musically talented at a young age, she played the piano and the French horn; the former she would continue to play—both during active duty and in church—her whole life. Hays graduated with honors from high school in 1937 and then enrolled at the Allentown General Hospital School of Nursing, from which she graduated with a degree in nursing in 1941. Then she began working at the Allentown General Hospital. Hays, like many other nurses, joined the Red Cross immediately after graduation. She then joined the ANC just a few months before Pearl Harbor, entering active duty in 1942.

Upon completion of her training, Hays shipped out to Assam, India, in 1943 to provide medical care to soldiers building the Ledo Road to China. In April 1945, she was promoted to first lieutenant, and after the war, Hays elected to remain in the ANC. She was initially stationed at Tilton General Hospital at Fort Dix in New Jersey. On January 22, 1947, she was promoted to captain. Before the onset of the Korean War, Hays attended the University of Pennsylvania to learn the latest neonatal training—including on prematurely born babies—and thereafter was accepted to Columbia University. The onset of hostilities in 1950s, however, interrupted her plans. She would complete a bachelor's degree in nursing science at Columbia in 1957.

The 1950s brought for Hays, as it did for the rest of the world, a turbulent time filled with war. She served at the 4th Field Hospital after landing at Inchon in September of 1950. Korea, Hays attested in later interviews, was far worse than World War II. During her service in both wars, Hays worked in cold, shorthanded, undersupplied conditions. In April 1951, she was transferred to the Tokyo Army Hospital to streamline the care, administration, and supplies there. A year later, she was again transferred, this time to Fort Indiantown Gap, Pennsylvania, as an obstetric and pediatric director. Hays graduated first in her class from the Nursing Service Administration Course at Fort Sam Houston in Texas and in 1956 was appointed head nurse at Walter Reed General Emergency Room in Washington, D.C. She would marry in 1956, only to become a widow six years later.

After completing her degree at Columbia in 1957, Hays was assigned to Walter Reed Army Institute of Research as head nurse of the Radioisotope Clinic; it was a position she found herself uninterested in, however, and shortly thereafter she was reassigned as supervisor of the clinic. The posting would only last seven months; in October 1960, Hays became chief nurse of the 11th Evacuation Hospital in Pusan. The 1960s saw great gains for Hays, both personally and for her career, though the decade would begin, sadly, with the death of her husband in 1962. By 1963, she had earned the rank of lieutenant colonel, and in September, Hays was appointed assistant chief of the ANC.

When the Vietnam War began, Hays's organization, administrative, and leadership skills were again called upon to make a valuation of nursing conditions. She was instrumental in the establishment of the WRAIN in 1965, which sought to recruit quality nurses and educate them with the latest training. In many ways, her work with WRAIN foreshadowed the goals she would set for the ANC at large upon her promotion to chief two years later.

In 1966, she began work on a master's degree in nursing service administration at Catholic University of America. In July 1966, she was promoted to colonel, and a month later she graduated with her master's of science. In 1967, Hays was promoted once again, to 13th chief of the ANC, where she served until 1971. During this period, she not only developed long-term goals for the ANC but also made three visits to the Vietnam front in order to evaluate the situation and develop strategies for the ANC to respond. During this time, Hays played a pivotal role in developing the ANC at both an organizational level and in recruiting and instituting training and education programs for new nurses.

Although she was one of thousands of women who joined first the Red Cross and then the ANC, Hays is unique for the level of talent and dedication she brought to her duties. On June 11, 1970, Gen. William C. Westmoreland promoted her to brigadier general, making Hays the first woman in the history of the U.S. armed forces so promoted.

Hays retired on August 31, 1971; she was 51 years old. Her retirement would be filled with all of those things that had characterized her life: a passion for helping others, music, and church. She remained active to a degree in the ANC while vacationing for extended periods in Marbella, Spain.

Ry Marcattilio-McCracken

See also: American Red Cross; Army Nurse Corps (ANC); Korean War (1950–1953); Nursing; Vietnam War (1965–1973); World War II (1941–1945).

References and Further Reading

"Brigadier General Anna Mae Hays." Army Heritage Center Foundation, 2010. Accessed February 20, 2012. http://www.army heritage.org/education-and-programs/educational-resources/soldier-stories/214-brigadier-general-anna-mae-hays.html.

"Embracing the Past: First Chief, Army Nurse Corps Turns 90! Brigadier General Anna Mae V. McCabe Hays." U.S. Army Medical Department, Office of Medical History, March 11, 2011. Accessed February 20, 2012. http://history.amedd.army.mil/Hays Bio/HayesBio.html.

Hays, Anna Mae. "Hays on Enlisting," "Hays on Korea," "Hays on the Draft," "Hays on India and Ledo Road," "Hays on Opportunities for Women in the Army," and "Hays on Vietnam." Interviews by Amelia J. Carson. *Voices of the Past*. U.S. Army Senior Officer Oral History Program, 1983.

Hutchinson, Kay Bailey. *Leading Ladies: American Trailblazers*. New York: Harper Collins, 2007.

Sarnecky, Mary T. *A History of the U.S. Army Nurse Corps*. Philadelphia: University of Pennsylvania Press, 1999.

HEAVREN, ROSE (1870–1968)

Nurse Rose Heavren served in the Spanish-American War and in World War I.

Heavren was born to Irish immigrant parents in New Haven, Connecticut, on January 19, 1870. She attended Connecticut Training School for Nurses in New Haven and later received post-graduate degrees from Kings Park State Hospital in New York and the Summer Course in Public Health Nursing at Teacher's College at Columbia University.

Heavren worked in a New Haven hospital from the time of her graduation until the Army issued a call for nursing volunteers to aid in the Spanish-American War. Heavren promptly enlisted in the military as a nurse on August 17, 1898. The Army initially assigned Heavren to work at Montauk Point in Long Island, accompanied by 12 other nurses and some Catholic nuns. In a later speech, Heavren noted the humiliation of becoming a nurse during this period as nurses were instructed to line up outside the colonel's tent and doctors would pick which nurse they wanted. Heavren noted in her memoirs that she could not abstain from giggling, leaving one doctor to have to accept the giggler. She also documented how difficult the work was, citing that the nurses worked continuously for long hours with limited food. Montauk housed approximately 1,500 patients, who, according to Heavren, were dying like flies. The hospital also had problems keeping adequate supplies, and the nurses were always running out of medicine. After her stay at Montauk, the Army sent Heavren to a brief tenure in Alabama.

In February 1899, Heavren went with the Army to Cuba and shortly thereafter, on August 1, 1899, signed a contract committing to work as the chief nurse of the Santiago de Cuba U.S. General Hospital. Contract nursing, a system implemented by the Army during the Spanish-American War, demanded that Heavren would work as many hours and whenever the Army deemed necessary. The military paid her $60 a month, plus food rations and medical attention. Heavren was also guaranteed transportation to and from Cuba. Heavren and other military nurses noted that conditions in Cuba were far from adequate. Infection spread rapidly as the military failed to provide ample disinfectants and sterilizers. Heavren also complained that the government did not deliver enough food supplies, allowing only 23 cents a day per man.

While in Santiago, Heavren contracted yellow fever, probably from one of her patients. Malaria and yellow fever were such common occurrences among the troops that some nurses noted the men were more likely to be afflicted by either of the two illnesses than to be wounded. Upon her recovery, the Army sent Heavren to Havana, where she served as chief nurse in the Las Animas yellow fever hospital. At the end of the war, in August 1900, Heavren returned to her mother in Connecticut, where she continued her career as a nurse. A few years after her return, in 1908, she served as treasurer of the Graduate Nurses Association of Connecticut, a trend that would become emblematic, as Heavren served in a variety of civic positions after her military career concluded.

On October 25, 1917, Heavren returned to the military in the Army Nurse Corps. This second call to duty occurred during World War I, and Heavren served with the American Expeditionary Forces. She worked in various locations in France until July 6, 1918, when she returned to the United States. The military discharged her from service in September of the same year, and she returned to nursing in New Haven.

As a result of the conditions she had experienced in the two wars, Heavren became an advocate for veterans and nurses. Heavren served as commander of the Allen M. Osborn Camp 1 in New Haven, Connecticut, an organization dedicated to commemorating the service of Spanish-American War veterans. Heavren also remained committed to the nurses who had served in the Spanish-American war and was twice elected president of the Annual Meeting of the Spanish-American War Nurses. She presented a paper titled "Mental Nursing" at the 1915 convention for the Alumnae Association of the Connecticut Training School Nursing, of which she was also a member.

On her return to the private sector, Heavren continued her dedication to nursing, serving as superintendent of nurses at the Homeopathic Hospital in Albany, New York, and at the Fergus Falls State Hospital in Minnesota. She was appointed the public health nurse in New Haven and Essex, Connecticut, in 1920. Heavren also worked in rural school nursing. She retired in 1948 and died in 1968.

Emily Meyer

See also: Army Nurse Corps (ANC); Nursing; Spanish-American War (1898); World War I (1914–1918).

References and Further Reading

Bellafair, Judith. *Women in the United States Military: An Annotated Bibliography.* New York: Routledge, 2011.

Nathan, Amy. *Count on Us: American Women in the Military.* Washington, D.C.: National Geographic Society, 2004.

Zenor-Lafond, Holly. "Women and Combat: Why They Serve." *Inquiry Journal* (Spring 2008): 32–38.

"HELLO GIRLS"

"Hello Girls" were the bilingual switchboard operators who served in Europe during World War I. They served in the U.S. Army Signal Corps from March 1918 until the Armistice in November 1918.

During World War I, the Allied and Axis forces were entangled in trench warfare in France; English-speaking troops from the United States and Great Britain were working alongside French-speaking troops. The new American Expeditionary Forces (AEF) telephone system, established in October 1917, was ineffective as the American soldiers and the French women were unable to communicate. The language barrier hindered efficient correspondence between the troops near the front line and the commanders in the rear. The need for bilingual telephone operators precipitated the recruitment of American women; one of the first tasks of the U.S. Signal Corps was to establish a bilingual battlefield telephone system to improve communications.

In November 1917, Gen. John J. Pershing, U.S. commander and chief of the AEF, appealed to the federal government for permission to hire 100 bilingual telephone operators for the Army Signal Corps to run the battlefield switchboards. He charged the Signal Corps with the assignment of recruiting them. Named the Emergency Appeal,

Hello girls operated military switchboards in Europe during World War I. (U.S. Army Signal Center Command History Office, Fort Gordon, Georgia)

the campaign specifically requested single women who spoke French, had college degrees, and held the position of switchboard operators exclusively in the new Bell Telephone Company. Pershing wanted women to be sworn into the Army on an emergency need because, he stated, women had the patience and perseverance to do long, arduous, detailed work. He found that the men in the Signal Corps had difficulty operating the switchboards. In addition, he thought that men would serve better in the field stringing the wire necessary for communication from the trenches to the AEF at Chaumont. It was the first time in the history of warfare that soldiers in the front lines were connected to the general command.

Initially, the Corps recruited applicants from the French-speaking areas in North America, including Louisiana and Canada, but of the more than 300 applications received, only six were found qualified. Subsequently, the Signal Corps ran advertisements in newspapers throughout the United States. They received 7,600 applications. Some requirements were waived; on rare occasion, the recruits were as young as 16 and had not worked as switchboard operators. Of the women who responded, 550 received military and Signal Corps training and were issued arm patches, gas masks, and steel helmets. Each recruit had to provide $300 to $500 to purchase an Army regulation uniform complete with U.S. crests, Signal Corps crests, and dog tags. They also had to purchase bloomers to be worn under their dresses.

Like other military personnel, the Hello Girls carried rank. Their white armbands identified their ranks. An operator first class wore the white armband with an outlined blue telephone mouthpiece. A supervisor, who rated as a platoon sergeant, wore the same armband with a wreath around the mouthpiece. A chief operator or "Top" had the emblem with the mouthpiece, the wreath, and blue lighting flashes shooting out above the receiver. Over time, arm patches of the rank were created in variations of olive-drab green.

For their work, Hello Girls were paid the same salaries as male soldiers in comparable positions; chief operators earned $125 per month, and regular operators earned $60 per month. Similarly, U.S. Army Signal Corps operators stood inspection in the soldiers' ranks for Pershing's visiting dignitaries, including Woodrow Wilson. Passes were also distributed to Hello Girls in the same way that they were given to any soldier. These women were subject to all Army regulations, including court-martial, as well as another 10 rules designed to ensure their moral character.

In March 1918, the first contingent of 33 Hello Girls was sent to France. Like the others that were to follow, these women were sent to numerous locations throughout the theater of war. A small group of six, which included operators Helen Hill, Berthe Hunt, Esther Fresnel, Marie Large, and Suzanne Prevot and led by Chief Operator Grace Banker, a Barnard College graduate and former instructor at AT&T, was sent forward to the front and assigned to the First American Army headquarters. They arrived just in time to be part of the September 12, 1918, push in the Battle of St. Mihiel. For eight days, these six Hello Girls worked around the clock behind the front lines handling communications on eight lines. During the battle, the building where the women operated the switchboards caught on fire, and the women were ordered to leave. They believed the order for their safety to have been in consideration of their sex and thus continued to operate until the fire was so threatening that General Headquarters threatened court-martial if they did not leave their posts. The fire was extinguished, and within the hour the operators returned, manning the remaining one-third of operational switchboards. On September 26, 1918, they were chosen for a new offensive and reassigned to the front, which at that time was northwest of Verdun.

By the end of the war, more than 200 Hello Girls had served overseas, and training centers had been established in New York City; Chicago; San Francisco; Philadelphia, Hershey and Lancaster, Pennsylvania; and Atlantic City, New Jersey. Women served in 75 towns in England and France and were often sent to operate equipment just behind the front lines. Pershing praised the Hello Girls for their outstanding work, but when the war was over the operator regiments were disbanded, and the Hello Girls returned to their civilian lives.

Upon returning, Hello Girls requested veteran's status, honorable discharges, and World War I Victory Medals. Their requests were turned down because Army regulations addressed males, not females, and there was a consensus that the Hello Girls were civilian volunteers and not military members. From 1930 to 1977, Merle Egan-Anderson, who worked for the Mountain States Telephone and Telegraph Company before serving in France, and other Hello Girls petitioned Congress for military status. In 1977, President Jimmy Carter signed the bill that gave Citations for Bravery to the women who operated in St. Mihiel. The bill also gave the Hello Girls their recognition as the first female veterans of the U.S. Army.

Ashanti White

See also: Army Signal Corps; World War I (1914–1918).

References and Further Reading

Frahm, Jill. "The Hello Girls: Women Telephone Operators with the American Expeditionary Forces during World War I." *Journal of the Gilded Age and Progressive Era* 3 (2004): 33–42.

Raines, Rebecca Robbins. *Getting the Message Through: A Branch History of the U.S. Army Signal Corps.* Washington, D.C.: Center of Military History, United States Army, 1999.

"Six Hello Girls Help First Army." *Stars and Stripes*, October 4, 1918.

Southall, Sally. *Hold the Line Please: The Story of the Hello Girls.* Studley, UK: Brewin Books, 2003.

"Uncle Sam Presents 'Hello Girls!' " *Stars and Stripes*, March 29, 1918.

HERZ, ALICE (1883–1965)

German-born U.S. peace activist Alice Herz immolated herself in 1965 to protest the escalating war in Vietnam. This action led to seven other antiwar protestors committing the same act.

Born in Germany in 1883 (the exact date of her birth is unknown), Herz, a widow and a Jew, fled Germany with her daughter in 1933 when the Nazis seized power. Herz and her daughter, Helga, first relocated to France, living there until the German invasion of that country in 1940. Both mother and daughter were temporarily forced to live in an internment camp near the Spanish border. In 1942, Herz and her daughter were able to immigrate to the United States. They settled in Detroit, where Herz managed to secure work as an adjunct instructor of German at Wayne State University.

Herz's experience in an internment camp as well as the grim realities of Nazi persecution of Jews and World War II in general convinced her to join the Women's International League for Peace and Freedom (WILPF). After World War II, the increasing threat of nuclear war and the arms race between the world's two superpowers increased her pacifist activities. At first, she was denied U.S. citizenship because of her role in the WILPF, which was considered a radical organization. She later reapplied and was granted citizenship in 1954. Thereafter, her hopes for a world without war and the abolition of nuclear weapons motivated her increasing involvement in local peace activities in the Detroit area.

By the mid-1960s, mounting U.S. military involvement in Vietnam spurred Herz to consider committing a dramatic act of civil disobedience. Linking the peace and civil rights movements of the era as part of the growing social justice movement in the United States, Herz took to heart President Lyndon B. Johnson's speech before Congress urging passage of the 1965 Voting Rights Act. It was at that point, however, that Herz decided to protest publicly the war in Vietnam. She was prompted to take the drastic measure of self-immolation by the example set by Buddhist monk Thich Quang Duc, who had burned himself to death in June 1963 in protest of the Republic of Vietnam government's oppression of Buddhists. The Buddhists in South Vietnam opposed violence and publicly criticized the U.S.-backed government there.

Prior to her dramatic act, Herz wrote a note to friends and fellow activists: "I choose the illuminating death of a Buddhist to protest against a great country trying to wipe out a small country for no reason." Herz commented that she had exhausted all the traditional methods of protests such as marching, civil disobedience, and writing numerous articles and letters. On March 16, 1965, at a busy intersection in Detroit, the 82-year-old Herz set herself on fire. Passersby in an automobile stopped and put out the flames, but she died 10 days later on March 26, 1965.

Herz's decision to follow the protest methods of Vietnamese Buddhist monks was designed to attract national attention. Her actions were soon imitated by pacifists Norman Morrison and Roger Allen LaPorte as well as by five others. Herz is considered the first American martyr of the anti–Vietnam War movement.

Charles F. Howlett

See also: Vietnam War (1965–1973); World War II (1941–1945).

References and Further Reading

Cooney, Robert, and Helen Michalowski. *The Power of the People: Active Nonviolence in the United States*. Philadelphia: New Society Publishers, 1987.

DeBenedetti, Charles, and Charles Chatfield. *An American Ordeal: The Anti-war Movement of the Vietnam Era*. Syracuse, NY: Syracuse University Press, 1990.

Shibata, Shingo. *Phoenix: Letters and Documents of Alice Herz: Thought and Practice of a Modern-day Activist*. New York: Bruce Publishing Co., 1969.

HESTER, LEIGH ANN (1982–)

A military police officer in the Army National Guard, Leigh Ann Hester became the first woman since World War II to earn the Silver Star for valor during combat operations in support of Operation Iraq Freedom.

Born in Bowling Green, Kentucky, on January 12, 1982, Hester was a stand-out high school athlete and manager of a Nashville, Tennessee, shoe store before her enlistment in the Kentucky National Guard at the age of 19, just four months prior to the 9/11 attacks. Upon joining the ranks in April 2001, Hester was assigned as a sergeant to the 617th Military Police (MP) Company in Richmond, Kentucky, which was later deployed to Iraq in November 2004.

Once deployed, the 617th MP Company was attached to Fort Bragg's 503rd MP Battalion, 18th MP Brigade, and stationed at Camp Liberty outside of Baghdad. Hester's unit, Raven 42, was responsible for route security for 15 to 25 miles of roads southeast of Baghdad. Serving as team leader from November 2004 to March 2005, Hester continued to train and prepare for potential threats under the direction of Staff Sgt. Timothy Nein. Hester's squadron was routinely entrusted with protecting supply trains, searching for improvised explosive devices, guarding against potential ambush threats, and ensuring the overall safety of the crucial road system.

During one such operation on March 20, 2005, Hester and her unit were escorting a logistical convoy of over 30 trucks down a four-lane highway known as Supply Route Detroit, east of Salman Pak, Iraq. Hester's squad shadowed the motorcade, following at a distance so as not to be spotted by potential ambushers. After a routine morning, Hester and the troops of Raven 42 began to notice a significant disturbance in the convoy ahead of them. Although initially unaware of what was happening, the members of Raven 42 quickly recognized that the cavalcade was under attack. The lead vehicle in the convoy had been struck by a rocket-propelled grenade (RPG), blocking the roadway and trapping the trailing vehicles. With the convoy unable to move, insurgents began firing upon the motorcade from a system of trenches located north of the highway.

In response, the troops of Raven 42, led by Nein, were directed to flank the enemy from the west, blocking off any potential escape route. In doing so, the squadron became caught between two groups of heavily armed enemy fighters. At this point, engaged in heavy fighting, Hester's unit attempted to go on the offensive. In an effort to break out of the two-front assault, Hester and Nein first turned their attention to their enemies to the south. They exited their vehicles and entered into the enemy trench system, firing their M4 rifles and throwing grenades, killing their attackers along the way. Hester and Nein eliminated the insurgents to the south and then turned their attention to the primary attack on the convoy to the north. Again, Nein and Hester slowly fought their way through the trench system, killing or flushing out the enemy.

Thirty minutes after it had begun, Hester had killed at least three insurgents and, along with Nein, had helped bring the firefight to an end. During the confrontation, 27 insurgents were killed, while 9 more were injured. In addition, the U.S. forces were also able to remove 22 AK-47 assault rifles, 13 RPK light machine guns, 6 RPG launchers, 16 RPG grenades, 40 hand grenades, and 2,700 rounds of ammunition from the enemy's possession. In the aftermath of the ambush, an investigation concluded that subversives had sought to both kill and kidnap as many American soldiers as possible. Through the efforts of Hester, Nein, and the other forces present that day, the enemy's plots were foiled and a significant military victory had been attained.

Following the clash, Hester was presented the Silver Star, the United States' third highest medal for bravery, by Army lieutenant general John R. Vines. Hester became the first woman since World War II to be awarded such an honor. Further, Hester became the first woman in U.S. history to be granted the award for her action in close combat operations. In addition to the Silver Star, Hester was also presented with the Army Good Conduct Medal and the National Defense Service Medal.

Moreover, the U.S. government's formal recognition of Hester's actions caused many to begin to question the military's policy of prohibiting women from taking part in close combat operations. Specifically, internal and external sources have refuted the Pentagon's 1994 combat exclusion policy, arguing that the actions of Hester, and of numerous other women in combat, have made such policies obsolete. Further, the less conventional nature of modern warfare, particularly in Iraq and Afghanistan, has made it more difficult to keep any soldier off the front lines. As a result, Hester's actions may prove to have long-term consequences.

Blake A. Duffield

See also: Brown, Monica Lin (1988–); Campbell, Kim Reed (1975–); Iraq War (2003–2011).

References and Further Reading

Doubler, Michael D. *The National Guard and Reserve: A Reference Handbook*. Westport, CT: Praeger, 2008.

Fainaru, Steve. "Silver Stars Affirm One Unit's Mettle." *Washington Post*, June 26, 2005.

Montag, C. J. "SSG Timothy Nein and the Convoy 678N Engagement." Fort Bliss, TX: U.S. Army Sergeants Major Academy, 2008–2009.

Wood, Sara Wood. "Woman Soldier Receives Silver Star for Valor in Iraq." American Forces Press Service, June 16, 2005.

HIGGINS (HALL), MARGUERITE (1920–1966)

An influential female reporter and war correspondent, Marguerite Higgins's

War correspondent Marguerite Higgins gained fame for her frontline reporting during the Korean War. (Hulton Archive/Getty Images)

coverage of three U.S. wars advanced the cause of female correspondents in combat zones. Her coverage of the Korean War earned her the Pulitzer Prize for international reporting as well as the Associated Press's Woman of the Year award. During the Korean War, she married Lt. Gen. William Hall of the U.S. Air Force. She expressed grave reservations about the Vietnam War in a book titled *Our Vietnam Nightmare* (1965).

Higgins was born on September 3, 1920, in Hong Kong. Her father worked for a shipping company, and three years after her birth the family returned to the United States. Higgins's penchant for writing and her interest in foreign languages first led to a bachelor's degree in French from the University of California at Berkeley in 1941, where

she also wrote for *The Daily Californian*, and then to a master's in journalism from Columbia University a year later. In 1942, she was hired by the *New York Herald Tribune* and married Harvard philosophy professor Stanley Moore. The marriage evaporated quickly after he was drafted and public reports of Higgins's own romantic encounters surfaced.

After pleading with Helen Rogers Reid, wife of the *Tribune*'s owner, to cover the war, Higgins was assigned to the London and Paris bureaus in 1944. In March 1945, however, when it appeared that an Allied victory was imminent, Higgins was reassigned to the battlefront, where she accompanied the U.S. Seventh Army, which liberated the Dachau and Buchenwald concentration camps. At the end of the war, she was awarded an Army campaign ribbon for distinguished service and the New York Newspaper Women's Award as the best foreign correspondent for 1945. She remained in Europe after the war to cover the Nuremberg War Trials. She also covered the escalating Cold War tensions between the United States and the Soviet Union. In 1947, she was promoted to bureau chief in Berlin. During this period, she began dating Lt. Gen. William Hall. They married in 1953 and had two children.

Higgins became chief of the *New York Herald Tribune*'s Tokyo bureau. In 1950, shortly after war broke out in Korea, she set out for the war zone to cover the conflict. Gen. Walton Walker ordered her out of the country, insisting that women did not belong on the front lines. UN commander general Douglas MacArthur overruled Walker and sent a telegram to the *Herald Tribune*, noting that female correspondents would be allowed in Korea and that Higgins, in particular, was well respected.

In May 1950, Higgins went to Japan as bureau chief. A month later, communist North Korea invaded South Korea. Higgins traveled to the capital city of Seoul and recounted the final days before the North Koreans entered the city. She barely escaped in time. The *Tribune* sent its top war reporter, Homer Bigart, to South Korea and ordered Higgins to return to Tokyo because the military had ordered all female reporters banned from the front lines. This order did not deter her, and once more, with Helen Reid's urging, MacArthur granted Higgins's request to report on the front lines. Wearing combat fatigues and intermingling with the soldiers, Higgins's coverage in dangerous situations earned her the respect of male reporters and combat soldiers. She daringly joined U.S. Marines during the Inchon landing, and her *Tribune* stories were often placed alongside those of Bigart.

Higgins's wartime exploits led to the 1951 publication of *War in Korea: The Report of a Woman Combat Correspondent*, which became a best seller. In 1951, she became the first woman to win a Pulitzer Prize for international reporting, which she shared with five other male journalists. In addition, that year the Associated Press named her Woman of the Year. For her courage and bravery, she also received the Marine Corps Reserve Officers Award.

In 1953, she covered the French army's defeat at the Battle of Dien Bien Phu, Vietnam. While covering this engagement, she escaped serious injury when photographer Robert Capra was killed by a landmine a few feet away. In the mid-1950s, she was the first female reporter granted a visa to the Soviet Union in many years, reporting on life under communism, which led to the 1955 publication of *Red Plush and Black Bread*. In 1961, she covered the civil war in the Congo. In 1963, now working for the Long Island paper *Newsday*, Higgins returned to Vietnam, interviewing hundreds of villagers and leaders. These interviews resulted in *Our Vietnam Nightmare* (1965). The book questioned the U.S. military presence in Vietnam.

While in Vietnam, Higgins contracted a tropical disease, resulting in her death on January 3, 1966, at the age of 45. She remains one of the nation's most distinguished war correspondents. She was buried in Arlington National Cemetery.

Charles F. Howlett

See also: Cold War (ca. 1947–1991); Korean War (1950–1953); Vietnam War (1965–1973); World War II (1941–1945).

References and Further Reading

Edwards, Julia. *Women of the World: The Great Foreign Correspondents*. Boston: Houghton Mifflin, 1988.

Elwood-Akers, Virginia. *Women War Correspondents in the Vietnam War, 1961–1975*. Metuchen, NJ: Scarecrow Press, 1988.

Higgins, Marguerite. *Our Vietnam Nightmare: The Story of U.S. Involvement in the Vietnamese Tragedy, with Thoughts on a Future Policy*. New York: Harper & Row, 1965.

Higgins, Marguerite, and Carl Mydans. *War in Korea: The Report of a Woman Combat Correspondent*. Garden City, NY: Doubleday, 1951.

Higgins, Marguerite, and Carl Mydans. *Red Plush and Black Bead*. Garden City, NY: Doubleday, 1955.

Kluger, Richard. *The Paper: The Life and Death of the New York Tribune*. New York: Alfred A. Knopf, 1986.

May, Antoinette. *Witness to War: A Biography of Marguerite Higgins*. New York: Penguin Books, 1985.

HISPANIC AMERICAN WOMEN

Of the more than 200,000 women in the U.S. armed forces today, 11 percent are Hispanic women. Despite the continuing presence of Hispanic women in the United States, their relationship with the military has been somewhat sporadic. It was often difficult for women of color to join military forces because of racial, ethnic, sexual, and gender discrimination. In addition, many Hispanic women did not consider military service a viable option, instead sticking to a cultural norm that held that women should work only in the home, where they would cook, clean, and raise children. Most participation by Hispanic American women in the military, therefore, began with World War II.

Despite cultural and social restraints, some Hispanic women took active, if largely hidden, roles in the military much earlier. For example, Maria Gertrudes Barceló was an entrepreneur during the Mexican War from 1846 to 1848. Residing in New Mexico during the time, Barceló loaned money to the military and was a well-respected informant for U.S. military personnel. Other Hispanic women served as cooks for the soldiers during the Mexican War. In addition, from 1859 to 1862, Maria Andre, also known Maria Mestre de los Dolores, served as the keeper of the St. Augustine Lighthouse in Florida, making her the first Hispanic American woman to serve in the Coast Guard and the first Hispanic American woman to oversee a federal shore installation. Another woman, Loretta Janeta Velasquez from Cuba, disguised herself as a man and fought for the Confederacy during the American Civil War in the early 1860s. As Lt. Harry T. Buford, Velasquez spied for the Confederate Army.

More typically, Hispanic American women, like women of all backgrounds, served as nurses during wartime. In this capacity, they could serve on the homefront as well as near a combat zone, and in hospitals as well as in homes. As the medical profession and women's role in the military expanded in the 20th century, women could be found serving as military medical aides, anesthesiologists, and nurses to wounded soldiers.

During World War I, the nation's small Hispanic American population was concentrated in the southwestern United States. Their location did not preclude them from military service. Many Hispanic men served in the armed forces. Women also did their part for their nation. During World War I, the Army began to recruit young women to assist with medical jobs. One of the first women to join was of Puerto Rican descent. Dr. Dolores Piñero was the first female doctor to be hired under a contract by the U.S. military during World War I. She served in the U.S. Army Medical Corps. Piñero was the only woman who served in the Army in Puerto Rico, working at the base hospital in San Juan, specializing in anesthesia, and helping during the influenza epidemic.

However, it was not until World War II that Hispanic American women and women in general became fully active in the U.S. military. The creation of women's branches in the military, including the Women's Army Corps (WAC), the Army Nurse Corps (ANC), and the Marine Corps Women's Reserve (Women Marines) allowed women to enlist in an official capacity. These female branches gave Hispanic women the opportunity to increase their participation and contributions to the U.S. war effort. Two hundred Puerto Rican women served in the WAC. In addition, women of Mexican descent, such as Maria Menefee, served in the U.S. Navy. Carmen Contreras-Bozak was the first Hispanic to serve in the WAC, where she served as an interpreter and also served in numerous administrative positions.

Hispanic women, however, often faced difficulties in being fully incorporated into the women's service. They frequently experienced segregation in military hospitals and nursing services, oftentimes because it was unclear whether they were white or black. Despite these setbacks, Hispanic women still made progress in their public role. For example, Ernestine Evans, one of the first women to be voted into a state legislature, in 1941, served as the administrator in a military hospital and treated wounded World War II soldiers. Hispanic American women also served as translators, interpreters, and interrogators during military conflicts.

Another way Hispanic American women participated in war efforts was domestically, often taking up jobs in the defense industries. They worked producing war goods in steel, meatpacking, sewing, and ammunition industries. For example, many took jobs in munitions factories, working alongside American women from all backgrounds. During World War II, California's large aircraft manufacturing industry turned to the women in the large local Hispanic population to fill jobs vacated by men. As a result, Hispanic American women's work in these factories contributed to the building of military commodities.

Other Hispanic American women played a nonmilitary but crucial role in World War II by taking low-paying jobs as physicians and thereby freeing up male doctors to join the overseas war effort. Many served as Red Cross nurses.

Hispanic women's mutual aid homefront organizations also helped them contribute to the war effort. In 1944, Hispanic women created the Association of Hispanic American Mothers and Wives to help with the war effort. The organization helped contribute to the war by printing newsletters, saving scrap metal, selling war bonds, and collecting used fat for explosives. It also provided a support system for women who had sons, brothers, or husbands overseas by offering day care services, translation services, and clothing. Other organizations similarly raised funds, bought war bonds, and supported members of the Hispanic community who had relatives fighting in the war. Women's exertions through these channels contributed to war efforts on a national level and a personal level, both directly and indirectly.

After World War II, the military reduced its demands for servicewomen of all ethnicities. However, the Korean War again offered opportunities for women to participate in the military. For example, Rose Franco, who served in the Marine Corps, became the first woman to become a chief warrant officer. The Vietnam War again produced a need for servicewomen in the WAC, the Navy's Women Accepted for Volunteer Emergency Service (WAVES), and the Women Air Force Service Pilots (WASP). Hispanic women actively participated in these branches of the military.

In the 1990s, approximately 20,000 Hispanic Americans, some of them women, were active in the military. Hispanic American women have participated in military campaigns around the globe, including those in Iraq and Afghanistan. Although not allowed in combat roles, women still face the dangers on the front lines. For example, in 2005, Cpl. Ramona M. Valdez became one of the first Women Marines to die in action in Iraq after an improvised explosive device exploded near her convoy.

Over time, Hispanic women, like women of all backgrounds, have become increasingly involved in and accepted by the U.S. military. In August 2006, Angela Salinas made history by becoming the first Hispanic woman promoted to brigadier general in the Marines.

Brittany Erin Elwood

See also: American Red Cross; Army Nurse Corps (ANC); Civil War (1861–1865); Cold War (ca. 1947–1991); Cubero, Linda Garcia (1958–); Espionage; Gulf War (1991); Iraq War (2003–2011); Korean War (1950–1953); Nursing; Republic of Texas; Spanish-American War (1898); Spanish Influenza (Influenza Pandemic); Valdez, Ramona M. (1984–2005); Velazquez, Loreta Janeta [Harry T. Buford] (1842–1897); Vietnam War (1965–1973); War on Terror (2001–); Women Accepted for Volunteer Emergency Service (WAVES); Women Air Force Service Pilots (WASP); Women Marines; Women's Army Corps (WAC); World War I (1914–1918); World War II (1941–1945).

References and Further Reading

Jensen, Kimberly. *Mobilizing Minerva: American Women in the First World War.* Urbana: University of Illinois Press, 2008.

Ruíz, Vicki, and Virginia Sánchez Korrol, eds. *Latina Legacies: Identity, Biography, and Community.* New York: Oxford University Press, 2005.

Skaine, Rosemarie. *Women at War: Gender Issues of Americans in Combat.* Jefferson, NC: McFarland & Company, 1999.

Telgen, Diane, and Jim Kamp, eds. *Notable Hispanic American Women, Volume 68.* Detroit: Gale Research, 1993.

Villahermosa, Gilberto. "America's Hispanics in America's Wars." *Army Magazine,* September 2002.

Weinstein, Laurie Lee, and Christie C. White, eds. *Wives and Warriors: Women in the Military in the United States and Canada.* Westport, CT: Bergin and Garvey, 1997.

HITT, GENEVIEVE YOUNG (1885–1963)

Genevieve Young Hitt was the first woman to work for the U.S. government as a cryptologist, initially as an unpaid volunteer code- and cipher-breaker during the Punitive Expedition and later as a salaried cryptographer during World War I.

Born in La Grange, Texas, on May 29, 1885, Genevieve Young was raised in San Antonio, Texas, and completed her secondary education at St. Mary's Hall in May 1903. In July 1911, she married Capt. (later Col.) Parker Hitt and moved to Fort Leavenworth, Kansas, where he was first a student and then an instructor at the U.S. Army's Signal School.

Genevieve Hitt was exposed to the arts of cryptanalysis and cryptography through her husband's studies. She learned to use a sliding-strip cipher device he developed and may have assisted with the preparation of his groundbreaking *Manual for the Solution of Military Ciphers*, which was published by the Army in 1916.

That same year, U.S. Army forces under the command of Gen. John J. Pershing pursued the Mexican rebel Pancho Villa into Mexico and sought to evade Mexican government forces in what is known as the Punitive Expedition. These troops intercepted Mexican government radio messages, some of which were in code or cipher. Because the United States had no cryptologic organization, the coded and enciphered messages were forwarded to a small group of amateurs for analysis. Both of the Hitts were among this group. Genevieve's unpaid code and cipher work is the first known instance of a woman providing this type of military support to the U.S. government.

In May 1917, shortly after the U.S. entry into World War I, Parker Hitt was selected for the initial staff of the American Expeditionary Force, and Genevieve moved back to San Antonio. Before leaving for France, Parker spoke to Maj. Ralph Van Deman, chief of the Military Intelligence Section, and advised him that Genevieve was available for cryptologic work. In June 1917, on her husband's behalf, Genevieve made

a trip to George Fabyan's Riverbank Laboratories in Geneva, Illinois, an early center of cryptanalytic research. There she demonstrated Hitt's cipher device to Fabyan and his employees, among them the future U.S. government cryptologists William F. and Elizabeth S. Friedman.

By August 1, 1917, cipher messages intercepted by the U.S. Army's Southern Department were being sent to Hitt's home at Fort Sam Houston for analysis, and she again supported the Army as an unpaid cryptanalyst. This work resulted in her appointment, on April 23, 1918, to lead the code work for the Southern Department's Intelligence Office at a salary of $1,000 per year. She worked five and a half days a week with frequent overtime, coded and decoded official intelligence correspondence, controlled the Army codebooks, and broke intercepted coded and enciphered messages. Her efficiency, aptitude, and leadership led to her team taking on all the code work for the entire Southern Department in late July 1918. She was recommended for a salary increase in September 1918, but due to paperwork delays, the November 11, 1918, Armistice, and her subsequent resignation, she never received the increase.

For a few months in 1920, Hitt worked as an abstractor in the Radical Section of the Bureau of Investigation (BOI), the predecessor to the Federal Bureau of Investigation (FBI). Her supervisor was J. Edgar Hoover. After leaving the BOI, she never again worked for the government. Genevieve received a patent for an illuminating device for dial telephones on February 18, 1930, but there is no record of the device ever being used. The Hitts's personal correspondence reveals that she was likely the uncredited coauthor of her husband's 1935 work *The A B C of Secret Writing.*

Although her career was brief, Hitt broke ground for women in cryptology. Her natural ability and willingness to take on challenging and untraditional work at a time when the United States had no formal cryptologic service enabled her to make a small but significant contribution to early military intelligence efforts as the U.S. government's first female cryptologist.

She died at her Front Royal, Virginia, farm on February 6, 1963.

Betsy Rohaly Smoot

See also: Espionage; Friedman, (Clara) Elizebeth Smith (1892–1980); World War I (1914–1918).

References and Further Reading

Center for Cryptologic History. *The Friedman Legacy.* Fort George G. Meade, MD: National Security Agency, 2006.

Hatch, David A. "The Punitive Expedition Military Reform and Communications Intelligence." *Cryptologia* 31, no. 1 (2007): 38–45.

Smoot, Betsy R. "An Accidental Cryptologist: The Brief Career of Genevieve Young Hitt." *Cryptologia* 35, no. 2 (2011): 164–75.

Smoot, Betsy R. "Pioneers of U.S. Military Cryptology: Colonel Parker Hitt and His Wife, Genevieve Young Hitt." *Federal History* 4 (2012).

HOBBY, OVETA CULP (1905–1995)

Oveta Culp Hobby was a prominent figure in Texas politics, a U.S. Army

During World War II, Oveta Culp Hobby helped create the Women's Auxiliary Army Corps (WAAC). She served as the first director of both the WAAC and the Women's Army Corps (WAC). In this role she became the Army's first female colonel. (Dwight D. Eisenhower Library)

officer, and the first commander of the Womens' Army Corps (WAC) during World War II.

Oveta Culp was born in Killeen, Texas, on January 19, 1905, the second of seven children to a prominent political family. Her father, Ike W. Culp, was a lawyer and state legislator. She learned early the concepts of service to family, community, state, and nation. She attended Mary Hardin Baylor College in Killeen and went on to study law at the University of Texas in Austin. She served as parliamentarian of the Texas State Legislature—a position that served as a starting point for her rise in Texas politics. In 1931, she married former Texas governor William P. Hobby, a man more than 25 years her senior. She gained prominence as a newspaper and radio executive in Houston, lawyer, writer, president of the Texas League of Women Voters, and civic activist in various civic organizations in Houston and elsewhere in Texas.

Hobby's wartime service began in June 1941, when, at President Roosevelt's request, Army chief of staff George Marshall appointed her chief of the Women's Interest Section of the War Department's Bureau of Public Relations. In that position, she was responsible for issues concerning the wives and dependents of Army personnel. She was also active in the initial organization of the Women's Army Auxiliary Corps (WAAC) and in negotiations with Congress over drafting of the legislation creating the WAAC. Congress approved the WAAC authorization bill on May 14, 1942. In the course of her work in the Bureau of Public Relations, the negotiations with Congress, and the planning for the organization of the WAAC, Hobby so impressed Marshall that he recommended to the secretary of war that she be appointed the WAAC director. She was sworn in on May 16, 1942.

As WAAC director, Hobby faced a host of problems in organizing the new service, especially overcoming the traditional stereotypes of women held by the conservative males who dominated the U.S. Army officer corps. Both Hobby and Marshall sought to build an image of the WAAC as an organization of sober, sensible, and hard-working women carrying out tasks vital to the war effort. Hobby had to fight for adequate funding and supplies to build barracks and to supply the needs of the WAAC's female personnel. Both the Army Corps of Engineers and the Quartermaster Corps initially resisted

cooperation, arguing that support for the WAAC was more of a drain on funds and resources that it was worth.

The most serious problem Hobby had to deal with were the sensationalist allegations spread by word-of-mouth gossip and private letters that women in the WAAC were engaging in sexual misconduct. One newspaper columnist charged that the Army was encouraging loose morals by issuing women with contraceptives and prophylactics. These rumors provoked a strong reaction from President Roosevelt as well as from others. Hobby undertook a vigorous campaign to discredit such accusations. She testified before Congress, citing statistics proving that the incidence of pregnancy and sexually transmitted diseases among women in the WAACs was lower than those in the civilian population.

As the war continued, support for women serving in the armed forces strengthened. Manpower shortages and an inadequate pool of male replacements for both combat and support positions led to calls for the recruitment of more women and the opening of more occupational specialties for women. Hobby undertook a vigorous campaign to discredit accusations of loose morals and successfully lobbied for congressional passage of a bill converting the WAAC from an auxiliary civilian organization into a full unit of the U.S. Army. Congress approved legislation creating the WAC in July 1943. Hobby was named as director and given the rank of colonel.

The two biggest problems Hobby had to deal with throughout her tenure as director of the WAC were continuing sex discrimination, with its attendant impacts on morale and resource allocation, and recruiting. Even so, she was instrumental in nearly quadrupling the number of Army occupations open to women over the course of the war.

Recruiting and training of personnel proved to be a daunting task. From the inception of the WAAC and, later, the WAC, Hobby was involved in contests with other War Department and civilian bureaucracies over the recruitment of women both for the Army and civilian sectors. Her first battle was with the Army Service Forces for control of recruiting. With Marshall's support, she prevailed in April 1944. She also had to overcome reservations from the War Manpower Commission that recruiting women for the WAC would threaten industrial production.

Hobby's most important target was the integrity and quality of personnel and the marketing of the WAC. The War Department's initial recruiting goal was 1 million women for the WAC—a target she felt was unrealistic. In addition, Hobby was concerned that mass recruiting would force a lowering of standards. When the War Department lowered the recruiting goal to 400,000 to 500,000, she made every effort to reach it even though she realized that chances for reaching that number were also remote.

Hobby also sought to control advertising for the WAC. The original recruiting theme, "Release a Man to Fight," proved ineffective and offensive to some. It generated resistance from male soldiers in noncombat occupations as well as from the families of servicemen who felt that more women in the Army would put more men in combat units. Hobby consequently launched a campaign emphasizing the WAC as the preserver of the American home. In this campaign, Hobby stressed that the WAC allowed men who otherwise might be drafted, despite the occupational needs of the economy or medical limitations, to remain in the civilian sector. Hobby's recruiting efforts paid off, although not to the extent that the War Department had hoped. As of January 1, 1944, membership in the WAC reached nearly 63,000, as opposed to 21,000 the year before. Membership in the WAC stayed at this level for the duration of the war.

Hobby also took the lead in recruiting African American women. From the inception of the WAAC forward, she sought to be as fair to black women as the values of the time allowed. In May 1942, she announced that black women would be recruited in proportion to their numbers in the total U.S. population (about 10 percent). There was some initial success. The first graduating class of female officers from WAC officer candidate class contained 36 African Americans out a total of 360. Ultimately, however, the total of black women was never more than 4 percent of the total population. Hobby and her staff still had to deal with the realities of pursuing fairness in the face of deeply held racial and gender prejudices in wartime U.S. society. Nevertheless, the WAC under Hobby's leadership was virtually alone among the women's services willing to take a chance on African American women.

Hobby resigned as WAC commander in July 1945, citing exhaustion and the need to spend more time with her family. She left at the rank of colonel—a grade equal to that held by men who often commanded no than 500 servicemembers—despite having had responsibility for more than 60,000 individuals. Hobby had built the organization almost from scratch, solving a myriad of problems in the face of male prejudice. Shortly before her departure, there was discussion of promoting her to brigadier general, but neither Congress nor the War Department took any action. This underranking reflected the extent to which sex discrimination still existed in the military at the end of the war.

The end of her military service did not mean an end to Hobby's career in public service. She resumed her political career in Texas as a lawyer and as publisher of the *Houston Post*. President Dwight D. Eisenhower named her to his cabinet as the first secretary of health, education, and welfare in 1953, making her only the second woman in United States history to achieve cabinet rank. Her son, William P. Hobby Jr., served as lieutenant governor of Texas. Hobby died in 1995.

Walter F. Bell

See also: African American Women; Women Accepted for Volunteer Emergency Service (WAVES); Women's Air Service Pilots (WASP); Women's Army Auxiliary Corps (WAAC); Women's Army Corps (WAC); World War II (1941–1945).

References and Further Reading

Treadwell, Mattie. *The Women's Army Corps.* U.S. Army in World War II, Special Studies. Washington, D.C.: U.S. Army Center of Military History, 1953.

Weatherford, Doris. *American Women and World War II.* New York: Facts on File, 1995.

HODGERS, JENNIE [ALBERT D. J. CASHIER] (1844–1915)

Jennie Hodgers served in male disguise as Albert D. J. Cashier to fight in the Union army for three years during in the American Civil War—the longest verifiable service by a female soldier in that war. In fact, one of the unique things about Hodgers is that her service in male disguise is extremely well documented.

Born December 25, 1844, in Belfast, Ireland, little is known about Hodgers's early years. As a young girl in Ireland, she apparently worked as a farmer and shepherd and wore male clothing while performing her chores. Hodgers took on a male identity when she boarded a U.S.-bound ship as a stowaway. She ended up working in Illinois, and by the outbreak of the Civil War was already living under the identity of "Albert D. J. Cashier." She never explained her reasons for assuming male identity, but some sources indicate that she had an uncle in the United States who was able to get a job for his "nephew" in a shoe factory. Undoubtedly it was easier and safer for a runaway like Hodgers to earn a living as a young boy rather than as a girl.

In 1862, when Hodgers was 17, she joined the 95th Illinois Volunteer Infantry. Five feet tall, Cashier was one of the shorter soldiers to be accepted into the Army; lack of height, however, did not keep her from being a good soldier. During her service, the 95th Illinois was an active regiment, part of Ulysses Grant's Army of Tennessee. Former comrade C. W. Ives regarded Cashier as a good soldier and recalled several incidents in which she gained distinction. Cashier's captain considered the soldier —who participated in 40 battles without being wounded—fearless and dependable. Not one of her comrades seems to have suspected that Cashier was anything but "a brave little soldier," although they saw him as a bit of a loner who kept to himself.

Like many other Civil War soldiers, Hodgers contracted chronic diarrhea, which plagued her from mid-1863 on, though she managed to avoid hospitalization, which might have exposed her identity. Cashier remained with the 95th Illinois until "he" was honorably discharged in August 1865.

After the war, Hodgers continued to live as Cashier for many decades. By 1869, she had settled down to work as a custodian and handyman in Saunemin, Illinois. Hodgers lived a solitary life, though she seems to have been accepted as almost a member of one local family for whom she worked. There is no evidence that she was ever sexually active or romantically involved with another person. In 1890, she applied for a government pension, but it was denied when she refused to submit to a physical examination. In 1911, when she was 67 years old, Hodgers had an accident and seriously injured her leg. In the course of treatment, locals discovered her sex, but they kept the secret. Because she was unable to continue working, her only recourse was to apply for a government pension and nursing care in the Illinois Soldiers and Sailors Home. The aid of Ira M. Lish, a state senator, was enlisted, but everyone still kept Cashier's secret while helping

the illiterate veteran gain admittance to the home.

However, Cashier's identity did not remain secret long in the nursing home. Once revealed, she attracted a great deal of attention. The state of Illinois had her declared insane, at least in part because of her long masquerade in male identity, and transferred her to an asylum. She was forced thereafter to wear women's clothing, which she hated; she even pinned her skirt into the shape of pants. She died less than two years after her transfer to the asylum. In the meantime, investigations by the military pension bureau confirmed that "Albert D. J. Cashier" had indeed served in the 95th Illinois. Her former comrades were uniformly surprised to hear of her true identity, but each corroborated to the investigators that she had performed all the duties of a soldier and in interviews then and for years to come continued to refer to Hodgers as "he" even after learning that "he" was a woman.

Hodgers had been a member of the Grand Army of the Republic (GAR), and upon her death on October 10, 1915, at East Moline State Hospital, Illinois, she was buried by the GAR in her uniform with full military honors. Her tombstone bore the inscription "Albert D. J. Cashier, 95th Ill. Inf."

Gayle Veronica Fischer

See also: Civil War (1861–1865).

References and Further Reading

Blanton, DeAnne, and Lauren McCook. *They Fought Like Demons: Women Soldiers in the American Civil War.* Baton Rouge: Louisiana State University Press, 2002.

Larson, C. Kay. "Bonnie Yank and Ginny Reb." *Minerva: Quarterly Report on Women and the Military* 8, no. 1 (1990): 35–61.

Leonard, Elizabeth. *All the Daring of a Soldier: Women of the Civil War Armies.* New York: W. W. Norton and Co., 1999.

National Archives, Washington, D.C., RG 15, Records of the Veterans Administration, Albert D. J. Cashier Pension File, and RG 94, Military Service Records and Medical Records of Albert Cashier.

HOEFLY, E. ANN (1919–2003)

Brig. Gen. E. Ann Hoefly was the first woman to rise to star rank in the U.S. Air Force Medical Corps. She was also the first woman in the Air Force Medical Service to be promoted to general. Over her long military career, Hoefly's responsibilities expanded to include 180 medical facilities around the world from 1,000-bed hospitals to small dispensaries. In 30 years of nursing, she worked in anesthesia and psychiatric care and was a qualified flight nurse.

Hoefly was born in Long Island, New York, in 1919. She graduated from high school in Hackettstown, a small community on the banks of the Musconetcong River in northwest New Jersey. In 1943, she graduated from the Methodist Hospital School of Nursing in Brooklyn, and the following year she enlisted in the U.S. Army. When she entered the U.S. Army Nursing Corps in 1944, the law finally allowed women to be commissioned as officers. However, there was not total equality for women in service. For the first two decades of Hoefly's career, women who married or became pregnant while serving in the armed forces were forced to resign their positions. These restrictions did not worry Hoefly, who prioritized her career over marriage and family.

Hoefly's military career included an extensive amount of education. Four years after joining the Air Force, Hoefly completed a course in postgraduate work in neuropsychiatric nursing at the Medical Field Service School in Texas. She attended Flight Nurse School at the U.S. Air Force School of Aviation Medicine in 1952, completed her BS in nursing at Florida Southern College in 1953, graduated with an MS in nursing administration at Columbia University in 1955, and passed a medical management of mass casualties course in 1956. In 1967, she attended and graduated from the Air War College and, in 1971, completed a degree at the Industrial College of the Armed Forces. In her off time, Hoefly sculpted, fished, and became a competent carpenter.

Hoefly's first assignment was with England General Hospital in Atlantic City, New Jersey. During World War II, she volunteered to go overseas and was assigned to the Army's 235th Field Hospital in the European Theater. After the end of World War II, she worked at Halloran General Hospital in Staten Island, New York. After returning to the United States, she exited the Army. Eighteen months later, she reenlisted in the newly formed U.S. Air Force as a general duty nurse and began training in the field of neuropsychiatric nursing. She was attracted to the neuropsychiatric domain after her experiences with patients in a U.S. field hospital in France who had suffered from neurological illnesses as a result of head trauma.

There were a relatively small number of people who recognized the need for such medical specialties, so Hoefly and her colleagues had to overcome great obstacles in attempting to move the discipline forward.

As the Korean War came to an end and the Cold War emerged, she was assigned to Valley Forge General Hospital in Pennsylvania and later to the 306th Medical Group at MacDill Air Force Base in Florida. She moved to the Department of Psychiatry of the Medical Field Service School and was assigned as a flight nurse for the 1724th Air Transportation Squadron at Brooks Air Force Base in Texas. She enjoyed the arena of flight nursing, which required a talent for developing and directing aeromedical evacuation crews on airplanes and planning for and preparation of aeromedical evacuation and mass casualty missions. Later, she became a training instructor for the flight nurse program. From Texas, she transferred to the Psychiatric Nurse Section of the 3883rd School Group at Gunter Air Force Base in Alabama.

In the 1960s and 1970s, Hoefly established "well baby" and cancer clinics. She also expanded the role of nurses in the Air Force by developing new instructional and health education programs for medical enlisted and officer personnel. During the austere zero-draft phase of the early 1970s, she created a nurse midwives facilities program for Air Force personnel and their families. During the Vietnam War, Hoefly was sent to the Office of the Surgeon General in Washington, D.C., and shortly after became the chief nurse of the 5th Nursing Division of the Air Force Hospital, Tachikawa Air Base, in Japan. From 1968 until her retirement in 1974, she made yearly visits to Vietnam.

Near the end of her career, she was stationed at the Air Force Systems Command at Andrews Air Force Base in Maryland and oversaw nursing operations at the Office of the Surgeon General. Her last duty was as chief of the U.S. Air Force Nurse Corps in 1968, and she was promoted to brigadier general in July 1972. Her military decorations included the Legion of Merit and Air Force Outstanding Unit Award Ribbon with Oak Leaf Cluster.

Hoefly retired May 1, 1974, and settled in Summerfield, Florida, with her two white Arabian horses, five dogs, five cats, and a 21-foot boat.

Hoefly died on August 3, 2003. At her death, the Air Force established the General E. Ann Hoefly Award for excellence in clinical nursing.

Mary Raum

See also: Air Force Nurse Corps (AFNC); Army Nurse Corps (ANC); Cold War (ca. 1947–1991); Korean War (1950–1953); Nursing; Public Law 90-130 (1967); Vietnam War (1965–1973); World War II (1941–1945).

References and Further Reading

Baron, Scott. *They Also Served: Military Biographies of Uncommon Americans.* Spartanburg, SC: Military Information Enterprises, 1997.

Holm, Jeanne M. *Women in the Military: An Unfinished Revolution.* New York: Presidio Press, 1992.

Reeves, Connie. *The History of the Air Force Nurse Corps.* N.p.: Amazon Digital Services, 2011.

HOISINGTON, ELIZABETH P. (1918–2007)

Brig. Gen. Elizabeth Hoisington was the second woman to be promoted to the rank of one-star general (brigadier general) and the first woman in the Army to receive that honor. The member of a military family, which included a father and three brothers who graduated from West Point, Hoisington enlisted in the military in 1942 and retired in 1971.

Hoisington was born in Newton, Kansas, on November 3, 1918. Following her 1936 high school graduation from Notre Dame of Maryland High School in Baltimore, she attended the College of Notre Dame of Maryland. Hoisington graduated from college in 1940 with a bachelor's degree in chemistry. Before her 1942 enlistment in the Army, Hoisington spent nearly two years working in Alaska, where her father was stationed.

Hoisington completed basic training in the Women's Army Auxiliary Corps (WAAC, later the Women's Army Corps, or WAC) in December 1942 and received her first assignment to the 9th WAAC Filter Company—Aircraft Warning Service in Bangor, Maine. Her commanding officer assigned her as first sergeant after only two weeks on the job. In May 1943, she completed Officer Candidate School as a third officer, the equivalent of a second lieutenant in the male Army. As an officer, she commanded WAC units in Fort Oglethorpe, Georgia, and Camp Cooke, California, and graduated from the Army Exchange School in 1944. Shortly after completing this training, Hoisington transferred to Europe.

As executive officer of the WAC Detachment for the European Headquarters Command, Hoisington served in London, Paris, and Frankfurt from 1944 to 1946. She left the WAC briefly in 1946 to support her family after her father suffered a heart attack. Hoisington returned to WAC service in early 1948, several months before the Women's Armed Services Integration Act ensured women a permanent place in the military.

Beginning in 1948, Hoisington served as executive officer of the WAC Battalion, General Headquarters of the Far East Command, in Tokyo. She held this position for two years and then commanded a WAC detachment in Virginia. While on assignment at the Pentagon from 1951 to 1954, Hoisington worked under WAC directors Col. Mary Hallaren and Col. Irene Galloway. This experience helped Hoisington learn more about staff work and writing as well as about WAC history.

During the next 10 years (1954 to 1964), Hoisington's military career took her to a number of assignments. Her duty stations included the Sixth Army Headquarters in San Francisco, the Office of the Deputy Chief of Staff for Personnel at the Pentagon, and the U.S. European Command Headquarters in Paris. Hoisington graduated from the WAC Officer Advanced Class in 1954, the U.S. Army Command and General Staff College in 1957, and the U.S. Army Management Course in 1964. In late 1964, Hoisington's second-to-last military assignment as commander of the U.S. WAC Center and commandant of the U.S. WAC School in Fort McClellan, Alabama, involved supervising officer training, operations, and staffing.

In 1966, Hoisington succeeded Galloway as the seventh director of the WAC. Over the next five years, she led WACs through numerous changes and helped expand the number of women in service. The passage of Public Law 90-130 in 1967 offered the opportunity to begin promoting female officers above the rank of lieutenant colonel for the first time. Under Hoisington's leadership, the WAC also grew by nearly one-third, from 10,000 to 13,000 members. In December 1968, six WAC officers became the first to receive permanent promotion to full colonel, and in 1969 the first group of WAC officers graduated from the Army War College.

Hoisington viewed the WAC director role as a public relations position and devoted extensive attention to publicity opportunities to help improve the WAC's image and raise recruitment numbers. Hoisington led the creation of a training film and revised women's uniforms in an effort to improve public perception of the WAC. Because of the negative military press resulting from the Vietnam War, Hoisington reinstated a marriage discharge policy that allowed servicewomen to separate from service voluntarily upon marriage, even if they had not completed their terms of service. Hoisington believed that this policy would help improve morale during the war, although the policy also increased discharge rates slightly.

Although plans to do so began before Hoisington became WAC director, the first WACs arrived in Vietnam in 1966, and the detachment remained active until late 1972. In 1967, Hoisington toured Vietnam to see how WACs were adjusting to their roles in the war zone. She remained adamant that women did not need weapons in the war zone because she believed U.S. combat soldiers offered sufficient protection. Moreover, Hoisington continually insisted that servicewomen wear their issued green cord uniforms instead of fatigues in order to ensure that women remained feminine at all times.

Hoisington believed firmly that the image the WACs projected was important to ensuring Americans accepted women in uniform. To that end, she endorsed ways to ensure women remained feminine rather than expanding into male-only fields. For example, she rejected the idea that women who had illegitimate children should be allowed in the military, believing that it represented a lowering of standards. She also did not believe that women needed to attend the military academies.

In 1970, Hoisington and Anna Hays of the Army Nurse Corps became the first women promoted to brigadier general. The following year, Hoisington retired in a ceremony at Fort McClelland, which was attended by Gen. William Westmoreland.

Seven years after Hoisington's retirement, the Army abolished the WAC and integrated women completely into the Regular Army. In 1985, despite her beliefs that women did not need to be in the military academies, Hoisington became a visiting member of the Board of the Virginia Military Institute. She continued to disapprove of women's movement towards combat roles and felt that women were unsuited for such positions. Although she supported equal pay for equal work, Hoisington was not an advocate of the Equal Rights Amendment.

Hoisington never married. She died of congestive heart failure in 2007 at the age of 88.

Tanya L. Roth

See also: Army Nurse Corps (ANC); Defense Advisory Committee on Women in the Services (DACOWITS); Galloway, Irene O. (1908–1963); Hallaran, Mary (1907–2005); Hays, Anna Mae McCabe (1920–); Public Law 90-130 (1967); Vietnam War (1965–1973); Women's Armed Services Integration Act of 1948 (Public Law 80-625); Women's Army Auxiliary Corps (WAAC);Women's Army Corps (WAC); Women's Army Corps (WAC) Officer Basic Course; World War II (1941–1945).

References and Further Reading

Holm, Jeanne. *In Defense of a Nation: Servicewomen in World War II*. St. Petersburg, FL: Vandamere Press, 1998.

Holm, Jeanne. *Women in the Military: An Unending Revolution (Revised Edition)*. Novato, CA: Presidio Press, 1993.

Morden, Bettie J. *The Women's Army Corps, 1945–1978*. Washington, D.C.: Center of Military History, 1989.

HOLM, JEANNE M. (1921–2010)

Maj. Gen. Jeanne Holm was one of the first women to be promoted to the flag ranks and the first to be promoted to major general. Holm began serving in the U.S. military during World War II, and her career in the armed forces spanned more than three decades, including high-level positions in the Women in the Air Force (WAF) service component. During her career in the service, she worked constantly to improve servicewomen's status in the military. Holm was also known for her writing on military women's history.

Although Holm served most of her career in the Air Force, she began as a member of the Women's Army Auxiliary Corps (WAAC) during World War II when she enlisted in 1942. After training at Fort Des Moines, she served as a truck driver. Within a year, Holm was among the first enlisted women accepted to attend officer candidate school to become a commissioned officer. In 1943, she began commanding basic training companies as a second lieutenant and decided to stay in the services when the WAAC became an official part of the Army, the Women's Army Corps (WAC), in 1943. From 1943 to 1944, she continued to hold command positions in Georgia and West Virginia and was ultimately promoted to the rank of captain. Over the course of the war, Holm trained more than 14 basic training companies. When the war ended, Holm returned briefly to private life and used the G.I. Bill to attend school at Lewis and Clark College in Portland, Oregon, from 1946 until after the passage of the Women's Armed Services Integration Act in 1948.

Although initially recalled to Camp Lee, Virginia (now Fort Lee), in 1948 to command WACs during the Berlin Airlift, Holm transferred soon to the newly created Air Force. As a woman, she served specifically in the WAF component of the branch. While stationed in Europe from 1949 to 1952, Holm received a promotion to major.

In early 1952, Holm became the first woman to attend the Air Command and Staff School at Maxwell Air Force Base in Alabama. Following this training, she received assignment to Air Force Headquarters in Washington, D.C., where she spent one year as an administrative officer in the Office of the Director, Women's Air Force, and three years as a plans and programs officer in the Office of the Deputy Chief of Staff, Personnel. Holm returned to Lewis and Clark College as a student officer to complete her degree in 1956 and 1957 before being assigned to Naples, Italy, until 1961. In March 1959, Holm advanced to lieutenant colonel, which was at that time the highest permanent rank female officers could hold in any service branch.

As lieutenant colonel, Holm returned to Washington, D.C., as a planning and program officer and was assigned as congressional staff officer. In 1965, she received a temporary promotion to colonel when assigned to the position of director of WAF to oversee women's roles in the Air Force and to recommend policy related to their service. She held this role for eight years, during which time she worked with servicewomen and the civilian Defense Advisory Committee on Women in the Services (DACOWITS) to expand women's opportunities in the services. During her time in this position, she helped open the Air Force Reserve Officer Training Corps (ROTC) program to women and supported legislative efforts to remove women's rank limitations. Holm instituted a sex education program that helped lower the number of pregnancies among WAFs. She also helped secure a broader range of career opportunities for women in the services and fought to prevent pregnant servicewomen from being automatically discharged from

service. Under Holm's directorship, the number of WAFs doubled.

In 1967, Congress passed Public Law 90-130, which removed rank limitations on women. In 1968, Holm became one of the first two Air Force women promoted to the permanent rank of colonel. Three years later, Holm became the first female Air Force officer to be promoted to brigadier general.

Two years later, in 1973, she became the first woman in the military to attain the rank of major general. After completing her tour as director of WAF in 1973, Holm became director of the secretary of the Air Force Personnel Council. By 1975, she retired formally from the military but continued to serve as an advocate for servicewomen and civilian women in a new appointment as special assistant for women under President Gerald Ford. In 1976, Holm also joined the DACOWITS for a three-year term as a member of the organization with which she had worked for so many years. While Holm served on DACOWITS, the organization recommended women be allowed to serve in combat and sought the end of sex discrimination provisions in military policy.

Holm received many awards and recognitions during her years in the military. She was recognized with the Distinguished Service Medal, Legion of Merit, Women's Army Corps Service Medal, American Campaign Medal, World War II Victory Medal, Army of Occupation Medal (Germany), Medal for Humane Action, National Defense Service Medal, Small Arms Expert Marksmanship Ribbon, and the Air Force Longevity Service Award.

Following Holm's retirement from public life, she began work on a comprehensive history of women's roles in the U.S. military. *Women in the Military: An Unending Revolution*, first published in 1981, examined women's service roles since the American Revolution. By the early 1990s, Holm had revised the publication to include information on the continued expansion of women's roles through the 1970s and into the early 1990s. Holm also served on and chaired the Veterans Administration Committee on Women Vets during the 1980s. In 1997, she published *In Defense of a Nation: Servicewomen in World War II*.

The U.S. Air Force and the armed services in general recognized Jeanne Holm as a pioneer in women's military service. Through her career and activism, she helped increase women's military roles substantially.

Holm died on February 15, 2010.

Tanya L. Roth

See also: Defense Advisory Committee on Women in the Services (DACOWITS); Public Law 90-130 (1967); Reserve Officer Training Corps (ROTC); Women in the Air Force (WAF); Women's Armed Services Integration Act of 1948; Women's Army Auxiliary Corps (WAAC); Women's Army Corps (WAC); World War II (1941–1945).

References and Further Reading

Holm, Jeanne. *In Defense of a Nation: Servicewomen in World War II*. St. Petersburg, FL: Vandamere Press, 1998.

Holm, Jeanne. *Women in the Military: An Unending Revolution (Revised Edition)*. Novato, CA: Presidio Press, 1993.

Witt, Linda, Judith Bellafaire, Britta Granrud, and Mary Jo Binker. *"A Defense Weapon Known to Be of Value": Servicewomen of the Korean War Era*. Hanover, NH: University Press of New England, 2005.

HOPPER, GRACE MURRAY (1906–1992)

Computer scientist and programmer Grace Murray Hopper joined the military during World War II. As part of the Navy, she became a programmer for Mark I, a sequenced digital computer. She and her assistants inputted codes used for aiming naval guns. She also created the first compiler and invented the computer language that became the basis for COBOL. She was closely involved with the development of the first digital computers (the Mark series) and the UNIVAC I and II.

Grace Brewster Murray was born on December 6, 1906, in New York City. She grew up listening to her father's encouragement to leave behind the traditional female roles of the period, so she did her best in school and excelled,

Computer scientist Grace Hopper served in the Navy, retiring with the rank of admiral in 1986. (U.S. Department of Defense)

especially in mathematics. Sometimes her intense curiosity about how things worked got her into trouble. After she graduated from high school in 1924, when most young women would have started looking for a husband, Grace followed her father's advice and went to college. She attended Vassar College, graduating with a bachelor's degree in math and physics in 1928.

She did so well at Vassar that she won a fellowship, allowing her to continue her education. She chose Yale University for her graduate work, earning a master's degree in mathematics in 1930. Later that year, she married Vincent Hopper, an English professor at New York University. They honeymooned in Europe, after which Vassar offered its former pupil a job as an assistant math teacher. Because jobs were hard to find during the Depression, she readily accepted.

In her spare hours, Hopper began working on her mathematics doctorate, which she earned from Vassar in 1934. That year, the school promoted her to math instructor, starting her on a path of advancement that included promotion to assistant professor in 1939 and associate professor in 1944. In the meantime, though, Hopper had decided to enlist in the Navy to help her country win World War II. After much difficulty, as the government wanted mathematicians to stay home and help as civilians, Hopper was permitted to enter the naval reserve in 1943 as an apprentice seaman and midshipman.

Immediately after enlisting, Hopper started training for her naval reserve job at the Midshipman's School for Women in Northampton, Massachusetts. She did

well at the school and, on graduating, received an assignment to the Bureau of Ordnance Computation at Harvard University. It was at that point that Hopper first saw the Mark I, which she was told was a "computing engine." Her first assignment was to program the machine to produce "the coefficients for the interpolation of the arc tangents by next Thursday."

A little panicked, Hopper asked some of her new colleagues for help. What she was doing was writing one of the first computer programs. Her program was designed to calculate the angles at which the Navy would aim its new guns. When she finished, Hopper was the third person ever to program the world's first large-scale, automatically sequenced digital computer.

In 1945, Hopper discovered the first computer "bug" when she found that a moth had flown into one of the new Mark II's relays and caused the whole machine to shut down. The term caught on and now means an irritating code problem that makes a program fail.

When the war ended, most of Hopper's female friends in the Navy returned to their families or boyfriends. However, by then, she was divorced and still had no children, so she wanted to remain in the service. Although she was 40 and the Navy's cut-off age was 38, she was allowed to remain in the reserves, so she took a new position as research fellow in engineering and applied physics at the Harvard Computational Laboratory and resigned from her position at Vassar in 1946.

Hopper finally left Harvard in 1949 to take a job as a senior mathematician in the UNIVAC Division of the new Eckert-Mauchley Computer Corporation in Philadelphia. It was a bold move because most people believed there was no market for computers and that the new-fangled technology was just a fad. When she joined Eckert-Mauchley, it was just completing its famous Binary Automatic Computer (BINAC). She remained with the company through its 1950 buyout by the Rand Corporation and its subsequent merger into the Sperry Corporation in 1955.

In 1952, Hopper created the first compiler, a program that translates a high-level language into a language a computer can understand. Her compiler, the A-0 System, translated symbolic mathematical code into machine language and was the first such program to be widely used. A-0 paved the way for the programming languages we know today. Despite its efficiency, however, no one would even think about using the program outside Sperry.

In 1953, Hopper became director of Sperry's automatic programming. By the end of 1956, she had become the first person to write computer programs in English. The basis of her work in that area was that because the English alphabet is really just another set of symbols, a computer should be able to translate letters into machine code. Although everyone told her not to try it, she stuck by her belief that "it's easier to apologize than get permission." So she went ahead with her English experiment and produced the B-0 System, which soon came to be known as FLOW-MATIC. That program was targeted for such business applications as accounting, payroll, and automatic billing. In 1959, Hopper became Sperry's chief engineer and in 1961 was promoted to staff scientist.

In the early 1960s, computer scientists decided to create a universal computer language that would work on any computer. The main source of code for their new language, COBOL, was FLOW-MATIC. Meanwhile, the Navy was again asking Hopper to resign because of her age. Finally, in 1966, she gave in and retired, having attained the rank of rear admiral. However, seven months later, she got a frantic call from the Navy asking her to return to service with the Naval Data Automation Command (NDAC) so she could fix their disastrous payroll program. She accomplished that by producing a universal COBOL certifier, which allowed all the Navy computers to speak the same language.

Hopper retired again from the Navy in 1971. Never one to sit around, she accepted a position as professor at George Washington University, which lasted until 1978. She also continued in her post as special adviser to the NDAC commander until she retired from the Navy for the last time in 1986. At that point, at age 80, she pared down all her responsibilities until she was only working as consultant to Digital Equipment Corporation. She retained that job until her death.

Hopper died in her sleep on January 1, 1992.

Amanda de la Garza

See also: Women Accepted for Volunteer Emergency Service (WAVES); World War II (1941–1945).

References and Further Reading

Billings, Charlene W. *Grace Hopper: Navy Admiral and Computer Pioneer.* Hillside, NJ: Enslow, 1989.

Dickason, Elizabeth. "Remembering Grace Murray Hopper: A Legend in Her Own Time." *Chips* 12, no. 2 (April 1992): 4–7.

Godson, Susan H. *Serving Proudly: A History of Women in the U.S. Navy.* Annapolis, MD: Naval Institute Press, 2001.

Williams, Kathleen Broome. *Grace Hopper: Admiral of the Cyber Sea.* Annapolis, MD: Naval Institute Press, 2004.

HOWARD, MICHELLE (1960–)

Michelle Howard was the first African American woman to graduate from the U.S. Naval Academy, attain the rank of rear admiral in the U.S. Navy, and command a U.S. naval vessel.

Michelle Janine Howard was born at March Air Force Base in Riverside, California, on April 30, 1960, to retired Air Force master sergeant Nick Howard and his wife, Phillipa. She is is one of four siblings. In 1978, she graduated from Gateway High School in Aurora, Colorado. She graduated from the U.S. Naval Academy in 1982 and from the Army's Command and General Staff College in 1998 with a master's in military arts and sciences.

At the beginning of Howard's career in the Navy, less than 5 percent of the total force was female. She faced resistance from those who did not believe that a woman, especially an African American one, could do the job.

In the 1990s, Howard served aboard several naval vessels, including submarine tender USS *Hunley*, aircraft carrier USS *Lexington*, dock landing ship USS *Tortuga*, and ammunition ships USS

The first African American woman to graduate from the U.S. Naval Academy, Michelle Howard also became the first woman to attain the rank of rear admiral and to command a U.S. naval vessel. (AP Photo/Chief Petty Officer Shawn P. Eklund)

Mount Hood and USS *Flint*. While aboard the USS *Mount Hood*, Howard and her crew were actively engaged in sealift responsibilities for Operations Desert Shield and Desert Storm. As first lieutenant aboard the USS *Flint*, with a crew of 400 personnel, her responsibilities were to oversee the stowing of missiles, rocket boosters, and munitions and to conduct weapons transfer at sea. In 1996, as executive officer aboard the USS *Tortuga*, Howard was engaged in Operation Joint Endeavor, an Adriatic peacekeeping effort for the Republic of Yugoslavia. In 1999, she took command of the USS *Rushmore*, a 15,000-ton assault ship, where she led a crew of 400 sailors and 350 battle-trained marines. The *Rushmore* was later involved in Operation Iron Magic, an exercise with the United Arab Emirates, and Operation Red Reef, with Saudi Arabia. Her vessel was the first naval warship to visit Doha, Qatar, in 10 years. The trip was part of the first Navy effort to utilize smart ship technology. She enjoyed being in command.

From 2004 to 2005, Howard was assigned to command Amphibious Squadron 7, which entailed oversight of three ships that actively transported troops and equipment to support assaults by the U.S. Marines or other armed forces. The squadron was involved in tsunami relief efforts in Indonesia and maritime security operations in the North Arabian Gulf. Four years later, she took command of one of 12 existing expeditionary strike groups. In 2010, she commanded Task Force 151 and Baltic Operations for the Navy's 6th Fleet, which included 40 ships, 175 aircraft, and 21,000 personnel.

Within a week after Howard took command of the U.S. Navy counterpiracy task force, a group of Somali pirates attacked the U.S.-flagged ship *Maersk Alabama* and took the ship's captain, Richard Phillips, and his crew hostage. The ship carried 15,000 metric tons of cargo. At the end of a five-day standoff, Howard had led a successful capture-and-rescue mission that ended with all hostages safe. Howard returned to Washington, D.C., to serve as the senior military advisor to the secretary of the Navy and was additionally assigned as the chief of staff to the J5 Joint Staff, where she was responsible for advising national security leaders on military strategy and policy. Howard was promoted to rear admiral upper half in 2010.

Howard's career spanned numerous shifts in naval policy. Her career began during the Navy's post–Cold War missions from 1986 to 1994. She earned promotions through the largest downsizing of the Navy since World War II and commanded operations during the global War on Terror and the increase in global piracy on the high seas early in the 21st century. A recipient of the Navy League's Captain Winifred Connors Award in 1987, she was recognized for inspirational leadership for her outstanding contributions that reflect credit on women in the naval service. She is also the recipient of the Defense Superior Service Medal, the Legion of Merit Medal—three awards, the Meritorious Service Medal, the Navy Commendation Medal—four awards, and the Navy Achievement Medal.

Mary Raum

See also: African American Women; Gulf War (1991); Iraq War (2003–2011); War on Terror (2001–).

References and Further Reading

Harris, Gail, and Pamela J. McLaughlin. *A Woman's War: The Professional and Personal Journey of the Navy's First African American Female Intelligence Officer.* Lanham, MD: Scarecrow Press, 2010.

Scheller, Robert John Jr., and Mary Strange. *Breaking the Color Barrier: The US Naval Academy's First Black Midshipmen and the Struggle for Racial Equality.* New York: New York University Press, 2005.

HUNTON, ADDIE WAITES (1866–1943)

Addie Waites Hunton was one of three African American women to staff Young Men's Christian Association (YMCA) huts for black soldiers during World War I. She later became an activist for civil rights, women's rights, and peace.

Born in Norfolk, Virginia, in 1866, Addie Waites attended the Boston Girls Latin School and the Spencerian College of Commerce in Philadelphia. She held several academic positions, including one at the State Normal and Agricultural College (Normal, Alabama), before she married William Alpheus Hunton in 1893. Her husband, an employee of the YMCA, was appointed to oversee the YMCA's interactions with African Americans. In addition to writing for the *Atlanta Independent*, *Voice of the Negro*, and *Crisis*, as well as raising two children, Addie Hunton also worked with the YMCA and other organizations, including the National Association of Colored Women (NACW) and the National Association for the Advancement of Colored People (NAACP). Following Atlanta's 1906 race riots, the Huntons moved to Brooklyn, where she worked with the Young Women's Christian Association (YWCA) while maintaining strong ties to the NACW. By 1916, the eve of American entry into World War I, Hunton had a national reputation.

After her husband's death in 1916, Hunton became more involved in the international scene. To ensure that American soldiers in France remained moral and upright, the YMCA provided places for soldiers to rest and relax, as well as educational opportunities. These activities took place in YMCA huts, which YMCA secretaries and other volunteers ran.

Despite the 150,000 African American soldiers serving overseas, few volunteers staffed YMCA huts for black men. Hunton, Kathryn Magnolia Johnson, and Helen Curtis were the only three black women sent to France to staff the segregated huts for the duration of the war. In contrast to YMCA huts for white soldiers, which may have had six women, Hunton, Johnson, and Curtis worked separately, each going to one of the YMCA huts for black soldiers. These three women worked 12-hour days; they organized entertainments, served refreshments at the canteen, wrote and read letters, educated illiterate soldiers, ran the libraries, and hosted discussions, lectures, religious services, and social hours.

Hunton and Johnson published their experiences in *Two Colored Women with the American Expeditionary Forces* (1922), an invaluable resource for understanding African Americans' experiences in wartime France. In addition to recounting their duties, they recorded their observations of the discrimination and racial injustices suffered by African Americans. They encountered prejudice from U.S. military officers and YMCA leaders and secretaries. For example, the U.S. military warned the French that African American soldiers were semihuman, diseased cowards, not fit to be associated with, and only useful for building roads, unloading ships, and (re)burying the dead. African American soldiers were often refused leave, segregated in camps, treated last in medical situations, and denied opportunities for promotion or the opportunity to fight the enemy. At some YMCA huts, posted signs read "No Negroes Allowed" or workers refused to serve black soldiers, and Hunton recorded instances when leaders appeared to conspire to keep the women from working with black soldiers. In spite of such hardships, African American men continued to serve, hoping that their bravery and patriotism would be recognized at home.

Her World War I experiences firmed Hunton's resolve to work towards equality for black women as well as for international peace and democracy; for her the two issues were inseparable. Hunton became involved in the causes espoused by the Pan-African Congress, which included an end to the exploitation of Africa by colonial powers, independence for African countries, equal access for all to educational opportunities, and an end to the United States' policy of segregation. Hunton was one of the few female representatives to the First Pan-African Congress (Paris, 1919) convened by W. E. B. Du Bois. Although unable to attend the 1921 and 1923 congresses, Hunton and the Circle for Peace and Foreign Relations were instrumental in organizing and funding the 1927 Congress.

Hunton was also a founding member of the International Council of Women and Darker Races (ICWDR) and actively involved with the Women's International League for Peace and Freedom (WILPF). At the 1921 National Women's Party (NWP) convention, she was instrumental in publicizing how Southern black women were being denied their right to vote. As a result of Hunton's activism, the Department of Justice and the Federal Bureau of Investigation kept files on her.

Hunton's children also had distinguished careers: Eunice Hunton Carter was New York City's first black assistant district attorney, and William Alphaeus Hunton Jr. earned an MA and PhD, taught at Howard University, was imprisoned for refusing to cooperate with the House Un-American Activities Committee, and wrote *Decision in Africa: Sources of Conflict* (1957).

Addie Waites Hunton died in Brooklyn, New York, in 1943.

Jenna L. Kubly

See also: African American Women; World War I (1914–1918); Young Men's Christian Association (YMCA); Young Women's Christian Association (YWCA).

References and Further Reading

Chandler, Susan. "Addie Hunton and the Construction of an African American Female Peace Prospective." *Affilia* 20, no. 3 (Fall 2005): 270–83.

Hunton, Addie W., and Kathryn M. Johnson. *Two Colored Women with the American Expeditionary Forces*. New York: G.K. Hall and Co., 1997.

Lutz, Christine. "Addie W. Hunton: Crusader for Pan-Africanism and Peace." In *Portraits in African-American Life since 1865*, edited by Nina Mjagkij, 109–128. Wilmington, DE: Scholarly Resources, 2003.

Plastas, Melinda. *A Band of Noble Women: Racial Politics in the Women's Peace Movement*. Syracuse, NY: Syracuse University Press, 2011.

I

INDIAN WARS

Warfare between Native Americans and the European newcomers and then later the people of the United States was a recurring reality for women in both Native and non-Native communities. The arrival of Europeans to the North American continent brought a direct threat to Indian sovereignty, as their lands, resources, and physical presence were often deemed roadblocks to American development. As a result, raids and skirmishes between Native Americans and Europeans frequently escalated, and the communities organized competing military forces to pursue full-scale warfare. In these wars, Europeans and then the people of the United States frequently found Native American allies to help them fight their causes.

Throughout the colonial era, fighting erupted between Native Americans and colonists. Many of these wars resulted from Indian tribes fighting to resist the Europeans who intruded on their land. Other fighting occurred from trading disputes and other disagreements. In these battles, colonists frequently attacked and destroyed Indian villages and often killed Indian women, men, and children. Native Americans similarly attacked European towns and outposts as they attempted to stop the advances of the white settlements. In these attacks, women and children were taken captive and often killed. Both sides often lost property.

The decision to initiate a war or authorize a war party belonged to women in many Native American communities. This was especially true for the Iroquois and Algonquin tribes. In addition, Indian women commonly served as mediators between the white colonists and the Indian tribes. One of the most famous was Pocahontas, who often warned the English colonists about their behavior and worked to create peace between the communities. Her position as a mediator grew after she married Virginian John Rolfe.

During the American Revolution, women continued to have an important role in warfare as their communities remained neutral or allied themselves with either the revolutionaries or the British. Legend has it that an Oneida woman, Tyonajanegan, went with her Dutch husband into the battle of Orinsky. During the battle, her husband was shot, and she continued to load his rifle so that he could continue firing at the British.

After the Revolution, Americans settled and developed the land between the Appalachian Mountains and the Mississippi River. This settlement resulted in warfare between the American settlers and the Indians who lived in the region. In these conflicts, women often found themselves acting as diplomatic mediators. For example, in the late 1780s, as the land in Tennessee and North Carolina became settled by Anglo-Americans, the Cherokees grew frustrated with the white settlers. Nancy Ward, the daughter of Cherokee civil chief Attakullkulla, proved to be a great mediator of peace. Ward had fought alongside her husband and other Cherokees in battles against the Creeks, and she earned the name "Beloved Woman" among her people. Because the Cherokee believed that the Great Spirit spoke through Ward, they named her head of the Women's Council of Chiefs. Throughout the 1780s and 1790s, she negotiated peace treaties between the white settlers and the Cherokee tribe.

After the 1803 Louisiana Purchase, President Thomas Jefferson sent Army officers Meriwether Lewis and William Clark to explore the newly purchased western lands. The two men and their crew of 40 started up the Missouri River on May 14, 1804. In April 1805, Lewis and Clark hired a Shoshone woman named Sacagawea to guide them and to negotiate with the tribes they encountered along the route. The pregnant Sacagawea became the first female Indian scout hired by the U.S. Army. Her relationship with other tribes helped the expedition gain passage and protection through much of the land.

While Lewis and Clark forged amicable relations with tribes along the Missouri River, fighting with American Indians continued to the east. In Ohio territory, the Shawnee chief Tecumseh tried to unite all the Indian tribes north and south against the white intruders. As they allied themselves with the British during the War of 1812, they also attempted to purge their communities of what they deemed to be cultural impurities. This included ridding the communities of newly acquired commodities—many of which belonged to women. Among the Creeks, in the South, Red Stick followers of Tecumseh's plan attacked Native American women who had adopted European dress and customs. They broke and often burned spinning wheels and looms, and on occasion stripped women of their European-style clothing. Tecumseh and the Red Sticks both eventually lost their battles, as Gen. William Henry Harrison defeated Tecumseh at the Battle of Fallen Timbers in 1811 and later Gen. Andrew Jackson defeated the Red Sticks at the 1814 Battle of Horseshoe Bend in Alabama.

During the 1830s, the U.S. government established a new Indian policy—Indian removal. In hopes of creating lasting peace, the U.S. government created a permanent Indian territory west of the Mississippi River. With the assistance of the U.S. military, the federal government forcibly moved most of the Native Americans who lived east of the Mississippi and relocated them to a permanent location in present-day Oklahoma. Dozens of tribes were moved, most notably the southern Cherokee, Creek, Choctaw, Chickasaw, and Seminole tribes. Removal had a particularly devastating effect on women—many of whom were excluded from the removal negotiations and yet were the owners of the land that was involved. As a result, Native American women lost thousands of acres of land and rarely received compensation for the improvements they left behind. In addition, thousands of Indians (both men and women) suffered and died on the journey west in what became known as the Trail of Tears.

Peace and the idea of permanent separation of whites and Indians did not last long. In the 1840s, the United States acquired the Oregon Territory from the British and more territory from Mexico. The acquisition of more land and the discovery of gold in California led to a flood of settlers headed west into the lands set aside for the Indian tribes. In California, small tribes were overrun by the gold seekers, and in the Washington and Oregon territories warfare erupted. The U.S. Army, in attempt to keep peace and allow settlers into the territory, pursued a military offensive against tribes in the Yakima and Rogue River Valleys between 1854 and 1856. By 1858, the U.S. Army had crushed the tribes of the Pacific Northwest. In all of these instances, Native American women struggled as their homelands were overrun by newcomers.

During the Civil War, volunteer units replaced Regular Army units in the West. Although most of the nation's attention was focused on the fighting in the East, warfare between Native Americans and the United States continued. Much of this warfare was considered irregular war in that it rarely consisted of pitched battled and hardly distinguished between Native civilians and soldiers, women or men. In 1862, bands of Sioux led attacks on white settlements in Minnesota. Gen. Henry H. Sibley led troops to put down the uprising. However, throughout the Dakotas and in the Southwest, the Army continued to fight Indians and place them onto permanent reservations. In the Southwest, the Army forged a war against the Navajo and Mescalero Apache in an attempt to relocate them onto a reservation.

After the Civil War, regular troops returned to military outposts and the Army focused on relegating tribes to reservations and enforcing treaties. The Medicine Lodge Treaty and the Fort Laramie Treaties of 1867 and 1868 forced the Plains Indians to settle on reservations and accept government supervision. Warfare returned in 1868 and 1869, when the Army waged a war against the Cheyenne, Kiowa, and Comanche. In 1876, the discovery of gold in the Black Hills of the Dakotas brought a flood of gold seekers and more conflict. The Army mounted an offensive war against the Sioux in an effort to force leaders such as Crazy Horse, Sitting Bull, and others to settle on the Sioux reservation. As the U.S. Army continued to pursue Indian tribes in the West, they often hired Indians to serve as scouts and interpreters. This often included women.

By 1866, whites had settled in Nevada territory, causing clashes between ranchers and the Paiute Indians. During the Pyramid Lake War, Paiute woman Sarah Winnemucca worked to negotiate peace between her tribe and the federal government. After the war in 1869, the Army hired Winnemucca to work as an interpreter at Fort McDermitt. In this role, Winnemucca convinced members of her tribe to move to the reservation, and she worked to bring attention to the corruption of agents at the agency. By 1878, tensions came to boil between the Bannock tribe and the white ranchers in the Nevada territory, and warfare erupted. Gen. Oliver Otis Howard, the military general detailed to bring peace and force the Bannocks back onto their reservation, hired Winnemucca as an interpreter and charged her with convincing the Paiutes to not join the Bannocks in the war. Unfortunately, she was unable to convince all her fellow tribesmen to follow her lead, and some of the Paiutes joined the Bannocks. Howard retained Winnemucca and used her as a guide and a scout against the warring Bannocks. Her knowledge of the environment and of the Indians helped Howard and his 480 men gain a victory over the hostiles at Birch Creek. After the Bannock War, she continued to work for the Army as an interpreter and as a schoolteacher for Indian children. After her employment with the Army ended, Winnemucca traveled the country giving presentations on the living condition of the Indians on reservations.

During 1872 and 1873, war erupted between the federal government and the Modoc tribe in Northeastern California. The government had tried to force a band under Captain Jack and other leaders onto to a reservation. Winema, a Modoc woman who had been married to Frank Riddle, served as a mediator and intermediary between the Indians and the U.S. Army during the Modoc War. Earlier in 1864, Winema and Riddle had negotiated a peace treaty between the Modocs and the whites that resulted in the formation of a reservation near the Kalamath River. During this time, Winema worked as an interpreter for the U.S. Army. Fleeing after being forced onto the reservation, Captain Jack and other Modoc leaders took refuge in some lava beds. During a peace meeting, Winema saved one of the peace commissioners from being killed by the angry Modocs. After four months, the Modocs were forced to flee their hiding place and were captured. As a result of her service as an interpreter, the U.S. government awarded Winema a military pension.

By the late 1870s and early 1890s, most of the tribes on the plains had been removed to reservations and the Army turned its attention back to the Southwest. Although Howard had made peace with the Apaches in 1872, new fighting erupted due to the poor living conditions on the reservation. The Army scoured the deserts of New Mexico and Arizona in an effort to subdue and return to the reservation Victorio, Geronimo, and their followers. War with the Apaches ended in 1881, when Geronimo surrendered with between 30 and 50 men, women, and children. The final chapter of the Indian wars occurred in December 1890 on the Sioux Reservation. During the Ghost Dance, a revivalist movement, unexpected violence erupted. Confused, the 7th Cavalry opened fire on Sioux leader Big Foot and his people. Nearly one-third of the Sioux were killed or wounded. This was the last major encounter between the whites and the Indians and the closing of the American West.

Although the U.S. Army held a policy that it was illegal for women to serve, at least one woman did serve in combat against hostile Indian tribes in the late 19th century. Cathay Williams, a former slave, managed to disguise her gender and enlist in the Regular Army. During the Civil War, Williams had been captured and pressed into service as a cook and laundress by an Indiana regiment. In 1866, with no family, hope for a job, or a home, Williams disguised herself as a man and enlisted in the U.S. Army at Jefferson Barracks in St. Louis, Missouri. Due to her race, she was assigned to the 38th Colored Infantry. This was one of the all-black regiments formed during the Civil War and transferred to the western frontier. Williams served for two years with the 38th in Kansas against various Plains tribes and in the Apache Wars in Arizona. Near the end of her service, she developed poor health and grew tired of the Army life and feigned illness, thus allowing a doctor to examine her and discover her sex. With this knowledge, the U.S. government discharged Williams in October 1868. For years after her discharge she continued to work for the Army as a laundress and a seamstress.

Beyond disguising oneself as a man and enlisting in the Regular Army, few women served in the military during the Indian wars. Although few fought, many found employment in support roles. Women were hired as laundresses and hospital matrons. Due to the isolation of the western posts, these women were usually the wives of enlisted men. These women lived on or near the military posts and were recognized as being in the employ of the U.S. Army. Despite not being on the front combat lines, these women supported the Army with their services and added a female presence to the isolated western frontier.

Stacy Reaves

See also: African American Women; American Revolution (1775–1783); Civil War (1861–1865); Duston, Hannah (1657–1730); Jemison, Mary (ca. 1742–1833); Johnson, Susannah (ca. 1730–1810); Native American Women; Nonhelema [Grenadier Squaw] (ca. 1720–ca. 1786); Parker, Cynthia Ann (ca. 1824–ca. 1870); Sacagawea (ca. 1787–1812); Tyonajanegen (n.d.–ca. 1820); War of 1812 (1812–1815); Ward, Nancy (ca. 1738–ca. 1824); Williams, Cathay [William Cathey] (ca. 1844–n.d.); Winema [Tobey Riddle] (ca. 1848–1920); Winnemucca, Sarah [Thocmetony "Shell Flower"] (1844–1891).

References and Further Reading

Ellington, Charlotte Jane. *Beloved Mother: The Story of Nancy Ward*. Johnson City, TN: Over Mountain Press, 1994.

Horn, James. *A Land as God Made It: Jamestown and the Birth of America*. New York: Basic Books, 2005.

McClary, Ben H. "Nancy Ward, Beloved Woman." *Tennessee Historical Quarterly* (December 1962): 352–64.

Meacham, A. B. *Wi-ne-ma: (The Woman-Chief)*. New York: AMS Press, 1980.

Quinn, Arthur. *Hell with the Fire Out: A History of the Modoc War*. Boston: Faber & Faber, 1997.

St. George, Judith. *Sacagawea*. New York: Putnam, 1997.

Stallard, Patricia Y. *Glittering Misery: Dependents of the Indian Fighting Army*. Norman: University of Oklahoma Press, 1992.

Tucker, Phillip Thomas. *Cathy Williams: From Slave to Buffalo Soldier*. Mechanicsburg, PA: Stackpole Books, 2009.

Utley, Robert Marshall. *Frontier Regulars: The United States Army and the Indian, 1866–1891*. New York: Macmillan, 1974.

Utley, Robert Marshall. *Frontiersmen in Blue: The United States Army and the Indian, 1848–1865*. Lincoln: University of Nebraska Press, 1981.

IRAQ WAR (2003–2011)

Operation Iraqi Freedom, the U.S. codename for the war in Iraq, was launched on March 20, 2003, by a coalition composed primarily of soldiers from the United States and the United Kingdom. Initially, these countries committed around 248,000 and 45,000 soldiers respectively—far fewer than had been deployed for the First Gulf War and a force numerically inferior to the Iraqi Army. The United States and United Kingdom led the prowar movement as the leaders of each country, President George W. Bush and Prime Minister Tony Blair, claimed that an invasion was necessary to prevent Saddam Hussein from developing weapons of mass destruction. Much smaller contingents from Australia, Denmark, Poland, and various other allies supported American and British forces.

The Iraqis were warned that the attack would come, so the invading force had to compensate for its lack of surprise and its size with overwhelming fire superiority and speed. Preceding the attack, operatives from the Central Intelligence Agency (CIA) and special operations forces infiltrated the country to identify key targets, encourage some of Saddam's top leaders to defect, and make contact with local resistance groups. In all, 48 British, Australian, and American special operations groups were deployed. One of the infiltrating units' central objectives was to meet with the Kurdish Peshmerga and help them attack from the north. Other groups destroyed Scud missile launchers, and Army Rangers formed a blocking position to cut forces in the western desert off from Baghdad. At around 3:30 a.m., coalition planes began bombing Saddam Hussein's residences while 40 Tomahawk missiles struck his command centers. All of the bombs and missiles fired during this invasion were precision guided, far more than the roughly 10 percent that were during the 1991 Gulf War, and the bombing campaign was much shorter than that in 1991. These factors helped to minimize civilian casualties during the initial invasion.

The U.K. 1st Armored Division along with commandos and air assault units took control of southern Iraq and Basra. U.S. Marines assisted them in the capture of the Al Faw peninsula. Two U.S. columns advanced on Baghdad along different routes. The I U.S. Marine Expeditionary Force moved northwest from Kuwait, following a course between the Tigris and Euphrates Rivers through Al Kut. This traditional invasion route provided the attacking marines with a highway that facilitated rapid movement and resupply. The U.S. 3rd Infantry Division, along with the 82nd and 101st Airborne divisions, advanced along the west bank of the Euphrates River toward An Nasiriya, Najaf, Karbala, and Ar Ramadi. The 3rd Infantry Division was the main force for the assault of Baghdad from the west, while the 82nd and 101st were assigned to take Samawah, Najaf, and other cities along the way to the capital.

Coalition forces moved quickly, avoiding major engagements with the Iraqi Army. Their plan was an advance of unprecedented speed that would bypass many of the large contingents of Iraqi military in a race to the capital. The goal was decapitation—remove Saddam and his commanders without engaging in any major fighting. This attempt was largely successful. The Iraqi Army deployed around 400,000 men, including 60,000 Republican Guards, but many of the units vanished as coalition forces drove into rearward areas.

By April 2, the two U.S. columns were within 35 miles of Baghdad. The advance came to a halt as marines paused to wait for the Army V Corps, which was taking a longer route and lacked paved roads. The final stage of the attack was a pincer movement against the capital that required the columns to strike simultaneously. This delay was one of the few moments of caution in the rapid advance, but one that military leadership though necessary. Many commentators, including Saddam himself, predicted a major urban battle of attrition in Baghdad. The army supply lines were also under sporadic attack from Saddam loyalists, although these failed to have any significant effect on the advance.

U.S. forces opened their attack on the capital by taking Saddam International Airport, later renamed Baghdad International Airport. This was a major symbolic and logistical victory; its capture meant that fewer supplies would have to cross the desert and pass the remaining pockets of Iraqi resistance. Over the following days, American soldiers battled to gain control of the city and to expel Republican Guards from Saddam's palaces. The Iraqi defense was determined but failed to live up to Saddam's predictions. On April 8, the British army secured Basra after a two-week battle for the city, and on April 9, the Americans staged a symbolic victory by pulling down a massive Saddam statue in Baghdad. The armies lost 122 American and 33 British soldiers, and only 6 of the British were actually killed in action.

On April 4, a car bomb exploded at a checkpoint near the Hidathah Dam, killing three American soldiers. Even before the conventional war was over an insurgency began. This attack set the tone for the fight to come. President Bush declared an end to the war on May 1, 2003, yet hostilities never ceased. Some of the soldiers bypassed in the drive on Baghdad continued to resist. They were left cut off from supplies and leadership, but their isolation allowed them to slip into the civilian population and begin a covert war. There were frequent attacks along the coalition supply lines, and determined resistance emerged sporadically in many cities. In the years following the invasion, the Iraq War became a counterinsurgency war as members of Al Qaeda, Saddam loyalists, and other militants fought against coalition forces and against each other. By many accounts, the violence was a civil war; at times the fighting between Sunni and Shiites was more intense than that between them and the coalition soldiers. The insurgency proved much harder to defeat than the Iraqi Army because the primary methods of attack were roadside bombs, car bombs, and armed raids by small groups—all tactics the U.S. military was unaccustomed to defending against.

Although women were formally excluded from participation in ground combat because of restriction of combat service to males, many were directly involved in fighting. Even before the war transformed into a counterinsurgency mission, there were no frontlines. The rapid advance on Baghdad left all coalition soldiers open to attack from bypassed Iraqi units. The role of women in combat became clear on March 23, when 12 members of the U.S. 507th Maintenance Company were attacked near An Nasiriyah. Three women, Jessica Lynch, Shoshana Johnson, and Lori Piestewa, were part of the supply column. All three were taken prisoner. While in captivity, Piestewa died from wounds sustained during the ambush, making her the first female combat fatality of the war. Lynch was injured in the attack and spent a week in an Iraqi hospital until U.S. special operations forces rescued her in a night raid. She became the most famous symbol of women in the war, and upon returning home, she made numerous television appearances and was the subject of the biography *I Am a Soldier, Too: The Jessica Lynch Story*. Johnson was held at a different location along with the men captured in the ambush and was rescued after 22 days in captivity. Although Lynch and Johnson were captured together and held under similar circumstances, the latter received very little attention. This led to accusations of racism because the media ignored a black woman and focused on the white one. The attack on the 507th was the war's first incident of American

women in combat, and it spread awareness of the limitations of the U.S. military's policy of excluding women from combat roles.

Lynch was widely admired and considered a symbol of women's new role in combat. By contrast, Lynndie England, the only other female soldier to generate as much scrutiny, showed that women could also commit the same illegal acts as male soldiers. She was among those serving in the 372nd Military Police Company caught abusing Iraqi prisoners at Abu Ghraib in 2003. England appeared in many of the graphic photos that documented the abuse. Her participation added to the outrage felt by many Arabs, as it sexualized the abuse in a way that conflicted with the prisoners' religious values. England was not alone in violating Islamic sexual norms for the sake of interrogation. Many female soldiers were willingly and unwillingly used for interrogation, to help humiliate captured male soldiers. Their ability to transgress Islamic norms makes women valuable psychological weapons.

Col. Janis Karpinski was also implicated in the Abu Ghraib scandal. As the commander of that prison and 14 others, she was in the chain of command responsible for ensuring that prisoners were treated fairly. She was demoted from brigadier general and relieved of her command for dereliction of duty because of her failure to prevent the mistreatment. However, she maintained that she was a scapegoat, possibly because she made an easier target than men with authority over the prison.

Coalition soldiers went to great lengths to be culturally sensitive. England's violation of sexual norms fueled outrage at the U.S. occupation, but many other women performed services essential to maintaining good relations with the Iraqis. One of the most serious security concerns was the searching of Iraqi women. For cultural reasons, men could not perform these searches, but female soldiers could. With women conducting raids and checkpoint security, coalition forces found it far easier to perform searches without cultural disrespect.

Women's greater role in searches and fighting was partly due to personnel shortages. Before the war, there was debate over how many soldiers were needed to occupy the country. The 150,000 troops Gen. Tommy Franks had to fight the insurgents was a much smaller force than the coalition of 550,000 led by Gen. Norman Schwarzkopf in 1991. With so few to call on for security missions, soldiers in noncombat roles often performed assignments typically reserved for the infantry. As of 2009, more than 206,000 women served in the Middle East and most of these in Iraq—more women than in any conflict since World War II. The number of women serving fluctuated, but they generally made up around 10 percent of the total U.S. forces.

Women serving in Iraq often suffered from harassment and sexual assault by the male soldiers. While there is no reliable estimate of how many incidents occurred, there were enough reports to initiate a formal investigation in 2004. The Department of Veteran Affairs estimates that around 30 percent of female soldiers were raped, 71 percent sexually assaulted, and 90 percent sexually harassed. To make matters worse, the Department of Defense estimates that only around 10 percent of sexual assaults

are reported. There are strong incentives for women to remain quiet as reporting a crime leads to a transfer, harsh informal sanctions, and possibly violence. Whatever the actual numbers, the attacks have led other women to fear for their safety. Even women who are not sexually abused face discrimination and labeling because they are a minority serving in a nontraditional role.

Despite the prominence of women in the Iraq War, little has been done to change military regulations. The typical way around the ban on women in combat is for commanders to attach mixed units to combat arms units as support personnel. This allows the women to fight, but it also prevents the military from officially changing its policy.

Under President Barack Obama, the United States officially ended its war with Iraq on December 15, 2011. All troops were withdrawn by the end of the year.

Marcus Schulzke

See also: Afghanistan; African American Women; Asian American Women; Campbell, Kim Reed (1975–); Charette, Holly A. (1983–2005); Clark, Regina Renee (1962–2005); Dunwoody, Ann E. (1953–); Gulf War (1991); Hester, Leigh Ann (1982–); Hispanic American Women; Howard, Michelle (1960–); Johnson, Shoshana Nyree (1973–); Lynch, Jessica (1983–); Native American Women; Piestewa, Lori (1979–2003); Sheehan, Cindy Lee Miller (1957–); Valdez, Ramona M. (1984–2005); Vega, Sarah (1981–); War on Terror (2001–).

References and Further Reading

Allawi, Ali. *The Occupation of Iraq: Winning the War, Losing the Peace.* New Haven, CT: Yale University Press, 2008.

Benedict, Helen. *The Lonely Soldier: The Private War of Women Serving in Iraq.* Boston: Beacon Press, 2010.

Holmstedt, Kristen. *Band of Sisters: American Women at War in Iraq.* Mechanicsburg, PA: Stackpole Books, 2008.

Keegan, John. *The Iraq War.* New York: Vintage Books, 2005.

Murray, Williamson, and Robert H. Scales Jr. *The Iraq War: A Military History.* New York: Belknap Press of Harvard University Press, 2005.

Oliver, Kelly. *Women as Weapons of War: Iraq, Sex, and the Media.* New York: Columbia University Press, 2010.

Ricks, Thomas. *Fiasco: The American Military Adventure in Iraq, 2003 to 2005.* New York: Penguin, 2007.

J

JACKSON, GILDA A.
(1950–)

A highly decorated soldier, Gilda Jackson was the first African American woman to be promoted to colonel in the U.S. Marine Corps. She served for nearly 30 years and ultimately retired as a lieutenant colonel.

Gilda A. Jackson was born in Columbus, Ohio, in 1950. Her father died when she was 16. She graduated high school during the escalation of the Vietnam War, and not long after, on her 18th birthday, enlisted in the Marines. She promised her mother she would attend college after her three-year obligation to the military. She served three years as an enlisted marine—two of which she spent in Hawaii—and then earned the rank of sergeant. When her initial obligation to the military ended, she returned to college to fulfill her promise to her mother. She attended Ohio Dominican College, where she enrolled in the Marine Officer Candidate Platoon Leader Course.

After she graduated from college, Jackson returned to military life. She was commissioned as a second lieutenant in 1975. She then began a career in marine aviation that included stints as supply officer for the Stations Operation and Engineering Squadron in El Toro, California, as a Group Aviation Supply Support Center officer for the Marine Aircraft 12 in Iwakuni, Japan, and as a fiscal officer for the Marine Aircraft Group 16 for the 3rd Marine Aircraft Wing in Tustin, California.

These experiences prepared her for Marine command and convinced others to allow her to pursue more training. She attended and then graduated from the Amphibious Warfare School in 1983. From there, she served in the Headquarters and Maintenance Squadron of the Marine Aircraft Group 13 in El Toro and then, once again, in the Marine Helicopter Training Squadron 301 of the Marine Aircraft Group 16.

Jackson graduated from the Marine Corps Command and Staff College in Quantico, Virginia. She was then stationed at the Navy Aviation Supply Office in Philadelphia, where she served as weapons system manager. In 1993, the Marines promoted her to lieutenant colonel, and the following year she became commander of the Marine Aviation Logistics Squadron 13 in Yuma, Arizona, and then the Marine support requirements officer at the Joint Advanced Strike Technology Program Office.

Jackson continued to rise in the military, and the Marines selected her to attend the War College at Maxwell Air Force Base in Montgomery, Alabama. Upon her graduation, she reported to the 2nd Marine Aircraft Wing and shortly after earned a promotion to colonel and received the command of the Naval Aviation Depot at Cherry Point, North Carolina. The promotion and appointment were both firsts for an African American woman. In her final appointment in the military, Jackson commanded the largest industrial employer east of I-95 and one with a billion-dollar annual budget.

By the time she retired from active duty in 2001, Jackson had received the Defense Meritorious Service Medal, the Meritorious Service Medal with gold star, the Navy Commendation Medal, the Navy Achievement Medal, and the Marine Corps Good Conduct Medal.

After retirement, Jackson briefly pursued a career in politics, where she ran an unsuccessful campaign for a seat in the North Carolina House of Representatives. Afterward, she went to work for Lockheed Martin as part of its Joint Strike Fighter (F-35) Program, using her experiences and knowledge to help develop training systems and curriculum for future pilots and aviation mechanics. In 2009, she received a Lockheed Galaxy award for her commitment to community service, as evidenced by her work as a mentor to school-aged children of color.

Andrew K. Frank

See also: African American Women; Vietnam War (1965–1973); Women Marines.

References and Further Reading

"Around the Corps: North Carolina." *Marines* 27 (February 1998): 6–7.

Boulware, Dorothy S. "Gilda Jackson Becomes 'First' Colonel." *Baltimore Afro-American*, October 25, 1997.

Hopkins, Stella M. "Marine Officer Managing to Push Stereotypes Aside: Corps' First Woman Colonel Commands Largest Industrial Employer East of I-95." *The State*, April 28, 2000.

"Women of Color Award Winners." *Women of Color*, Autumn 2010, 33.

JEMISON, MARY (CA. 1742–1833)

Captured as a teen during the Seven Years' War, Mary Jemison was adopted by a Seneca family and remained among the Seneca for the rest of her life.

Although her exact birth date is unknown, Jemison was born on a ship in the Atlantic while her parents, Thomas and Jane Jemison, made the trip from Ireland to the colonies in 1742 or 1743. Her family, of Scots-Irish decent, settled in Pennsylvania near current-day

Gettysburg. In April 1758, a small party of French soldiers and Shawnee warriors attacked the Jemison family, which now contained six children. Although two of her brothers managed to escape, she and the rest of her family and some neighbors were taken captive. Separated from the group with the young neighbor boy, Jemison soon learned that everyone else had been killed.

When the party arrived at Fort Duquesne (near Pittsburg), the warriors gave Mary to two Seneca women who had lost a brother in battle. Renamed Degiwene's (spelling varies) or Two Falling Voices, Jemison became part of a Seneca family. Although white settlers tried to reclaim her after the war, Jemison's Seneca sisters fled to avoid turning her over. Jemison married a Delaware warrior named Sheninjee, whom her sisters had chosen for her. Her first child, a daughter, did not survive. She also bore a son and named him Thomas. After Sheninjee died, leaving her a young widow, Jemison had another opportunity to return to white society when a Dutch trader intended to redeem her for award money. Jemison resisted. She married a respected Seneca warrior named Hiokatoo in 1762 or 1763. They had six children, two sons and four daughters, all named after Mary's lost relatives.

During the American Revolution, the Six Nations of the Iroquois Confederacy initially pledged neutrality. Yet by the fall of 1776, four of the six, including the Seneca, supported the British. In 1779, George Washington sent Gen. John Sullivan and 3,000 men into Iroquois country. The Seneca fled ahead of the invading army, and Sullivan's troops burned the crops and destroyed the towns. Jemison and her children relocated to the spot along the Genesee River that would become her home—the Gardeau Flats. With the help of two fugitive slaves who were living there, Jemison survived the winter and constructed a cabin for her family. After the Revolution, Jemison's Seneca brother offered her the chance to return to white society. Her oldest son, Thomas, planned to go and help out with the younger children, but the chiefs would not agree to let Thomas leave. Jemison again chose to stay among the Seneca, fearing that her white relatives would not accept her children.

During the Council at Big Tree (1797), the Seneca sold all their land west of the Genesee River, retaining only reservations and a few individual land grants. Despite the opposition of Red Jacket, Jemison received a large tract of nearly 18,000 acres of rich land along the Genesee River, including the Gardeau Flats. Although this land offered her family some security, Jemison's later years were mired by tragedy as reservation life and the influence of alcohol took their toll on the Seneca. Hiokatoo died in 1811 at the age of 103, the same year her oldest son, Thomas, was killed in a fight with his brother John. A year later, John murdered Mary's youngest child, Jesse. John also died in a drunken fight. As change ravaged Seneca society, Jemison also found herself targeted by swindlers who wanted her land. One man, claiming to be a cousin, tricked her into signing over 400 acres of land because she could not read the deed. At the end of her life, Jemison retained only a small piece of land. She moved to the Seneca reservation at Buffalo Creek, near Buffalo,

New York, where she died in 1833 at the age of 90 or 91.

Her story lived on through the popularity of her narrative. In 1823, Jemison sat down with a local doctor named James Seaver, and over the next three days she told her story. A year later, *A Narrative of the Life of Mary Jemison* was published, selling over 100,000 copies in the first year. New editions continued to come out for over 100 years, including an award-winning children's book. Her grave and the land she once farmed is now part of Letchworth State Park in New York.

Tara M. McCarthy

See also: American Revolution (1775–1783); Indian Wars; Native American Women; North American Colonial Wars (17th–18th centuries).

References and Further Reading

Namias, June. *White Captives: Gender and Ethnicity on the American Frontier.* Chapel Hill: University of North Carolina Press, 1993.

Rosenberg-Naparsteck, Ruth. "The Legacy of Mary Jemison." *Rochester History* 68, no. 1 (2006): 1–32.

Seaver, James. *A Narrative of the Life of Mrs. Mary Jemison.* Edited by and with introduction by June Namias. Norman: University of Oklahoma Press, 1992.

JOHNSEN, HEATHER LYNN (1973–)

In 1996, Heather Lynn Johnsen became the first woman to guard the Tomb of the Unknown Soldier in Arlington National Cemetery in Washington, D.C.

She earned the silver tomb guard badge in 1996 when she was 23 years old, and she later received her honored assignment.

An athletic child, Johnsen was born and raised in Fremont in the San Francisco Bay area of northern California. She ran cross-country and track in high school and pursued other athletic and academic pursuits. For one year, she served as editor of her high school newspaper.

Upon graduation, she joined the military. She served as a member of the military police in Korea and at Fort Monmouth, New Jersey, before deciding to pursue the path that would enable her to become a tomb sentinel. In 1994, she joined the 3rd Infantry as a member of its military police. In June 1995, she applied to become a tomb sentinel. After nine months of grueling training—a course that is highly competitive to be accepted into and that 70 percent of applicants are reportedly unable to complete—she received her appointment. Training for the position as a guard not only consisted of physically exacting tests but also required a complete education about Arlington Cemetery and the Tomb. She was the 389th soldier to earn the silver tomb guard badge.

The Tomb of the Unknown Soldier contains three unnamed soldiers—one each from World War I, World War II, and the Korean War. A fourth soldier—from the Vietnam War—had been buried at the site but was formally disinterred in 1988 after the remains were identified. The Tomb of the Unknown Soldier also represents the burial of approximately 90,000 soldiers whose bodies were not identified or remain missing from those conflicts. The tomb is guarded around the clock by the 3rd U.S. Infantry, known

Heather Johnsen, the first woman to serve in this post, guards the Tomb of the Unknown Soldier. (AP Photo/Mark Wilson)

as the Old Guard. Guards are held to the highest standard, as they are expected to stand stoically at all times. The slightest exceptions are cause for dismissal from the post.

The Old Guard, the oldest active corps in the Army, did not accept applications from women until 1982. For the next 12 years, women were forbidden to apply to the tomb sentinels or the other two elite groups of the corps. This policy banning women changed in 1994, when the secretary of defense changed it.

Andrew K. Frank

See also: Korean War (1950–1953); Military Police; Vietnam War (1965–1973); World War I (1914–1918); World War II (1941–1945).

References and Further Reading

Fiore, Faye. "They All See Me as a Soldier Now." *Los Angeles Times*, July 26, 1996, 3.

"Marching into History." *Washington Times*, March 23, 1996, 1.

Tousignant, Marylou. "A New Era for the Old Guard: Woman Joins Elite Ranks of Soldiers Tending Tomb of the Unknowns." *Washington Post*, March 23, 1996, C01.

JOHNSON, OPHA MAE (1900–1976)

Opha Mae Johnson became the first woman in the Marine Corps Reserves on August 13, 1918. She enlisted during

World War I, when women were given the opportunity to fill in positions recently vacated by men.

Johnson was born February 13, 1900. During World War I, Johnson worked as a civil service employee at Headquarters Marine Corps prior to her official commitment to the Corps. When she enrolled in the Marine Corps Reserves on August 13, 1918, she became the first woman Marine. During World War I, the military encouraged women to enroll in the Corps to fill jobs usually performed by men who, during wartime, were needed overseas. Johnson immediately signed up for the Corps when the opportunity became available.

Johnson was initially tasked with taking charge of and guiding the future female recruits. She eventually served with 304 other women. Although the military encouraged female enlistment, men did not readily accept these women. They were derisively called the "Lady Hell Cats," "Skirt Marines," and "Marinettes." They worked in office jobs previously held by male marines. The women originally enlisted as privates but could work their way up to higher ranks. The female marines worked largely in public relations and payroll and finance. Many worked at military supply centers. They were also required to participate in daily drills, and some worked guard duty. Unfortunately, unlike their male counterparts, the women were not given health care or other veterans' benefits. They were also not allowed to serve in war zones.

Johnson eventually served as clerk in the office of the quartermaster general, Brig. Gen. Charles McCawley. By the end of the war, she was a senior enlisted woman and had reached the rank of sergeant. Despite her exemplary service, Johnson and all of the female marines were discharged by November 11, 1919. Johnson died in January 1976.

Some have questioned whether Johnson was, in fact, the first female marine. Notably, Lucy Brewer claimed to have served during the War of 1812 as a marine on the USS *Constitution*. Brewer penned a memoir, *The Female Marine*, wherein she detailed her experiences in the Marine Corps. In 1967, Women Marines, beginning with Barbara Dulinsky, first started to serve in war zones.

Emily Meyer

See also: Brewer, Lucy [Louisa Baker, George Baker, Lucy West, Eliza Bowen] (ca. 1793– n.d.); Dulinsky, Barbara J. (n.d.–n.d.); Women Marines; World War I (1914–1918).

References and Further Reading

Gavin, Lettie. *American Women in World War I: They Also Served*. Niwot: University of Colorado Press, 1997.

Women Marine's Association. *The History of the U.S. Women Marines*. Nashville, TN: Turner Publishing, 1992.

JOHNSON, SHOSHANA NYREE (1973–)

Shoshana Johnson, a food service specialist in the Army, became the first black female American prisoner of war. Iraqis captured Johnson and five other American soldiers on March 23, 2003. She was held prisoner for 22 days.

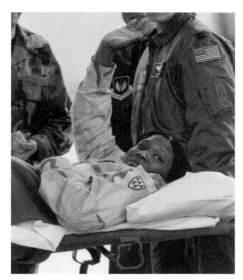

Army Specialist Shoshana Johnson, the first African American woman to be taken prisoner of war, waves goodbye as she is carried onto a military plane at the U.S. Air Base in Ramstein, Germany, on April 19, 2003. (AP Photo/ Michael Probst)

Born on January 18, 1973, in Panama to Eunice and Claude Johnson, Shoshana Nyree Johnson moved to the United States as a child. She came from a military family. Her father, a U.S. Army sergeant, deployed to the Gulf War as a nuclear, biological, and chemical specialist. One of her sisters, Nikki, was a commissioned lieutenant who graduated from the New Mexico Military Academy.

Shoshana served in her high school's Reserve Officer Training Corps (ROTC). She later attended the University of Texas at El Paso. Although she did not plan to have a long-term career in the military, she joined the Army in 1998 to cook for the soldiers as she earned money for culinary school. She prepared meals for the 507th Maintenance Company at Fort Bliss, Texas. Her

company's duties included fixing tankers, generators, and Patriot missile batteries. However, once the United States invaded Iraq, she and her company were deployed in early 2003. She left her two-year-old daughter, Janelle, in her parents' care.

On March 23, 2003, Johnson's supply convoy took a wrong turn. As the two trucks passed through the southern Iraqi town of Nasiriya for the second time, Iraqis ambushed them. Her truck rolled over, and she and another soldier took cover under it. When they tried to return fire, they discovered that their guns were jammed. Johnson got shot in both ankles during the firefight. After it became clear that their situation was hopeless, Johnson's superior officer surrendered the group. Eleven soldiers had been killed. The Iraqis took the seven remaining soldiers, including three women, as prisoners. Johnson and four male soldiers—Edgar Hernandez, Joseph Hudson, Patrick Miller, and James Riley —were imprisoned together. Jessica Lynch and Lori Piestewa were imprisoned elsewhere. Piestewa died of her wounds. Lynch was rescued by special forces troops on April 2, 2003.

A video of Johnson's interrogation by her captors was broadcast all over the world. Her parents learned of her capture after seeing the clip. During their 22 days as prisoners of war, Johnson and the others were moved seven times. While a prisoner, Johnson had surgery on one of her ankles. She was kept in a separate cell from her male counterparts but was not sexually harassed or assaulted while being held prisoner.

On April 13, 2003, Johnson and the four other captured soldiers were found by a group of marines. The marines instructed the captives to run for safety, but because of her injuries Johnson had to be carried to the vehicle. The soldiers were taken to safety, treated for their wounds, and debriefed before they were flown home to their families.

Johnson's experiences in Iraq earned her a Bronze Star, Purple Heart, and Prisoner of War Medal. It also shaped her career. In addition to her damaged ankles, Johnson also suffers from posttraumatic stress disorder and depression. As a result, she applied for a medical discharge from the Army in August 2003. She retired from the Army on a temporary disability honorable discharge in December 2003.

Lisa Tendrich Frank

See also: Iraq War (2003–2011); Lynch, Jessica (1983–); Piestewa, Lori (1979–2003); Prisoners of War; Reserve Officer Training Corps (ROTC); War on Terror (2001–).

Reference and Further Reading

Johnson, Shoshana. *I'm Still Standing: From Captive U.S. Soldier to Free Citizen—My Journey Home*. New York: Touchstone, 2010.

JOHNSON, SUSANNAH (CA. 1730–1810)

Susannah Willard Johnson was an English woman held captive by Native Americans and the French during the French and Indian War (1754–1763).

Susannah Willard was born around 1730, probably in western Massachusetts. She married James Johnson, and they lived just outside the Fort at Number Four at Charlestown, New Hampshire.

In a dawn attack on August 30, 1754, a group of Abenakis raided the Johnson home. The assault was the beginning of a life-changing saga that was similar to the stories of many of those captured along the frontier. The entire Johnson family (Susannah, her husband James, and their three children), Susannah's younger sister, and two other local men were taken. During her second day of captivity, Susannah gave birth to a girl. She and her husband named the child Elizabeth Captive Johnson.

Following an arduous trip, the family arrived at St. Francis, a native settlement in Canada. The Abenakis sold James, the two middle Johnson children, and the two local men to the French. The family of Joseph Louis Gill adopted Susannah, her daughter Elizabeth, and her son Sylvanus. Several months later, after living among the natives, whom she grew to respect, Susannah and the young Elizabeth were sold to the French. During their years in captivity, the Johnsons sought ransom money so that they could return home. They regularly petitioned various government entities in New France seeking better treatment and freedom. Finally ransomed, Susannah, her sister, and her two youngest children returned to New England in late 1757. James was also released and was reunited with his wife on January 1, 1758. Sylvanus arrived home in November 1758. Johnson's remaining captive child returned home late in the summer of 1760.

In March 1758, James joined the Massachusetts Militia. He died in the Battle of Ticonderoga in July 1758.

Susannah remarried in 1760 and published her account of the events she endured in 1796. Johnson (now Hastings) lived near Charlestown, New Hampshire, where she died on November 27, 1810.

Marcia Schmidt Blaine

See also: Indian Wars; North American Colonial Wars (17th–18th centuries).

References and Further Reading

Johnson, Susannah. *A Narrative of the Captivity of Mrs. Johnson.* Bowie, MD: Heritage Classic, 1990. Originally published 1796.

Steele, Ian K. "Susannah Johnson, Captive." In *The Human Tradition in Colonial America*, edited by Ian K. Steele and Nancy L. Rhoden, 257–71. Wilmington, DE: Scholarly Resources, 1999.

JOHNSON-BROWN, HAZEL WINIFRED (1927–2011)

In 1979, Hazel Johnson-Brown became the first African American woman promoted to general and the first to become chief of the Army Nurse Corps (ANC). Prior to her promotion to general, when she earned promotion to colonel, she had been the highest-ranking African American woman in the military.

Born October 10, 1927, in West Chester, Pennsylvania, Hazel Winifred Johnson was one of seven children. She spent her childhood on her family's farm in Chester County, near the town of Malvern. She attended school in Berwyn. Her compassionate nature and passion for education were passed down to her by her parents and her Quaker teachers, who advocated that she received the best education possible despite backlash from others in her West Chester ocmmunity. She found her calling in life early from hands-on experience in taking care of others. After she graduated from high school, she continued her education in New York and trained as a registered nurse at Harlem Hospital's School of Nursing.

Never one to let opportunity go untapped, Johnson joined the Army in 1955, hoping to use her nursing experience to travel the world. Her first post was in Japan. In addition, while in the Army, she received a bachelor's degree in nursing from Villanova University in 1959. She continued her education by earning a master's degree from Columbia University's Teachers College (1963) and a doctorate in educational administration from Catholic University (1978).

Despite the racial tensions of the time, Johnson's leadership skills in the field of nursing and her insatiable curiosity helped her rise through the ranks in the military. During the Vietnam War, Johnson helped to train surgical nurses before they headed to war. In 1967, Johnson became part of the staff of the Army's Research and Development Command, which did scientific and technological research for the Army and the Department of Defense. During Johnson's time in the department, she worked on ways to sterilize medical instruments and apparatus in the field. She became the director of the Walter Reed Army Institute of Nursing in 1976.

In 1977, when Johnson was promoted to colonel, she became the highest-ranking African American woman in the U.S. military. She served for a time as chief nurse with the U.S. Army Medical Command in South Korea. Then, on September 1, 1979, Johnson was promoted to brigadier general and to chief of the ANC. She was the first African American woman in both positions. As chief of the ANC, Johnson directed over 7,000 nurses in the Army, set policies, and oversaw operations in 8 Army medical centers, 56 community hospitals, and 143 free-standing clinics in the United States, Japan, Korea, Germany, Italy and Panama.

Johnson received much recognition for her exemplary service. She was twice named Army Nurse of the Year. She also received several medals, including the Distinguished Service Medal, Legion of Merit, Meritorious Service Medal, and Army Commendation Medal with Oak Leaf Cluster.

On August 31, 1983, she retired from the Army but continued to work within the medical field. She became the director of the Center for Health Policy at George Mason University. She also headed the government relations unit of the American Nurses Association. She married David Brown in 1984, and the couple settled in Clifton, Virginia. They later divorced. Johnson-Brown served as professor of nursing for several universities before retiring in 1997. She then chaired the Board of Advisors of the College of Nursing and Health Sciences at George Mason. She also served as an advisor to doctoral candidates in nursing.

Late in life, she developed Alzheimer's disease. Johnson-Brown died on August 5, 2011, in Wilmington, Delaware.

Aineshia Carline Washington

See also: African American Women; Army Nurse Corps (ANC); Nursing; Vietnam War (1965–1973).

References and Further Reading

Haskins, Jim. *African American Military Heroes*. New York: John Wiley and Sons, 1998.

Hine, Darlene Clark, ed. *Black Women in America*. New York: Carlson Publishing, 1993.

"Resolution 88: Honoring Brigadier General Hazel Winifred Johnson-Brown." Congressional Bill 88, November 16, 2011.

K

KEICHLINE, ANNA WAGNER
(1889–1943)

Anna Wagner Keichline was the first certified female architect in the state of Pennsylvania, a women's suffrage leader, and an agent for the U.S. Military Intelligence Division, an organization whose origins stemmed from the American Protection League. Keichline served in this agency from May 1918 to the end of World War I in November of the same year.

Born the youngest of four children in Bellefonte, Pennsylvania, in 1889, Keichline developed an early talent for and interest in carpentry from a patient at a tuberculosis sanitarium, where her mother was recovering from the illness. In 1903, at age 14, Keichline won first place in a local fair for her walnut chest and oak card table, shocking everyone by declaring she wanted to devote herself to it. In her pursuit of studying architecture, Keichline received tremendous support from her parents, who did not quell her ambitions to pursue what was traditionally a field restricted to men.

In 1906, Keichline graduated from Bellefonte High School and enrolled at Penn State to study mechanical engineering. A year elapsed, and Keichline transferred to Cornell University, where she studied architecture. Initially the university was reluctant to grant her a degree. When her classmates refused to graduate without her, the university issued her a diploma and Keichline became the fifth woman to receive an architecture degree from Cornell. In 1913, Keichline, a strong supporter of women's rights, led a march for women's suffrage during Bellefonte's July Fourth parade.

In 1918, the United States was in the middle of World War I. Twenty-eight-year-old Keichline yearned to serve her country. In February 1918, she volunteered for service and petitioned Capt. Harry A. Taylor of the Military Intelligence Division in Washington, D.C., expressing her qualifications for a position. Acknowledging that the mentality of the era toward women in the workforce might lead Taylor to recommend her for a clerical position, in her letter Keichline expressed her desire to work in a more prominent position, even if it was difficult or dangerous.

Keichline's qualifications for wartime work included her knowledge of German, a language she learned when her father, John, a prominent lawyer in Bellefonte, dealt with German clients. Her qualifications impressed Taylor, and Keichline was assigned to the Military Intelligence Division. The organization had investigated the loyalties of German Americans since the beginning of U.S. participation in the war.

Keichline quickly acquainted herself with German Americans working in munitions factories while secretly investigating their views on the war. The specifics of Keichline's investigations have yet to be discovered. Keichline served for the final six months of the war and sent her letter of resignation to the agency at the end of 1918.

Keichline continued to have a remarkably distinguished career in architecture in the years following World War I. In her lifetime, she was granted six utility patents and one design patent. The first of these patents was awarded in 1912 for her improved sink design. In addition, using traditional brick and stone, she designed 24 commercial buildings and residences. Among the more famous of her designs are the Bald Eagle and Nittany Valley Presbyterian Church in Mill Hall, Pennsylvania (constructed in 1915), the Juniata Colony Country Clubhouse in Mount Union Pennsylvania (built in 1927), and the Decker Home in Bellefonte, Pennsylvania (constructed in 1931).

Among the other Keichline inventions were her efficient kitchen designs to accommodate women of the 1920s and reduce the amount of time women needed to spend in the kitchen. Keichline is also famous for her development of the K-Brick, a clay building block for hollow wall construction and predetermined fracture points.

Keichline achieved the status of celebrated architect, World War I special agent, and women's suffrage activist during an era when women were expected to remain in domestic capacities. In the 1920s, she was a delegate to the Better Housing Conference, where she met and became friends with President Herbert Hoover.

On February 3, 1943, Keichline died from cancer. There is a historical marker located in her hometown of Bellefonte honoring her legacy.

Alison Vick

See also: Espionage; World War I (1914–1918).

References and Further Reading

Bidwell, Bruce W. *History of the Military Intelligence Division, Department of the Army General Staff: 1775–1941.* Frederick, MD: University Publications of America, 1986.

Kephart-Sulit, Beth. "Anna Wagner Keichline: A Portrait of Pennsylvania's First Registered Female Architect." *Pennsylvania Architect* 5, no. 1 (Winter 1992).

Perkins, Nancy J. "It's Already Been Done: Contexts of Achievement." *Innovation: Quarterly of the Industrial Designers Society of America,* Summer 2000.

KENNEDY, CLAUDIA J.
(1947–)

Claudia J. Kennedy was the first female three-star general in the U.S. Army. During her 31 years in the military, she worked extensively in Military Intelligence (MI), eventually holding the office of Deputy Chief of Staff for Intelligence.

Kennedy, one of four children, was born in Frankfurt, Germany, on July 14, 1947. Her father, Cary, was a major in the U.S. Army Transportation Corps, and her mother, Tommie, dedicated her time to raising their children. Due to her father's career, Claudia's family relocated frequently throughout her formative years. During Claudia's childhood, the Kennedy family lived in several countries around the world including Japan, Israel, and Germany.

In 1964, Cary became a full colonel, and the family returned to the United States. Claudia completed her final year of high school near her father's base in Fort Hamilton, New York. In 1965, she began attending college at Southwestern at Memphis, Tennessee. While at college, Claudia's father was posted to Saigon, and many of her male friends were drafted into the Vietnam War. These events inspired Claudia to consider the possibility of military service.

In 1967, Kennedy saw an advertisement in *Cosmopolitan* for the Women's Army Corps (WAC). Around the same time, a professor introduced her to Betty Friedan's *The Feminine Mystique*. Friedan's feminist message convinced Claudia that women should be not shut out of any part of public life, including the military. Asking a sorority sister to join her, Kennedy signed up for a four-week WAC orientation and training program.

In 1969, Kennedy enlisted in the U.S. Army and received her commission as a second lieutenant. She served as a WAC on various army bases for two years, performing a variety of somewhat menial tasks. Her frustration over gender bias and the lack of stimulating job duties made her think about leaving the military. She changed her mind in 1973, however, when she was given command of an Army company at Fort McClellan. One year later, she married a fellow soldier.

In 1974, Kennedy received approval for an assignment to MI. Due to the sensitive nature of Kennedy's occupation, much of her MI work remains classified. However, it is public knowledge that she specialized in cryptology. After completing her cryptology training, Kennedy reported for duty at an army base in Seoul, South Korea. There, she worked to gather intelligence and maintain the security of the Demilitarized Zone between North and South Korea.

The long period of separation between Kennedy and her husband, as well as her decision to remain a career officer, strained the marriage, and they decided to divorce.

After completing her tour of duty in South Korea, Kennedy joined the National Security Agency (NSA), achieving the rank of major within three years. In 1979, she attended the Command and General Staff College, which is considered a necessary step toward advancement to high-ranking positions in the U.S. military. She then worked as an intelligence officer in Germany before being named a battalion commander in 1985.

From 1988 to 1990, Kennedy commanded San Antonio's recruiting battalion. She then commanded the 703rd MI Brigade in Kunia, Hawaii; at the time, this base contained some of the most sensitive MI in the country. While commanding the unit, Kennedy made several changes to the training program, including requiring foreign language training for all intelligence officers in order to improve their cryptography skills.

In 1993, Kennedy became a brigadier general and joined the U.S. Army Forces Command. By 1996, she had achieved the rank of major general and had become the Pentagon's assistant deputy chief of staff for intelligence. She received a promotion to the rank of lieutenant general in 1997 and advanced to the office of deputy chief of staff for intelligence.

In 1999, Kennedy accused Brig. Gen. Larry G. Smith of sexual harassment. She felt compelled to report the incident, which had occurred three years earlier, when she discovered that Smith had been promoted to a position in which one of his duties would have been investigating sexual harassment cases. In addition, she had recently become aware of a scandal involving the sexual abuse of female Army recruits by superior officers. An investigation validated Kennedy's claims and concluded that Smith had acted inappropriately. The complaint and subsequent investigation became subjects of significant publicity and media attention.

Kennedy retired on June 2, 2000. Since retirement, she has vocally opposed the military's now-defunct "Don't Ask, Don't Tell" policy and has been an outspoken advocate for gender equality in the armed forces.

Jamie Stoops

See also: Espionage; Vietnam War (1965–1973); Women's Army Corps (WAC).

References and Further Reading

Kennedy, Claudia J. "Redefining the Warrior Mentality: Women in the Military." In *Sisterhood is Forever: The Women's Anthology for the New Millennium*, edited by Robin Morgan, 409–17. New York: Washington Square Press, 2003.

Kennedy, Claudia J., and Malcolm McConnell. *Generally Speaking*. New York: Warner Books, 2001.

KEYS (EVANS), SARAH LOUISE (1929–)

An African American woman who served in the Women's Army Corps (WAC) from 1951 to 1953, Sarah Louise Keys became the subject of racial discrimination when traveling home on leave from service in 1952. Her case became a predecessor for understanding civil rights issues in public transportation, predating Rosa Parks's efforts in the Montgomery Bus Boycott.

Born in Washington, North Carolina, in 1929, Keys was the second of seven children. She graduated high school in 1948 and moved to the New York metropolitan area, where she attended nursing school briefly before pursuing other employment. Keys enlisted in the WAC in 1951, three years after President Truman ordered the desegregation of the armed forces. Keys's basic training at Fort Lee, Virginia, was in a fully integrated environment in which women of all races trained and lived alongside one another.

While stationed at Fort Dix, New Jersey, Pvt. 1st Class Keys took a 10-day leave to visit her family in North Carolina in August 1952. Wearing her dress uniform with heeled shoes, Keys boarded the bus in Trenton, New Jersey, and selected a seat near the middle of the bus. Around midnight, the bus stopped in Roanoke Rapids to take on new passengers and change drivers. When the new driver came to collect tickets, he told Keys to move to the back of the bus and refused to take her ticket.

When Keys did not move, the driver requested the other passengers to disembark for another bus. Keys also got in line for the new bus, but the driver refused to allow her on board. Instead, he advised two policemen that Keys had been causing problems, and Keys was taken to the local jail for the night.

Although the police threatened to charge her with disturbing the peace, she was imprisoned on no charges overnight and was not allowed to make a phone call. The police released Keys the following morning, after charging her a $25 fine, and put her on a bus to her parents' home. The chief advised her that she could come back to court the following Thursday if she contested the fine.

With her father's support, Keys found a lawyer through the local minister and went to the court, but the judge upheld the fine. After her return to Fort Dix, Keys secured permission to return to North Carolina for an appeal the following month. When the appeal efforts failed, Keys's father began looking into other legal options.

A family friend in Washington, D.C., recommended a new lawyer, Dovey May Johnson Roundtree, a black woman who served in the WAC in World War II. After the war, Roundtree completed law school at Harvard University. Roundtree had developed a network of contacts with the NAACP, and with Roundtree's guidance, Keys first filed for a civil suit in February 1953. When that was denied, she filed a complaint with the Interstate Commerce Commission (ICC) in September 1953.

Sarah Keys v. North Carolina Coach Company alleged that the North Carolina Coach Company discriminated against Keys, which led to her false arrest. She testified in front of the ICC in 1954, and the complaint was initially settled against her in a ruling by one ICC representative. Roundtree petitioned to have the case considered by all 11 ICC members. With support from New York congressman Adam Clayton Powell Jr., the ICC agreed to reconsider the case. In November 1955, with one member dissenting, the ICC settled in Keys's favor. The ICC ruled that segregation in interstate travel was illegal, affirming that passengers who paid the same fare, regardless of race, must have access to the same seats. Additionally, just as the ICC handed down their decision in Keys's case, they also upheld the same principles in a concurrent NAACP case regarding discrimination in interstate railway travel. The ICC stipulated that desegregation of interstate travel must be accomplished by January 10, 1956.

The NAACP hailed the decision as an important landmark in civil rights, coming just one year after *Brown v. Board of Education* in Kansas. The ICC rulings presented a major challenge to the 1896

Plessy v. Ferguson "separate but equal" guidelines that had helped develop segregation in southern states, including practices such as forcing African Americans to sit in designated areas of buses and railcars. One week after the ICC settled Keys's case, Parks initiated the Montgomery Bus Boycott in Montgomery, Alabama, which lasted more than one year.

After completing her service in 1953, Keys used military benefits to attend beauty school for one year while working as an office clerk. Keys married George Evans in 1958 and had a career as both a stylist and beauty consultant for many years.

Tanya L. Roth

See also: African American Women; Roundtree, Dovey May Johnson (1914–); Women's Army Corps (WAC).

References and Further Reading

Holm, Jeanne. *Women in the Military: An Unending Revolution (Revised Edition).* Novato, CA: Presidio Press, 1993.

Morden, Bettie J. *The Women's Army Corps, 1945–1978.* Washington, D.C.: Center of Military History, 1989.

Nathan, Amy. *Take a Seat, Make a Stand: A Hero in the Family.* New York: iUniverse, 2006.

KINNEY, DITA HOPKINS (1855–1921)

Dita Hopkins Kinney was the first superintendent of the U.S. Army Nurse Corps (ANC) and the author and staff collaborator for the *American Journal of Nursing*.

Born in New York City on September 13, 1855, Kinney attended Mills Seminary before graduating from Massachusetts General Hospital training school in 1892. After teaching child care classes, training nurses' assistants, and nursing at several institutions, including Almshouse Hospital in Boston and French Hospital in San Francisco, she began her Army career in September 1898, at the outset of the Spanish-American War. In decline since the American Civil War, military nursing was revitalized in April 1898 when Congress permitted the appointment of female nurses under contract status. Stationed at the Presidio in San Francisco, California, Kinney was quickly released from this assignment so that she could take charge of a soldiers' convalescent home established by the Red Cross in Oakland, California. She stayed there until the home was closed, and then she resumed work at the French Hospital. Frustrated by what she called the impossible conditions there, she signed another Army contract and worked as an operating room nurse at the Presidio.

Her work in the operating room was first rate, and Kinney was recommended for promotion just as an 1,800-bed hospital was being planned in Nagasaki, Japan. Kinney was appointed chief nurse of this proposed facility, which would care for the allied injured in the Boxer Rebellion in China. However, the hospital never came to fruition due to deteriorating stability in the region. Kinney reported instead to Fort Bayard, New Mexico, where she served as chief nurse at the Government Hospital for Consumptives, the first hospital committed to the treatment of U.S. Army soldiers suffering from pulmonary tuberculosis. According to the July 13, 1901, edition of the *Journal of the American Medical Association*, the sanatorium made great strides in treating its patients, many who were reportedly able to return to duty.

From Fort Bayard, Kinney was ordered to report to Washington, D.C., where she worked alongside Anita Newcomb McGee in the surgeon general's office. In Washington, Kinney administered the inclusion of women nurses in the Army through the newly developed ANC. The ANC developed as a result of recognition of the valuable service of contract nurses during the Spanish-American War. Realizing the need for an on-call corps of trained nurses who were also acquainted with military procedures, the Nurse Corps became a permanent part of the Medical Department under the Army Reorganization Act of 1901. Officially assuming the role of superintendent of the ANC on March 16, 1901, Kinney served honorably in this position for more than eight years.

During her tenure as superintendent, Kinney led an inspection tour of the majority of the Army hospitals in the United States and the Philippines, which resulted in several improvements in the Nurse Corps regulations. Prior to Kinney's inspection tour, for instance, the Nurse Corps did not require any examinations for promotion. Based on her recommendation, however, the Nurse Corps established and made requisite an examination in nursing, cooking, and related subjects. Corps nurses with demonstrable leadership ability who passed this exam could be promoted to chief nurse. This measure brought the Nurse Corps more into line with regular Army promotion practices and gave the Corps greater integrity. Also during these years, Kinney served as staff collaborator for the *American Journal of Nursing*, contributing many professional articles to this publication including one based on her experiences in the Philippines, entitled "Glimpses of Life in Manila."

Her time as superintendent was not without controversy, however. At the time of Kinney's appointment, the professional nursing leadership was still at odds with Anita Newcomb McGee because McGee had drafted ANC legislation in 1900 without consulting with them. Thus, as McGee's appointee, Kinney suffered some of the backlash of this conflict and did not receive the professional nursing leadership's support. Further, some male physicians and soldiers strongly opposed having female Army nurses, creating an unpleasant working environment for all. This workplace tension coupled with low pay for nurses reduced the number of ANC members, and when Surgeon General George H. Torney took over in 1909, Kinney was forced to resign as superintendent.

Undaunted, Kinney resumed study at the Massachusetts General Hospital training school and worked as a hospital superintendent in Gloucester, Massachusetts. Retiring due to declining health in 1914, Kinney died in Bangor, Maine, on April 16, 1921. She was buried in New York City's Trinity Cemetery.

Dana Nichols

See also: American Red Cross; Army Nurse Corps (ANC); McGee, Anita Newcomb

(1864–1940); Nursing; Spanish-American War (1898).

References and Further Reading

Sarnecky, Mary T. *A History of the U.S. Army Nurse Corps*. Philadelphia: University of Pennsylvania Press, 1999.

Shearer, Benjamin F. *Homefront Heroes: A Biographical Dictionary of Americans during Wartime*. Westport, CT: Greenwood Press, 2007.

KOREAN WAR
(1950–1953)

In June 1950, when the Korean War began, 22,000 women were serving in the U.S. armed forces as a result of the Women's Armed Services Integration Act of 1948. Of this number, nurses comprised 7,000. The remainder served in the ranks of the Women's Army Corps (WAC); Women Accepted for Volunteer Emergency Service (WAVES), or the Navy Women's Reserve; Women Marines; and Women in the Air Force (WAF). As the U.S. government moved more men to the front, women again assumed vacated clerical and administrative, engineering, and technical positions.

Before recruiting began in earnest, 1,600 servicewomen of the Organized Reserve Corps (which in 1952 became known as the U.S. Army Reserve) returned to the Army Nurse Corps (ANC), Women's Medical Specialist Corps, and the WAC. A total of 640 military nurses served in Korea (540 from the Army, 50 from the Navy, and 50 from the Air Force). Seventy percent of the

Army nurses were attached to mobile Army surgical hospital (MASH) units. In the United States, 120,000 military servicewomen served during the war, primarily as clerks and administrators.

In 1950, 629 WAC personnel served in the Far East Command Headquarters. By 1951, their numbers had increased to 2,600. Women were able to rise in the ranks and to move into arenas formerly occupied only by men. Women were ward masters in military hospitals in Japan and senior noncommissioned officers in motor pools, mess halls, and post offices. Women could be found in administration, in communications, and in intelligence. They worked as censors, interpreters, draftsmen, weather personnel, and even aides-de-camp.

The ANC numbered 3,450 in 1950. By 1951, it had grown to 5,397 women, the majority of these being World War II veterans. Five hundred and forty nurses volunteered to serve in Korea. One, Capt. Viola McConnell of the U.S. Military Advisory Group/Republic of Korea, assisted in the evacuation of 700 Americans from Seoul. For her actions, McConnell received a Bronze Star and the Oak Leaf Cluster.

Four days after U.S. troops joined UN forces, 57 female nurses arrived in Korea. Twelve Army nurses in the first MASH unit moved out on July 8, 1950, to the front line at Taejon. One month later, over 100 Army nurses were stationed near the front lines within Korea, positions they would occupy throughout the war. Three African American nurses served in Korea: Lt. Martha E. Cleveland and Lt. Nancy Greene Peace were posted at the 11th Evacuation Hospital, and Lt. Evelyn Decker served with the 8055th MASH. Still others served in hospitals in Japan and Hawaii.

MASH nurses also adopted the protective clothing of the male soldiers for whom they were caring. Combat boots, fatigues, and steel helmets replaced more traditional nursing uniforms, and the women lived in tents like other military personnel. Amazingly, despite their proximity to battles, not a single Army nurse died in Korea.

At the beginning of the war, the Navy's WAVES hoped to enlist 1,000 officers and 10,000 servicewomen in their ranks. That initial goal was not met. To increase their numbers, Capt. Joy Bright Hancock implemented a voluntary recall. When that failed to provide the desired numbers, an involuntary recall followed. It was the first time in U.S. history that women, as well as their male counterparts, were called up, voluntarily or not. To further add to the ranks, unreasonable deterrents were eliminated. The ban against married women serving was dropped; additionally, the age of enlistment was lowered to 18, following the successful 1948 model of the Army and Air Force. As a result, WAVES numbers went from 3,239 in 1950 to a high of 9,466 in November 1952.

Recruited WAVES were sent to a six-week training program, initially held at the Great Lakes Training Center; in October 1951, the program moved to the Naval Training Center in Bainbridge, Maryland. Petty officer leadership schools were established at San Diego and at Bainbridge, Georgia, in 1953, while officer candidates trained at Officer Indoctrination Unit (W) at Newport, Rhode Island. Finally, a Reserve Officer Candidate Program began at the Great Lakes Training Center.

The Navy Nurse Corps consisted of 1,921 women when the Korean War broke out in June 1950. It peaked at 3,405 in November 1951, but only 2,600 remained at the end of the war. The growth included an involuntary recall of 926 navy nurses. The Navy Nurse Corps also recruited and commissioned civilian nurses. Capt. Winnie Gibson oversaw the Nurse Corps, which served in 126 stations in the United States, at 25 foreign stations, on 8 Military Sea Transport Service (MSTS) ships, in 3 MSTS ports, in 15 civilian schools, and on 3 hospital ships. In fact, 35 percent of the U.S. battle casualties from the Korean War were evacuated directly to the USS *Consolation*, USS *Haven*, and USS *Repose*. In August 1950, a fourth ship, the USS *Benevolence*, was accidentally rammed and sank before leaving port. One nurse died as a result.

The women's auxiliary unit of the U.S. Coast Guard, the SPARs (Semper Paratus—Always Ready), had been demobilized in 1946. The unit began recruiting again in late 1949, and by 1950, 200 former SPARs had voluntarily reenlisted. They served mostly in U.S. territory. The Air Force Nurse Corps was involved in the evacuation of approximately 350,000 patients during the course of the war. Within the Marines, many of the 2,787 women in the corps earned entry to a broader range of occupational specialties than did those in other branches of military service.

In all, the Navy lost 12 nurses as well as 18 enlisted WAVES. Eleven Navy nurses were killed when their plane crashed on takeoff from Kwaejon Island, and another one died as a result of the sinking of the USS *Benevolence*. The deaths of the WAVES were also not combat related. Three nurses received the Bronze Star, six the Commendation Ribbon, and 90 the Navy Unit Commendation. In addition, U.S. Army major Genevieve Smith died in a plane crash in transit to her post as chief nurse in Korea. Three Air Force nurses also died.

Prior to 1950, American women had a limited presence in Korea, primarily as missionaries. During the war, women were captured, marched, and treated as brutally as their male soldier counterparts. Nellie Dyer from North Little Rock, Arkansas, and Helen Rosser, from Atlanta, Georgia, were held as POWs along with members of the 24th Infantry Division.

Although most servicewomen were confined to traditional "female" jobs, the Korean War afforded a unique opportunity for a few civilian women to break the mold. Anna Rosenberg had been a political consultant and labor relations expert working for President Roosevelt as his personal observer during World War II. Building on her career as one of the first women to hold various directorial posts in the U.S. government, Rosenberg was appointed assistant secretary of defense for manpower and personnel in 1950. During her tenure she oversaw all defense department policies and created the Defense Advisory Committee on Women in the Services (DACOWITS), a committee of 50 professional women (chaired by Mary Lord) that aggressively recruited women for military service. Rosenberg, a lifelong civil rights and women's suffrage

advocate, also effectively integrated formerly segregated African American and white troops into cohesive combat units. For her service, Rosenberg received the Department of Defense's Exceptional Civilian Award in 1953.

The war provided unique opportunities for both U.S. civilian women and women in the military, who were now an integral part of the armed forces. Marguerite "Maggie" Higgins, a reporter for the *New York Herald Tribune*, had the distinction of being the only female war correspondent during the Korean War. Margaret Bourke-White, a photographer with World War II experience, was sent by *Life* magazine in the spring of 1951 to photograph bomber planes belonging to the Strategic Air Command in Korea. Bourke-White was the first woman to fly in a B-47 jet, and she subsequently accompanied South Korean police as they moved against guerrilla fighters.

Sarah Hilgendorff List

See also: African American Women; Air Force Nurse Corps (AFNC); Army Nurse Corps (ANC); Asian American Women; Bourke-White, Margaret (1904–1971); Cold War (ca. 1947–1991); Defense Advisory Committee on Women in the Services (DACOWITS); Espionage; Hancock, Joy Bright (1898–1986); Higgins (Hall), Marguerite (1920–1966); Military Sea Transport Service (MSTS); Mobile Army Surgical Hospital (MASH); Navy Nurse Corps; Prisoners of War; Reserve Officer Training Corps (ROTC); Smith, Genevieve M. (1905–1950); United States Coast Guard Women's Reserve (SPAR); USS *Benevolence*; Women Accepted for Volunteer Emergency Service (WAVES); Women in the Air Force (WAF); Women Marines; Women's Armed Services Integration Act of 1948; Women's Army Corps (WAC); Women's Medical Specialist Corps (WMSCP); World War II (1941–1945).

References and Further Reading

Godson, Susan H. *Serving Proudly: A History of Women in the U.S. Navy.* Annapolis, MD: Naval Institute Press, 2001.

Goldberg, Vicki. *Margaret Bourke-White: A Biography.* Reading, MA: Addison-Wesley, 1987.

Higgins, Marguerite. *War in Korea: The Report of a Woman Combat Correspondent.* Garden City, NY: Doubleday, 1951.

"1950s." Women in Military Service for America Memorial. http://www.womens memorial.org (accessed January 21, 2005).

L

LADIES' ASSOCIATION

The Ladies' Association of Philadelphia was one of the most influential women's groups that supported the American cause during the American Revolution.

In June 1780, Esther de Berdt Reed, the wife of Pennsylvania's governor, published *The Sentiments of an American Woman*. In it, Reed called upon women to support the troops with more than just good wishes. Invoking historical examples of female heroines, especially those who demonstrated patriotism, she urged patriotic women to support the war effort. She especially called for women to embrace the home manufacture movement and boycott British-made products. In addition, she called for women's material and financial support of American troops.

Three days after the publication of the *Sentiments*, three dozen Philadelphia women of high social standing came together to form the Ladies' Association of Philadelphia. Their plan of female mobilization and contribution to the American Revolutionary War was published on June 21, 1780, in the *Pennsylvania Gazette* as "Ideas, Relative to the Manner of Forwarding to the American Soldiers, the Presents of the American Women." Although Reed became president of the Ladies' Association, Sarah Franklin Bache, daughter of Benjamin Franklin, became one of the leading figures in this national organization.

Its founders set up the Ladies' Association of Philadelphia as a national organization with the main objective of raising funds for American troops. Thus, guidelines held that in each county a treasuress should be appointed. The task of each treasuress was to oversee local fund-raising and keep record of the money gathered in her area. On the next organizational level, each state should be headed by treasuress-general, a task prescribed to the governors' wives. The money raised by all local organizations was to be sent to Martha Washington. The money was designated to support the armed forces, and the

Ladies' Association required that the money not be spent on items the soldiers should receive from Congress or the states.

In order to collect the money, the Philadelphian women divided the city into equal districts and assigned a woman responsibility for each of the resultant 10 districts. Thus, these women of higher social standing went from house to house requesting contributions from every woman and girl. On completion of the collection of the Philadelphia canvass, Reed wanted to use the money collected to give a certain amount to every soldier. Thereby, she came into conflict with George Washington. Reed and Washington finally agreed on using the money to buy linen that the women of the Association sewed into shirts, redirecting the activities of their initiative to traditionally gendered tasks.

Eva Katharina Sarter

See also: American Revolution (1775–1783); Bache, Sarah "Sally" Franklin (1743–1808); Reed, Esther de Berdt (1746–1780).

References and Further Reading

Erkkila, Betsy. "Revolutionary Women." *Tulsa Studies in Women's Literature* 6, no. 2 (1987): 189–223.

Gundersen, Joan R. *To Be Useful in the World: Women in Revolutionary America, 1740–1790.* New York: Twayne Publishers, 1996.

Kerber, Linda K. *Women of the Republic: Intellect and Ideology in Revolutionary America.* New York: W. W. Norton and Company, 1980.

Norton, Mary B. *Liberty's Daughters: The Revolutionary Experience of American Women, 1750–1800.* Boston: Little, Brown, and Company, 1980.

LAMARR, HEDY (1914–2000)

Hedy Lamarr was an Austrian-born actress who coinvented an early concept of "frequency hopping," a form of spread-spectrum technology, with musical composer George Antheil.

Lamarr was born Hedwig Eva Maria Kiesler in Vienna, Austria, as part of an upper-class Jewish family. Her father was a bank director, her mother a concert pianist. She studied ballet and piano from an early age, entering the German film industry in her teen years. In early 1933, under the name Hedy Kiesler, Lamarr starred in the controversial film *Ecstasy*, which garnered notice for the young actress.

Lamarr married Austrian arms dealer Fritz Mandl, one of the most important armament manufacturers in Europe. During the four years of their marriage, Lamarr acted as a society hostess,

During World War II, actress Hedy Lamarr helped create an antijamming radio control for naval torpedoes. Her idea developed into the spread-spectrum technologies that the military uses today. (AP/Wide World Photos)

entertaining military personnel, Nazi sympathizers, and foreign leaders, including Mussolini and Hitler, on her husband's behalf. Mandl was interested in control systems and, during the couple's parties, frequently discussed the difficulties in guiding torpedoes towards evasive targets. Lamarr listened in on his conversations, picking up more than her husband and his acquaintances realized.

In 1937, Lamarr left her husband and fled to Paris to obtain a divorce. She then went to London, where she met Louis B. Mayer, studio boss of Metro-Goldwyn-Mayer (MGM). It was Mayer who forced Lamarr to change her name in an attempt to cleanse her image, replacing her surname with "Lamarr" and shortening Hedwig to "Hedy." During her career at MGM, Lamarr went on to star in such films as *Boom Town* (1940), *White Cargo* (1942), and *Tortilla Flat* (1942). She left the studio in 1945, her biggest success a post-MGM film, *Samson and Delilah* (1947).

Lamarr met George Antheil in 1940 when they were neighbors in Hollywood. She told the composer that she was considering leaving her film career in order to join the National Inventors' Council in Washington, D.C. This council had been set up to gather ideas from the general public, although few submitted inventions achieved any prominence. As a woman with natural mathematical talents, Lamarr wanted to put her mind, rather than her physique, to work for the government in order to combat what she saw as a growing Nazi threat to Europe.

The inspiration for Lamarr and Antheil's invention came when Lamarr attended one of Antheil's concerts at which 16 player pianos were utilized simultaneously. The constantly moving notes on the piano sparked Lamarr's idea of how to create an antijamming radio control for naval torpedoes. Lamarr determined that radio frequencies needed to be randomly changed so that the enemy couldn't intercept or jam the signal. Antheil suggested that punched player piano rolls be used to keep the radio transmitter in sync with the torpedo receiver. Lamarr and Antheil's design utilized a band of 88 possible frequencies for transmission, 88 being the number of keys on a piano.

In December of 1940, Lamarr and Antheil submitted their idea to the National Inventors' Council. After receiving encouragement, the inventors filed a patent on June 10, 1941, for a device named "Secret Communication System." Lamarr filed the patent under the name "Hedy Kiesler Markey," her married name at the time. The proposed object of the device was to provide a simple and reliable method of secret communication that would be difficult to detect or discover, using the piano roll system the pair had devised.

The U.S. Navy scorned the idea of using player piano rolls in torpedoes and shelved the idea after the patent was granted. The mechanical device proposed by the patent would have been difficult and expensive to construct under the constraints of military technology and knowledge of the 1940s. Lamarr and Antheil's system was rediscovered in 1957 when engineers from Sylvania Electronics unearthed the patent and altered the invention to utilize electronic signals instead of the piano rolls initially devised. This system in turn evolved into what the U.S. Navy dubbed "spread-spectrum" technology, a method used to keep military communication channels secure. By 1962, the Navy was using spread spectrum in communication systems placed in ships sent to blockade Cuba during the Cold War.

Spread-spectrum technologies continue to be used by the military today, notably in the Military Strategic and Tactical Relay (Milstar) defense communications satellite system. The Milstar satellite system provides secure, jam-resistent communications for the U.S. military's use in wartime. Lamarr's influence can also be seen in cellular communications and wireless Internet networks, both of which rely on the use of spread spectrum to encrypt and pass on information.

Like many female inventors of her time, Lamarr saw little renown and less revenue for the concept that she had helped create. Lamarr's contributions to military technologies went largely unrecognized until 1997, when she was honored by the Electronic Frontier Foundation.

Lamarr died in her home in Altamonte Springs, Florida, on January 19, 2000.

Gwen Perkins

See also: Cold War (ca. 1947–1991); World War II (1941–1945).

References and Further Reading

Braun, Hans-Joachim. "Advanced Weaponry of the Stars." *American Heritage* 12, no. 4 (1990): 10–16.

Lamarr, Hedy. *Ecstasy and Me: My Life as a Woman.* New York: Fawcett Crest Books, 1967.

Lewis, Ted. *Critical Infrastructure Protection in Homeland Security: Defending a Networked Nation.* Hoboken, NJ: John Wiley & Sons, 2006.

Stallings, William. *Data and Computer Communications.* Upper Saddle River, NJ: Pearson Communications, 2007.

Walters, Rob. *Spread Spectrum: Hedy Lamarr and the Mobile Phone.* Seattle, WA: BookSurge Publishing, 2006.

LANE, ANNA MARIA
(N.D.–1810)

A Continental Army soldier who was wounded at the Battle of Germantown in 1777, Anna Maria Lane was the first and only female veteran to receive a pension from the state of Virginia for her services as a soldier in the American Revolution.

Details about her early life have been lost. Lane's birth date is unknown. Sources suggest that she and her husband, John Lane, were originally from New Hampshire. In 1776, they joined the Continental Army, serving under Gen. Israel Putnam. Enlisting as a disguised woman at that time was relatively easy as there was no physical examination required for enlistees. In September 1777, after the Battle of Brandywine, Putnam's troops joined the main body of the Continental Army. It was during this campaign that Lane performed the services that later merited her a veteran's pension.

The Pennsylvania Campaign had gone poorly for the Americans. By October 1777, the British had taken Philadelphia, the capital city of the rebelling colonies. Following the Battle of Brandywine (September 11, 1777) and the Paoli Massacre (September 20, 1777), morale in the Continental Army was low. Gen. George Washington, commander in chief of the American army, needed a victory to rally his troops.

The British had occupied the nearby town of Germantown, just outside Philadelphia. On October 4, 1777, Washington deployed his troops to approach the town from several angles. In this coordinated assault, Washington hoped to catch the enemy by surprise in the early hours of the morning. A heavy fog foiled this plan; Washington and his generals scrambled to recover despite losing the advantage of surprise. The British had taken up in the Chew House, an old stone house owned by a Loyalist family, which withstood artillery fire. After several hours of fighting and the Americans' failure to push the British out of their stronghold at the Chew House, the tide turned and the officers were hard pressed to keep their soldiers from running in a disorganized retreat.

In a last-ditch effort, Washington rallied a contingent of troops to attempt to take the Chew House. Scholars argue that it may have been during this push to take the Chew House that Lane performed her extraordinary service, pressing onward when many men had backed down. The force of the onslaught and ferocity of the British defense would explain the severe wounds that she sustained during the battle. Despite an inspiring effort, the Americans were unable to overcome the British and retreated from Germantown. The retreat, while disappointing, was not altogether demoralizing; the Americans had demonstrated a growing militaristic confidence and tenacity that, with proper training during the winter of

1777–1778, would ultimately result in victories for the Americans.

Lane recovered from her wounds and continued to serve alongside her husband in subsequent campaigns after her husband reenlisted with the Virginia Light Dragoons. Lane was with her husband when he was wounded during the siege of Savannah (September 16–October 18, 1779). Her wound from the Germantown battle left her lame for the rest of her life.

After the war, the Lanes remained in Virginia, where John served in the Public Guard, first guarding the arsenals at Point of Fork in Fluvanna County. In 1801, he transferred to the arsenal in the capital city of Richmond. Anna and their three children lived with John in the barracks for the Public Guard and drew daily rations. Despite her lameness, Anna volunteered as a nurse at a hospital, for which she received a small stipend at the recommendation of Dr. John H. Foushee to Gov. James Monroe and the Council of State.

In 1804, her name disappeared from the council journal records; due to her deteriorating health, she could no longer work. In 1808, John Lane was discharged, leaving the couple without any income. Gov. William H. Cabell requested that the General Assembly provide pensions for disabled male veterans and a few women who had served the Army. John Lane received $40 per year for life. Anna, however, for her extraordinary services as a disguised female soldier, received $100 per year for life.

Lane passed away June 13, 1810. In 1997, the state of Virginia erected a state marker in Richmond in her honor.

Ashley L. Shimer

See also: American Revolution (1775–1783); Gay, Samuel [Ann Bailey] (n.d.–n.d.); Nursing; Samson [Sampson] (Gannett), Deborah. [Robert Shurtliff] (1760–1827).

References and Further Reading

Treadway, Sandra Gioia. "Anna Maria Lane: An Uncommon Common Soldier of the American Revolution." *Virginia Cavalcade* 37, no. 3 (1988): 134–43.

Ward, Harry M. *For Virginia and for Independence: Twenty-Eight Revolutionary War Soldiers from the Old Dominion.* Jefferson, NC: McFarland & Company, 2011.

Wolfe, Margaret Ripley. *Daughters of Canaan: A Saga of Southern Women.* Lexington: University Press of Kentucky, 1995.

LATIN AMERICAN MILITARY INTERVENTIONS

In the late 19th century, U.S. military interventions came to dominate relations between Latin America and its neighbor to the north. The importance of the military persists in U.S. policy towards Latin America, and women form an essential part of this history of interventions. Women have labored as civilian employees, volunteers, military personnel, and policy makers. They have been wives and mothers to military members, providing financial and psychological support, and they have served as combatants, even though the law still limits their participation. The American populace has not uniformly supported U.S. military involvement in Latin America, and women themselves did not inevitably agree on U.S. policy. Some women voiced opposition to military interference at the same time that other women expressed support for U.S. intervention in Latin American affairs. Although women did not always share the same opinions or participate to the same degree in U.S. occupations, many women faced discrimination and disregard for their involvement in politics and the military, sectors traditionally reserved for men.

Prior to 1942, nursing was one of the few occupations that allowed women to formally participate in military activities. During the Revolutionary War, George Washington requested one female nurse for every 10 patients. Nearly a century later, during the American Civil War, Dorothea Dix supervised both black and white nurses in the Union Army. Sally Louisa Tompkins of the Confederacy ran a private hospital where she cared for wounded soldiers. By the time of the Spanish-American War, the U.S. military was aware of the need for nurses during wartime, and in April 1898, Congress authorized the surgeon general to hire male and female nurses to serve in Cuba.

In 1898, Cuban colonists were fighting their third war of independence from Spain, and the United States worried that the revolutionaries would finally succeed in liberating the island. The U.S. government had long expressed interest in the territory and investments of Cuba, and it did not believe the Cuban people capable of governing themselves. On the basis of this presumption and under the guise of aiding the colonists, the United States intervened in Cuba's war of independence. The American public largely supported the war effort, and service personnel and nurses both rallied to defend Cuba from Spain.

Between April and August 1898, American nurses traveled to Cuba, both as volunteers and as contract workers. Hired by the surgeon general, contract nurses earned $30 per month plus a daily ration. Thirty-two African American women were hired by the military to serve as nurses in Cuba. Contract nurses were not official members of the military, however, and they could not earn veterans' benefits. They tended to the sick and wounded alongside volunteer nurses who worked under the auspices of the Red Cross. The volunteers received no pay and were not always welcomed by the American troops. When U.S. Army officers refused the aid of Red Cross volunteer Clara Barton, she dedicated herself to caring for the fallen Cuban soldiers.

Female physicians also volunteered their services in the Spanish-American War; however, the U.S. government would only hire them as nurses. These women distinguished themselves as contract workers and volunteers, distributing supplies and assisting male surgeons. Although they agreed to relinquish their status as doctors and serve instead as nurses, at least 10 of these nurse-physicians asserted their professional identity by writing "physician" on their identification cards. Only one woman, Dr. Anita Newcomb McGee, was granted the title of acting assistant surgeon. Her job was to select contract nurses to care for typhoid-infected soldiers in the army camps.

American women remaining in the United States also contributed to the war effort. Thousands of women's organizations raised money and purchased supplies to send to Cuba. They also tended to the soldiers in U.S.

military camps. When the military failed to provide provisions to new recruits, female-run Soldiers' Aid Societies distributed food to the recruiting posts. The Women's Christian Temperance Union also ran rest stations where soldiers could nap and write letters. Women unaffiliated with any organization donated their services by delivering cookies and coffee to the men at the U.S. camps. These women also tended to soldiers who returned home weak and often suffering from tropical diseases. The United States finally departed Cuba in 1902, shortly before establishing the Guantanamo Bay Naval Base on the east end of the island.

The same year, President Theodore Roosevelt began to collaborate with the Colombians to purchase rights to the Panama Canal. When negotiations failed, the United States provided warships to Panamanians fighting for independence from Colombia. The U.S. military intervened in Panama, replicating its actions in Cuba. In both cases, the success of each independence effort resulted in huge financial gains for the United States. Two weeks after Panama secured independence from Colombia, the newly independent state granted the United States permission to complete the Panama Canal. The U.S. government also secured sovereignty over 450 square miles surrounding the canal and stretching from the Atlantic to the Pacific Oceans.

American nurses arrived at the Panama Canal Zone in 1904, the same year that male military personnel began serving on the isthmus. The early arrival of female nurses to a zone otherwise deemed unsuitable or dangerous for women illustrated the degree to which officials and politicians viewed nursing as an extension of women's natural role. Nurses experienced greater restrictions than did male employees. Canal officials set a curfew for these female workers and forbade them from traveling to Panama City. Despite these difficulties, nurses felt empowered by their employment. They also resisted the attempts at gender-specific regulation. In 1911, nurses at Ancon Hospital protested new rules that imposed uniform attire and prohibited French heels. Other nurses worried hospital officials by consuming alcohol and dating canal workers.

Other American women, both single and married, who traveled to Panama in search of adventure, companionship, and better wages, soon joined the nurses. Many married women arrived alongside their husbands, and they sought to make a home for themselves according to U.S. customs and norms. In this way they helped solidify the cultural divide between the Canal Zone and the rest of Panama. Zone officials welcomed American wives because they hoped the female presence would have a civilizing effect on the canal workers. However, they were more apprehensive about the arrival of single women from the United States. Experienced telephone operators, cashiers, and teachers arrived at the peninsula, willing to fill empty positions and replace men who could earn better wages working on the canal. Mary Chatfield was one of these adventurous hopefuls, traveling to the Canal Zone from New York City in 1905. She hoped to find work as a stenographer but quickly became outraged that so many employers refused to hire women. Like other recent arrivals, Chatfield was forced to combat prejudices that stereotyped

single American women as flirtatious, modern, and incompetent.

Although the U.S. occupations of Cuba and Panama established a precedent for future military interventions, a singular moment of noninterventionism occurred between 1933 and 1945. A spirit of isolationism permeated international politics following World War I, and the United States was not immune to these changes. In the midst of the Great Depression, the American public began to demand that the federal government limit foreign interventions and prioritize domestic concerns. President Franklin D. Roosevelt soon implemented the Good Neighbor Policy, a plan to improve Latin American relations by removing U.S. troops from countries such as Nicaragua and promising not to interfere in Latin American affairs.

The work of First Lady Eleanor Roosevelt exemplified this era. She both championed and interpreted U.S. foreign policy, highlighting the importance of mutual respect and hemispheric cooperation. During World War II, Roosevelt targeted American housewives in her radio broadcasts on pan-American cooperation. In March 1944, she traveled to U.S. military installations throughout Central America, South America, and the Caribbean, seeking to improve the morale of U.S. service personnel. Many Latin Americans approved of her trip and viewed Roosevelt as a symbol of female involvement in the war effort. Her departure from the White House in 1945 did not end her investment in hemispheric solidarity. Following the Cuban Revolution, Roosevelt encouraged presidential candidate John F. Kennedy to engage in dialogue with other Latin American countries before making official his policy on Cuba.

The end of World War II and the beginning of the Cold War signified a return to the interventionism of previous years, and women participated in these interventions in more formal capacities than before. In 1942, women began serving as military personnel. The Navy, Coast Guard, Marines, and later the Army accepted and trained females, granting them full rank and status. In order to limit the recruitment of African American women, the Army initially stated that black females could comprise only 10 percent of the Women's Army Auxiliary Corps (WAAC). The other branches of the military were no less prejudiced. By 1947, nurses in the all-female Army Nurse Corps also received permanent commissions and rankings. Motivated by the desire to eliminate communism, the U.S. military deployed these women throughout Latin America and the world.

For the next several decades, the United States aggressively sought to promote democracy; indeed, the opinions of UN Ambassador Jeane Kirkpatrick illustrated the persistence of anticommunist ideology into the 1980s. As the first female ambassador to represent the United States, Kirkpatrick also exemplified women's advancement in the political sphere. She gained the attention of presidential candidate Ronald Reagan when she published an article advocating U.S. support of authoritarian regimes, as they were more open to reform than totalitarian (communist) governments. For this reason, she defended the conservative military junta of El Salvador and refused to negotiate with its opponents, the Farabundo Martí

National Liberation Front (FMLN). By 1991, over 70,000 Salvadorans were dead, many of them innocent peasants killed by the U.S.-trained and U.S.-funded Salvadoran military. The Marxist-inspired Sandinistas gained control of Nicaragua in 1979, and they also faced resistance from U.S.-armed troops. Kirkpatrick herself raised funds for the *contras* fighting against the ruling Sandinistas.

The end of the Cold War in the early 1990s changed U.S. priorities in Latin America. Rather than combating communism, the United States turned its attention towards drugs, undocumented immigration, and, later, terrorism. U.S. military bases remained in Latin America, tangible manifestations of U.S. foreign policy in the region.

Women continued to play essential roles in U.S. military occupations, serving as military personnel, contract workers, volunteers, and policy makers. Some faced deployment, while others remained in the United States to support families and care for children. For over 100 years, American women have both facilitated and challenged U.S. interventions in Latin America. They have done so in both formal and informal capacities, and historians are only beginning to tell their stories.

Rachel Hynson

See also: African American Women; American Red Cross; American Revolution (1775–1783); Army Nurse Corps (ANC); Asian American Women; Barton, Clara Harlowe (1821–1912); Civil War (1861–1865); Cold War (ca. 1947–1991); Dix, Dorothea Lynde (1802–1887); Hispanic American Women; McGee, Anita Newcomb (1864–1940); Native American Women; Nursing; Roosevelt, Eleanor (1884–1962); Spanish-American War (1898);

Tompkins, Sally Louisa (1833–1916); Women's Army Auxiliary Corps (WAAC); Women's Army Corps (WAC); World War I (1914–1918); World War II (1941–1945).

References and Further Reading

Bellafaire, Judith, and Mercedes Herrera Graf. *Women Doctors in War*. College Station: Texas A&M University Press, 2009.

Crapol, Edward, ed. *Women and American Foreign Policy: Lobbyists, Critics, and Insiders*. Westport, CT: Greenwood Press, 1987.

D'Amico, Francine, and Laurie Weinstein. *Gender Camouflage: Women and the U.S. Military*. New York: New York University Press, 1999.

Enloe, Cynthia. *The Morning After: Sexual Politics at the End of the Cold War*. Berkeley: University of California Press, 2000.

Finger, Seymour Maxwell. *American Ambassadors at the UN: People, Politics, and Bureaucracy in Making Foreign Policy*. New York: Holmes and Meier, 1988.

Greene, Julie. *The Canal Builders: Making America's Empire at the Panama Canal*. New York: Penguin Press, 2009.

Hoganson, Kristin L. *Fighting for American Manhood: How Gender Politics Provoked the Spanish-American and Philippine-American Wars*. New Haven, CT: Yale University Press, 1998.

Monahan, Evelyn M., and Rosemary Neidel-Greenlee. *A Few Good Women: America's Military Women from World War I to the Wars in Iraq and Afghanistan*. New York: Alfred A. Knopf, 2010.

Moore, Brenda L. "African-American Women in the U.S. Military." *Armed Forces and Society* 17 (April 1991): 363–84.

Morgan, Paul W., Jr. "The Role of North-American Women in U.S. Cultural Chauvinism in the Panama Canal Zone, 1904–1945." Ph.D. dissertation, Florida State University, 2000.

Pérez, Louis A. Jr. *The War of 1898: The United States and Cuba in History and Historiography*. Chapel Hill: University of North Carolina Press, 1998.

Schoultz, Lars. *Beneath the United States: A History of U.S. Policy towards Latin America*. Cambridge, MA: Harvard University Press, 1998.

LAUWERS, BARBARA (1914–2009)

Intelligence operative and Women's Army Corps (WAC) corporal Barbara Lauwers attained recognition during World War II for her creative uses of propaganda and psychological strategy during the Italian campaigns of 1944–1945.

Born Božena Hauserová in Brno, Austria-Hungary, on April 22, 1914, Lauwers later proved an adept student at the University of Paris, earned a law doctorate at Masaryk University, and subsequently became an attorney and journalist. Seeking to escape Nazism's reach, she and American husband Charles Lauwers relocated to the Belgian Congo in 1939. Working briefly with Bata Shoes, the couple eventually immigrated to the United States on the eve of that nation's entrance into World War II. Charles was drafted into the Army in 1941, and Barbara became a liaison assistant in the Czechoslovakian Embassy in Washington, D.C. Lauwers soon entered the WAC. She viewed military service as a chance for adventure and an opportunity to strike back at the fascist powers oppressing her homeland. She enlisted on June 1, 1943, only hours after officially being inducted as a U.S. citizen. Lauwers's superiors quickly realized that she was a valuable asset to Army intelligence given her foreign upbringing, bilingual abilities, and tested diplomatic experience.

Immediately following her basic training in Georgia, she was appointed to the Office of Strategic Services (OSS), an espionage component of the Army. After receiving further orientation in Washington, she was posted to the Algerian port of Oran. By this time, the North African Campaign had concluded and the invasion of Sicily was underway. By the summer of 1944, Lauwers found herself on the cusp of the Allied advance toward Rome and heavily involved with Morale Operations (MO), a unit specializing in propaganda to weaken Germans' will to fight. Following the capture of Rome on June 5, 1944, Lauwers helped implement Operation Sauerkraut, a counterintelligence mission that capitalized on the chaos following the failed assassination of Adolf Hitler by subordinates. By dispersing propaganda, rumors of Army rebellion, and conflicting orders behind the German lines, Americans could effectively cripple Nazi capabilities with minimal loss of life. At a prisoner of war processing station near Naples, Lauwers began interrogating recently captured Germans, weeding out dissenters from loyal Nazis. Those willing to collaborate with the Allies were provided forged identification papers in order to return to their own lines and distribute thousands of leaflets relaying false intelligence.

Another successful component of Operation Sauerkraut credited to Lauwers was the creation of the League of Lonely War Women. The brochure advertising the fictitious club to German troops featured a heart logo soldiers back home could affix to their uniforms with the understanding that wearing it would win them romantic favors by lovelorn females on the homefront. Word of the league seared through the German ranks and created homesickness and further dissention with the war. At least 10,000 Germans defected as a result. Initial outcomes were so successful that the League's "advertising" was extended through the duration of the war. Nearly 300,000 copies were released and proved so convincing that even the *Washington Post* was duped by the deception.

Perhaps Lauwers's greatest achievement during the war came in the spring of 1945. The Allies' final push to crush German resistance began in April as multiple U.S. divisions advanced into the northern regions of Italy. Lauwers hoped to appeal to the better nature of conscripted Czechoslovakians forced into the German army, coaxing them to surrender by arguing that Germany was their enemy, not their benefactor. Through propaganda handbills and radio broadcasts, Lauwers persuaded over 600 Czech and Slovak combatants to surrender to Allied forces. For this feat, she was awarded the Bronze Star in Rome on April 6, 1945.

Following a welcomed journey to reconnect with family in Czechoslovakia, Lauwers returned to the United States. She later divorced Charles when she realized they had become estranged. In the following years, she worked various jobs in radio broadcasting, the National Academy of Sciences, and finally the Library of Congress, where she met her second spouse, Joseph Podoski. Retiring in 1968, she spent nearly a decade in Vienna, Austria, becoming an advocate for international refugees. Returning to the United States in the late 1970s, she lived a peaceful life until her death at age 95. Boasting a very colorful and multifaceted life, Lauwers helped create new dimensions of counterintelligence efforts in World War II.

Jared Frederick

See also: Espionage; Women's Army Corps (WAC); World War II (1941–1945).

References and Further Reading

Liptak, Eugene, and Richard Hook. *Office of Strategic Services, 1942–45: The World War II Origins of the CIA*. Oxford, UK: Osprey, 2009.

Mauch, Christof. *The Shadow War against Hitler: The Covert Operations of America's Wartime Secret Intelligence Service*. New York: Columbia University Press, 2003.

McIntosh, Elizabeth P. *Sisterhood of Spies: The Women of the OSS*. Annapolis, MD: Naval Institute, 1998.

Wise, James E., and Scott Baron. *Women at War: Iraq, Afghanistan, and Other Conflicts*. Annapolis, MD: Naval Institute, 2006.

LEE, HAZEL YING (1912–1944)

Among the very first Chinese American woman aviators, and the first Chinese American woman to pilot aircraft for the U.S. military, Hazel Ying Lee served with the Women Air Force Service Pilots (WASP) program during 1943 and 1944, ferrying both single and multiengine aircraft and flying transport planes. She was killed in active duty in November 1944.

Chinese American Hazel Ying Lee was a member of the Women Air Force Service Pilots (WASP). She was killed on active duty in November 1944. (National Archives)

Lee was born August 24, 1912, in Portland, Oregon, one of eight children of Chinese immigrant parents. After graduating from high school in 1929, she worked a menial job in Portland because during that era there existed only limited opportunities for Asians.

Lee became enamored of flying after her first airplane ride in 1932, so she joined the Chinese Flying Club of Portland. Although women comprised less than 1 percent of all pilots in the United States at the time, in October 1932 she became one of the first Chinese American women to qualify for a pilot's license.

In 1933, Lee traveled to China, hoping to join the Nationalist air force so that she could participate in China's struggle against Japanese military incursions. However, despite a critical shortage of trained aviators, the Chinese military refused to accept a female pilot. Although frustrated, Lee remained in China for nearly five years, living in the southern city of Guangzhou and flying for a commercial airline. Not long after Japan's 1937 invasion of China, Lee returned to the United States, where she found a job assisting the Chinese government in its acquisition of war materiel.

After the United States declared war in December 1941, the nation faced a shortage of labor. The wartime demand for skilled personnel in the military drained many talented people from the civilian workforce, even from those positions affiliated with the military. As a result, all service branches developed specialized opportunities for qualified women. The primary goal of the WASP program, founded in 1943 and commanded by Jacqueline Cochran, was to use trained female pilots for stateside duties such as transporting aircraft, training, and towing aerial targets. Utilizing female pilots for these jobs subsequently freed male pilots for front-line duties. Eventually 1,074 women completed the WASP training school and entered service.

Lee entered the WASP program in 1943 and trained with over 100 other women in class 43-W-4 at Avenger Field, a U.S. Army Air Forces facility in Sweetwater, Texas. After successfully completing the six-month course, Lee was assigned to the Air Transport Command's 3rd Ferrying Squadron, based at Romulus Army Air Base (AAB), near Detroit, Michigan. Here Lee mainly flew training and transport aircraft. Then, in April 1944, she began instrument training, Officer Candidate School (OCS), and pursuit school. The latter qualified Lee to pilot fast, single-engine fighter aircraft such as the Bell P-39 Airacobra and P-63 Kingcobra, the Republic P-47 Thunderbolt, and the North American P-51 Mustang. By the first days of October 1944, Lee had successfully completed both the courses of instruction and OCS, whereupon she returned to duty with the 3rd Ferrying Squadron at Romulus AAB.

Now qualified to fly fighter aircraft, Lee immediately began to do so. In November, she was dispatched to Niagara Falls, New York, to pick up a new P-63 from Bell, the manufacturer, and fly it to Great Falls, Montana. Severe weather delayed everyone scheduled into that airport and led to a backlog of incoming flights when conditions cleared and flights resumed on November 23. A radio malfunction on another approaching P-63 caused confusion in the control tower. Consequently, both Lee's plane and this second P-63 were directed to the same runway at the same time. The two fighter planes collided, and Lee was badly burned in the crash. She died of her wounds on November 25, 1944. Lee became the last of 38 WASP pilots killed during World War II. Twenty-seven of these fatalities occurred during active duty.

Lee is buried in Portland next to her brother Victor, who in late 1944 was killed in action in France as a member of the U.S. Army.

Thomas Saylor

See also: Asian American Women; Cochran, Jacqueline (ca. 1910–1980); Women Air Force Service Pilots (WASP); World War II (1941–1945).

References and Further Reading

Merryman, Molly. *Clipped Wings: The Rise and Fall of the Women Airforce Service Pilots (WASPs) of World War II*. New York: New York University Press, 1998.

Official WASP Archive. Woman's Collection, Texas Woman's University, Denton.

Verges, Marianne. *On Silver Wings: The Women Air Force Service Pilots of World War II*. New York: Ballantine Books, 1991.

LEFTENANT COLON, NANCY (1921–)

Nancy "Lefty" Leftenant Colon became an Army nurse during World War II and in 1948 became the first African American woman to be commissioned into the Regular U.S. Army Nursing Corps.

Born in 1921 in North Amityville, New York, to Eunice and James Leftenant, she was one of 12 children. Her parents had grown up in the South and had moved to New York to give their children better educational opportunities than they had in the South. After graduating from high school, Nancy spent a year working as a maid to save the $100 necessary to pay for nursing school. In 1942, she graduated from the Lincoln School for Nurses in the Bronx, New York. Despite having some concerns about how people viewed women in the military, she joined the U.S. Army Reserves in January 1945. After she completed basic training and received her commission as a second lieutenant in March 1945, Leftenant began serving as an Army nurse.

Leftenant was selected as one of the first African American nurses to treat white soldiers. Until 1945, Army regulations had confined African American nurses to caring for African American soldiers, but a shortage of qualified nurses led the Army to attempt an integration experiment. Leftenant was one of a group of 37 African American nurses sent to Framingham, Massachusetts, to care for white soldiers at the Fort Devens Army Hospital. Despite meeting opposition from white nurses, Leftenant and many of her colleagues vastly exceeded expectations. She was promoted to first lieutenant after only 11 months of service.

President Harry Truman's progressive desegregation of the military, which culminated in Executive Order 9981, opened new opportunities for African Americans in the armed forces. Until then, African American women had only been able to serve as nurses in the U.S. Army Reserves, but the Truman administration's reforms opened up the prospect of Regular Army commissions. Leftenant, who was then stationed at Lockbourne Air Force Base in Ohio, received her commission in the Regular Army Nursing Corps on February 12, 1948. In 1949, Leftenant secured a transfer to the Air Force in hope of becoming a flight nurse. Her decision was partially motivated by the memory of her brother Lt. Samuel Leftenant, a Tuskegee Airman, who had died in April 1945 when his P-51 Mustang was lost on a combat mission over Austria. He had encouraged Nancy to pursue her interest in a military career. His service with the 99th Pursuit Squadron strengthened her interest in aviation and inspired her life-long devotion to the memory of the Tuskegee Airmen.

After joining the Air Force, Leftenant immediately applied to be an Air Force flight nurse. However, despite having the highest nursing aptitude test results in the service, she was repeatedly rejected. It was not until 1952 that she was selected to begin training as a flight nurse. As a flight nurse, she was at the pinnacle of the Air Force's nursing hierarchy. Her first posting was to Tachikawa Air Force Base in Japan. Leftenant was the flight nurse on missions to Korea, Taiwan, Okinawa, and French Indochina. In 1954, Leftenant was onboard the first U.S. flight that evacuated wounded French soldiers from the besieged air base at Dien Bien Phu, the fall of which on May 7, 1954, led to France's defeat in the Indochina War. After being promoted to major, she served as an administrator at bases in the United States and West Germany.

Leftenant retired from the Air Force in 1965 and returned to Long Island. Soon after returning to New York, she married Bayard A. Colon, a captain in the Air Force Reserves. They lived on Long Island, where he co-owned a funeral home and worked as a school counselor, while she worked as a nurse at Amityville High School. Neither her retirement from the military nor the death of her husband in 1972 reduced her interest in the military or African Americans' contributions to it.

Leftenant's dedication to the Tuskegee Airmen led to her involvement as a national officer of Tuskegee Airmen Incorporated (TAI). She served as national treasurer from 1978 to 1987 and as first vice president from 1987 to 1989. From 1989 to 1991, she was Tuskegee's first female president. As an officer of TAI, she worked to teach future

generations about the Tuskegee Airmen's experiences and accomplishments. In 1998, Tuskegee University awarded her an honorary doctorate of humanities in recognition for her service and work to preserve the Tuskegee Airmen's legacy.

Andrew Orr

See also: African American Women; Air Force Nurse Corps (AFNC); Army Nurse Corps (ANC); Cold War (ca. 1947–1991); Executive Order 9981 (July 26, 1948); Korean War (1950–1953); Nursing; World War II (1941–1945).

References and Further Reading

Decker, Evelyn. *Stella's Girl: The Autobiography of Captain Evelyn Decker, a World War II and Korean War Veteran.* New York: iUniverse, 2008.

Webster, Raymond. *African American Firsts in Science and Technology.* Detroit, MI: Gale Cengage, 1999.

LOVE, NANCY HARKNESS (1914–1976)

An early pioneer of female aviation, Nancy Harkness Love helped organize the Women's Auxiliary Ferrying Squadron (WAFS) and later served in the Women's Air Force Service Pilots (WASP) division. For her service in World War II, she received an Air Medal.

Nancy Harkness was born in Houghton, Michigan, on February 14, 1914. She grew up in an affluent household, attending the Milton Academy and Vassar College. Her love of flying and desire to be a pilot, although contrary to the accepted social norms of the time for

Nancy Harkness Love, director of the U.S. Women's Auxiliary Ferry Squadron (WAFS), later served in the Women's Air Force Service Pilots (WASP) division. (National Archives)

women, would not be squelched. Soon after experiencing her first flight at 16, she earned her pilot's license. She married Robert Love, an Air Corps Reserve major, in 1936. The two shared a love of flying and created their own aviation company in Boston, Inter City Aviation. Love flew as a commercial pilot for their company. The Bureau of Air Commerce also hired her to fly. She flew as a test pilot in 1937 and 1938.

Although her upbringing had prepared her for a life of ease and grace within the upper echelons of American society, Love instead used her connections to work in aviation and war industries. Her social standing allowed her to catch the attention of high-ranking military officers and federal legislators, which helped

her bring her ideas into fruition. In May 1940, before the United States entered World War II, Love wrote to Lt. Col. Robert Olds, the man charged with creating the Ferrying Command for the Army Air Corps. Love offered to him the names of 49 women, including her own, who were ready and capable of executing the duties of a ferrying pilot for the U.S. government. Each of these women had more than 1,000 flying hours. Although Olds was in favor of the idea, his superior, Gen. "Hap" Arnold, refused it.

In 1942, when Love's husband was deputy chief of staff of the Ferry Command, she accompanied him to his post in Washington, D.C. She soon found herself with a civilian job within the Air Transport Command's Ferrying

Division Office in Baltimore, Maryland. Love finally convinced Col. William Taylor, the man in charge of the domestic wing of the Ferrying Division, to allow experienced female pilots to ferry new and repaired military planes to U.S. bases.

Love's determination and successful navigation of Washington, D.C.'s political and military labyrinths led to the creation of the WAFS. By the time the squadron was officially created, she had recruited 29 experienced female pilots to join. These aviatrixes were based out of New Castle Army Air Field in Wilmington, Delaware, and placed under the command of the Air Transport Command's 2nd Squadron. Love became the commander of the WAFS at this air base. Quickly her command expanded to encompass another squadron located at Love Field in Dallas, Texas, along with others in Michigan and California. The success of the training course at Avenger Field in Sweetwater, Texas, helped increase the ranks of the WAFS.

Under Love's command, the WAFS merged with the Women's Flying Training Detachment at Avenger Field to create the WASP. Throughout the duration of combat operations in Europe, WASPs ferried over 12,650 aircraft for the U.S. military. The ferried aircraft came from over 75 different makes and models, ranging from bombers and transports to fighters. During this period, Love became the first female pilot to qualify on the P-51 Mustang. She was also the first woman to qualify to fly both the B-25 and the B-17.

The government disbanded the WASP on December 20, 1944. However, their legacy and service did not end. In honor of their efforts and service to the United States, both Love and her husband were simultaneously decorated after the war. She received the Air Medal, while he received the Distinguished Service Medal. Her medal recognized her leadership in training over 300 qualified female pilots to fly military aircraft.

As a civilian, Love continued to push for an increasing role for women in military service and aviation. She also championed the recognition of the WASPs and WAFS pilots for their wartime service.

Love died on October 22, 1976.

Ryan C. Davis

See also: Cochran, Jaqueline (ca. 1910–1980); Women Air Force Service Pilots (WASP); Women's Auxiliary Ferrying Squadron (WAFS); Women's Flying Training Detachment (WTFD); World War II (1941–1945).

References and Further Reading

Haynsworth, Leslie, and David Toomey. *Amelia Earhart's Daughters: The Wild and Glorious Story of American Women Aviators from World War II to the Dawn of the Space Age.* New York: Harper, 2000.

Rickman, Sarah Byrn. *Nancy Love and the WASP Ferry Pilots of World War II.* Denton: University of North Texas Press, 2008.

LOVELACE'S WOMAN IN SPACE PROGRAM (WISP)

The Lovelace's Woman in Space Program (WISP) began in 1960 and ended in 1962. The program was designed to encourage the involvement of women in the space exploration program.

Dr. W. Randolph Lovelace II of the Lovelace Foundation for Medical Education and Research and Brig. Gen. Donald Flickinger of the U.S. Air Force Air Research and Development Command (ARDC) were the driving forces behind the program. Lovelace and Flickinger discussed the possibility of sending women into space. In 1959, Flickinger established the program Woman in Space Earliest (WISE) at ARDC and planned to test women aviators. After the Air Force decided to cancel WISE in mid-1959, Flickinger asked Lovelace to take over the project. Lovelace used his foundation's private funds as well as donations from female aviator Jacqueline Cochran and her wealthy husband Floyd Odlum to support the new program. Lovelace renamed the program WISP.

In 1960, Lovelace invited women pilots to apply to participate in WISP. It was a rare opportunity for female aviators because at the time there was little support for female aerospace experimentation. Invited applicants had to be between 22 and 35 years old and have at least 1,500 hours of flying time. In early 1961, after screening the applications, Lovelace invited 25 women for the initial medical examinations. Only 19 women completed the full set of tests. Beginning in summer 1961, Lovelace gave physical and physiological testing to these 19 women aviators at the Lovelace Medical Clinic in Albuquerque, New Mexico. The tests were the same as those that the National Aeronautics and Space Administration (NASA) used for choosing the Project Mercury astronauts.

Thirteen women aviators passed the tests; these women became known as the Mercury 13. In May 1961, Jerrie Cobb, the only female aviator invited to participate in both WISE and WISP, became the only woman in the program who took the space flight simulation testing at the U.S. Naval School of Aviation Medicine in Florida. Cobb's score was as good as that earned by experienced Navy pilots. After Cobb's test, Lovelace began to make informal arrangements for other participants to take this test. In 1962, the program ended as the result of repeated cancellations of the space flight simulation testing. Lovelace did not conduct any more tests.

Although Cobb lobbied for the continuation of WISP, NASA was not interested in a woman-in-space program. Even Lovelace and Cochran did not support the testing. As a result, WISP officially disbanded in 1962.

Edy Parsons

See also: Cochran, Jaqueline (ca. 1910–1980).

References and Further Reading

Ackmann, Martha. *The Mercury 13: The Untold Story of Thirteen American Women and the Dream of Space Flight*. New York: Random House, 2003.

Ryan, Kathy L., Jack A. Loeppky, and Donald E. Kilgore Jr. "A Forgotten Moment in Physiology: The Lovelace Woman in Space Program." *Advances in Physiology Education* 33 (September 2009): 157–64.

Weitekamp, Margaret A. *Right Stuff, Wrong Sex: America's First Women in Space Program*. Baltimore, MD: Johns Hopkins University Press, 2004.

Woodmansee, Laura S. *Women Astronauts*. Burlington, ON: Apogee Books, 2002.

LUDINGTON, SYBIL (1761–1839)

Sybil Ludington became a heroine of the American Revolution as a result of her 40-mile horseback ride to alert American militia of the presence of British troops nearby.

Born April 16, 1761, Ludington lived in Fredericksburg, New York, near Danbury, Connecticut. She was 16 years old when she made her fateful ride. On the night of April 26, 1777, Ludington rode 40 miles to warn American troops of the British presence, twice the distance covered by another famous rider, Paul Revere. From her family farm, Ludington could hear the sounds of skirmishing and see the light from the flames in nearby Danbury. Two thousand British troops had captured the town and were burning it. As a result, she rode toward Carmel, New York, in order to warn others of the approaching British soldiers and an impending attack.

According to reports, Ludington took off on her horse for Carmel around 9:00 p.m. She was familiar with the local area and also knew where the Tories lived so she could easily find her way around without alerting the enemy to her message. Along her route, she made stops in neighboring Mahopac, Mahopac Falls, Kent Cliffs, and Farmers Mills before returning to her family farm. She quietly knocked on doors, alerted locals to the presence of the enemy, and mustered the militia. From her family's farm, her father, a colonel and commander of the Dutchess County militia, and his detachment of approximately 400 men began to spread throughout the countryside.

Ludington's father, Col. Henry Ludington, held high rank not only in the state militia but also within the community. He was a veteran of the French and Indian War. His experience garnered his rank in the colonial militia. Within the community, he was esteemed as a mill owner and community leader. Col. Ludington realized he would need to muster his troops quickly to meet the British and keep them from moving further into the countryside. His daughter knew of the impending danger awaiting the slumbering colonists. She volunteered to ride throughout the surrounding area not only to warn the colonists but also to help muster the militia. After completing the circuit of her ride through the New York countryside, she arrived home to witness the militia marching off to confront the British.

By the time the militia began its march, it was too late to save Danbury, Connecticut. However, as a result of Ludington's ride, other towns were spared similar destruction by British troops. In fact, the 400 militiamen under her father's command were able to push the British troops back to their boats moored at Danbury. In this engagement, known as the Battle of Ridgefield, Ludington's militia joined forces with other patriots under Gen. David Wooster. The battle ended as a successful rout by the colonial militia. The victory resulted, in part, from the young Ludington's ride and her efforts to rouse the militia. Gen. George Washington later formally recognized Ludington's vital role in the battle.

Her 1777 ride was the pivotal moment in Ludington's military career. Not much is known in regards to her other actions during the Revolutionary War. In any case, her contribution to the war effort was not only pivotal in the victory of the Battle of Ridgefield but also showed the martial spirit was not limited to men. Ludington continued to assist in the war effort in the following years. As with most female revolutionaries during this time, she served as a messenger for the colonial army.

After the war, Ludington settled down to enjoy American independence. She married Edward Ogden, a lawyer by trade, in October 1784. The newly married couple settled down in Unadilla, New York. Ludington would live the rest of her life in this growing town.

Although her deed seemingly was overshadowed in popular memory by Revere's similar ride, Ludington was honored by her hometown in New York. The town renamed itself Ludingtonville in remembrance of her heroic dash through the countryside. Also, a statue of Ludington astride a galloping horse commemorates her martial deed of bravery stands outside of the Danbury public library.

Ryan C. Davis

See also: American Revolution (1775–1783); Corbin, Margaret Cochran (1751–ca. 1800).

References and Further Reading

Berson, Robin Kadison. *Young Heroes in World History.* Westport, CT: Greenwood, 1999.

Bohrer, Melissa Lukeman. *Glory, Passion, and Principle: The Story of Eight Remarkable Women at the Core of the American Revolution.* New York: Atria, 2003.

LYNCH, JESSICA (1983–)

A U.S. Army soldier who was taken prisoner early in Operation Iraqi Freedom, upon her rescue Jessica Lynch became a national celebrity and controversial symbol of the Iraq War.

Born in Palestine, West Virginia, on April 26, 1983, Lynch joined the Army largely because she was interested in traveling. On the eve of the war, she was deployed to Iraq as part of the 507th Maintenance Company. On March 23, 2003, after an element of her supply convoy became separated from other vehicles and became disoriented, she was injured in a Humvee accident during an ambush and taken captive by the Iraqis. The attack took place in the city of Nasiriyah.

After the engagement ended, Pvt. 1st Class Lynch lost consciousness. She later awoke in an Iraqi military hospital. There, and subsequently at Saddam Hussein General Hospital, Iraqi doctors and nurses treated Lynch for the severe injuries she had sustained. She remained hospitalized until April 1, 2003, when a U.S. special forces team raided the hospital and freed her, carrying her out on a stretcher and delivering her to military authorities for medical treatment. Footage of the rescue operation was released to the media, and Lynch quickly became a symbol of American fortitude and resolve in the early days of Iraqi Freedom.

Although much of the media portrayed Lynch as a hero, the details of her ordeal remain unclear. Some reports, for example, suggested that during the ambush she had fired her weapon in an effort to fend off the attackers; others maintained that the firing mechanism of her assault rifle was inoperable because it was jammed with sand. The nature of her captivity also became a source of speculation. Although there is a great

U.S. Army soldier Jessica Lynch became one of the first American female prisoners of war when she was captured in March 2003 during Operation Iraqi Freedom. (AP/Wide World Photos)

deal of evidence that the Iraqi medical staff treated her professionally and in accordance with the provisions dictated for prisoners of war, questions persist about the possibility that she had been interrogated and abused. Additionally, many critics are skeptical of whether or not the operation to reclaim her was as dangerous as it appeared to be, and there are conflicting reports about whether or not the soldiers encountered any resistance as they entered the hospital. Some have suggested that the George W. Bush administration and the media embellished the story to increase public support for the war and turn her rescue into compelling headlines.

Beyond the disagreement about the details of her captivity, Lynch's story reignited much larger debates about gender, race, and the military. For opponents of the combat exclusion that bars women from front-line duty, Lynch's courage indicated the fitness of women for combat situations. Conversely, for those who support the ban on women in combat, her apparent helplessness proved the rightness of their claims. Other observers wondered why Lynch was the only captive whose cause became famous, particularly because there were two other female casualties of the Nasiriyah ambush, Pvt. 1st Class Lori Piestewa and Specialist Shoshana Johnson. Piestewa died of injuries sustained during the skirmish, while Johnson was held captive for 22 days. Despite being the first Native American woman to die in combat and the first female African American prisoner of war, respectively, neither woman received as much media attention as did Lynch, and some have claimed that this disparity was a result of race and that mainstream America was more interested in the suffering of a white woman than her nonwhite peers.

Whatever the reasons, Lynch became an instant celebrity. Multiple television networks developed her story into full-length programs. In an effort to capitalize on her iconic status, some media outlets may have exaggerated certain aspects of the story, and Lynch later contested the accuracy of an NBC-TV dramatization in particular. Seeking to make her own voice heard, Lynch told her story to Pulitzer Prize–winning journalist Rick Bragg, who developed it into the popular book *I Am a Soldier, Too: The Jessica Lynch Story* (2003). Throughout the text, which covers everything from Lynch's idyllic childhood to her postwar return to her home in Palestine, West Virginia, Lynch resists being labeled a hero and instead tries to provide an accurate account of her life and her time in Iraq. Now a decorated veteran, Lynch has returned to civilian life and is pursuing a college education. She became a mother for the first time in January 2007.

Rebecca A. Adelman

See also: African American Women; Iraq War (2003–2011); Johnson, Shoshana Nyree (1973–); Native American Women; Piestewa, Lori (1979–2003); Prisoners of War; War on Terror (2001–).

References and Further Reading

Bragg, Rick. *I Am a Soldier, Too: The Jessica Lynch Story*. New York: Alfred A. Knopf, 2003.

Conroy, Thomas. "The Packaging of Jessica Lynch." In *Constructing America's War Culture: Iraq, Media, and Images*, edited by Thomas Conroy and Jarice Hanson, 61–84. Lanham, MD: Lexington Books, 2008.

Holland, Shannon L. "The Dangers of Playing Dress-Up: Popular Representations of Jessica Lynch and the Controversy Regarding Women in Combat." *Quarterly Journal of Speech* 92 (2006): 27–50.

Takacs, Stacy. "Jessica Lynch and the Regeneration of American Identity and Power Post-9/11." *Feminist Media Studies* 5 (2005): 297–310.